PEOPLES
OF THE WORLD

NATIONAL GEOGRAPHIC
PEOPLES
OF THE WORLD

INTRODUCTION BY DAVID MAYBURY-LEWIS
AFTERWORD BY WADE DAVIS

NATIONAL
GEOGRAPHIC

WASHINGTON, D.C.

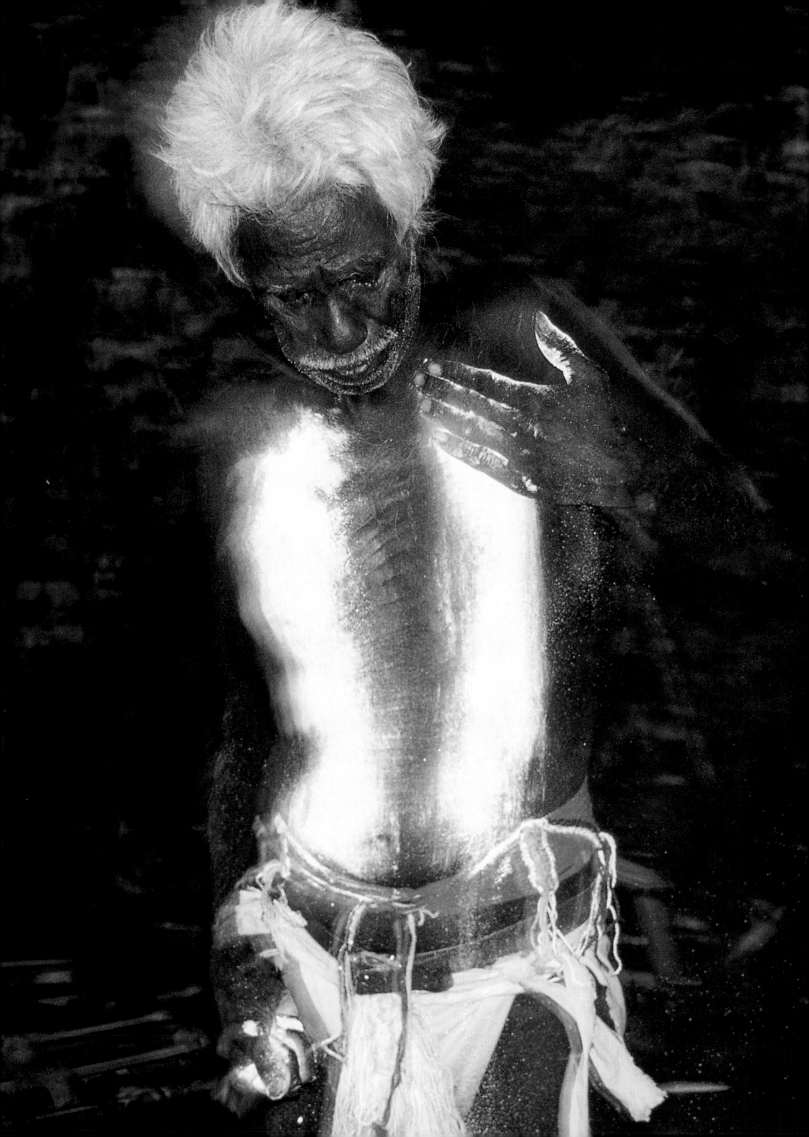

CONTENTS

Applying pigment to his body, an Aboriginal performer gets ready for a corroboree, a festive gathering featuring traditional songs and dances. *Preceding pages:* A pilgrim in Morocco walks through a shrine to Moulay Ismail, the 17th-century sultan who united the country.

EDITOR'S NOTE

P EOPLES OF THE WORLD is unquestionably an ambitious topic for a single book. The anthropologists and demographers consulted on this project estimate that there are thousands of ethnic groups—or peoples—worldwide, more groups, in fact, than have ever appeared on any one list or in any single database, volume, or series of volumes. But beyond the sheer numbers is a more ineffable problem: What exactly is a "people"? What elements must coalesce to produce an ethnic group, to create a culture?

As David Maybury-Lewis explains in his thought-provoking introduction to this book, "Ethnicity is a kind of fellow feeling that binds people together and makes them feel distinct from others, yet it is difficult to say precisely what kind of feeling it is and why and when people will be strongly affected by it." Our objective in selecting the groups for inclusion in this book was to identify when that "fellow feeling" created a distinctive culture. Almost always ethnicity arises out of a shared history and language, shared traditions and values. But sometimes a shared religion creates a sense of not just spiritual but also cultural distinctiveness. On the other hand, nationality, in its strictly political sense, was never a basis for inclusion. While ethnic groups occasionally lay claim to their own nations, political boundaries in and of themselves do not create—or confine—cultures.

Placing each group geographically posed its own problems. We have organized the book into nine major areas that have their own broad cultural cohesion, and within each area we have featured groups that historically have been a prominent part of the ethnic mix. Many of the groups that we placed in one region may also have a strong presence in other regions or may have formed immigrant communities far from their homelands; others may be in the process of returning to their homelands, as political boundaries reopen or are redrawn. Owing to the mobility of humans across the face of the globe and to the space limitations of a single volume, we could not, in most cases, cover immigrant groups and the hybridized cultures that they have formed—though, on occasion, when an immigrant group has evolved into its own highly distinctive culture, we have included it. Finally, as a coda to the book, we have also provided an exhaustive list of more than 5,000 ethnic groups worldwide.

In Wade Davis's afterword, he warns that cultures and languages are vanishing at a rate unprecedented in history. But, despite the threat that globalization poses to diversity, it is clear from the wealth of photographs in this book that humans relish their distinctiveness and their ability to express themselves as part of a particular group, whether that expression takes the form of the elaborately hennaed hands of a bride in the Middle East or the pig-tusk nose ornament of a man in Melanesia. *Peoples of the World* celebrates that diversity and the National Geographic's long fascination with the rich and colorful play of human cultures.

K. M. Kostyal

CONTRIBUTORS

DAVID MAYBURY-LEWIS, Edward C. Henderson Professor of Anthropology, has taught at Harvard since 1960. He and his wife have made various field expeditions to central Brazil and carried out research on problems of social change and development in that country. In 1972 they founded Cultural Survival, an organization that defends the rights of indigenous societies worldwide, and Maybury-Lewis has been its president ever since. He is the author of *The Savage and the Innocent* and *Millennium: Tribal Wisdom and the Modern World*.

WADE DAVIS, an Explorer-in-Residence at the National Geographic Society, received his Ph.D. in ethnobotany from Harvard University. Davis's fieldwork has taken him throughout the world. He is the author of many books, including *The Serpent and the Rainbow* and *One River*. Recently, his work has taken him to Peru, Borneo, Tibet, the Arctic, the Orinoco Delta, and Kenya. His most recent book, *Light at the Edge of the World*, was published by National Geographic.

BEEBE BAHRAMI is a cultural anthropologist and freelance writer. She has done extensive research in Morocco, where she was a Fulbright scholar, and in Egypt, Iran, and Spain. She contributed to *Charting Memory: Recalling Medieval Spain; City and Society; Iranian Studies;* and *Edebiyyat*.

PATRICK BOOZ, a graduate of the University of Wisconsin, has spent half his life in Asia and speaks Chinese and Indonesian. He is based in southern Sweden, where he writes and edits on Asian topics, especially China and the Himalaya.

BRIAN FAGAN is a professor of anthropology at the University of California, Santa Barbara. Among his extensive writings on pre-Columbian America is *Kingdoms of Jade, Kingdoms of Gold*, an account of ancient American civilizations.

TRUDY GRIFFIN-PIERCE is an adjunct faculty member in the Anthropology Department of the University of Arizona. In addition to publications about Navajo religion, she has written *The Encyclopedia of Native America; Native America: Enduring Cultures and Traditions;* and *Native Peoples of the Southwest*.

ROY RICHARD GRINKER, a professor in the Department of Anthropology at George Washington University, is the author or editor of numerous publications on Africa, including *Houses in the Rainforest: Ethnicity and Inequality among Farmers and Foragers in Central Africa; Perspectives on Africa: A Reader in Culture, History and Representation;* and *In the Arms of Africa*.

CATHERINE HERBERT HOWELL, an anthropologist by training, has contributed to dozens of National Geographic publications, including *Wonders of the Ancient World* and the *Expeditions*

Atlas. She was also the editor of *Out of Ireland*, a companion volume to the PBS documentary of the same name.

ROBERT LEE HUMPHREY, professor emeritus at George Washington University, served as Chair of Anthropology for 12 years. A specialist in Paleo-Indian cultures, his archaeological research has taken him from northern Alaska to South America. He has written about the Paleo-Indian in North America; the Arctic; the ancient cultures of Washington, D.C.; and the Mesoamerican ball game.

IAN MCINTOSH is the director of Cultural Survival Inc., an indigenous peoples research-and-advocacy nonprofit based in Cambridge, Massachusetts. An Australianist and specialist in indigenous issues, he resided in the Aboriginal (Yolngu) community of Galiwin'ku from 1986 to 1992. He has worked with Aborigines in Queensland's far north and in Kakadu National Park, where he was the Northern Land Council's senior anthropologist.

EUGENE OGAN, professor emeritus of anthropology at the University of Minnesota, is currently based in Honolulu. He has conducted research into Pacific anthropology and history for almost four decades, and his most recent article, "The Nasioi of New Guinea," appears in *Endangered Peoples of Oceania*.

PHILIP SCHER, assistant professor of anthropology at George Washington University, has done fieldwork in the West Indies and conducted research on religion and performance in West Africa. His book, *A Moveable Fete: Caribbean Carnival as Transnational Cultural Process*, is scheduled for publication in 2002.

GEORGE STUART serves as president of the Center for Maya Research, Barnardsville, North Carolina. Over a professional career that spans more than 40 years, his contributions to the scholarly literature and popular press have included writings on the archaeology and anthropology of the Americas, particularly Mesoamerica and the southeastern United States.

KEITH AND ELISABETH WARD are a husband-and-wife team whose European heritage inspires their work. Elisabeth has explored her Icelandic roots as a co-editor of the Smithsonian exhibition catalogue, *Vikings: The North Atlantic Saga*, while Keith's heritage has spurred him toward a Ph.D. in medieval English literature at George Washington University.

JAMES F. WEINER has spent more than three years in Papua New Guinea, mostly with the Foi of the Southern Highlands Province. Author of three books and many articles on the Foi, he is currently a visiting fellow at the Research School of Pacific and Asian Studies, Australian National University.

ETHNICITY AND CULTURE

BY DAVID MAYBURY-LEWIS

ETHNICITY IS A KIND OF FELLOW FEELING that binds people together and makes them feel distinct from others, yet it is difficult to say precisely what kind of feeling it is and why and when people will be strongly affected by it. Some people under some circumstances are willing to die and certainly to kill on behalf of their ethnic group. Other people, under other circumstances, are hardly aware of their own ethnicity and pay it little attention in their everyday lives. So what is ethnicity and why does it have this evanescent quality?

Ethnicity is like kinship. When people recognize each other as belonging to the same ethnic group, they feel like distant kin, vaguely related to each other through common descent but so far back that no one can trace the precise relationship. Ethnicity is a group's idea of its own distinctiveness from others. It is invariably based on a sense of common history, and other shared characteristics such as skin color, religion, language, culture. Some groups may have a common ethnicity imputed to them, without feeling or recognizing it themselves. A classic example in the Americas is a diverse series of distinct populations who were lumped together and called Indians by newcomers to the hemisphere. Ethnicity is thus a sense of relatedness that is ascribed to peoples, either by themselves or by others or both.

Like families, ethnic groups may or may not have a strong sense of identity, and may or may not stick together. Yet there is one important difference between family ties and ethnic ties. Everybody everywhere normally starts life as the member of a family and must at some time or other act as one. This is true even in societies that have tried to curtail the functions of the family, as the former Soviet Union once did, or in societies where families seem reduced to the vanishing point, as in some parts of the United States. Family ties, however defined, could be said, in this sense, to be truly primordial links. This is not so of ethnic ties. Everyone has a latent qualification for ethnic association in that we all speak a language, have a skin color, live in places that have a history, and so on; but these (or other) criteria do not necessarily make us members of ethnic groups. Ethnicity comes into play only with the recognition of certain criteria that give rise to a group identity.

Based on collective memories and countless journeys, this freehand map represents the rain forest world of Suriname's Tirió people, who seek title to lands they have lived on for hundreds of years.

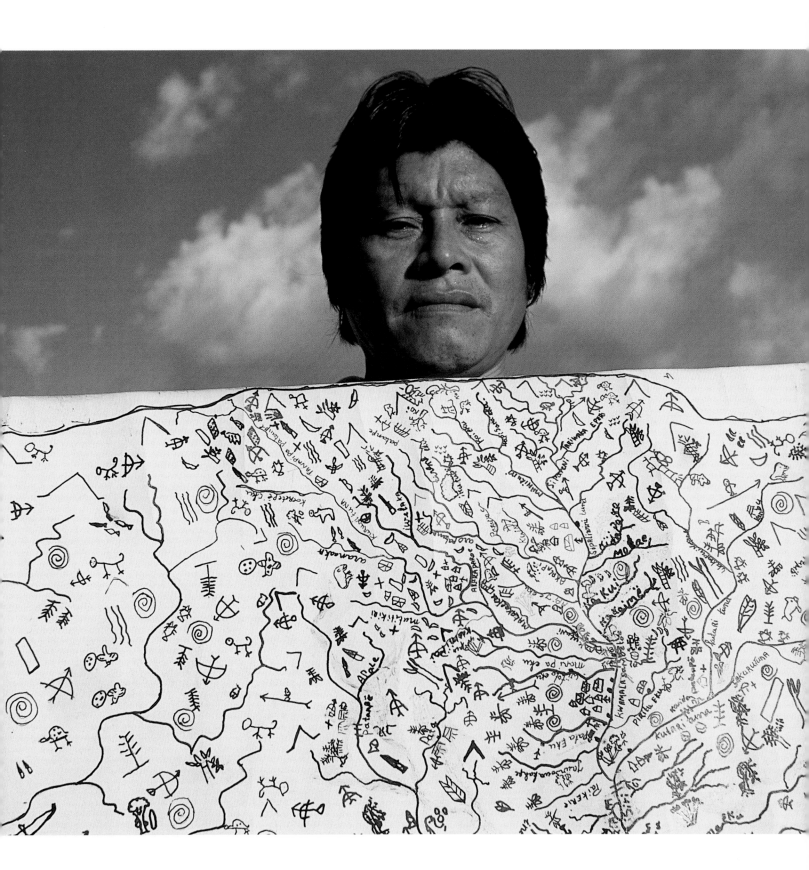

Religion may serve to distinguish an ethnic group in some places and be an unmarked criterion in others. Ethnicity may depend on skin color in some places and not in others. A common language may distinguish an ethnic group—or may not. French speakers as such do not, for example, constitute an ethnic group, yet being primarily French speaking in Quebec is the most important aspect distinguishing the ethnic group that wishes to turn Quebec into an independent country. Similarly, language is the most important criterion for distinguishing the major ethnic groups of Belgium (the French-speaking Walloons and the Dutch-speaking Flemings) from each other. But perhaps the most sensitive and malleable criterion is the sense of common history. Ethnic groups must have a shared sense of their past, but that past is open to construction or reinterpretation in a variety of ways that may have tragic consequences in the present.

Ethnic groups, then, do not form because people share the same race or language or culture. They form because people who share such characteristics *decide* they are members of a distinct group, or because people who share such characteristics *are lumped together* and treated by outsiders as members of a distinct group. People considered to be ethnically related establish rules and understandings concerning the essence and limits of what they have in common, concerning their culture, in fact. They also try to agree on who is part of their group, and who is not.

These mechanisms for maintaining the boundaries of the group are critically important, because they perpetuate the group. People must know whether others can be admitted to the group and whether it is possible to "pass" as one of the group, either formally or informally. They also need to know how far an individual can deviate from the norms and behaviors of the group before he or she will be no longer considered a member of it. Above all, they need to know how much and what kinds of interaction members of the group may have with outsiders if the group is not to lose its identity. Some groups, such as the Amish in the United States, maintain their separateness from the surrounding culture by an elaborate set of rules designed to limit the outside contacts of their community members. Jews are often likewise concerned about how much members of their communities can adopt the customs of surrounding gentiles, and particularly whether they can marry non-Jewish partners without losing their Jewishness.

Ethnic groups are never isolated. They invariably have contact with others, and their members invariably interact with other groups, even hostile ones. That is why the understandings about boundaries and their maintenance are absolutely critical; the stronger the ethnic sentiment that binds the group together, the more strictly will its members try to enforce the boundaries, which explains why interethnic marriages often meet resistance from the families concerned. In fact, the way such marriages are regarded—as unthinkable, to be discouraged, of no consequence, or encouraged—says a great deal about people's ideas of their own ethnicity and the interethnic situation in which they find themselves. Immigration, exile, and other situations that transplant peoples often force new ethnic identities to form, as these people establish relationships with those of the countries that receive them.

While there are few societies left that have no contact with the rest of the world, there are some remote peoples who have comparatively little. Such peoples are sometimes referred to as "tribal," because they live in relative isolation and choose to manage their own affairs without the centralized authority of a state. Other ethnic groups are called "indigenous," because their territories have been taken over by people who differ from them in such characteristics as race, language, or culture. It is therefore characteristic of indigenous peoples that they are marginal and dominated by the states that claim jurisdiction over them.

Ethnic groups cover a wide spectrum—from indigenous to tribal to substatal societies that may even be referred to as nationalities and aspire to nationhood. China's national minorities, for example, meet the criteria for being considered indigenous. They are, however, unlike most indigenous peoples in that many of them have populations that run into many millions. The Zhuang number about sixteen million, the Manchu about ten million, the Hui approximately nine million, and the Miao and the Uygurs eight million each. These national minorities occupy about half the territory of China and have played an important role in Chinese history. In other respects, their situation is very similar to that of indigenous peoples the world over. For example, the Tibetans, like the Uygurs and Muslims of China's far western province of Xinjiang, are considered by the central government to be peoples who cling to their backward cultures, refusing to join the Chinese mainstream and constantly trying to secede from the state altogether.

THIS CONCERN ABOUT ETHNIC minorities who are unwilling to join the mainstream is something relatively new in human history. Most organized states throughout history have been multiethnic and multicultural. In empires, one people typically dominated the others. In most states, one ethnic group normally dominated the others. States, in effect, very often contained peoples speaking different languages and living according to customs and traditions that differed from those of the dominant majority. The idea that the state should correspond to a single nation or culture is a fairly recent one. It derives from two major tendencies in Western thought that came to this conclusion by different paths. One stems from the theorists of the French and American Revolutions. Writers like Rousseau, in his *Social Contract*, published in 1762, and James Madison, in *The Federalist Papers* #10, published in 1787, argued for a concept of the state in which government derived its legitimacy from the people. This revolutionary state would respect the dignity of its citizens as individuals, equal before the law, but it would do nothing to assist them to maintain their ethnicity, should they wish to. On the contrary, the revolutionary theorists thought that ethnicity would disappear as the modernizing tendencies of the postrevolutionary age rendered it irrelevant. The state would thus establish a uniform, modern culture for all its citizens.

An alternative tendency in Western thinking was championed largely by German scholars like Herder and Fichte, writing in the early 19th century. They were preoccupied with Germanness, with the problem of how German culture could flourish when the Germans themselves were scattered through a number of different European states. These writers came to the conclusion that ideally a state should represent the culture of a single people, from which it followed that a people with a distinctive culture could and perhaps should aspire to have its own state. This idea was at the heart of 20th-century nationalism, a devastating kind of ideology that has led to endless conflict and untold suffering as it caused what has come to be known (unflatteringly) as Balkanization.

This kind of ethnic nationalism in eastern and southeastern Europe supplied the tinder that eventually blazed up in the conflagration of the First World War. At the end of that war, a serious effort was made to defuse ethnic tensions by allowing some of the suppressed ethnic groups to form their own states. President Woodrow Wilson led this effort, on the grounds that it was only logical for those who believed in democracy to support the cause of freedom for peoples as well as for people. The campaign on behalf of "self-determination," as it was called, had to deal with major difficulties. It was neither politically nor practically possible to allow every people with a sense of nationalism to form their own state. Yet the map of Europe was redrawn, permitting the Czechs and the Slovaks to form the new state of Czechoslovakia, the southern Slavs to form Yugoslavia, and so on. Inevitably, though, most states, including the new ones, still retained substantial minorities who were not of the dominant nationality or nationalities. These were often minorities who were also glowing with the prevailing spirit of nationalism and who felt neglected when their particular nationalistic aspirations could not be met. The League of Nations was supposed to offer protection to minorities, but it proved incapable of doing that. Worse still, it could not even protect states such as Czechoslovakia, which had cooperated with the League and tried to live up to its precepts by actually putting its protective policies toward minorities into practice.

I T IS CLEAR THAT THE THEORISTS who predicted ethnicity would evaporate in truly modern societies have been proven wrong. They are wrong in two ways. Ethnicity does not evaporate in modern states. On the contrary, we have witnessed an upsurge of ethnic pride and reaffirmation in recent years. Indigenous peoples such as Native Americans, Hawaiians, Australian Aborigines, and New Zealand Maori are now insisting on their right to maintain their own cultures and administer their own lands—insisting furthermore that such demands do not make them outsiders in their own countries, and should not be used to treat them as second-class citizens. Even more striking is the fact that, after 500 years of denial, state after state in the Americas has proclaimed itself multiethnic and thus willing to tolerate semiautonomous nations within itself. Mexico, Colombia, Ecuador, and Bolivia, all states with large indigenous populations, have declared themselves constitutionally multiethnic. Nor does this new spirit apply only to indigenous peoples. European nations such as Britain, Spain, and others have granted local autonomy within the decentralized state to ethnic provinces. This willingness to tolerate distinct ethnic groups within the state is not only politically wise, it is also culturally beneficial. Such tolerance protects the most important resource that is available to humankind, namely the extraordinarily rich variety of cultures and ways of living that human beings have developed. This diversity is currently threatened by the forces of globalization that tend to eliminate cultural differences and turn nations into shopping malls that are barely distinguishable from each other. Cultural variation makes the world interesting. Tolerance of it makes the world a pleasanter and more peaceful place in which to live.

The other way in which people nowadays systematically misunderstand ethnicity is by assuming that, if it is tolerated, it leads inevitably to conflict. There is, furthermore, an international tendency nowadays for people to throw up their hands in the face of ethnic conflicts and proclaim that nothing much can be done about them, since they result from primordial ethnic enmities that are irrupting in our retribalized world.

The conclusion is too pessimistic, however. It "reads" ethnic conflicts as resulting from primordial hatreds, when in most cases they are nothing of the sort. Most of the ethnic conflicts in the world today have been created by people who sought to profit from them. Even the worst-case scenarios, such as the genocidal warfare between the Tutsi and the Hutu in Rwanda, or the ethnic cleansing in the former Yugoslavia, were hardly examples of spontaneous ethnic combustion. The Tutsi and the Hutu were originally members of a single society who were separated into antagonistic pseudo-castes by the policies of the colonial powers (Germany and later Belgium) and then set against each other. The peoples of Yugoslavia had a long history of coexistence before they were torn apart by outside powers during World War II, and before they were recently torn apart again by the opportunistic nationalism of their ex-Communist leaders.

These examples show that Hutu and Tutsi, Serb and Croat have not always "been at each other's throats." On the contrary, each pair of peoples shares a similar culture, speaks mutually intelligible languages, and has lived peacefully intermingled with each other for long periods of time. How, then, are we to understand the recent bloodletting between them?

The immediate cause of the killings was that they were instigated by unscrupulous politicians, of the kind that Valery Tishkov, a Russian specialist on ethnic matters, has labeled "ethnic entrepreneurs." Since ethnicity is a matter of manipulating definitions, ethnic entrepreneurs become specialists in such manipulation—in the creation of situations, even genocidal ones, that enhance their own power and their own economic gain. Yet this does not explain why and under what circumstances ethnic entrepreneurs are successful. Serbs and Croats may have lived together in relative peace for long periods of time, yet why did they, at a given moment, follow leaders who led them into conflict with each other? Why, to put it more generally, do people follow ethnic entrepreneurs? The answer is that they do so at times of stress and fear, in fact in times like the ones we live in.

This is an era when uncertainty and instability have affected many states that emerged from the old colonial empires. Similar instabilities have also affected many states that are trying to adjust to the collapse of communism and the disappearance of the arrangements that were locked in place during the Cold War. On top of these political instabilities people are having to deal with economic instabilities, occasioned by the revolutions in technology and information processing and the globalization that brings these revolutions into the lives of even the remotest peoples. With the former Soviet Union, which was until recently one of the world's two superpowers, now in desperate economic straits, it is not surprising that other nations are also feeling the pinch of poverty and uncertainty. In stressful times, when people often do not know whether their nation will survive and, if so, in what form; in times when people fear the loss of their jobs, their savings, their social safety net, if they had one; in times such as these, people may follow leaders who promise them security, on condition that they stick with the fellow members of their ethnic group.

It is important, though, to understand how and why such uncertainties may lead people in different parts of the world into ethnic conflict, and equally to understand that such conflicts are neither inevitable nor primordial. It is important to understand that indigenous peoples and ethnic minorities do not subvert the state by maintaining their own cultures, provided that the state treats those cultures as a resource and not as a threat. Above all, it is important to understand that states can be, and have been, both peaceable and multiethnic, so that we can learn how to make such states the models for our future, rather than helplessly accepting the ethnic conflicts of the present.

ASIA'S CULTURAL MAKEUP fully matches the geographic complexity and richness of the world's largest continent. From Japan to Georgia, from Mongolia to Malaysia, Asia is home to more ethnic groups than any other major region. These groups have evolved over a very long time; some of them developed in isolation, while others have complex histories of interaction and sharing, either through peaceful migration or military conquest.

China, India, and Indonesia—the first, second, and fourth most populous nations—are home to 40 percent of Earth's people, and in these three countries reside extraordinary numbers of ethnic groups. Language, a major measure of ethnicity, reveals in its diversity the range of a country's human wealth: Indonesia counts more than 700 languages, India over 400, and China more than 200.

In China, at least 90 percent of the people consider themselves to be Han. This term is commonly used interchangeably with "Chinese" and dates from the Han dynasty, China's first long-lasting period of unification. For more than 2,000 years, smaller ethnic groups have been driven into mountains and marginal areas by the Han Chinese, whose approximately one billion people now constitute the world's largest ethnic group.

ASIA

A woman's hard stare reflects the difficult but independent life of the Rana Tharu people, who live along Nepal's border with India.

China's population has tens of millions of minority members constituting hundreds of ethnic groups, yet officially the Chinese government recognizes only 55 "national minorities." Some groups have been lost through a steady acculturation, which continues to threaten Tibetans, Mongolians, and others whose lands abut heavily populated Chinese regions. One group, the Manchu, ruled China as the last imperial dynasty (until 1911) but did so at the expense of ethnic identity: By assimilating Chinese ways, the Manchu lost their own language and culture. While millions survive, their language now has as few as a hundred speakers.

Throughout history, religion has given cohesion and meaning to ethnic groups, so much so that it often seems inseparable from an overall way of life. This is clearly true with Tibetan Buddhism, where belief and culture have evolved intertwined. Many parts of Asia have been touched by Islam, brought by Arabs from the seventh century onward. The religious, political, and social forces of this faith continue to dominate hundreds of millions of people every day. In Armenia, Christianity has been a foundation of society and a balm during the long and difficult history of its people. But religion can also inflame local hatreds: Ethnic hostilities erupt between Muslims and Hindus in India, between Hindus and Buddhists in Sri Lanka, and between Christians and Muslims in Indonesia.

Buddhism developed into a world religion from Indian origins 2,500 years ago. Eventually it all but disappeared in its homeland, but by traversing the Himalaya and streaming along Silk Road trade routes, the religion reached China and from there spread to other parts of East Asia. In Japan especially, Buddhism and contacts with China's mature civilization helped shape the character of the people. While holding fast to their indigenous traditions, the Japanese borrowed and adapted foreign ways to great benefit: Landscape gardening, flower arranging, and the art of serving tea, for example, all began in China, with Japan bringing them to full bloom. The tea ceremony involves the graceful serving of tea with simple implements in impeccable surroundings, combining aesthetic and spiritual aspects to express the Japanese love of beauty and inner calm. Despite Japan's modern ways, this ritual survives and continues to grow in popularity.

Through government and architecture, painting and sculpture, science and warfare, even the use of chopsticks, Chinese institutions also influenced the cultures of Korea, Vietnam, and other areas of East and Southeast Asia. Even so, local peoples created and maintained vital, thriving cultures of their own, while acknowledging their debt to a common written language and elements of Confucianism. In fact, the Confucian ethical system of social relations still underlies the modern state in China, Korea, Singapore, and elsewhere.

India has left its mark, too, dramatically spreading its civilization and religions into South and Central Asia. Aspects of its culture reached into Sri Lanka, Pakistan, and Afghanistan, to name a few present-day countries, and traveled sea routes all the way to Bali, which remains Hindu to this day. Indian scholars and priests introduced many of Asia's peoples to the classical languages of Sanskrit and Pali, which were used in early writings and historical records.

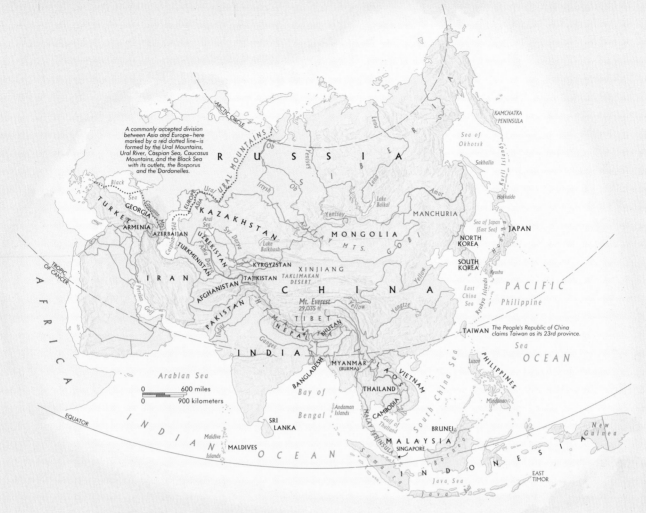

A commonly accepted division between Asia and Europe–here marked by a red dotted line–is formed by the Ural Mountains, Ural River, Caspian Sea, Caucasus Mountains, and the Black Sea with its outlets, the Bosporus and the Dardanelles.

The People's Republic of China claims Taiwan as its 23rd province.

One of history's most important developments remains a shared legacy and a critical component of many Asian cultures: wet-rice cultivation. For millennia, Asians from Japan southward have shared the common inheritance of rice, a staple that is central to the survival of groups large and small. People eat it every day and rely on it for a hundred other uses. Versatile rice straw, for example, supplies material for thatch, basketry, floor mats, sandals, brooms, bedding, rough cloaks, and hats; it also serves as feed for the animals.

People in all of Asia's rice-growing countries honor this grain through seasonal festivals and ceremonies. For them, rice has a sacred, even divine significance, so offerings of cooked and uncooked rice, rice cakes, rice stalks, and rice wine serve to ensure good harvests and to rejuvenate the vital forces of the Earth itself.

Rice cultivation demands many hands and a spirit of cooperation to prepare fields, sow seeds, transplant shoots, maintain irrigation systems, and harvest, husk, and polish the grains that will be cooked and eaten (almost all Asians prefer polished, white rice rather than brown rice). Accompanied by pickles or chilies, or served with other dishes, a bowl of rice represents the enduring hopes and expectations of Asia's billions. To grow this grain in submerged fields, farmers have reshaped entire landscapes with hand-built terraces, dikes, water channels, and carefully constructed beds stretching to the horizon. Stepped emerald fields, such as those of the Ifugao people in the mountains of northern Luzon in the Philippines, stand as a lasting image of Asia.

Following Pages: Still cheerful in the face of lashing monsoon rains, Burmese women transplant bundles of rice shoots in carefully spaced rows under water. Myanmar (Burma), once the world's largest rice exporter, today just holds its own to feed a population of some 48 million.

ASIA

CLOCKWISE FROM TOP LEFT: KAZAKH FALCONER, ARMENIAN STUDENT, WIFE OF DAYAK CHIEF, AND CHINESE ELDER

CAUCASUS

CENTRAL ASIA

EAST ASIA

SOUTHEAST ASIA

SOUTH ASIA

CAUCASUS
ARMENIANS • AZERIS

⊛ ARMENIANS

LANDLOCKED ARMENIA, a mountainous country slightly smaller than Maryland, with many rivers and narrow, fertile valleys, counts 3.5 million people within its borders. But this population represents only half of the world's Armenians; the rest—officially considered part of the nation—live in the former Soviet Union, India, the Middle East, Poland, Romania, Western Europe, and North America, where many have achieved success in business, crafts, and other occupations. Independent only since 1991, the Republic of Armenia faces major challenges: Nearly half the people are under age 25; the economy is grim; many skilled workers are emigrating; and an ethnic war with Azerbaijan has killed tens of thousands.

Armenians remember a time during the Middle Ages when they were part of a major kingdom that also included what is now northeastern Turkey. Yet the greatest events in Armenia's collective memory are invasions, suppressions, and forced exiles over the past thousand years. The worst was the 1915 massacre, when Turks drove the people from eastern Anatolia; more than 600,000 died.

Among diaspora Armenians, cosmopolitan attitudes coexist with a great love of home, family, and age-old traditions. The people strongly value their distinct language; although it belongs to the large Indo-European family, it has no close linguistic relatives and stands alone with a unique 38-letter alphabet.

A distinctive brand of Christianity is the foundation that underlies the unity of all Armenians, who converted to the faith early and in the fourth century declared that Christianity was their state religion. This tie has produced an invaluable corpus of religious literature, as well as remarkable art and architecture. The people are renowned for their mosaics and tiles, and the circular dome of their churches is thought to have had a strong influence on Byzantine and Ottoman buildings.

On theological grounds, primarily the interpretation of Christ's divinity, the Armenian Apostolic Church stands independently and proudly next to the Roman Catholic and Orthodox Churches. It has been a pillar of Christianity and a primary force in maintaining Armenian culture.

⊛ AZERIS (Azerbaijanis)

THE SEVEN MILLION Azeris of Azerbaijan form the largest group in the ethnic jumble of the Caucasus. A hundred years ago, their homeland was the world's top oil producer; today, it is again actively tapping the immense Caspian Sea reserves, with the oil industry advancing the trend toward urbanization. While most Azeris now live in cities, many

are farmers and nearly all are Muslims, in contrast to neighboring Armenia and Georgia, which are Christian. According to local custom, Azeri Muslims may drink wine, and women are free to work and go unveiled.

Islam arrived with 7th-century Arab conquerors, the first of many waves that included Turks, Mongols, Persians, and Russians—who began dominating the area in the 19th century. A hybrid people, Azeris were ethnically and linguistically Turkic by the 11th century, yet their roots go deep into ancient Caucasia and Iran. To the south lies an Iranian region also named Azerbaijan, larger in both size and population but lacking a nation's cohesiveness.

Azeris also honor Zoroaster (circa 628-551 B.C.), the founder of Zoroastrianism, a religion with a central belief in the cosmic conflict between good and evil. But today the quality of their Islam sets them apart. Of Islam's two main branches, the Shiites began to dominate after the departure of the Sunnis, who had allied themselves with Ottoman Turks in the 19th century. Later there was reconciliation as Azeri nationalism stressed a common heritage and downplayed sectarian differences. With improved relations came a cultural flowering from the mid-1800s to the early 1900s, bringing new libraries, hospitals, schools, art academies, and charities. A spirit of emancipation was spreading to Turkic peoples throughout the Russian Empire and elsewhere.

The Soviet era suppressed this awakening, closing Azerbaijan's 2,000 mosques, crushing intellectuals and artists, and forcing the people to abandon Arabic and adopt the Cyrillic alphabet. Then, under glasnost and following independence in 1991, writers and historians returned to resurrect past glories. In recent years, Azeris have reopened or rebuilt their mosques. After 70 years of Soviet rule, few reminders of Russian culture remain, though broad education policies and the country's 95 percent literacy rate are by-products.

As a boy watches quietly, Azeri men stand to worship in a restored mosque. Since 1991, when decades of Soviet religious suppression came to an end, Azerbaijan's moderate expression of Islam has increasingly come under pressure from hard-line Muslims in neighboring Iran.

CENTRAL ASIA

BALUCHI • BURUSHO • KAZAKHS • PASHTUN
• TURKMEN • UZBEKS

BALUCHI

FIERCELY INDEPENDENT seminomads whose origins may go back to Middle Eastern and Caspian Sea nomadic peoples, the Baluchi have for centuries integrated marginal groups from many cultures under their tribal name. Today, this broad ethnic group comprises dozens of tribes and occupies a vast area of Pakistan, southeastern Iran, and southwestern Afghanistan. Although arid and largely inhospitable, with dramatic landscapes and few roads, the region also encompasses green valleys, juniper forests, and lofty mountains with wildflowers, as well as irrigated gardens and orchards producing dates, apples, cherries, almonds, and cumin. Where the land meets the Arabian Sea, a 500-mile-long coastline has fine, sandy beaches.

About 70 percent of the Baluchi live in the province of Baluchistan, which takes in nearly half of Pakistan's land surface but supports only five million inhabitants. Worldwide, the group numbers some seven to ten million individuals, including people who speak Baluchi, an Indo-Iranian language similar to Kurdish and Pashtu; people who consider themselves to be Baluchi but speak a different language, such as Urdu or Farsi; and even people whose disparate ancestors historically found solidarity among the Baluchi. Each tribal group follows a head chief or a *pir*, a Sufi mystic or Muslim holy man.

Nearly 80 percent of all Baluchi raise sheep and other livestock and rely on small-scale farming activities for part of their livelihood. True nomadism has almost disappeared,

and the pastoral life has given way to cultural assimilation within larger nations. The people are increasingly entering the mainstream, frequently as migrant laborers. Even so, they retain a vibrant storytelling tradition that includes age-old songs with themes emphasizing courage, heroism, protection of the weak, and veneration of ancestors. Another notable aspect of Baluchi culture has also survived: In Afghanistan and eastern Iran, the tribal name is still applied to intricate rugs with rich, dark reds and blues, highlighted sparingly with white.

BURUSHO (Hunzakuts)

THE HUNZA REGION of northern Pakistan's Karakoram Range is home to the Burusho, a people who claim descent from soldiers in the fourth-century B.C. army of Alexander the Great. As fanciful as the story may be, many Burusho do appear European; some people say they look specifically Celtic. The Burushaski language, with just 60,000 speakers, is unrelated to any other world tongue.

Over the years, misconceptions about the Burusho diet and a romantic ideal held by gullible Westerners gave rise to stories about exceptional life spans in the Hunza region. While it is true the people have traditionally relied on apricots during the long winter, the stories connecting their eating habits to great longevity are merely myths.

The Burusho once lived in a much larger area but were eventually driven into the mountains, where they established their virtually impregnable homeland. Hunza was ideally situated, allowing the Burusho to tax—or raid—caravans traveling between India and China. Governed by the same family of *mirs* (rulers) since the 11th century, the remote outpost converted late to Islam; in 1904, it pledged loyalty to the Aga Khan and his Ismaili sect, a branch of Islam with no mosques, no imams. This sect defers to a *pir*, a religious leader who exhibits sanctity or special charismatic powers.

In 1974, Hunza became fully integrated with Pakistan, ending the long rule of the mirs, and four years later the Karakoram Highway arrived to relieve the severe isolation. Most important, the Aga Khan Foundation's programs for health, education, agriculture, transport, and small businesses have given new hope to the people. Money has slowly replaced barter, and schooling, especially for girls, is seen as the necessary way forward for Burusho society.

KAZAKHS

THE MOTIF OF Kazakh history has been the struggle and interplay between Mongol and Turkic tribes across the vast stage of Central Asia, from the Gobi desert to the Caspian Sea. Kazakhs speak a Turkic language, but some scholars consider them to be Turko-Mongols; in appearance they seem more Mongoloid than their Turkic brethren.

United under the Mongols in Uzbek lands, Kazakh clan leaders in the 1460s broke away to return to coveted pastures in the east, where they prospered as nomads. At that time they became known as Kazakhs, which means "secessionists" or "independents," and their ethnic identity firmly took shape.

The arrival of Russian soldiers and traders in the 1600s spelled a slow doom for indigenous culture. From Moscow to Kazakhstan is not much farther than from Washington to Boston, so Russian penetration came steadily. In the modern era, Kazakhstan played a main role in Soviet industrial and military development, with its northeast region subjected to more nuclear tests than any other place on the planet.

Today, Kazakhstan's seven million ethnic Kazakhs do not form a clear majority in their own land (just 44 percent); nearly as many Russians live there. Two and a half million more Kazakhs reside in China, Uzbekistan, Mongolia, and Russia. The largest country in Central Asia and the ninth largest in the world, Kazakhstan is sparsely populated and three-fourths desert or semidesert. Deep in the ground, though, lie rich reserves of oil, gas, and coal.

Kazakhs in all regions can communicate fairly easily, but their language never developed a modern technical vocabulary and thus lives in the shadow of Russian, the language of education, business, and technology. The issue of language and ethnicity has come to the fore as the two official languages—Kazakh and Russian—vie for position and symbolize the deep rifts between two peoples living in entirely different spheres. Russians are skilled, technically capable, and international; Kazakhs seem unsure of the way forward as they struggle to balance the needs of a young nation, Islam, and modern mass culture.

Even in a modern state, the people find security by relying on traditional ties that go back 500 years. Each Kazakh holds allegiance to one of three ancient groups, or *zhuz* (hordes): the Lesser Horde in the west, Middle Horde in the north and east, and Great Horde in the south. Because clan and national politics, as well as economic decisions, depend on such affiliations, the ancient hordes remain important in the makeup and functioning of Kazakh society.

PASHTUN (Pathan)

IN SOUTHEASTERN Afghanistan and adjacent regions of Pakistan live the Pathan or, as they call themselves, the Pashtun or Pakhtun. The Persian name "Afghan" referred specifically to this group long before the word became a geographic designation. In multiethnic Afghanistan, where over 45 languages are spoken, these people form the largest ethnic group, with eight million members. Pakistan is home to more than ten million Pashtun. *(Continued on page 28)*

At a geographic crossroads—where the borders of Russia, Kazakhstan, Mongolia, and China meet—the Altay Mountains still shelter the seminomadic Kazakhs and their age-old ways: Below, a dancer helps celebrate a circumcision ceremony. ***FOLLOWING PAGES:*** Burusho villagers in northern Pakistan sort sun-dried apricots, long a staple of the Hunza region. Using the Karakoram Highway as a link to the outside world, the people now sell this fruit elsewhere in Pakistan and also in China. Meanwhile, motor transport, television, and tourism bring more of the outside world to Hunza. ***PAGES 26-27:*** Founded in the 4th century B.C. by Alexander the Great, the former garrison town of Herat dominates a densely populated region in northwestern Afghanistan. Persians and Central Asians brought commerce, science, and culture to the region.

Pashtu, an eastern Iranian tongue incorporating numerous loanwords from Persian and Arabic, forms one of Afghanistan's two national languages. Written in a type of Arabic alphabet since the early 1500s, this language has inspired many poets and writers, including Ahmad Shah Durrani, 18th-century founder of the Afghan nation.

Pashtun lands have witnessed tides of invasion by Persians, Alexander the Great, Turks, Moghuls, British, and most recently Russians, who invaded Afghanistan in 1979. But undaunted and self-assured, the people have always resisted external control and gained fame as fierce fighters.

The Pashtun make up some 60 tribes, all with separate territories, and together they form the largest tribal society in the world. Central to their lives as farmers, herders, traders, and warriors is the *pakhtunwalimale*, the Pashtun code of conduct embodying core values of pride, honor, and hospitality. The code's strict rules concern tribal property, succession, the right to speak in gatherings, even slights.

Most of the men carry guns, and blood feuds frequently erupt over land, water, injury, and women. A severe beating or death could be the price a stranger pays for talking to a Pashtun woman. While this seems severe to outsiders, such strict adherence to rules has kept the society independent and intact. Tribal ways do erode, though, as electricity, roads, schools, and government officials steadily encroach. Above all, legitimate commerce, paralleling the age-old occupation of smuggling, is opening the Pashtun to a larger world.

TURKMEN

TO BE TURKMEN is to claim lineage through a male Turkmen, to be a Sunni Muslim, and to speak the Turkmen language, related to modern Turkish and Azeri. In the past, Turkmen were famous as horsemen and warriors from the steppes of Central Asia. As nomads, they herded on lands that supported little besides herd animals and occasionally raided settled areas; their transient lifestyle enabled them to avoid taxes and control by larger governing powers. Today, more than four million Turkmen live in northeastern Iran, Turkmenistan, Afghanistan, Turkey, Syria, and Iraq.

Though tribal ties are very strong, fewer Turkmen are nomadic now; most are either sedentary farmers who grow wheat, barley, and cotton or seminomads who divide their economic labors between raising crops and herding sheep, cows, goats, horses, and camels. The importance of nomadism and animal husbandry is seen in the higher status held by a *chorva* (herder) compared with the lower status of a *chomur* (farmer). It is widely held among Turkmen that a farmer is someone who does not have the wealth to remain a herder and is therefore no longer independent of larger political powers.

Using wool gathered from their own sheep—and occasionally adding silk to the weave—Turkmen women create carpets that are internationally sought after for their quality, design, and colors. Their designs are geometric

and make repeated use of polygonal shapes called *guls*. Each tribe has a distinctive gul that communicates the tribal affiliation of the weaver, and this design is passed from one generation to the next within the tribe. Weaving styles produce knotted carpets with a thick pile, and colors range from saturated rusty hues to deep shades of red, black, and tan. Turkmen use their many woven goods for everyday living, as can be seen in their tents, ground coverings, and saddlebags.

UZBEKS

THE UZBEKS OCCUPY a Central Asian land famous through the centuries for its wealth, learning centers, and culture. Two thousand years ago, the Uzbeks' successful merchant ancestors traded along the Silk Road with Russia, China, India, and Afghanistan, creating a brilliant commercial hub whose riches inevitably attracted invaders.

Arab conquerors in the seventh century brought Islam and helped usher in a golden age, with Bukhara becoming one of the world's greatest cities. From the ninth century onward, Turks came from the northern grasslands. Mongols arrived in the 13th century, but Turkic language and culture predominated because Genghis Khan's armies were in fact mostly Turkic soldiers, many of whom settled here and married local women. One Mongol chieftain, Öz Beg, left the legacy of his name, which survives as "Uzbek."

In the 1380s, the Turkic conqueror Timur (Tamerlane) captured much of Asia and brought more scientists, artists, and architects to the region; he also established Turkish as a written language. But after 1501, as Tamerlane's empire was crumbling, a tribe from north of the Aral Sea invaded and became the core of people we now call Uzbeks.

In the 1900s, artificial ethnic and regional boundaries imposed by the Soviets dramatically altered Uzbek life: Until the Soviet Republic of Uzbekistan was set up in the 1920s, the people had seen themselves as members of tribes and clans, not as part of a nation. The Uzbek language, too, has only a short history as a distinct tongue. Before the 1920s, it was not considered a separate state language; instead, it was one of many Turkic dialects. All of the trappings of nationhood were achieved in 1991, when the Soviet empire ended and Uzbekistan became an independent country.

Uzbekistan's population of 25 million, the largest in Central Asia, is more than 70 percent Uzbek. Sizable Uzbek populations also reside in Afghanistan, China, and Kazakhstan. While its geographic position and ethnic clout lend Uzbekistan some claim to being Central Asia's leader, the country is beset with economic and environmental ills. Reckless expansion of cotton-growing areas and overuse of water have led to the shrinking of the Aral Sea, which now has just one-third its volume of 40 years ago. Fierce storms throw tons of salt and sand into the air, causing severe health problems. Many people worry about the future of the Uzbeks, who once lived so gloriously on the land.

East Asia

AINU ● BAI ● DONG ● KOREANS
● MONGOLS ● TIBETANS ● UYGURS

The People's Republic of China claims Taiwan as its 23rd province.

AINU

AMONG ASIA'S most enigmatic ethnic groups, the Ainu live on Japan's Hokkaido Island and on Russia's Sakhalin and Kuril Islands. For countless generations, these Caucasoid-like people led outwardly simple lives that relied on fishing, hunting, and primitive agriculture. They were once known as the "hairy Ainu," because men grew large beards and women were adorned with moustache-like tattoos around their mouths. Traditionally, they dressed in animal skins and beautiful robes of elm bark and feathers. Where the people came from remains a mystery.

Only some 24,000 Ainu survive today, and few are considered true, or pure, Ainu. Into the 18th century most lived on Honshu, Japan's main island, but they were so different from the rest of the population that the Japanese majority marked them for destruction. Official policy and population pressures eventually drove the people northward. Now, however, the Japanese hold their culture to be worth protecting, perhaps because of the Ainu's

almost total assimilation through intermarriage and domination, especially in the past 50 years.

For the Ainu, the focus of spiritual life has long been the bear-spirit ceremony, or *iyomante*, a ritual involving a sacred space and objects such as prayer sticks, carved staves, and elaborate shaved-wood animals. During the ceremony, a specially raised bear is killed to allow its soul to return to the spirit world. This offering affirms Ainu devotion to, and respect for, nature's hidden forces. The skin and meat of the bear are treated as gifts from the gods.

Traditionally, daily life centered on the village and its immediate territory, or *iwor*, which determined the limits of the Ainu world; within it, the people were largely self-sufficient, relying on salmon, deer, and the cultivation of millet. They excelled in the construction of bows, arrows, spears, traps, and harpoons, and they retained a deep knowledge of the forests and waters of their homeland.

Now many Ainu work in the Japanese construction industry, and their plight clearly exemplifies the precarious survival of an ethnic group within a dominant majority.

BAI

THE 1.75 MILLION Bai of Yunnan Province are among China's most assimilated, prosperous, and successful minorities. For centuries they have maintained close ties with the majority Han Chinese, and because they lacked a written language of their own, they have always relied on Chinese characters. While their name means "white" and they call themselves Speakers of the White Tongue, the Bai's actual origin and language affiliation are not known for certain; ethnolinguists remain undecided about whether their spoken language belongs with Tibetan, Khmer, Thai, or Chinese.

Dali, the Bai capital, is known to have once stood at the center of a kingdom that endured for nearly 500 years, separate from dynastic China until the mid-13th century. This well-documented independent history is the reason for the people's status as a recognized ethnic group.

The geography of their homeland has greatly affected the Bai, who dwell along the shores of sparkling Erhai Lake, beneath a range of snowcapped granite peaks. A 35-mile-long lakeside plain seems specially designed for a protected and bountiful life: Rich, productive rice fields and dazzling yellow rapeseed flowers contrast with the blue lake and red hills of the far shore, planted with peach and pear orchards. Towns and villages of weathered gray stone look across the entire plain, once covered with hundreds of pagodas standing as beacons to the Buddhist faithful. A trio of thousand-year-old pagodas still stands today as the emblem of the Bai.

In the past, horses were very important in this remote, mountainous region, and the Bai became known for strong, small ponies that they supplied to members of various dynasties. Only with the coming of the Burma Road in the 1930s did the style of Bai life and transport truly change, and today's airports, highways, and trains have brought the Bai people into the mainstream of modern Chinese life.

Still, the old love of horses lives on in an annual fair hosted by the Bai. The event has grown enormously, with mountain dwellers and minorities from many parts of China coming not only to trade animals and traditional medicines but also to race horses, eat and drink, and enjoy the mountain scenery. The Bai continue to believe their horses and their land are the most blessed in China.

✪ DONG

DOTTING THE BORDER regions of South China's Guangxi, Hunan, and Guizhou Provinces are the fascinating villages of the 2.7 million Dong, an official minority of the People's Republic of China. Considered the northeasternmost extension of the greater Thai peoples, the Dong speak a Tai language that requires more than 15 separate tones and is thus one of the world's most difficult to speak.

In this culture, new parents commonly plant a grove of pines called "18-year trees," which will later supply their son or daughter with timber for a home. Such obvious concern for building needs extends beyond individual houses—generally two stories tall, with the firewood and farm animals downstairs, the belongings and sleeping quarters upstairs—to communal projects and public architecture. All major settlements proudly raise one or more drum towers, elaborate constructions up to 13 stories high, with tight, overlapping pagoda-like roofs containing tiles and decorations. People paint the eaves with scenes from myths, legends, and daily life: Cooking, farming, weaving, hunting, and the playing of musical instruments are often shown. Statues of beasts and birds decorate the roofs. From afar these towers resemble stylized fir trees, sacred to the Dong.

In ancient times, a huge drum suspended inside each tower helped warn of danger; now its beating calls people together for meetings, celebrations, and festivals, during which songs of praise may be sung for the towers. Dong architecture also includes "wind and rain bridges" of elegant proportions, each bridge having up to five separate pagoda structures. Originally built for shelter, these covered bridges and their special roofing now add beautiful touches to the landscape. Locals have discovered yet another use for them: Leafy vegetables are hung from the railings to dry.

This attention to creative design can also be seen in Dong embroidery. On hot days, women may be found sitting in the shade of wind-and-rain bridges, dabbling their feet in cool streams while painstakingly adding bright stitches to bags, collars, aprons, or baby carriers.

✪ KOREANS

THE ROBUST KOREANS occupy East Asia's strategic Korean Peninsula. With 55 percent of the land, mountainous North Korea has only half as many people as South Korea;

combined, the countries have a population of 68 million. The 1945 division of the peninsula along a 150-mile border led eventually to the Korean War, which raged from 1950 to 1953, and half a century later tensions remain high.

Despite their separation, Koreans historically have had a feeling of shared identity reinforced by geography: Water borders them on three sides, and mountains are to the north. Their location between China, in the north and west, and Japan, in the east, has also played a major role in the shaping of their national character. Early colonization by China encouraged Korea to form institutions based on Chinese models of administration, writing, and the arts, yet the Koreans never relinquished their own identity. They excelled in arts, crafts, and construction, and their contribution to East Asian painting, calligraphy, sculpture, and pottery is of great aesthetic beauty, with an artistic spirit that is natural and spontaneous. Many collectors prize the pale green porcelains known as celadon, created during the 10th- to 14th-century Koryo dynasty.

Language also has helped shape the Korean identity. As a probable member of the Altaic language family and thus closer to Mongolian, the present language is far removed from Chinese. It evolved from the time of Korean unification in the seventh century and, like Japanese, has hierarchies of usage and a sensitivity to social position. Koreans used Chinese characters for writing into the 15th century, when they invented a script called hangul; its 40 symbols are extremely accurate in representing spoken sounds. This break with Chinese literary tradition allowed Koreans to develop their own popular forms dealing with life, love, humor, and even social criticism; at this time, the people began to record colorful folktales possessing funny, ribald qualities. Today, Koreans enjoy one of the highest literacy rates in Asia, and South Koreans have one of the world's highest rates of university attendance.

Korean religion, diverse and complex, has roots in the old traditions of Confucianism and Buddhism, later overlaid with Christianity. The indigenous Ch'ondogyo faith, with elements of Confucianism, Buddhism, Daoism, shamanism, and Catholicism, has been joined in recent times by hundreds of new charismatic sects, such as the Unification Church of Sun Myung Moon and his millions of followers.

Finally, diet is a point of pride for Koreans, who enjoy grilled meats and vegetable dishes such as kimchi—a fiery pickled cabbage that accompanies every meal.

✪ MONGOLS

THE MONGOLS BURST onto the world scene in the 13th and 14th centuries and left a short but audacious legacy that is remembered to this day. After Genghis Khan unified diverse clans in the heart of Asia's steppelands, swift mounted warriors known as the Mongols went on to conquer much of Eurasia. But their overextended empire, from the Pacific to the borders of Egypt and Western Europe, lasted a mere

175 years before breaking up. The stereotype of cruel hordes, however, has survived much longer, even though peaceful herding has been the norm ever since those long-ago days.

On the vast grasslands where they lived, Mongols found success as nomadic pastoralists, horsemen, and herders. They made their homes in circular tents (yurts, or *gers* in Mongolian) of felt and canvas, supported by wooden frames. Women and children also took an active part in the pastoral life, caring for animals and collecting dung that would be burned for fuel. A toughness born from their exposed, windswept life prepared the Mongols well for survival, which required the skillful handling of small horses while tending sheep, goats, cattle, camels, and yaks. Today, such animals continue to support a diet made up of dairy products and meat; milk, cheese, and yogurt appear in a hundred different forms, and there is even a distilled "milk-vodka" for festivities. All parts of the animals are used, with large chunks of fat considered a delicacy.

Mongol culture has been strongly influenced over the years by Buddhism, a foreign faith introduced from Tibet and combined with indigenous shamanism. The nomads learned to use portable altars and devotional scroll-paintings that could be rolled up and easily transported. In the 16th century, the bond between Tibet and Mongolia became so strong that a Mongol khan bestowed the title of Dalai Lama, meaning "ocean of wisdom," on the Tibetan leader.

Today, Mongols have their own country in north-central Asia. Known as the Republic of Mongolia, it encompasses a high, rolling plateau nearly three times the size of France and embraces a population of 2.6 million. Even more Mongols—3.5 million—live across the southern border, in China's Inner Mongolia and other Chinese provinces; additional clusters survive in Kazakhstan, Siberia, and the Kalmyk region of Russia's lower Volga River.

On Japan's Hokkaido Island, Ainu men and women in ceremonial dress perform a ritual crane dance and make offerings of sake, rice cakes, and shaved-wood talismans. Though their origins remain unknown, the culture probably dates from the late Ice Age.

FOLLOWING PAGES: Kazakhs long skilled in hunting with golden eagles occupy barren lands in far western Mongolia. Fierce eagles with seven-foot wingspans can swoop at 100 miles an hour to capture fur-bearing prey, a source of income for their masters.

Mongolia achieved its status as a republic and as the world's second communist country, after Russia, in 1924. Antireligious revolutionaries murdered many thousands of monks and forced changes in lifestyle, limiting nomadism and setting up collectives. Most Mongols now reside in towns and settlements, though many prefer to live in gers, even in the suburbs of Ulaanbaatar, the capital.

The popular revival of wrestling, archery, folk dancing, and horse racing reveals the Mongols' deeply rooted desire to maintain their age-old traditions.

TIBETANS

WITH THEIR NUMBERS estimated at between five and six million, the Tibetan people inhabit an immense plateau, a high-elevation desert bordered by barren cold expanses and the world's highest mountains, the Himalaya.

Cultural Tibet is far larger than the territory within China called the Tibet Autonomous Region. This "Greater Tibet" includes Bhutan, Sikkim, northern Nepal, and sections of Kashmir in northern India. Significant parts of China's Gansu, Qinghai, Sichuan, and Yunnan Provinces are ethnically Tibetan as well. Groups indelibly influenced by Tibetan culture are the Sherpas of Nepal, the Drukpas

of Bhutan, and the Ladakhis of northern India; dozens of smaller groups speaking diverse dialects contribute to the complex Tibetan world. Within China, Mandarin Chinese has become a lingua franca for many Tibetans who otherwise could not converse with one another.

Harsh physical barriers, along with official isolation, allowed Tibetans to maintain a nearly medieval way of life into the mid-20th century. Their culture developed in the relatively well-watered southern part of the plateau, where raising barley proved possible, while in the great north, nomads living in black tents tended livestock, primarily the ubiquitous yak. In the seventh century, Buddhism was introduced from China and was soon followed by the arrival of Buddhist missionaries from India. Spiritual and secular institutions blended together, touching all aspects of life. The land eventually supported 6,000 monasteries, which required most families to have at least one son as a monk.

Although Tibetan Buddhism has several branches, the Gelukpa sect has been dominant since the 17th century, when the fifth Dalai Lama reached the apex of Tibet's theocracy. Buddhism fostered a sophisticated civilization of advanced learning and philosophy that survives to this day, albeit in limited form. Tibet's de facto independence from 1912 to 1950 ended when China occupied the country and in 1959 forced the exile of the Dalai Lama and 80,000 of his followers to India. Suppression of religion and destruction of monasteries followed, and a steady influx of Chinese immigrants has diluted the indigenous population.

☸ Uygurs

THE MORE THAN 7.5 million Uygur people of western China's Xinjiang region inhabit desert and mountain expanses that were once known as eastern Turkestan. Two million more live in Pakistan, Afghanistan, Saudi Arabia, Turkey, Europe, and North America.

Uygur origins date from the third and fourth centuries, when Turkic tribes roamed as nomads in search of pastures and oases. In time, the people created empires extending

A laughing Sherpa girl in Tibetan-style striped apron (top left) lives just south of Mount Everest. Famed as skillful climbers, hardy Sherpas came from eastern Tibet some 400 years ago. In southwestern China, Bai women and children (top right) watch fireworks that accompany the raising of a house in their agriculturally rich homeland. A Uygur man (above) eyes motorcycles in Kashgar, once a fabled stop on the Silk Road in far western China. A highway to Pakistan and a train link with eastern China have brought modern transportation while supermarkets have begun replacing ancient bazaars.

east to the Yellow River, north to Siberia, and south to Pakistan. Positioned at the Silk Road's midpoint, Uygurs slowly abandoned their nomadic lifestyle, took up farming and trade, and enhanced their culture with religious and intellectual exchange. They became scholars, administrators, inventors of a versatile script, and creators of magnificent cave art. Their contributions to architecture, music, printing, and medicine have enriched the whole region.

Uygur life, long tied to oases, centered on Buddhist Turfan in the northeast and on Muslim Kashgar in the southwest—both in today's Xinjiang region. The Muslims conquered their northeastern brethren at the end of the 1300s and were able to remain independent from China until 1759, when the Qing dynasty took over. China has determined the larger fate of the Uygurs ever since.

Although Uygurs have ostensible autonomy in their homeland, ethnic unrest is prevalent. For decades, large numbers of Han Chinese have been migrating to Xinjiang to relieve population pressures elsewhere and to develop the region. For the Uygurs, this has meant curtailment of their religion and dilution of their communities.

Today, the markets of Xinjiang are a mix of Arab souk, Chinese bazaar, and Central Asian trading station, filled with animals, tack shops, pungent spices, furs, carpets, brilliantly hued silk dresses, and vendors selling kebabs and huge flat breads. Beyond the markets, farmers still irrigate their fields with an ingenious system of underground channels that bring water from the distant Tian Shan mountains.

SOUTHEAST ASIA
BALINESE • DAYAK • JAVANESE • KHMER • MINANGKABAU • THAIS • VIETNAMESE

⊛ BALINESE

THE TINY, VOLCANIC island of Bali, east of Java in the Indonesian Archipelago, has long enthralled visitors and residents alike. For the three million Balinese, this tropical island is an entire world, with physical and spiritual attributes important for existence. The Balinese believe that because their cosmos is so rich, the psychic, unseen forces constantly spill over into the mundane. Daily life becomes a vibrant expression of propitiation and praise for gods and nymphs, demons and witches. Hardly a day goes by without a procession or a temple festival, and at night villages far and wide come alive with the hypnotic music of gamelan percussion orchestras.

In the otherwise Muslim expanse of Indonesia, Bali has remained a Hindu holdout. Hinduism arrived with Indian traders and found such a firm foothold in the seventh and eighth centuries that Bali was later able to resist all attempts at conversion, even after Islam dominated Java and other islands in the sixteenth century.

Beneath a holy volcano known as the Gunung Agung, "navel of the world," spread the emerald rice fields and myriad villages forming the heart of Balinese life. Here, sophisticated artists continually create, remake, and teach their traditions. Myths, rituals, painting, carving, acting, and dancing all seem to come together in Bali, where more than 5,000 dance troupes testify to the importance of creative and religious expression. The Balinese also encourage trance states as a way to communicate directly with the spirit world.

Bali's most powerful drama revolves around the clash between two mythical creatures, Barong and Rangda. The lion-beast Barong—representing sunshine, medicine, life, and light—provides the antidote for evil. He likes to dance for sheer joy, but his playfulness is interrupted by the appearance of Rangda, hideous witch and queen of death. In a climactic struggle, trance dancers rush to Barong's aid, only to have their own daggers turned against them by Rangda's evil magic. But Barong's power prevents the daggers from piercing the flesh. Slowly, the dancers are brought out of their trances by Barong's beard, his power center. Neither creature wins this cosmic struggle; goodness gains only a temporary victory.

Since the 1930s, Bali has seen growing numbers of tourists, and now half a million each year swarm through temples and villages. The threat of cultural breakdown and commercialization of the entire island is always present, yet Bali's dynamic, adaptable people keep a firm view of themselves and their unique culture.

⊛ DAYAK

LIVING ALONG large, meandering rivers flowing through the forests of Borneo, the Dayak are a people whose name covers numerous non-Muslim ethnic groups. Most of the two million Dayak inhabit southern and western Borneo, in both East Malaysia and Indonesian Kalimantan.

Traditionally, Dayak communities were made up of several hundred people who maintained few ties with other groups. Family clusters lived in longhouses and led a largely self-sufficient way of life that took raw materials and animals from the forest and fish from the rivers. Slightly back from the riverbanks, they practiced simple agriculture, growing dry rice for a few seasons in one field, then abandoning the site for another. Ritual warfare, including head-hunting, was also part of their lives.

In recent decades, the Dayak have been confronted with major changes. Beginning in the 1960s, the Indonesian government poured resources and people into Kalimantan in an effort to exploit the forests and relieve overcrowding elsewhere. A program called *transmigrasi* relocated ethnic

groups from other parts of the densely populated nation, especially the Madurese from Madura and East Java. The extraction of hardwood timber, felled and transported out of Dayak regions, paralleled the growth of farms, plantations, and towns. Placed near native Dayak animists, Muslim immigrants caused economic disparity and distrust, fueling tensions between themselves and the Dayak, who feared the newcomers would take tribal lands as well as any town jobs they held.

Fighting has broken out periodically, but it became fierce in early 2001, when Dayak used spears, axes, and old hunting rifles to attack and displace thousands of Madurese. Hundreds were killed, and head-hunting reappeared during the frenzied bloodletting. Many Madurese left Borneo or fled to refugee camps; in towns, counterattacks caused more deaths. Historic neglect and insensitivity to Dayak needs had set the stage for misunderstandings and conflicts that have since exploded into full-scale ethnic trauma.

⊛ JAVANESE

AN INDONESIAN ISLAND smaller than Florida, Java is home to more than 100 million people, two-thirds of whom are ethnic Javanese living in the central and eastern parts of the island. Beneath Java's backbone of volcanoes and crater lakes, people have engaged in agriculture for 4,500 years. Here, rich soil and abundant water have allowed industrious villagers to turn their homeland into a wet-rice miracle, able to support the dense population.

Throughout their history, the Javanese have evolved an ability to adapt and transform outside forces into a profound inheritance. Layers of cultural history, vital and varied, have created a complex and sophisticated people. Invaders, immigrants, traders, and colonists from Polynesia, India, China, Arabia, Portugal, the Netherlands, and Great Britain left their imprint on the culture, bringing along

many of the world's main religions: Hinduism, Buddhism, Islam, and Christianity.

Indian civilization on Java culminated between A.D. 750 and 900 in a great age of temple building, the legacy of which can still be seen in Hindu and Buddhist monuments sprinkled across the countryside. Borobudur, a massive carved stupa, is Java's most magnificent structure. The refinement of court life during this era also encouraged a language hierarchy that remains to this day. With separate vocabularies reflecting the social positions of its speakers, the Javanese language displays varying levels of speech: coarse, ordinary, modestly respectful, and fully respectful.

In the 15th and 16th centuries, maritime merchants introduced Islam, but the ascendancy of this faith was less a formal conversion than an adaptation of Islam to earlier Hindu-Buddhist institutions. Javanese also practice animism and ancestor worship, believing in the supernatural and acknowledging a world of spirits and ghosts, magic and malevolence. Their religious epics, mytho-heroic stories, and comedies—presented as plays for *wayang kulit* (shadow puppets), *wayang golek* (wooden puppets), and *wayang wong* (human actors)—find enthusiastic audiences.

In arts and crafts, the kris, a double-edged sword with a wavy blade, has an aura of holiness. Many believe krises can fly or that the original owner's soul lives in the blade. Javanese masters of batik, a wax-and-dye process on silk or cotton cloth, create masterpieces based on themes that are secular and sacred, ancient and modern. Batiks can be fine art of subtle styles, colors, and symbols, or they may be purely functional productions for shirts, sarongs, and bags.

⊛ KHMER

CAMBODIA'S KHMER, an ethnic group of more than 11 million people, live in a fertile land watered by the Mekong River and the Great Lake, Tonle Sap.

For more than a thousand years, the Khmer have been animated by Buddhism—influenced by earlier Hinduism—as both a personal faith and state religion. Under a line of Buddhist kings who combined just administrations with huge building projects, the people established a civilization of profound creativity and grand accomplishments. The carved stone complex at Angkor, not merely a temple but a city, represents the flowering of the Khmer from the 9th to 13th centuries. This high point of culture focused on a courtly life of ritual and classical dance, a slow, graceful art form that portrayed Indian epics, romances, and Buddhist themes. Temple dancers served as the earthly counterparts of celestial nymphs, and Angkor's stone carvings record this tradition, which not only entertained the gods but also embodied Khmer ideals.

Incredibly, this land of beauty and refinement was transformed into a place of utter darkness between 1975 and 1979. The Khmer Rouge embarked on a bloody revolution that killed more than 1.5 million people, brought the Khmer close to cultural suicide, and almost destroyed all traces of the past; it took the lives of artists, dancers, and musicians, and threatened to erase the nearly thousand-year-old classical dance tradition. Every Khmer was changed by the mass death, forced labor, disease, and famine. Many fled, with nearly 150,000 finding refuge in the United States.

When the nightmare came to an end, a handful of survivors revived the classical dance and its slow, rhythmic music. Discipline and training started anew, with children as young as eight learning how to dress in opulent, glittering costumes and bring to life the ancient court dance. In their struggle to survive, the Khmer have preserved intact the nation's great arts, the living pieces of cultural memory that provide links to the past and hope for the future.

✥ MINANGKABAU

VIGOROUS AND SUCCESSFUL, the approximately five million Minangkabau inhabit the western section of Sumatra, sixth largest island in the world. Their region of verdant plateaus, forests, gorges, and escarpments supports many small villages where people farm or engage in handicraft, creating such articles as silver and gold filigree and fine embroidered shawls.

The Minangkabau form one of the world's largest matrilineal societies. This means that titles, property, family names, and inheritance go through the female line, even under Islam, which normally favors men. The arrangement provides a degree of social equality uncommon in Asia.

Traditionally, many families live together in a *rumah gadang* (longhouse), and every person stays through life as a member of the mother's original house. If people wish to marry, the prospective bride's family usually makes the proposal, and the new husband, not the wife, changes homes to enter the woman's clan house. In some rural places there is even a groom price. *(Continued on page 42)*

Wearing ceremonial batik waistbands and bearing offerings of flower garlands, food, crafted bamboo decorations, and other gifts, Hindu women and their children prepare to celebrate an annual festival in Bali.

FOLLOWING PAGES:

The funeral of a classmate brings Muslim girls together on Java, the principal island of Indonesia. In 400 years, Islam has become the major religion in a land comprising many cultural layers.

PAGES 40-41:

At Bangkok's Marble Temple (Wat Benchamabophit), candles light a procession of Thai monks. Buddhism permeates all aspects of Thai culture, and many men make retreats for weeks or months to become monks.

When a daughter takes a husband, an annex is added to the longhouse for the growing family. Such extensions, with swooping saddle-back roofs, have hornlike adornments that rise toward the sky and symbolize the horns of a water buffalo, sacred animal of the Minangkabau. By counting longhouse extensions, visitors can guess the number of daughters with husbands and children.

Because of the strong family ties and an emphasis on education, the Minangkabau have one of the highest literacy rates in Indonesia. This group shines in the world of Indonesian letters, having produced many well-known writers over the past century.

Overpopulation and a decline in traditional ways have caused many Minangkabau men to emigrate to other parts of the island nation. Most have gone to the capital, Jakarta, and become successful shop owners, respected teachers, or outstanding cooks who serve up the tasty, spicy dishes for which the people are famous.

✿ THAIS

IN THE DAILY bustle and roar of Bangkok, the capital of Thailand and one of Asia's megacities, all the elements of Thai society have been thrown together. Here coexist the four core groups making up the greater ethnic "nation": Central Thai, Thai-Lao, Northern Thai, and Southern Thai. They all share the faith of Theravada Buddhism, dialects of a common language, and a similar ethnic origin, and all face the same summer monsoon rains and long, dry periods from autumn to spring.

Today's 62 million Thais descend from ancestors who came from southwestern China's Yunnan Province. From the 9th to 13th centuries, a large, non-Chinese kingdom proved to be a buffer that allowed Thais to escape Chinese assimilation. Within this kingdom, Thais held high positions and could expand and migrate steadily into Southeast Asia, even into areas that extend far beyond the present-day borders of Thailand. As a result, most Laotians are Thai by descent, as are the Shan, who make up about 10 percent of the population of Myanmar (Burma). Other Tai-speaking people live in southern China and Vietnam.

Most of the early Thais settled in the fertile zone of the Chao Phraya River, which dominates Thailand's central valley. They officially emerged as a people in 1238, when diverse groups were unified under the Sukhothai kingdom and freed from the formerly dominant Khmer. Buddhism helped to bind them, and this in turn inspired a distinct art style reflecting prosperity and self-confidence, as still seen in carved temples and giant Buddha sculptures.

Today, one of the country's most popular activities is Thai boxing; in fact, it is a national pastime. For all its outward violence, this sport is layered with refinements and cultural meaning that aficionados have come to recognize and admire.

Many Thais follow the lunar calendar and look forward to the predictable and joyous yearly festivals. Perhaps the most popular festival is Loy Krathong. Under a November full moon, the country's rivers, streams, lakes, and canals become sites for honoring Mae Khongkha, goddess of rivers and waterways. People of all ages prepare little boats in the shape of lotuses or miniature temples, which are then blessed and decorated with candles, incense, flowers, and coins before being set afloat. All through the night, millions of tiny lights drift and bob on the waters.

✿ VIETNAMESE

AFTER FOUR DECADES of intermittent warfare against varied foes—Japanese, French, Americans, Cambodians, and Chinese—and following the successful unification in 1975 after a long civil war, the 79 million Vietnamese have settled down to the task of rebuilding their ancient land.

The Vietnamese people originated in the Red River Delta region of the north, but their early roots are very hazy. Sometime between 500 and 200 B.C., they emerged as an ethnic entity from a melting pot that contained seaborne travelers from Oceania and various migrants from Asia, with northern Mongol characteristics predominating. Once established, the Vietnamese marched slowly and steadily

To get salt for packaging and export, Vietnamese women use foot power to raise sea water into evaporation ponds. Such simple methods survive even as Vietnam modernizes.

PAGES 44-45: Perched above the surf in Sri Lanka, fishermen eke out a living. Two decades of civil war between Buddhist Sinhalese and Hindu Tamils have made life difficult here.

southward, settling plains and deltas along the way and reaching the southern Mekong region by the early 1700s. Today, their thousand-mile-long country extends like a huge, stretched letter *S* from the Chinese border to the Gulf of Thailand, taking in an area half the size of Texas.

The Vietnamese language, most likely a member of the complicated Austroasiatic language family of mainland Southeast Asia, was deeply influenced during a millennium of domination by China, when classical Chinese stood as the official discourse of Mandarins and scholars. Much later, in the 17th century, European missionaries created a new script based on the Roman alphabet, and this one replaced Chinese to become the common form of writing.

Confucianism from China held society together through interlocking relationships and duties, helping to establish four major groups: scholar-officials, artisans, merchants, and farmers. Then as now, the peasantry cultivated rice and secured protein by fishing. Today, nearly four out of five Vietnamese continue to reside in the countryside.

Both Mahayana and Theravada Buddhism took hold in Vietnam, the northern branch arriving from China, the southern from India. Buddhist institutions functioned freely until communism arrived in the 20th century and all aspects of religious life were curtailed. Catholics, presently three million strong, flourished for a century after French colonial dominance in the mid-1800s. In the early decades of the 20th century, Vietnam saw the establishment of Cao Dai—a mix of Daoism, Buddhism, Confucianism, and Christianity—in which utopian and cosmological ideals merged with an all-inclusive theology; Cao Dai saints include Victor Hugo, Napoleon, Louis Pasteur, and Winston Churchill.

SOUTH ASIA
BENGALIS • NAGAS • SINHALESE • TAMILS

BENGALIS

THE GREAT BRAHMAPUTRA River meets the expansive Ganges River Delta in the Bengali heartland, and here the people divide themselves into two main regions: the nation of Bangladesh and the Indian state of West Bengal. Though short on many resources, both areas have water and people in excess. Bangladesh, with nearly 126 million people, is the world's most densely populated country, while West Bengal, with 70 million, is India's densest state; the Bengali language ranks sixth in number of speakers.

In 1947, the partition of India split its Bengal Province into Indian and Pakistani sectors; eventually, Bangladesh (formerly East Pakistan) declared its independence and in 1971 became a nation. The division followed religious, not ethnic lines, for all of the people in the area speak the Bengali language and consider themselves Bengalis. India's West Bengal has always been overwhelmingly Hindu, but Bangladesh, with the largest concentration of Muslims in the world, follows a form of Islam that contains pre-Islamic Hindu and Buddhist elements.

Both sectors share a common history and acknowledge common successes, such as the 19th-century revival of literature, music, and the arts. Their shared language, an Indo-European tongue, preserves a rich literary heritage. The works of Rabindranath Tagore, beloved poet and 1913 winner of the Nobel Prize for Literature, are still read and memorized by Muslim and Hindu alike. Poet and playwright Kazi Nazrul Islam, "the voice of Bengali nationalism," grew to become a champion of poor farmers; his plays and tales on political and historical themes gave hope to long-subjugated Muslims.

While many Bengalis live in huge cities such as Calcutta and Dhaka, most of the people are villagers. To the north, they inhabit the hills, but elsewhere Bengalis dwell in a largely watery realm where fishermen, traders, and farmers depend on shallow inlets, fragile islands, and shifting fingers of land. Although the annual summer flooding rejuvenates the countryside with silt, every few years great inundations kill thousands of people.

Daily necessities for Bengalis (below), umbrellas provide protection against the rain in Bangladesh's summer monsoon and against the sun in the hot, dry season. The heavily populated Ganges-Brahmaputra Delta faces floods nearly every year. Bus passengers on India's Grand Trunk Road (opposite) delight in the company of an elephant. From Calcutta to Amritsar, traffic of nearly every variety crosses north India on the historic road established by British colonists.

NAGAS

IN NORTHEASTERN India, a strip of extremely rugged territory between Myanmar (Burma) and the Brahmaputra River Valley is home to the numerous tribal peoples of Nagaland. Although Nagas are difficult to distinguish from other Assamese and Burmese ethnic groups, these people acknowledge an unmistakable shared identity and speak Tibeto-Burman languages. And while their customs may vary, they commonly occupy small villages perched on hilly spurs. The land's jumbled isolation has allowed development of more than 50 dialects, requiring different Naga peoples to use either a pidgin form or Assamese to communicate with one another.

Historically, the Nagas obtained all they needed from the land, the forest, and minor trading. Farming and hunting, supplemented by fishing, supported them well inside their walled villages. Outside, beautiful gateways with bas-relief decorations greeted anyone approaching along the winding, sunken paths leading up to them.

A variety of local organizations distinguish the Nagas, from strong chiefs with near total power to democratic councils to gerontocracies. Throughout the Naga tribes, women have always enjoyed high status, with equality in work and at tribal meetings.

The British, by establishing control over the Naga Hill District in the 1870s, stopped ritual warfare and head-hunting—a practice that had grown out of the belief that a human head retains a vital force, or soul-power, after the victim's decapitation. By taking the head of an enemy, a warrior could gain status, win a bride, and bring to his village an increase in positive energy. Such acts also inspired dances and various forms of art, all with skull motifs. The last case of Naga head-hunting occurred in 1958, several years after the British had left the area.

In the late 19th century, American missionaries began converting Nagas to Christianity, and two-thirds are now Christian. Their religion has reinforced their identity in a region where the majority of people are Hindu.

SINHALESE

IN MULTIETHNIC Sri Lanka, a teardrop-shaped island off the southeastern tip of India, the majority Sinhalese number 15 million out of a population of 20 million. They have since earliest times coexisted with Tamils, then Muslim traders, Portuguese, Dutch, and British. In recent times, though, contention with Tamils has grown into warfare because the Tamils, inhabitants of the island's north and east, seek an independent homeland free of Sinhalese control. Points of division include religion and language as well as ethnic identity.

Indo-Europeans (Aryans) from northern India moved to Sri Lanka about the fifth century B.C. and in time became the Sinhalese, with their own distinct language, Sinhala. As early as the third century B.C., Buddhism had fully converted them, and their mutual faith and shared language bound the people together. Sinhalese kings played important roles as patrons of Buddhism. Because this religion was declining and disappearing in India, the island nation felt protective toward the faith, with its people stressing the need to preserve their special path to enlightenment. The Sinhalese also strongly influenced the development of Buddhism in Southeast Asia through the missionary efforts of their teachers and artists; they used religion and a distinct writing system to direct the flow of education, literature, Buddhist chronicles, and common aspirations. Today, the village monastery or temple still stands as the local center for culture, and to become a monk is considered a noble goal.

Throughout history, successful kingship has been marked by massive irrigation works for the growing of rice and by impressive art and architecture: A period of exceptional flowering in the 12th century produced Polonnaruwa, a magnificent royal Buddhist city that achieved greatness in art, sculpture, and architecture.

❀ TAMILS

THE TAMILS LARGELY inhabit Tamil Nadu, an Indian state created in 1956 to be a home for Tamil speakers, a group tending to be stockier and somewhat darker than northern Indians. Since before the arrival of the Aryans around 1500 B.C., these people have lived at the southeastern limit of the Indian subcontinent.

More than 50 million Tamils define themselves as Tamil-speaking Hindus who share in a great Dravidian culture. The term Dravidian describes an independent family of some 22 languages and the special culture of the south. Except for classical Sanskrit, Tamil is the oldest written language in India: Going back nearly 2,000 years, its rich literary repository includes epics, religious and secular poetry, philosophy, and moral instructions.

Of particular interest are the verses and hymns of devotional literature dating from the sixth to ninth centuries. Collectively, these works are considered to be among the great contributions to Indian civilization. Tamils believe that bhakti, meaning "devotion," elevates a devotee's personal relationship with a god to a level of ecstatic love and selfless praise. Above all, the path of bhakti leads to salvation.

Over the years, Tamils have vociferously resisted the encroachment of the Hindi language and northern cultural influences. They have done so even though they, too, are overwhelmingly Hindu, worshiping at more than 9,000 temples and celebrating a huge variety of riotous festivals.

Madras, the Tamil capital, was a weaving center when the British East India Company built a fort and trading station there in the mid-17th century. Later it became the administrative and trading capital of southern India. Because of British needs for labor elsewhere, emigration created Tamil communities as far away as Fiji, Malaysia, Singapore, South Africa, and Mauritius.

The people's presence in Sri Lanka consists of two groups: the Sri Lankan Tamils, who settled there more than 1,500 years ago, and the Indian Tamils, who came in the 19th and 20th centuries to work on tea and rubber plantations. Civil war in Sri Lanka has led Tamils to migrate to many other countries, but wherever they go, they build temples and develop strong local ties.

N THE 19TH CENTURY, European scholars recognized three broad geographical, cultural, and linguistic zones across the vast Pacific Ocean: Melanesia, immediately to the north and east of Australia; Polynesia, in the central Pacific; and Micronesia, east of the Philippines in the North Pacific. This largely artificial division, which downplays important similarities and connections among the islands, is said to have originated with French explorer Jules-Sébastien-César Dumont D'Urville (1790-1842), who based it on the mistaken notion that three separate races of people dwelled on the widely dispersed islands.

Australia, on the other hand, has always been viewed separately. Indeed, the Aboriginal languages and customs of this continent are not closely linked to those of other Pacific peoples, although archaeological evidence suggests that continuing migrations from Asia through Melanesia and onto the world's largest island began as early as 60,000 years ago.

In the past few centuries, the indigenous cultures of Oceania—a collective name for the Pacific islands and Australia—have been greatly affected by colonialism; at various times they were disrupted or even unified by their opposition to it. In New Zealand, for example, strong Maori resistance to settlement by Europeans

OCEANIA

Face of Melanesia: On the island of New Guinea, an aged warrior of Irian Jaya wears a curved pig-tusk nose ornament.

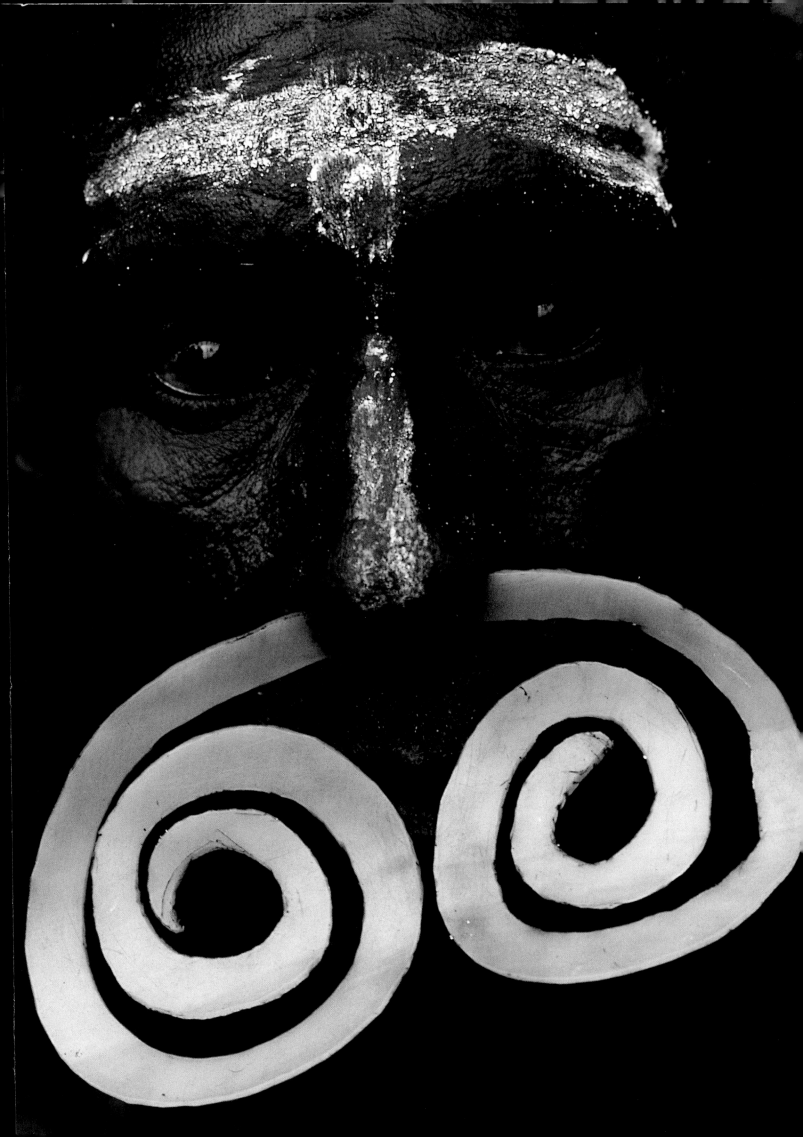

resulted in an 1840 treaty establishing terms of coexistence. Such a treaty was never contemplated with the Aborigines of Australia. The British considered Australia *terra nullius*, a "land without people," despite the fact that at the time of James Cook's 1770 expedition more than 500 tribes were living there. Because Aborigines had no recognizable system of land tenure in the eyes of British law, the British believed there was no one with whom they could conduct negotiations for the transfer of land.

Following the tragic excesses of the chaotic frontier period, Australia's policy in relation to the Aborigines ranged from protection to assimilation, integration, and finally self-determination. Not until 1992 was the terra nullius doctrine overturned by the Australian High Court. Now Aboriginal groups are reclaiming their homelands through federally enacted native title legislation, and Aboriginal reconciliation ranks high on the national agenda. Through it all, though, Aborigines have held on to many of their traditions, continuing to follow rituals and practices associated with the Dreaming or Dreamtime, a system of beliefs related to events at the "beginning of time."

Traditions are also important to Pacific islanders, providing links to the past and helping them maintain a sense of solidarity. Over countless generations and sometimes across great distances, islanders reached out and connected through trade and intermarriage to other Pacific peoples. Then, in the 16th century, European explorers sailed into their waters, and by the mid-1800s, most of their islands had been claimed by Germany, France, Spain, and England. The United States entered the colonial arena following the Spanish-American War of 1898, with acquisitions in the Philippines, Guam, Hawaii, and Samoa. After World War I, Japan took control of many former German territories.

The invasiveness of colonial rule varied widely among the islands: In some cases, contact was infrequent and did not threaten the cultural integrity of local populations, while in others, the islanders' rights of self-determination were curtailed. Some groups felt compelled to develop strategies of avoidance or resistance that often grew into anticolonial and protonationalist movements. The most famous of these responses were the Melanesian cargo cults, which held that a supernatural "cargo" of deities and ancestors would arrive among supplies delivered to the islands, thus bringing about an age of plenty and a new, moral world order devoid of a ruling European presence.

Between 1962 and 1980, most colonial territories achieved independence. But the postcolonial period for many of them has been marked by deep division and civil unrest. In Polynesia, where chiefdoms are largely determined by genealogy and seniority rather than personal prowess, island chiefs have readily made the transition to political leadership; however, the justice of their continued rule is sometimes challenged. In much of Melanesia, political organization centers on "big men" who achieve leadership through oratory skills, gift-giving, and marriage alliances. While Melanesians share a common religion (Christianity), they often resist forming alliances with strangers and former enemies. Military coups in Fiji in 1987, independence movements in Bougainville and Irian Jaya, and the 1985 assassination of the president of Palau are symptoms of the difficulties Pacific islanders face as they move toward democracy.

Although indigenous groups may achieve freedom from foreign rule, they sometimes find that national unity threatens their cultural distinctiveness. New states, often

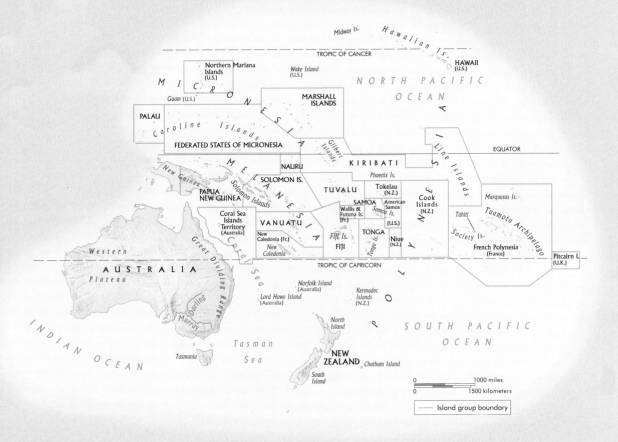

dogged by local demands for autonomy, may actively resist the notion of land rights for cultural or ethnic groups within their boundaries. Instead, governments try to promote a sense of shared identity, particularly in regard to *kastom* (custom or tradition).

In Melanesia, people have a long history of making and remaking kastom, creating and re-creating songs, myths, dances, and other cultural expressions associated with constituent groups. Such expressions are sources of prestige for their creators, and new variations are traded and exchanged following traditional practices—as exemplified by the Trobriand Islands *kula* ring. Members of this trading network travel in canoes around an island group off Papua New Guinea, and as they exchange arm rings, necklaces, and other items, they affirm ties between ring partners and their communities.

In some Oceanian states, population growth rates are among the world's highest; even so, survival of many groups is threatened by large-scale plantation agriculture, mining activities, migration and transmigration, and uncontrolled fishing and logging. Forced dislocation and illnesses stemming from atomic testing have been major problems in Micronesia, where many people are kept from their former homes by alarming levels of radioactivity. Traditionally, Micronesians have occupied small villages with a strongly hierarchical social order. Today, that order has not declined appreciably, despite the establishment of constitutional governments in places such as Palau. There remains a deep sense of attachment to homes and ancient customs—a feeling shared by many Oceanians.

Following Pages: In the Trobriand Islands, a coral archipelago off the coast of Papua New Guinea, people follow a traditional Melanesian lifestyle, including these two young women bathing in the warm, tropical waters surrounding Kaileuna Island.

OCEANIA

Clockwise from top:
Hawaiian hula teacher
and students, Papua
New Guinea villagers,
Australian Aborigine

AUSTRALIA

MELANESIA

POLYNESIA

MICRONESIA

AUSTRALIA

ARRERNTE • CAPE YORK PEOPLES • MARDU •
NGARRINDJERI • NYUNGAH • PALAWA • PINTUBI
• TIWI • TORRES STRAIT ISLANDERS • WARLPIRI •
WURUNDJERI • YOLNGU

ARRERNTE (Aranda or Arunta)

CENTRAL AUSTRALIA'S Arrernte are perhaps the most
famous Aboriginal Australians, thanks in part to the
writings of such distinguished European social scientists
as Sigmund Freud (1856-1939) and Émile Durkheim
(1858-1917). Their works were classic ethnographic studies
focusing on the concept and meaning of the Dreaming
or Dreamtime—traditional land-based Aboriginal
religion—and on the Arrernte kinship system, within
which a man marries his mother's mother's brother's
daughter's daughter (his second cousin).

The Arrernte are a collection of Arandic-speaking
peoples from the well-watered Macdonnell Ranges region
in the vicinity of Alice Springs. These peoples include the
Alyawarre, Anmatyerre, and Western Arrernte. All suffered
gravely after contact with Europeans, experiencing high
mortality rates, physical and emotional dislocation, and
ethnocide. Some groups became extinct.

In the 1860s, after 20,000 years of living in this region,
the Arrernte first encountered non-Aborigines. With
colonization came the conversion of their lands into grazing
lands, where they worked as ranch hands and domestic
servants; in return, they received rations and pocket money.
Since the 1970s, some of the lands have been returned to
the traditional landowners through federal land-rights
laws and excisions on ranches.

The Dreaming is still relevant for the Arrernte, even
though the beliefs and practices of Christianity are quite
prominent in their lives. Large families are common among
these former nomads, who now reside in permanent
settlements where more than half the population is made
up of minors. Joblessness is a serious problem, and a large
proportion of income comes from unemployment benefits
and pensions. Arrernte purchase most of their foodstuffs
from retail outlets, supplementing them with kangaroos,
emus, bush turkeys, goannas, rabbits, honey ants, witchetty
grubs, and bush fruits.

CAPE YORK PEOPLES

EXHIBITING CONSIDERABLE social, cultural, and linguistic
diversity, the 6,000 Aborigines living in Cape York make
up 35 percent of the cape's population and own 20 percent
of the land. Most of them dwell in Aboriginal-controlled
townships and outstations. According to archaeological
evidence, Cape Aborigines at one time tried farming
activities, but the benefits of agriculture did not outweigh
the costs in terms of labor. A nomadic lifestyle provided

much more time for leisure activities, the performance of rituals, and the forging and maintenance of inter- and intra-clan alliances.

The Wik of the central west coast may be the best known Cape Aborigines. Their participation in the momentous legal movement of the 1990s helped end the long fiction of *terra nullius*, "land without people," the policy that had facilitated dispossession of Aboriginal lands. In recent years, the Cape York Land Council was formed to pursue Aboriginal property rights on the cape, and it has embarked on a number of novel and groundbreaking regional comanagement schemes with conservationists, pastoralists, and miners. Even so, Cape Aborigines continue to endure poor health standards and have a life expectancy that is among the lowest in the country.

MARDU

AUSTRALIA'S WESTERN desert, one of the most inhospitable landscapes on Earth, is devoid of permanent streams or lakes. For this reason, the Mardu homelands were long considered undesirable by non-Aborigines and remained unsettled until well into the 1960s, thus enabling desert-dwellers to survive European contact with cultures intact.

Before contact, the Mardu—a collective term for the Giyadjarra, Mandjildjarra, and Budidjarra language groups—led a nomadic life in the desert. They moved from place to place, taking advantage of changing weather patterns and using stone, bone, and wood tools to provide for themselves. Population density was low, averaging only one person in 75 square miles.

Like other Aborigines, the Mardu believe that the continued existence of both the world and their people

Corroboree Rock, in Australia's eastern Arrernte homelands, marks a water hole frequented by kangaroos, emus, and bush turkeys. An Aboriginal woman recalls when people also came to sing, dance, and debate.

In the Great Sandy Desert, an Aborigine displays a wild turkey—a desert specialty and a prize catch—after a day's hunt in the heart of Australia's Outback, where temperatures reach 130°F.

depends on the maintenance of their relationship with all-powerful Dreaming entities, the objects of their religious life. These entities are said to have emerged from the flat, featureless void that was Earth at the beginning of time. With the outward appearance of either humans or animals, they moved across the landscape, shaping the territories of the Mardu as they traveled. These totemic beings performed rituals to be emulated by the people, and they imbued the landscape with the spirit that animates humans and all other living things. In addition, they instituted laws and procedures that were blueprints for social interaction, hunting, performing circumcision and subincision, and more. Eventually the entities transformed themselves into features of the landscape, which serve as eternal reminders of the sacred laws followed by all Mardu. Today, Mardu men still spend much of their time discussing spiritual matters, crafting sacred objects, and performing age-old rituals at sacred sites known as *jabiya*.

🌀 NGARRINDJERI

THE NGARRINDJERI of South Australia's lower Murray River were once best known for the near equality of their men and women, something unique in Aboriginal Australia. Although sacred rituals were usually the province of men, the Ngarrindjeri women also played important roles in the ceremonial life of the tribe.

Encompassing five different lowland zones, the tribe's rich environment was particularly attractive to colonists. As a result, the Ngarrindjeri became predominantly of mixed descent by 1900, and less than half a century later,

few people retained knowledge of the traditional ways and customs. This situation grew worse as the government increased pressure on the people to assimilate into the dominant Australian society.

Currently, the Ngarrindjeri are perhaps more socio-economically integrated than other Aboriginal groups. Nevertheless, they embrace their Aboriginality and are actively involved in attempts to revive traditions and beliefs. They also hope to remedy the social problems associated with alcohol abuse and economic disadvantage. One of their chief means of reinvigorating tradition is the clan-wide, ongoing opposition to the destruction of sacred sites by developers, particularly in the vicinity of Hindmarsh Island. Led by Ngarrindjeri women, the protest has brought worldwide attention to the plight of this marginalized group and forced debate on a great national concern: Has the tide of history washed away not only knowledge of ancestral beliefs and practices but also traditional attachments and rights to the land?

🌀 NYUNGAH (Nyoongah)

FOR AT LEAST 40,000 years, the Nyungah and their ancestors have occupied the Swan River area in the vicinity of Perth. The name of their language group, also Nyungah, forms part of the collective label for a body of languages—the Pama-Nyungan language family—spoken by 80 percent of Aborigines, from the tip of Cape York to the southwest corner of the continent.

Until 1829, when the British established a colony in the Nyungah's Western Australia homelands, the people had led a seminomadic life; they moved freely from one area to another, depending upon the availability of water, fish, game, fruit, and root vegetables. But colonization struck the Aboriginal economy at its core. Depleted or destroyed were the Nyungah's traditional food resources, and the people soon became dependent upon introduced goods. The first few decades of the settlement at Swan River saw large numbers of Aborigines dying after contracting measles, influenza, and other introduced illnesses.

Despite their violent 19th-century clashes with soldiers, convicts, and free settlers—and subsequent harassment by 20th-century bureaucrats—the Nyungah have maintained a sense of themselves as a distinct cultural entity. As an urban Aboriginal collective, they face immense problems, not the least of which is how to reinvigorate a land-based culture when areas of greatest significance are covered by asphalt and concrete.

Aboriginality in Australia is a matter of self-ascription, but recognition from the state requires two things: proof of descent and membership in a community of Aborigines. In the Nyungah case, various territorial and linguistic bands merged in the late 1800s, and new communities evolved that could claim descent from earlier groupings. Nyungah associations now provide a collective voice for speaking out on topics of common concern.

◉ PALAWA

ABORIGINES HAVE occupied Tasmania for as long as 32,000 years. Known as the Palawa, they thrived as one of the world's southernmost human populations during the last ice age. Then, as the ice age came to a close around 10,000 B.C., rising seas separated Tasmania and its people from the rest of Australia. The population would live in isolation until the arrival of Dutch, French, and English explorers.

The Palawa were divided into 70 to 85 bands of 30 to 80 people, with each band occupying a territory of around 200 to 300 square miles. These Tasmanians were grouped into nine larger social units or tribes that shared a common culture and language. Very little is known of their religious beliefs and practices, apart from the fact that 3,500 years ago, for unknown reasons, fish ceased to be part of their diet; instead, shellfish, crustaceans, and penguins became their nutritional mainstays.

In 1803, the English established a convict settlement at Hobart, and the massacre of local Aborigines began. Martial law was declared in 1828, culminating in a huge military operation, or "Black Line," which was designed to corral all surviving Aborigines onto offshore islands and into remote enclaves. By 1838, there were only 82 survivors from the original population; the last "full blood"—a woman named Truganini—died in 1876.

Today, thousands of people claim Palawa ancestry because they descend from Aboriginal women and non-Aboriginal sealers and whalers. Through their mothers, they have learned about the importance of their natural heritage and about the strength of the Aboriginal spirit, and they continue to use kinship, oral history, and traditions to keep the culture alive. In Aboriginal schools, old languages are again being spoken, and sacred sites are being honored.

◉ PINTUBI

BY 1965, THE GOVERNMENT of the Northern Territory had removed the so-called lost tribe of Gibson Desert Pintubi Aborigines from their homeland and settled them hundreds of miles to the east in Papunya. About 150 miles west of Alice Springs, the settlement was one of the last Aboriginal communities to be established. It was intended as a place for "re-educating" people to ensure their assimilation into mainstream society, but the Aborigines who were taken

there managed to retain their traditional language and culture. The Papunya community, now among the most well-known autonomous Aboriginal settlements, instead became the focus of an extraordinary 20th-century success story. Ceremonial sand designs, as well as designs inscribed or painted on the body during sacred and secret Pintubi rituals, became the centerpiece of a local arts movement that eventually spread throughout Australia. One of the most successful businesses owned and directed by the Aborigines is Papunya Tula Artists, a cooperative that began in 1971. Its art has done very well internationally, sometimes selling for record prices in such places as New York and Paris.

The increasing prominence of Pintubi designs has had a dramatic impact on art and craft production throughout Australia's center. To meet tourists' growing demand for the art, other Aborigines have been motivated to learn more about their Dreaming stories and designs and to seek out elders who could teach them, leading to a widespread cultural renaissance. Artists insist they are not selling their heritage; rather, they want the world to know about their culture. They keep the sacred knowledge for themselves, to be passed on to their children; while style may have changed, the sacred message has not, they say.

Since 1981, artists have established outstations at Warlungurra and Kiwirrkura, near the Northern Territory's border with Western Australia, and both are flourishing settlements. Kiwirrkura was the scene of a remarkable development in 1984, when first contact was made with perhaps the last of the traditional or "bush" Pintubi. Neither Aborigines nor non-Aborigines had believed that there were desert-dwellers who still followed a traditional nomadic lifestyle, and the reuniting of the nine bush Pintubi with family members—who had lost touch with them more than 25 years before—attracted substantial international media attention.

◉ TIWI

THE TIWI OF northern Australia's Melville and Bathurst Islands experienced their first recorded exposure to Europeans in the 18th century; it was an encounter that would be followed by many more over the years. After a false start in the 1820s, European settlement of the Tiwi islands finally began in earnest in the early 20th century. Since that time, however, the Aboriginal Land Rights (Northern Territory) Act of 1976 has been passed, and the Tiwi have regained full control of their islands.

Today, most Tiwi live in three townships: Nguiu, the former Catholic mission; Pularumpi, which had been a school for part-Aboriginal children; and Milikapi, the former government settlement. Some of the people here go on weekend kangaroo- and turtle-hunting excursions, but they now rely on outboard motorboats and shotguns rather than the traditional dugout canoes and spears.

The Tiwi's concept of Dreaming distinguishes them from other Aborigines. Divided into *murukupupuni,* or individual Tiwi "countries," their islands are "spirit-child" centers in which membership is determined by the burial place of one's father. Tiwi believe that when a new clan member is conceived, a spirit-child is transferred through a dream from a father to a mother of the same clan.

Celebrating the Tiwi culture, Nguiu's Tiwi Design Aboriginal Corporation is the base of operations for Tiwi Design, a collective of about a hundred artists involved in textile design, weaving, painting, printmaking, wood carving, and ceramics. Many consider it a good model for other Aboriginal art enterprises.

☙ TORRES STRAIT ISLANDERS

WHERE ONCE there was a land bridge, 90 miles of sea now separate Australia's Cape York Peninsula from Papua New Guinea. More than a hundred named islands and many thousands of islets, reefs, and sandbanks dot the Torres Strait, home to an indigenous population quite distinct from the original inhabitants of mainland Australia. Combining cultural and genetic influences from both Australia and Melanesia, the 30,000 Torres Strait islanders trace their ancestry to 14 island groups and claim rights of ownership to the lands and waters where their ancestors have dwelled for more than 4,000 years.

Before colonization by Europeans, the Torres Strait's eastern and northern islands, such as Mer and Saibai, were home to permanent villages of bamboo-and-thatch huts. Elsewhere, settlements were transitory and populated according to the seasonal availability of resources. In their large double-outrigger canoes, islanders engaged in extensive trading relationships not only with each other but also with Papuans to the north and Aborigines to the south. They sent out pearl-shell harpoons, ornaments, and human heads, and in return they received sago, yams, coconuts, tobacco, bird of paradise feathers, and outrigger canoes. Subsistence came from both the sea and horticulture: Positioned on platforms constructed in shallow waters, islanders fished or hunted turtles and dugongs; families also relied on defined garden plots inherited from their ancestors along the male line. If they wished, the owners could transfer or lend their lands to others for gardening and foraging purposes.

Unlike inhabitants of the Australian mainland, Torres Strait islanders have been able to maintain traditional production, exchange, and subsistence practices. Today, the strait is largely an autonomous zone, a situation unique in indigenous Australia. Islanders manage their own affairs through the Torres Strait Regional Authority, the Island Coordinating Council, and the Torres Strait Council. In addition, each island has a council with local government responsibilities.

Major issues include a significant out-migration to the mainland, poor health and education standards, and crowding in the limited available housing. Ties to coastal New Guinea communities, once strong, are now in decline or have been terminated: The international boundary limits communications, and there is growing disparity in wealth among the former trading partners. But pride in cultural heritage continues and is exemplified in annual cultural festivals that draw thousands of visitors.

WARLPIRI

AMONG THE most populous Aboriginal groups in Australia's Northern Territory, the Warlpiri were traditionally hunter-gatherers living in small groups of up to 30 people. They led a hydrocentric existence in the Tanami Desert, their movements around water sources characterizing life in their vast, arid homeland. Regular contact with Europeans commenced in 1911 with the establishment of the Tanami goldfields. Later, in the Coniston Massacre of 1928, as many as a hundred Warlpiri were killed by government forces; others fled northward from home territories to escape further depredations. Survivors were forced to settle in the 1940s, and today they and their descendants inhabit the small communities of Yuendumu, Lajamanu, Warrabri, Willowra, and Nyirrpi, as well as outstations.

Following the 1976 enactment of federal land-rights legislation, almost all of the country the Warlpiri owned prior to contact was returned to them. This has not restored the independence they once enjoyed, however. Most of the people are unemployed and getting by on various forms of government support, minimally supplemented by mining royalties and art sales.

The Warlpiri are known for their "dot paintings," which illustrate visions of their Dreaming, or *Jukurrpa*, narratives. By re-creating the individual and collective Dreamings and associated places in the landscape—with their customary U-shapes, concentric circles, and journey lines—artists assert their rights and obligations to the land. One of the best known Warlpiri artists is Michael Jagamara Nelson, who produced the design for, and also helped create, the forecourt mosaic of Australia's Parliament House in Canberra. In 1985, the Warlukurlangu Artists Aboriginal Association was incorporated after the works of Warlpiri women artists, who had transferred their body-painting designs to canvas, gained international attention.

WURUNDJERI

"KOORIE" IS THE popular name among Aborigines for the 17,000 indigenous people of southeastern Australia. The Wurundjeri, a Koorie group, live on the Yarra River plains now encompassed by the city of Melbourne, Australia's largest city after Sydney.

In the first decade of contact between the English colonists and the Wurundjeri, diseases decimated local populations. Survivors watched as their hunting grounds were cleared and drained and their sites of cultural significance were destroyed. Within ten years, only 300 to 400 people remained, and they soon became totally dependent upon the newcomers.

Very little is known about traditional religious and spiritual life, except that clan members belonged to one of two intermarrying moieties, or halves, called Eagle Hawk and Crow. The Wurundjeri also were part of a confederacy of clans known as Kulin; today, though, social life centers on the extended family. The Wurundjeri still maintain spiritual and cultural ties to the land, asserting their role as traditional caretakers of the territory created by the Dreaming entity known as Bunjil.

In response to the situation of urban Aborigines, the federal government established the Indigenous Land Council, which has since helped the Wurundjeri purchase the old mission site of Coranderrk and the surrounding 200 acres—a small portion of their former tribal lands. The Wurundjeri have also established a heritage walking trail and a bush-food trail in Melbourne, with the hope they can raise awareness among the general population about the region's history and its significance to the Koorie. Downtown Melbourne was built atop Aboriginal burial sites, resource extraction areas, ceremonial and sacred areas, and former campsites. Markers placed along the trails describe the old Aboriginal way of life.

YOLNGU

SPEAKERS OF Pama-Nyungan languages, the 4,000 Aboriginal people of northeastern Arnhem Land refer to themselves as Yolngu. They are well known not only for the richness of their cultural heritage, as expressed in traditional feathered ornaments and paintings on eucalyptus-tree bark, but also for their fundamentalist Christian beliefs. The Yolngu community of Galiwin'ku, which was the setting for the landmark Adjustment Movement in Arnhem Land, is especially noteworthy for the innovative ways people have incorporated Christianity into their worldview without compromising the sanctity of the Dreaming. Affirming their belief in both traditional religion and Christianity, residents publicly stated that neither would receive preference in their lives. Galiwin'ku is also the base of the touring Aboriginal Black Crusade, whose aim is to re-Christianize Australia's non-Aborigines.

Yolngu have a rich history of contacts with outsiders. From the late 1600s to the early 1900s, the Yolngu traded with Indonesian fisherfolk who were seeking access to fisheries and trade beyond the *(Continued on page 64)*

Cat's cradle: As children watch, Arnhem Land women (opposite) manipulate bark twine into the shape of a Dreaming ancestor—the turtle. During this popular pastime, women teach children about the traditional world, showing them images from a repertoire of about 250 patterns.
FOLLOWING PAGES: To clear the head and lungs of her newborn granddaughter, and thus give the child a healthy start to life, an Aboriginal woman passes the infant through the conkerberry-scented smoke of a ritual fire.
PAGES 62-63:
In Irian Jaya, a family shares a tree house, with men and women at separate hearths. They used palm fronds for the walls and roof and built fires on mud-covered lattices placed over holes in the floor.

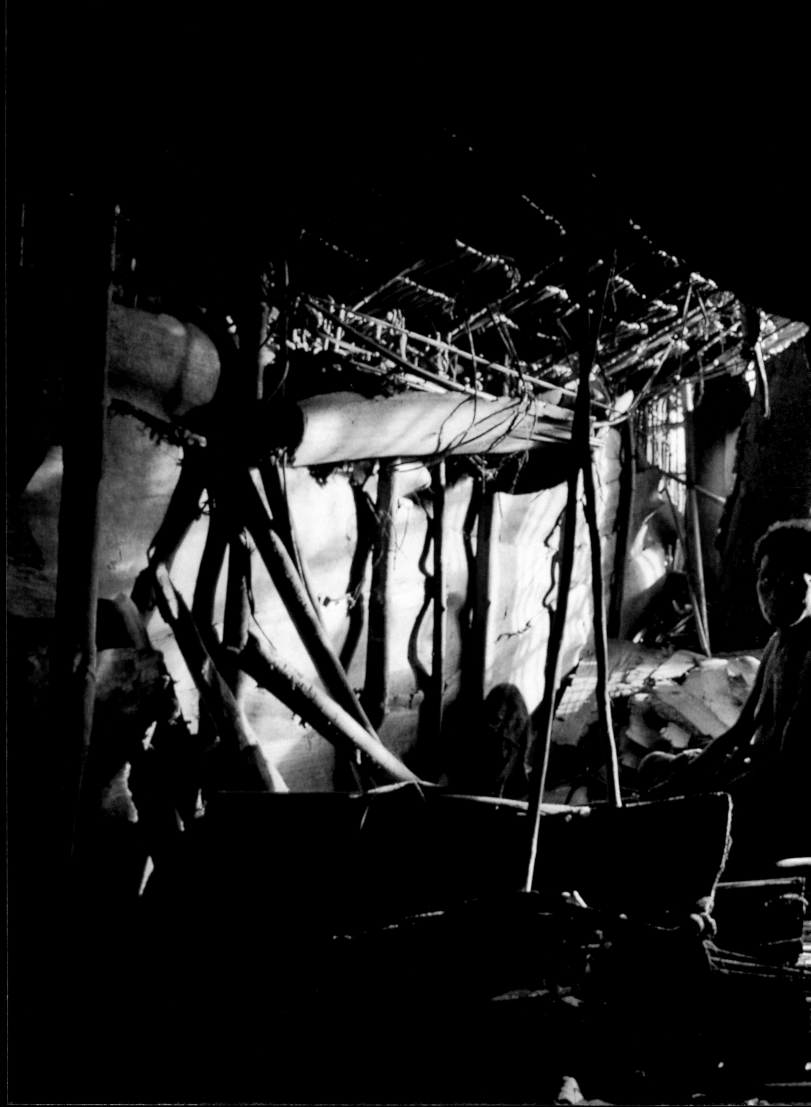

control of colonial European powers. These long-distance voyagers worked with the Yolngu in the procurement of trepang, a sea cucumber that was then sold at great profit, thereby establishing Australia's first international industry. It is widely held that these precolonial contacts enabled the Yolngu to better deal with the later arrival of missionaries, miners, and bureaucrats.

In the 1960s, the Yolngu mounted a sustained protest against bauxite mining by a multinational company at Yirrkala. Their efforts even included a bark petition to the government, but they still could not win the court case against mining on their sacred lands. The case did, however, set in motion a commission of inquiry into how land rights could be delivered to Aboriginal Australians, leading eventually to the proclamation of the Aboriginal Land Rights Act of 1976. More than 50 percent of the Northern Territory has now been returned to Aborigines.

MELANESIA
CHIMBU • ENGA • FOI • MARIND-ANIM
• MIDDLE SEPIK • MOTU • TANNESE • TOLAI
• TROBRIANDERS

CHIMBU

INHABITING THE Wahgi and Chimbu River Valleys of the eastern highlands, the Chimbu are one of Papua New Guinea's largest populations. They were first contacted by Jim Taylor and Michael and Dan Leahy, Australian explorers and gold prospectors, on their epic patrol into the New Guinea highlands in 1933—when the region was controlled by Australia.

Soon after contact, the Chimbu were missionized by Lutherans and Catholics. They also experienced rapid cultural change in the post-World War II period, when Australia placed the Territory of Papua and the Trust Territory of New Guinea under a single administration. In 1975, Papua New Guinea became independent.

Originally part of the Eastern Highlands District (now a province), the Chimbu broke away and later became the Simbu Province. Today, they and other eastern highlanders are successful coffee growers and a dynamic force in the economy and on the national political scene.

Along with western highlanders, the Chimbu were transformed by the agricultural revolution that introduced sweet potatoes into New Guinea almost 300 years ago. This crop, which allowed intensive cultivation, not only spurred growth of the human population but also supported a large domestic pig population. The Chimbu subsequently developed an elaborate ceremonial system based on the exchange of pigs, shell valuables, feathers, and other items.

Because of their expanding population, the people became chronically short of land. Early in the 1960s, in some parts of Chimbu territory, densities reached as high as 500 inhabitants per square mile. This led to endemic warfare and to expansion of the Chimbu into less densely populated lower-elevation areas south of their home area.

Like the western highlanders, the Chimbu have no hereditary positions of authority. They are very egalitarian, with men exerting authority on the basis of personal characteristics such as strength, bravery, and generosity.

ENGA

THE ENGA ARE one of the most numerous populations of the western highlands of Papua New Guinea. As is the case with the Chimbu of the eastern highlands, the Enga have their own province—Enga Province—with its capital at Wapenamanda. They survive on intensive sweet potato cultivation, which in turn supports vast pig herds. Other garden foods, including greens, sugarcane, bananas, and introduced vegetables, supplement the sweet potato.

The Enga do not supplement their daily diet with pork; instead, they use the pigs in a regional exchange cycle called the *tee*, which also involves trading ceremonial crescent pearl shells. The pigs are periodically slaughtered at great, highly ceremonialized events that are part of the tee.

Before Australian colonial pacification in the 1950s, warfare was endemic among Enga groups, with casualties from fighting claiming around 25 percent of the male population between 1900 and 1955. In many respects, the competitive display and acquisition of shell wealth and pigs is a peaceful substitute for actual warfare, and the tee has actually become enhanced and more important in local political life since the advent of the Pax Australiana.

The Enga are known for their strict separation of men and women. Like their Huli neighbors, Enga men feared contamination by women's sexual and menstrual fluids. Cohabitation was not permitted, and women were not allowed to enter men's space in the village during their menstrual periods. Feminine fertility, on the other hand, figured centrally in the Enga's precontact male cults, a general characteristic of groups in the western highlands.

Hereditary chiefs and other formal leadership positions are not part of Enga culture or the societies of most other large horticultural groups in the New Guinea highlands. Male leadership is acquired through prowess in warfare, success in tee exchange, skill in oratory and magic, and management of ceremonial wealth. Enga politics are thus mutable and dynamic, reflecting the egalitarian society.

FOI

TODAY NUMBERING about 6,000, the Foi inhabit the banks of Lake Kutubu and the valley of the Mubi River in the

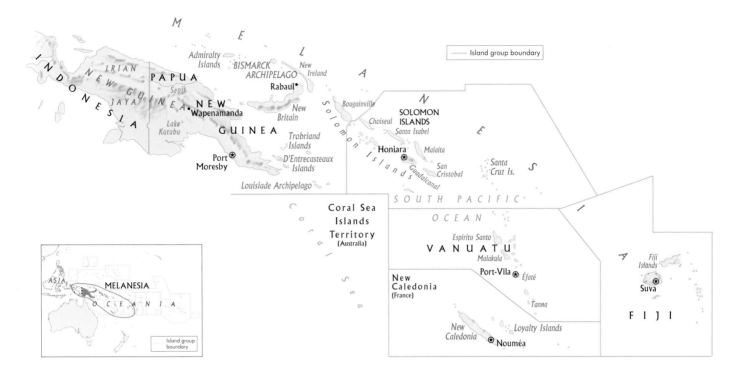

Island group boundary

Southern Highlands Province of Papua New Guinea. Their first significant contact was in 1936 with explorers Ivan Champion and William Adamson, who subsequently established a police camp from which to conduct their historic peacekeeping Bamu-Purari patrol.

The Foi's subsistence lifestyle relies on sago processing and on hunting, gathering, fishing, and gardening. At the center of each village is the communal longhouse, where all of the men live; the women inhabit smaller, individual houses flanking the longhouse. Each village is composed of between 3 and 11 clans related through the male line, and these clans prefer to intermarry with one another and with clans of neighboring longhouse villages. Traditionally, the Foi engaged in trade, intermarriage, and warfare with all of their neighbors. Most men also spoke at least one other language—that of their closest non-Foi neighbor.

Occupying a strategic position between the edge of the southern highlands and the interior south coast, the Foi had a highly fluid religion that readily adapted cult practices from neighboring groups. Knowledge and objects associated with fertility and sorcery cults passed through the Mubi Valley in exchange for wealth objects such as pigs, black palm bows, bird feathers, and a tree oil known as *digaso*. The Foi's main export, digaso is sap from the *Campnosperma brevipetiolata* tree, which is abundant in their territory.

Although the Foi lack the graphic-art traditions so prominent elsewhere in coastal Papua New Guinea, they do have a highly elaborate verbal art, expressed in poetic songs commemorating their dead kinsmen. Composed by women, these songs are performed by men in public ceremonies on the night following large-scale pork-and-shell exchanges. Men from neighboring ethnic groups also attend the ceremonies and often perform similar poetic songs in their own language and style.

MARIND-ANIM

TRADITIONAL INHABITANTS of New Guinea's southern coast, the Marind-anim lived in Irian Jaya, an Indonesian province that has recently declared itself to be independent West Papua. They were a flamboyant society known for head-hunting raids, often far afield, and for elaborate ceremonies and mythology. Their sexual practices drew the attention of many anthropologists and medical specialists.

The Marind-anim were divided into two groups, as were most of the south-coast peoples; each group had its own mythology and specific ceremonial responsibilities toward the other group. Each boy was appointed a *binahor* father from the opposite group, and the man would undertake to inseminate the boy anally on regular occasions until the boy attained physical maturity. In this culture, semen was considered the source of male growth, life, and fertility in general; its regular ingestion was thought to benefit both men and women, fortifying them and increasing fecundity.

The Marind-anim believed that the semen of a man's entire patrilineal lineage was needed for conception. As a result, a woman was obliged to copulate with her husband and his male kinsmen on a regular basis; she also did so on occasions when semen was needed by men for medicinal or ritual purposes. According to early 20th-century studies by a Dutch medical team, this custom led to a high incidence of genital tract infection and consequent sterility in women. The Marind-anim thus suffered from a very low birthrate, which they made up for by capturing children during head-hunting raids on neighboring tribes.

At a festival in the eastern highlands of Papua New Guinea, a young "mudman" of the Asaro Valley wears mud-based body paint, a typical adornment for the region's beauty-conscious males.

The ceremony, mythology, and sexual practices of the Marind-anim, as well as their cults of warfare and head-hunting, were brought to an end by the Dutch colonial presence and subsequent Indonesian dominance over Irian Jaya (since 1962). With their traditional culture severely repressed by colonial authorities, the Marind-anim embraced Christianity and were assimilated into Indonesian society.

MIDDLE SEPIK

BECAUSE OF THEIR highly developed art and architectural styles, the Middle Sepik River peoples are probably among the best known groups in New Guinea. Their now famous *haus tambaran* (spirit house), a ceremonial longhouse with a high over-hanging roof, was the model for the Papua New Guinea High Commission building in Canberra, Australia.

The peoples of the Middle Sepik—Kwoma, Arapesh, Manambu, and Iatmul—share many cultural similarities, including a totemic clan system organized into larger groups and an elaborate system of initiation for boys, organized around sacred bamboo flutes.

Secrecy is a major dimension of public life along the Sepik River, and as men grow older, they attain greater and greater knowledge of mythological names and significances. Iatmul and Manambu men debate in public, challenging each other's knowledge of secret totemic names. Among the Iatmul, the mythological journeys of ancestral creators are depicted by means of a knotted cord, each knot representing a place where an ancestor stopped along the creative journey; knowledge of these creators is a mark of ritual prominence.

Among the Kwoma and other lowland Sepik River peoples, the staple yam is the focus of fertility ceremonies. In recent times, these ceremonies and the boys' initiations have taken on new forms—nonsacred versions performed for the many tourists who visit every year. Art, too, has become important for the tourist market and is an integral part of the local economy. Sepik carvers are renowned for their masks and depictions of local animals and birds.

East Sepik Province has long provided prominent leaders for the nation of Papua New Guinea, including Michael Somare, who in 1975 was inaugurated as the first prime minister. The province was also one of the first in the country to incorporate traditional landowning clans, allowing them to become modern business organizations suited to the demands of commercial development.

MOTU

INDIGENOUS PEOPLE of the coastal area around Port Moresby, in southeastern Papua New Guinea, the Motu inhabit a tropical savanna that changes dramatically between dry and wet seasons. Traditionally, the people have been potters, traders, and fishermen, with gardening and hunting as supplementary activities. They have lived closely with the Koita people, who depend on horticulture, and have intermarried extensively with them, exchanging pottery and fish for the Koitans' garden produce.

The Motu became most famous for *hiri,* their annual trading voyages along the Papuan Gulf coast in outrigger canoes. Under the leadership of a man who had claimed a vision in a dream to organize such a journey, as many as 600 men would sail forth on a voyage. They took pots made by Motu women to Elema and the home of the Namau people. There they exchanged the pots for sago and for timber they would make into canoes. When the traders got back home, the Motu held a *koriko* feast, during which the return gifts were ceremonially distributed. As a result of these voyages, Motuan became a trade language along the south coast and today serves as the other indigenous lingua franca of Papua New Guinea. Tok Pisin, a mixture of Tolai, German, and English, remains the country's dominant language.

One of the Motu's central religious ideas is *irutahuna,* which can refer to the center of a house, an individual's heart or mind, the central part between two masts of an outrigger, or the base of a single-masted vessel. Clearly, the core or center of an important architectural or organic entity is a space of great sacredness for the Motu. This concept reflects a widespread preoccupation among Melanesians with the vital, germinal core of all things.

☺ TANNESE

THE ISLAND OF Tanna, in the southern part of the Vanuatu archipelago (formerly the New Hebrides), has a fascinating history as well as a rich ceremonial culture. As is the case with villages elsewhere in Vanuatu, a dancing ground called the *nakamal* is situated near each small group of huts. This site is where ceremonies, rituals, and communal social events occur, including gatherings of men who come to drink kava at the end of the day. The core of men who meet this way is called a "canoe," the local term for a small group related through the male line.

Because the Tannese have a long history of contact with the European world, their culture has in many respects evolved as a reaction to, and an incorporation of, colonial encounters. Among the most important encounters were the notorious "blackbirding" expeditions mounted in the late 1800s by seagoing Australian merchants. These expeditions transported thousands of Tannese, as well as indigenous Melanesian men from eastern New Guinea, the Solomon Islands, and other nearby areas, to Australia, where they were put to work in the cane fields of northern and central Queensland. During this period, more than 100,000 Melanesians were brought to Australia and to plantations and mines on Fiji, New Caledonia, and Samoa, leaving many of their home islands depopulated and culturally weakened. The name "Tanna" survives as a common surname among descendants of the original laborers.

Tannese efforts to preserve their heritage and maintain distinctiveness in the face of dominant outside forces can be summed up in the term *kastom* (custom), from the Bislama pidgin of Vanuatu. Used throughout the archipelago, the word describes a fusion of old, rediscovered traditions with new or re-created traditions.

The island of Tanna was home to the famous cargo cult started by John Frum. In the 1930s and '40s, Frum preached the return of traditional political power to Tannese and prayed for the departure of the Europeans. The British acted decisively to crush the movement in 1941, but the legend of John Frum and the influence of his followers have continued to this very day.

☺ TOLAI

THE TOLAI INHABIT the Gazelle Peninsula at the eastern edge of New Britain Island—site of Rabaul, the most important town in island Papua New Guinea and the location for a major Japanese naval base during World War II. This group experienced colonization relatively early in Melanesian terms: Before the Japanese, there were Germans who came in 1884 and Australians who arrived after World War I. As a result, the Tolai became one of the most literate,

sophisticated, and vocal groups in all of Papua New Guinea, and they are a dominant force on the national scene today.

Tolai society is organized into groups called *vunatarai*, a term that can refer either to clans—descendants of a particular ancestor associated with a particular everyday leader—or to groups into which the clans are placed. Members of vunatarai hold land, personal property, and ceremonial objects in common.

Because of the early plantation activity on New Britain, cash cropping has long been a primary component of the village economy, with copra and cocoa being the most important crops. The people are famous for the use of shell money known as *tambu*, which consists of nassa shells sewn into plaits about six feet long. A true local currency, tambu is used to purchase food and implements and is exchanged for ceremonial purposes such as bridewealth and mortuary payments.

Art created by the Tolai includes elaborate effigies and masks representing the female spirits of the *tubuan*, which were owned by the clans and considered the incarnation of ritual and sociopolitical power.

☺ TROBRIANDERS

INHABITING KIRIWINA and a number of smaller islands off the east coast of Milne Bay Province, Trobriand Islanders are probably among Papua New Guinea's most famous groups—thanks in large part to anthropologist Bronislaw Malinowski, who did pioneering fieldwork on them early in the 20th century. As he discovered and subsequently reported, Trobriand men and women engage in relatively uninhibited sexual activity from an early age. Sexuality is prized and admired as a desirable trait, with both men and women devoting time, attention, and resources to obtaining love and beauty magic.

The Trobrianders also are noted for their involvement in a regional inter-island trading network called the *kula*, which encompasses all of the coral and larger islands in the Massim group, off the east coast of Papua New Guinea. In the kula, valuable arm shells and shell necklaces are circulated among the islands by traders in seagoing canoes, traveling in opposite directions around the island group. This trading arrangement, essentially a competition for prestige among regional men of renown, is not limited to the valuable shell objects: Many islands also contribute specialty items such as clay pots to the trade.

Like most Massim area people, the Trobrianders are organized into clans based on descent through their mothers. But fathers also bequeath important property rights to their children, and these are from their own matrilineal connections.

In recent years, Trobriander artists have become internationally known for their traditional carving of canoe prow boards, figures, and masks, an art form that has caught the attention of the tourist trade.

POLYNESIA

HAWAIIANS • MAORI • SAMOANS • TAHITIANS •
TONGANS

HAWAIIANS

TELEVISION VIEWERS who watch reruns of *Hawaii 5-0* or
Magnum, P.I. may be unaware of the rich culture and
history of the Hawaiian archipelago's native inhabitants.
Identified as native Hawaiians or Kanaka Maoli, they are
the descendants of intrepid voyagers whose canoes reached
one of the most isolated island groups in the world. Though
scholars debate the details, the original Hawaiians probably
arrived from the Marquesas Islands at least 1,700 years ago.
There may also have been a subsequent migration from
Tahiti long before Captain James Cook's 1778 "discovery"
of the islands put them on maps made in Europe.

When Cook arrived, he encountered the most highly
developed political system in all of Polynesia. Like other
Pacific islanders, Hawaiians lacked metal technology,
but even without metal tools, their agricultural system
produced enough food to support a population that has
been conservatively estimated at 300,000. There was also
an array of chiefs, priests, and craft specialists whose

lifestyle set them apart from the rest of society. Thought
to be descended from the gods, Hawaiian chiefs, or *ali'i*,
theoretically inherited their positions as the firstborn in
a male line. In practice, however, ability—particularly for
making war—was a potent factor in establishing and
expanding a chiefdom. Women, too, could enjoy ali'i status.

A Hawaiian chief controlled land, especially irrigated
fields, and the labor of commoners. The complexity of
chiefdoms was supported by an ideology of supernatural
power: Kamehameha I, for example, inherited a war god's
title. He would go on to use his own skills and European
weaponry to unite all the islands by 1810, an unprecedented
feat in Hawaii. After the chief's death in 1819, his widow,
Ka'ahumanu, became a powerful figure in her own right.

American Protestant missionaries arrived in the
islands in 1820. Even before that time, native Hawaiians
had begun to suffer severe population losses from measles,
influenza, and other introduced diseases for which they
had no immunity; by 1854, their numbers had been reduced
by at least 75 percent. When foreigners began to establish
sugar plantations, they found it necessary to import labor
from Asia. These same commercial interests, as well as
missionary descendants, began assuming power in the
Hawaiian kingdom. In 1893, the last Hawaiian monarch,

Queen Liliuokalani, was deposed by a group of mostly American businessmen, who then established a republic in 1894. The United States annexed the islands as a territory in 1898, and in 1959 Hawaii became the 50th state.

Native Hawaiians, now mostly of mixed ancestry, began to increase in number in the 20th century; however, they generally remained socially inferior not only to "white" Americans but also to the descendants of Asian laborers, who moved into higher economic and political positions after statehood. In the past 40 years, though, a new sense of Hawaiian identity has emerged. Hawaiians have self-consciously revived their language and customs such as hula and traditional healing. In 1976, the sailing canoe *Hokule'a* was built according to traditional style. With the help of a navigator from the Caroline Islands, its crew sailed to Tahiti using only stars, wind, and waves to guide them. Subsequently, *Hokule'a* has voyaged to all the major islands in the Polynesian triangle, inspiring young Hawaiians as well as Tahitians and other Pacific islanders to assert their ethnic pride.

MAORI

THE MAORI were the last major group of Polynesians to settle their islands. Legend has it that Kupe, a fisherman and navigator, left his eastern Polynesia homeland of Hawaiki to pursue a huge octopus that had been stealing his bait. He caught up with the creature and killed it; then he began exploring what is now New Zealand. Kupe later sailed home to tell others of uninhabited land available for settlement. Regardless of the story's accuracy, modern scholars agree that Maori began settling in New Zealand about 1,200 years ago, after they had made the longest and last voyage of settlement in Polynesian history.

The new settlers, having come from a warmer climate, faced challenges in adapting to a different environment. In the early days, they depended in part on the moa, a large flightless bird that Maori hunters eventually destroyed. The people subsisted on fishing, cultivating sweet potatoes, and gathering forest products. Between sweet potato harvests, collecting such items as fern roots provided an important part of the diet.

The largest social unit in traditional Maori life was the *iwi*, often translated as "tribe." Each iwi occupied a distinct territory and was ideally based on descent through males or females from a founding ancestor. Within each iwi were several *hapu*, or sections, whose members also claimed common kinship. Because the Maori could claim descent through *(Continued on page 74)*

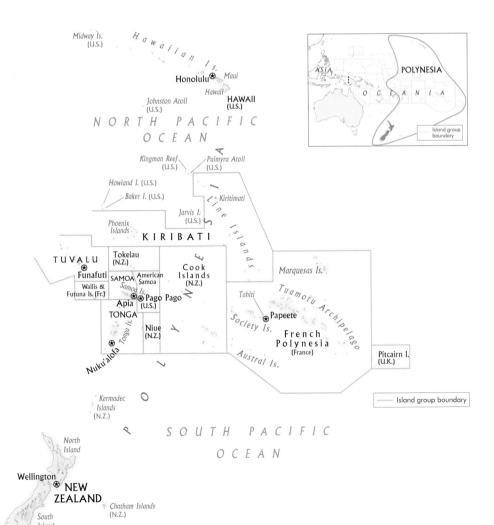

Trobriand Islanders (opposite) embark on a trading voyage off the east coast of Papua New Guinea. Sailing their decorated outrigger canoe to islands in the so-called kula ring—a roughly circular trading network—they will participate in a cycle of trade that not only exchanges ceremonial shell ornaments but also reinforces alliances between islands.

FOLLOWING PAGES: Tahitian dancing—shocking to early missionaries—now entertains appreciative tourists at Polynesian resorts.

PAGES 72-73: Formerly ceremonial platforms where religious leaders performed major rituals, *marae* now serve as sites where Maori show solidarity. People gather at the marae of their kin groups for any important occasion, such as this three-day funeral in Reporua, New Zealand.

either sex, individuals potentially could belong to more than one hapu. Actual membership depended primarily on one's residence and cooperation in group activities.

Each hapu had its own chief, and the chief of the most senior hapu was the paramount chief of the entire iwi. Ideally, the tribal chief was succeeded by his eldest son, but in some groups a senior daughter received special recognition. Conflict was frequent, even within the same iwi. When Europeans eventually reached New Zealand, the Maori quickly gained a reputation for ferocity. Maori tribes were known for enslaving their defeated enemies or perhaps even eating them as a final humiliation.

Like other Polynesians, Maori traditionally believed in an elaborate pantheon of supernatural beings, from which the highest ranking individuals were thought to derive their power. Chiefs presided over major ceremonies, but a specially trained priesthood also existed. Most public rites were celebrated on special open-air platforms that were associated with a particular hapu or iwi.

Europeans were drawn to New Zealand at the end of the 1700s, when they decided to exploit the rich sealing and whaling grounds off the North Island. Protestant missionaries arrived in 1814, and soon other Europeans and Australians followed. In 1840, many Maori chiefs signed the Treaty of Waitangi, which gave sovereignty to England. But from 1860 to 1865—sometimes called the period of the Maori Wars—battles were fought over land rights and questions of sovereignty. These issues remain controversial; now, however, Maori struggles to obtain their rights are usually played out in courtrooms.

People identifying themselves as Maori number about 525,000, or between 10 and 15 percent of New Zealand's population. Although they are a more cohesive and visible ethnic group than their Hawaiian relatives, they have followed some of the same strategies for cultural survival. Exhibits of traditional arts and crafts have toured overseas with success, while younger artists are making their own statements about ethnic identity. Maori language schools have provided models for those in Hawaii.

SAMOANS

SINCE 1900, Samoans have been divided into two polities. Eastern Samoa is a territory of the United States, while the western islands—ruled first by Germany, then New Zealand until 1962—are independent. Samoans settled here more than 3,000 years ago, and for centuries the people have regularly interacted with Tongans and Fijians. Today, their islands are home to the world's largest concentration of full-blooded Polynesians: More than 60,000 live in American Samoa, and some 165,000 are in independent (formerly Western) Samoa.

Traditional Samoan life was based on horticulture, with taro and breadfruit considered the primary crops. Men carried out more strenuous tasks, including clearing and planting the land, fishing beyond the reefs, and even cooking food. Women collected wild plants and gathered small sea creatures in the lagoons and reefs. They also wove mats, and these continue to be important exchange items on ceremonial occasions such as marriage.

Samoans typically lived in self-contained communities made up of a number of kin groups that were related through descent from either male or female ancestors, or by adoption or marriage. Still basic to the Samoan social structure is the *matai* system, in which chiefly titles are assumed on the basis of birth, ability, or a combination of the two factors. Titles are of two kinds, *ali'i* (head chiefs) and *tulafale* (orators), and are ranked within the village and in wider political contexts. The degree of authority exercised by titleholders varies according to rank; for example, a council of matai exercises supreme authority over village affairs. When Samoa became independent, only titleholders were allowed to vote and to be candidates in general elections. This changed in 1990, when a referendum created universal suffrage; however, only matai can be candidates for most of the parliamentary seats.

During aboriginal times, matai also served as religious practitioners who were responsible for the worship of family gods. But teachers from the London Missionary Society eventually began their work in Samoa, and today about half the people of independent Samoa are affiliated with the Congregational Church. About one-quarter are Catholics, and the rest are Methodists, Mormons, and members of other faiths.

Today, Samoans have become noteworthy for the way they have spread through the English-speaking world: More people live away from their home islands than they do on them. In New Zealand, there are more than 100,000, and about the same number live in Hawaii and the 49 other states. Several Samoans are, or have been, members of professional football teams. But no matter where Samoans live, they maintain ethnic identity through their own church congregations. They have also revived the practice of elaborate tattooing, which is done by using traditional instruments, such as toothed combs and mallets, to tap pigments into the skin.

TAHITIANS

MANY ROMANTIC images of the South Seas were created when French and English explorers first met Tahitians in the late 18th century. Before these early encounters, there may have been 30,000 islanders; afterward, however, the population declined for a time. (In 1999, estimates exceeded 100,000, including a number of people with mixed ancestry.) Like other speakers of Polynesian languages, the early Tahitians settled their homeland after making long canoe voyages from Southeast Asia. These voyagers passed through Tonga and Samoa before arriving in what is now called the Society Islands.

Traditionally, Tahitians divided their society into three classes: nobility *(ari'i)*, commoners, and servants. Nobles inherited their rank from their fathers; usually, the firstborn male would become the heir, though women might also enjoy high status. Because people at the highest level of society claimed descent from the gods, the culture was a complex mixture of religion, status, and power. Chiefs received tribute from lower ranks, but competition among those who were claiming power in different parts of the island group meant that no ruler could rise above all of the others. That situation changed when Europeans arrived and introduced new weapons and different political ideas to the islands.

Though Tahitians were among the first Polynesians to be converted to Christianity, they originally recognized a ranked series of gods. Some of these deities were worshiped by an entire region, while others received the devotions of families or individuals. Drawn from the ranks of the ari'i were the priests who officiated at major ceremonies involving whole districts; many of them were thought to have the power to practice sorcery. People believed that divine anger could cause untimely death, but they also recognized death through aging as a normal occurrence. Funeral rituals depended on the deceased's social status: For example, the body of a high-ranking Tahitian was exposed on a covered platform, or ghost house, before burial, and lengthy and elaborate expressions of mourning were a high chief's prerogative.

Tahitians used to support themselves by gardening and fishing. The men fished, did construction work, and made tools, weapons, and canoes. Women made bark

Samoans try to maintain the cornerstones of their identity—church and family— wherever they go. This father, wearing a traditional lavalava, hopes to pass along his skills as a church band leader and a talented trumpet player.

cloth, a very important item for trade, formal gift-giving, and clothing. They also wove mats, hats, and baskets from the leaves of the pandanus plant. Both sexes shared the gardening chores, raising a variety of crops that included yams and sweet potatoes. The numerous coconut trees provided not only food but also craft materials. Today, Tahitians participate in such modern economic activities as tourism and the cultivation of black pearls. Traditional dancing, featuring rapid hip movements accompanied by frenetic drumming, has become a staple of Pacific island tourist performances and a potent symbol of identity.

Tahiti has long been tied to France, which made it part of a protectorate in 1842 and today includes it within the Overseas Territory of French Polynesia. In recent decades, France was criticized for carrying out nuclear tests in other parts of the Society Islands. The tests ended in 1996, and now funds for compensation and other French government subsidies provide much of the income for Tahitians. For more than 60 years, the people have pressed France for greater freedom, and they have achieved some increase in local autonomy.

TONGANS

IN ALL OF POLYNESIA, only Tongans can boast that their islands were never ruled by a foreign power. Settled some 3,000 years ago—like Samoa, whose chiefs Tongan nobility once married—the Tongan archipelago is the largest group at the western end of the Polynesian triangle of islands. Approximately 100,000 Tongans live there today, almost 70 percent of them on the main island of Tongatapu.

Tongan society seems always to have been extremely centralized and stratified. Traditionally, the supreme ruler held the title of Tu'i Tonga; he claimed descent from the gods and had power that was originally both sacred and secular. As the population grew, however, the Tu'i Tonga delegated more responsibility to his close relatives, who became chiefs in their own areas. The political instability that ensued led to a separation of powers, with the Tu'i Tonga remaining sacred ruler and someone else becoming secular leader. Later, the secular leader delegated authority to his son, creating a new royal lineage and title. The Tu'i Tonga's sister—Tu'i Tonga Fefine—was also a powerful figure, but her oldest daughter—the Tamaha—was the most sacred being of all. Theoretically, all Tongans, including the reigning monarch, trace their kinship affiliations and relative rank from one of these four chiefly titleholders.

A significant feature of Tongan life was the superiority of women as sisters over men as brothers, meaning that brothers were expected to defer to their sisters and sisters' children. The higher status had a material basis in that women created valuable property such as mats, basketry, and bark cloth, which were and are exchanged at important events. They also prepared the pepper-plant-based kava drink featured on social and political occasions.

Missionization brought major changes to traditional Tongan life, including an increase in the political instability created by new European commercial interests. In 1826, a Wesleyan Methodist mission was established, and by 1845, a Tongan newly converted to Protestantism had defeated the Tu'i Tonga, who was supported by Catholic missionaries. Proclaimed King George Tupou I and guided by Methodist missionaries, he modeled his rule after British constitutional monarchy. A constitution was created in 1875, giving the sovereign ownership of all the land, while designating a class of hereditary nobles as trustees and guaranteeing all adult males a farm and village allotment.

Today, the independent Kingdom of Tonga remains centralized and traditional. The present king, fourth in the Tupou dynasty, appoints a cabinet that is the highest governing body. Although a pro-democracy movement emerged in 1994, the monarchy and its associated nobility appear firmly in control. Tonga relies heavily on foreign aid and on income that is earned elsewhere but sent back by Tongans who migrated; more than 30,000 of them now reside in New Zealand. A number of migrant men have achieved prominence in sports, including rugby and boxing.

MICRONESIA
CHAMORROS • CHUUK ISLANDERS • MARSHALLESE • PALAUANS

CHAMORROS

THE PACIFIC PEOPLE having the longest history of contact with the Western world are the Chamorros of Guam and the Mariana Islands. In 1521, Ferdinand Magellan landed on their islands while in command of the first expedition to circumnavigate the world. Spain claimed the islands in 1565 but established settlements there only in 1668. Three decades of war and disease followed, and by 1710 fewer than 4,000 Chamorros remained. Today, an estimated 150,000 people live on Guam, while 72,000 reside in the Commonwealth of the Northern Marianas. Many are of mixed ancestry, with forebears who may have been Spanish, Filipino, American, Asian, or perhaps Micronesian (from the Caroline Islands). Regardless of their ancestry, though, Chamorros are linked by a language believed most closely related to ones spoken in the Philippines.

The original Chamorros wore very little clothing, and early European observers were impressed with their physiques. They were fishers and gardeners, as well as the only Pacific islanders who, when first contacted, cultivated rice as a staple crop. Men did most of the gardening and some of the fishing, built houses and canoes, and created stone structures. Women made pottery, cooked, gathered food in the jungle, and fished with hand nets on the reefs. They were particularly skilled at working with pandanus fiber to create fine mats, sails, hats, baskets, and boxes, some of which were traded in places as far away as the Caroline Islands. The betel nut, chewed with pepper plant and lime, was the Chamorros' preferred stimulant.

Traditional Chamorro society was based on clans whose membership was inherited through females. These clans were ranked to form separate social classes, with women of the upper class holding high positions in society. Within the clans themselves, rank was determined by seniority, and the senior member of each group would use clan property for the benefit of all. Today, Chamorros are overwhelmingly Christians; the majority are Catholics, reflecting 17th-century Spanish missionization. Originally, a form of ancestor worship seems to have prevailed, and at that time some individuals were thought to be professional sorcerers.

Chamorro history has taken many turns since Europeans first made contact. Under early Spanish rule, the Marianas population was moved to Guam and not returned until 1815, when other Micronesians were also settled on the islands. After the Spanish-American War, the United States took over Guam while Germany purchased other Mariana islands. After World War I, Japan ruled Germany's old possessions as a League of Nations mandate. World War II brought bloody fighting to all the islands. Today, Guam is an unincorporated

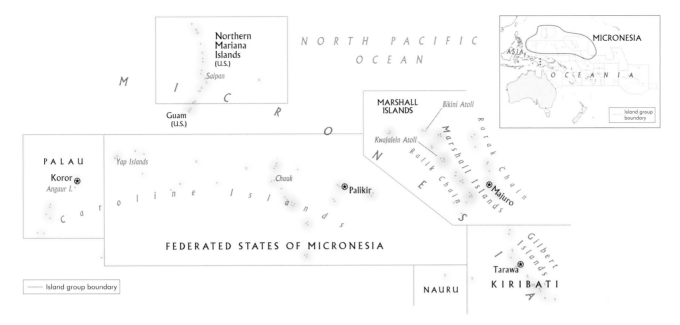

territory of the United States, while the Northern Marianas have been an independent commonwealth in association with the U.S since 1986. Chamorros operate in a modern political and economic world, and only their language links them to the lives they once led.

CHUUK ISLANDERS

CHUUK (FORMERLY TRUK) Islanders live on a group of islands surrounded by coral reefs enclosing a large lagoon. After sailing there in outrigger canoes, their ancestors settled these islands by the beginning of the Christian era. They eventually established and maintained trade relationships with nearby atolls, obtaining pandanus mats and sennit cord made from plant fiber and occasionally receiving canoes built to order. In return, they supplied the atolls with a plant dye used as a cosmetic.

Chuuk was divided into small districts, within which households spread out to form loose neighborhoods. These households were made up of extended families formed by a group of related women; husbands generally lived on their wives' land. Clans and smaller kin groups, such as lineages, were also based on descent through females. In each district, certain lineages claimed the right to particular lands, and for each district this claim was the basis for chieftainship. Though lineages were based on descent through women, the senior male in the line of senior women usually served as chief. The oldest man in the lineage generally acted as a kind of symbolic chief, receiving gifts of food as his right. Conflict often occurred over just which lineage member had the right to succeed as chief and thereby control land and other resources.

While coconuts provided food, drink, and fiber for cord, breadfruit was the traditional staple food, preserved by fermentation in pits. Gardens also included taro, plants for cosmetic dye, and sugarcane. Men gardened, prepared food in bulk, fished in deep waters, engaged in war and political affairs, built canoes and houses, and worked with wood, shells, and stone. Women wove with hibiscus and banana fibers on looms, and they plaited mats and baskets.

They also prepared routine meals, did inshore fishing, and took the main responsibility for child care.

Chuuk Islanders traditionally believed in a wide variety of spirits, some of whom lived in the sky and were especially important. Chiefly clans derived part of their power from association with these spirits and the magic lore they controlled. There were also spirits who controlled particular crafts and others who brought illness. Sickness was commonly believed to be caused by malevolent spirits, who might be invoked by a sorcerer to harm the infirm. Every person was thought to possess two souls—one good, the other bad—and at death, the good soul went to the sky world, while the bad one became a potentially dangerous ghost. Since the middle of the 20th century, the people have been either Protestant or Catholic Christians.

Like many other Micronesians, Chuuk Islanders became the subjects of successive colonial regimes. Between the First and Second World Wars, Japan administered Chuuk as a League of Nations mandate and developed the islands as a military base. United States troops mounted an invasion in World War II, bringing much suffering and loss of life; Chuuk later became part of the Trust Territory of the Pacific Islands, administered by the U.S. for the United Nations. After two decades of negotiation, in 1986 the Federated States of Micronesia (FSM) became self-governing in free association with the United States. Chuuk is one of the four states making up the FSM; its population of more than 50,000 includes people living on nearby atolls. Because "free association" means that the islanders can easily immigrate to the U.S., many have done just that. Today, a number of Chuuk communities are found in Hawaii and California.

MARSHALLESE

THE PEOPLE OF the Marshall Islands became best known to the wider world in 1946, when the United States began a series of nuclear tests on tiny Bikini Atoll. Descendants of seafarers who came to these islands almost 2,000 years ago, the Marshallese speak a language that is most closely related to those of Fiji, Nauru, and the nearby Caroline Islands.

The Marshalls' 5 small islands, 29 atolls, and hundreds of reefs form a double chain, with the islands in the south having a more favorable, reliable climate. Gardening, fishing, and collecting from the reefs were the activities that traditionally supported Marshallese life. On northern atolls, arrowroot, pandanus, and coconut were cultivated along with some breadfruit. Southern atolls enjoyed larger yields of breadfruit, together with some taro. Marshallese men always looked to the sea, where they fished from canoes they had made. Women dominated activities on the land, making mats, baskets, and clothing from pandanus and coconut fronds. They also prepared meals, cared for children, fished occasionally, and collected from the reefs.

On such small islands, land was inevitably a key factor in social life. On larger isles with more resources, the control of land permitted chiefs to exercise considerable power over those who depended on them for access. Links through females were basic to social organization—rights to land were inherited through women—but the paramount chiefs, who claimed descent from ancient gods, were male. Generally, social arrangements were flexible enough to provide people with what they needed for their livelihoods; residence and cooperation in socially valued activities could give individuals claim to resources that they might not have gotten through descent alone.

The Marshallese formerly believed in many kinds of spiritual beings, both male and female. Major deities were associated with constellations, while others were believed to inhabit specific local sites. For most people, ancestor spirits were thought to have a direct effect on their daily lives. The Marshallese were first missionized by American Protestants, and today almost all adhere to some form of Christianity.

After living under different colonial powers and surviving the trials of World War II, the Marshallese were included in the U.S.-administered Trust Territory of the Pacific Islands in 1947. A Compact of Free Association with the U.S. became effective in 1986, creating the Republic of the Marshall Islands (RMI). The United States pays for the use of a missile-testing base at Kwajalein; it also continues to compensate Marshallese for the health and social problems resulting from the nuclear testing. Today, more than 60,000 Marshallese live in RMI, while some have migrated to Hawaii and California.

☺ PALAUANS

THE WESTERNMOST Caroline Islands are home to the Palauans, whose proximity to Asia has strongly influenced their culture over the years. The first Palauans are thought to have arrived in these islands more than 2,000 years ago; they were voyagers who perhaps came directly from Southeast Asia and chose to settle here rather than venture farther east. Today, the people speak a form of Austronesian that is more closely related to languages of western Indonesia and the Philippines than to those of islands to the east.

They have also marked out a political patch separate from other Micronesians by establishing themselves as a self-governing nation: the Republic of Palau, or Belau.

In the prehistoric past, Palauans built inland villages on elaborate stone foundations. The village meetinghouse, or *bai,* was the center of the basic social unit, which not only controlled land for homes and taro patches but also had responsibilities regarding chiefly titles, certain valuables, and ceremonial functions. Members were related either through maternal or, less often, paternal ties, and adoption was common within this extended kin group. Rank governed relations between siblings, between houses within a village, between titles in a political council, and between villages in the largest political grouping. Chiefly titles were ranked according to the social value of local land holdings, and title-holders assigned land to families according to their needs.

Fishing and taro cultivation provided the basis for traditional subsistence, with fishing symbolizing male virtue and taro cultivation serving as the emblem of female productivity. This division was paralleled by the control of valuables: Women exchanged hammered turtle-shell trays, while men used beads of foreign origin. Other items exchanged between districts depended on local resources and included canoe sails, pottery, and wooden tools.

Like the rest of the Caroline Islanders, Palauans lived under a succession of colonial rulers: Spanish, Germans, Japanese, and finally Americans, who administered the Trust Territory of the Pacific Islands under the auspices of the United Nations. Because of its location, the Palauan archipelago was especially subject to Japanese influence during the period between the World Wars. Japanese men sometimes married Palauan women, and even today Japanese is spoken on Angaur Island, in addition to the local dialect. During World War II, Japan used the archipelago as a base from which to attack the Philippines.

Palau was the last of the four political units to emerge from what had been the Trust Territory of the Pacific Islands; the others were the Northern Marianas, the Federated States of Micronesia, and the Republic of the Marshall Islands. Negotiations were delayed because the Palauans, in 1981, adopted a constitution declaring their islands a nuclear-free zone—a sticking point for the United States, which hoped to maintain a strategic presence in the area. In 1994, the impasse was broken, and Palauans assumed a new national identity as citizens of a republic.

In Micronesia, food means more than just nourishment, and providing feasts remains central to social organization. Here, 25 men bring a huge yam to show respect at a deceased elder's funeral.

SOUTH AMERICA is a continent of dramatic environmental contrasts, with a remarkable diversity of indigenous human populations to match. In the north, a wide coastal plain borders the Caribbean Sea and is backed by a narrow branch of the Andes mountain range. The Andes themselves run from about 10 degrees north of the Equator southward for almost 5,000 miles, forming the western backbone of the continent. On the mountain flanks, complex environmental zones are stacked one above another, often in deep highland valleys. The celebrated Altiplano, or high plain, surrounds Lake Titicaca, and its grasslands provide good herding areas for llamas. East of the Andes, humid tropical forest stretches across the enormous Amazon Basin, encompassing more than 2.3 million square miles. But lying along the Pacific coast west of the mountains are some of Earth's driest deserts; they are dissected by a few river valleys made fertile by mountain runoff.

In the central part of South America, the Amazon Basin gives way to the Brazilian Highlands. Here is the huge sandstone plateau of the Mato Grosso region, where widespread forest clearance in recent decades has exposed lateritic soils that have hardened to a concrete-like consistency. Small-scale subsistence farmers once prospered in this area, the forest clearance for their gardens being

SOUTH AMERICA

In the rain forest of Venezuela, this Yanomami girl lives in a culture unchanged over many centuries.

too small to affect the soil. Southwest of the Mato Grosso is the Gran Chaco, a series of arid plateaus descending from the Andes. In this hostile, thicket-covered area, with a very low water table and sandy terrain, only migratory bands can survive. To the south lie the vast grasslands of the Pampas. Famous today for their ranching, but home to migratory hunter-gatherer bands in ancient times, the Pampas stretch to the arid plateaus of Patagonia. A mountainous landscape of islands, fjords, glaciers, and densely forested valleys lies to the west and extends into Tierra del Fuego. Here, at the remote, southern end of the continent, human groups arrived more than 8,000 years ago.

South America's environmental diversity led to an astounding range of human societies, which adapted brilliantly to their surroundings by developing an intimate knowledge of them. For example, at the time of the Spanish conquest in the 16th century, Andean peoples were cultivating 70 indigenous plant species—almost as many as the number being raised in all of Europe and Asia. Some of the 70, notably the potato, have become staple foods that now feed millions around the world. The South Americans have used their botanical knowledge for ritual purposes, too. Throughout the continent, hallucinogenic plants continue to play a central role in religious beliefs and rituals of all kinds, for many people still view their world as a place where the material and supernatural pass one into the other almost imperceptibly, where every landmark has intense symbolic significance. For this reason, shamans—men and women with the ability to journey in hallucinogenic trances through the supernatural realm—are of paramount importance in indigenous South American society.

The Andes were one of the great centers of ancient civilization, culminating in the Inca Empire of the 15th century A.D. The Inca called their vast domains Tawantinsuyu, "the land of the four quarters," and Cuzco, high in the Peruvian Andes, was where the four quarters met. When Spanish conquistador Francisco Pizarro landed on the shores of northern Peru in 1532, the supreme Inca ruler reigned over as many as six million people. His domains extended from Bolivia and Chile northward to Ecuador and from the deserts along the Pacific coast through the Andean highlands to the edges of the Amazon Basin. The Inca Empire eventually fell apart in the face of civil war and rapacious conquistadores, although many former Inca subjects continued their traditional lifeways in remote valleys and desert communities.

Elsewhere, the diversity and productivity of the natural environment offered few opportunities for more complex states. At the time of the Spanish conquest, many South Americans made their living by hunting and gathering and by fishing and fowling, especially in Patagonia and the Pampas, in the southern third of the continent. The Aché, Mataco, and other forest hunter-gatherers flourished in the southern Andes, while some groups on the edge of the rain forest to the north subsisted in similar fashion. Most native South Americans lived in small, egalitarian bands sustained by simple subsistence farming, often relying on tropical root crops such as manioc.

Much of the diversity of indigenous life was destroyed by Spanish colonization, which brought not only European crops, farming methods, and technology but also horses and the pervasive influence of Catholicism. Thousands died from epidemics of infectious diseases, thousands more from maltreatment and forced labor in mines or on enormous estates. Today, many once powerful Indian peoples eke out a poverty-stricken existence in the slums of South American cities or live close to the subsistence level in small peasant communities. Others still endure near serfdom on large estates, where they contribute labor and produce to support their powerful masters. Despite all of these changes, a surprising number of native South American groups have maintained their traditional ways, especially in the remoter parts of the Amazon Basin. But even there, land-hungry colonists and prospectors have been moving into tribal lands and threatening the continued existence of small groups.

There are no consistent policies regarding native rights to land throughout the continent. In many countries, such as Brazil and Venezuela, nominal tribal reserves have been established; these are shrinking rapidly, however, in the face of growing population densities among peasant farmers, chronic land hunger, and global demands for fossil fuels and minerals. For example, the Xingu National Park in Brazil was funded in 1961 as a home for 6,000 Indians of 18 culture groups, but by the time the reserve had been approved by the Brazilian government, it had shrunk from 120,000 to 12,000 square miles. Today, it is surrounded by commercial agriculture operations and expanding urban areas. If the pace continues, few, if any, native South Americans may be following their ancient lifeways a hundred years from now.

For the moment, the legacy of native American societies is still apparent in many surviving art styles and traditional crafts, as well as in the melding of indigenous religious beliefs with those of the Christian faith. Hallucinogenic trances and tribal shamans continue to play an influential role in indigenous societies everywhere on the continent, for, as both conquistadores and missionaries discovered, one can transform a society's technology, but the people will turn inward and prize their own deep-felt beliefs and rituals in the face of overwhelming odds. From the remarkable Aymara farmers to the skilled Otavaleño weavers, the often consulted Kallawaya coca diviners, and the creative Mapuche singers, much remains to admire and enjoy. And South American society is immeasurably richer as a result.

83

Following Pages: Using a traditional Peruvian form of food processing, a highland woman forces water from potatoes with her feet. Left to dry in the field, the potatoes eventually become *chuño*, an important staple food that can be safely stored for years.

CLOCKWISE FROM TOP LEFT: MAPUCHE HEALER, QUECHUA WOMAN, AND BRAZILIAN GAUCHO

CARIBBEAN COAST

KOGI

NORTHERN COLOMBIA'S Kogi people live in an environment of striking contrasts: Within a distance of only 22 miles, the land rises from sea level to peaks more than 18,000 feet high in the Sierra Nevada de Santa Marta. Here, land suitable for cultivation occurs in small pockets up to 11,500 feet, so the Kogi live vertically, traveling up and down among the hot, temperate, and colder zones of their environment. They cultivate bananas and manioc in the tropical lowlands, bananas and beans up to 8,200 feet, potatoes and onions in the temperate zone. No one zone can meet all their dietary needs. In earlier times, they staved off malnutrition by also eating fish from the Caribbean, but this resource became scarcer as the white population rose sharply.

Ironically, the Kogi would fare much better if they could cultivate maize in the fertile, terraced fields left by their prehistoric predecessors, the Tairona. But their ritual leaders, or *mámas,* place such fields off-limits for growing crops because they believe evil spirits occupy the lands. The Kogi's belief system thus limits their agricultural productivity and diet—despite their reputation as people who make full and "sensible" use of their environment, an image they cherish in their dealings with the outside world. This image is almost entirely a delusion, for their homeland's plains and slopes are eroded and degraded after centuries of slash-and-burn agriculture, and the people now complain that their environment will not feed them adequately.

An Embera family (opposite) from Bolivia unload their dugout canoe in the midst of a tropical downpour. For people in the dense rain forest, small canoes provide convenient transportation to village markets and from one community to the next.

To sustain themselves during hard work and arduous climbing, Kogi men rely heavily on coca leaves, chewed with lime to release narcotic alkaloids. They eat only small amounts of food. Women and children, on the other hand, seem to be well fed and do not munch coca. Their diet is always uncertain, though, because insufficient rains and the degraded soils often lead to poor harvests. In good years, people move frequently from one zone to another, with a preference for lower, more productive elevations. At these times, there is little hunger, the Kogi trade with mestizos and others on the coast, and ritual life comes to a virtual standstill. During hungry periods, the people move up the mountains and shift little from one elevation to another.

The largest settlements lie at different elevations, most of them between about 3,000 and 6,000 feet above sea level, but they are occupied only a few days a week when families come in from the fields. Village dwellings are circular, with thatched, conical roofs, and are scattered around a central building where the men usually reside. Women and children reside in family dwellings. Every family also has three or four field houses at different elevations, and these are used seasonally. Typically, two dwellings face each other across an open area, the husband and adolescent boys living in one, the wife and younger children in the other. In hard times, the Kogi tend to settle close to ritual centers, near the leaders who provide them with spiritual guidance.

Kogi society is divided into two main groups, with one comprising all the men and the other all the women, a pattern reflected in their housing arrangements. There are smaller kin groups, too, resulting in marriage arrangements that are so complex only mámas can decipher them. After marriage, a son-in-law works for his in-laws until he is deemed capable of starting fields on his own.

About 2,000 Kogi lived in an area of about 386 square miles in the 1940s, when their society was closely studied. Now that European settlement has blocked their access to the coast, many are becoming peasant farmers or laborers as their traditional lifestyle becomes less productive.

AMAZON AND ORINOCO BASINS

AMAHUACA • BORORO • CAMPA • CARIBS • DESANA • KUIKURA • MUNDURUCÚ • NUKAK • SARAMAKA • SHUAR • TAPIRAPÉ • XIKRÍN • YANOMAMI

◈ AMAHUACA

HUNTERS OF PECCARIES and rodents, and simple farmers of maize and some manioc, the Amahuaca are a remote group

AMAZON &
ORINOCO
BASINS

SOUTH
AMERICA

who live in tiny settlements of thatched dwellings in the border region of southeastern Peru and western Brazil. Their rugged homeland is tropical forest with difficult access, so even today they have only occasional contact with the outside world. The Amahuaca would prefer to continue their traditional ways, but international logging interests and prospectors threaten their homeland and their very simple material culture. Before steel axes and adzes arrived in the late 19th century, the people relied on stone axes, digging sticks, and tortoise-shell hatchets. Clothing is minimal.

As in other forest groups, the boundaries between the living and spiritual worlds are blurred, with shamans acting as intermediaries between them. To induce trances during group sessions, the Amahuaca use hallucinogens, especially ayahuasca—a narcotic beverage made from the *yagé* vine—which produces vertigo and visions. The people believe that a yagé taker's soul leaves the body and that spirits appear who can then be questioned.

This group is also remarkable for having practiced endocannibalism—consuming the flesh of their own kind. In 1960, anthropologist Gertrude Dole witnessed the death of an Amahuaca infant during the night. The body was buried under the house, then disinterred and burned in a pot. The baby's mother carefully removed the bones from the ashes and, after several days of grieving, ground maize and made gruel, which she mixed with bone powder and drank. Her period of mourning was intended to appease the deceased's spirit, just in case it had hung around to cause evil. Once the mother had consumed all the bones, she reportedly became voluble and happy.

◈ BORORO

IN THE MID-20th century, French anthropologist Claude Lévi-Strauss studied the Bororo of the southern Brazilian Highlands and found them to be a group with a highly complex social life. During the more productive times of year, the people came together into a large settlement, but during the drier months they dispersed over the landscape in small groups, searching for food.

In his work, Lévi-Strauss focused on 140 Bororo living what he described as a marvelously choreographed social ballet in the riverside village of Kejara. A line running parallel to the river divided the village into halves known as Tugaré and Cera; another line divided the community into upstream and downstream halves, with further subdivisions into clans and groups of rich and poor, each with its own religious symbols. The Tugaré half honored mythical heroes responsible for water, rivers, vegetation, fish, and human artifacts. The Cera heroes dated from the time of the creation, when they brought order to the living world. According to the natural hierarchy of things, at least in Bororo terms, the Tugaré were closer to the physical universe and therefore "strong," whereas the Cera were closer to the human world and "weak."

To Lévi-Strauss, the Bororo seemed to delight in making the affairs of a small-scale society extremely complex. Today, both halves of society are still intricately engaged: They bury each other's dead, exchange women in marriage, and live, as it were, one for the other. Paraphrasing Lévi-Strauss, one could say that Bororo life is an escutcheon with symmetry and asymmetry in equilibrium. The people delight in social complexity, for it preserves the social order and ensures that they stay in tune with their vision of the cosmos.

◈ CAMPA

THIRTY THOUSAND Campa dwell in the Peruvian Andes, across the watersheds of five rivers that flow into the Urubamba. Like many of South America's highland groups, they have a lifestyle that reflects the realities of their environment. The Campa are semiagricultural, depending chiefly upon yuca, maize, the plantain or banana, and maguey (*manhiot*), which requires little tending.

Campa dwellings are light, open structures thatched with palm leaves, and inside them are hammocks for sleeping, handmade earthen pots, and wooden *masato* troughs used for furniture. For clothing, a man wears a sort of shirt, while a woman dresses in a short skirt woven from locally made, dyed-black cloth. The people wear silver nose pendants and paint their faces black.

Traditionally, the Campa were a polygamous society that often raided weaker tribes for the purpose of carrying off women. They relied on bows and arrows before firearms were available. Like other groups, they have made frequent use of *yagé*, which produces hallucinogenic visions and provides a way of communicating with the spirit world.

The Campa believe their homeland is a well-defined region on a flat Earth that extends in all directions. Above them are the heavens' many strata and the good spirits who dwell there. An invisible river, perhaps the Milky Way, flows through the heavens. Clouds lie between heaven and Earth and are also populated with good spirits. Below Earth's surface are two layers; the upper holds benign spirits, but the lower is a stronghold of demons.

According to Campa beliefs, their earliest ancestors—immortal beings who possessed remarkable powers—were already living on the Earth at the time of creation. One by one, the primordial Campa were transformed into the first representatives of various species of animals and plants. Some escaped, however, and today's Campa believe they are descended from that group. Theirs is a world of constant transformations, where the animate and inanimate become visible, then invisible; it is a place where mortality reigns and the Campa are the weakest beings, destined to be crushed by larger forces in the universe.

The Campa have created a cosmos that reflects the opposing forces of good and evil. Facing these forces, both of which have great strength, the people strive through their behavior to balance the one against the other. This approach to life has been a strong psychological buttress against encroaching industrial civilization, just as it has been for other South American Indians.

◎ CARIBS

EXPERT CANOE navigators and warriors, the Carib Indians of the Caribbean's Lesser Antilles drove out the indigenous Arawak about a century before Columbus and settled on the northern and northwestern shores of South America. They were originally known as Galibi, a word corrupted by the Spaniards to "cannibal"; hence, they were thought to be eaters of human flesh. If the Caribs were indeed cannibals, their consumption of enemies may have had purely ritual significance. Decimated by Europeans fighting for control of the Caribbean, these people survive only in small enclaves today, notably in Venezuela and Guyana.

For all their reputed ferocity, Caribs were, and still are, expert fisherfolk. They built dugout canoes, equipped them with sails, and ventured far offshore. Blowguns as well as bows and arrows provided them with forest game, and they farmed maize, cassava, yams, and squash. Today, coastal Caribs live in spacious thatched houses close to river banks. The largest Carib settlement, Galibi, is a fishing town in Suriname; a cooperative there sells fish locally to help the community remain self-supporting.

The Barama Caribs of Guyana live in small farming communities of thatched, timber houses near the Barama River and along forest trails. They are hunters, fisherfolk, and subsistence farmers whose lands are now threatened by mineral prospectors and international logging companies. For centuries, they have relied upon simple, traditional

methods for catching fish, but they have not hesitated to use European fish hooks and nets when they could obtain them through trade. Much of the time, though, they resort to their ancient strategies: If there are rocks on which to stand, men will try spearing fish or shooting them with bows and arrows, but the murky water militates against success.

Barama Caribs also set fishing lines, using hooks made from thorn trees or even bent domestic pins, but their most effective method involves a poison made from *haiari* roots. Although the Guyana government forbids the poisoning of the country's streams, this method is still commonplace among the people. Almost every creek has a wickerwork fence lying across its mouth, placed there to catch the dead or stupefied fish that float downstream. Waiting women and children kill the sluggish fish as they float to the surface.

The Caribs are now Catholics. Until recently, however, shamans played an important role in Carib rituals after serving long apprenticeships. They used tight ropes to master the movements of their souls: Bound by the hands, they swung through the air and induced vertigo as a way of transporting themselves to the supernatural realm.

◎ DESANA

THE RAIN FOREST of Colombia's southeastern lowlands is home to the Desana, hunters and fisherfolk who also obtain much of their diet from manioc. Each household has to fend for itself and get food from a carefully delineated area surrounded by the territories of other groups. Because fish and game animals are such important foods, people try not to take too many fish from the rivers or to overhunt their prey. They also try to manage the size of their families by limiting the frequency of sexual relations.

The Desana live in local kin groups. Their dwellings are long, rectangular houses composed of wood and thatch and occupied by four to eight related families. Each family practices strict birth control, relying on oral contraceptives made from herbs and on men's sexual abstinence, especially before and during a hunt. For the Desana, the consequences of sex can present grave threats to their survival: People and animals share homelands with finite resources, they say, and thus both have the same limited potential for optimum reproduction. If the human population were to increase too much, then the animals and supernatural Master of Animals would grow envious of the humans' misuse of the limited sexual energy available to all. In this culture, men who sire more children than the norm are regarded with scorn, and their families are considered little more than those of dogs. The strong social controls, reinforced by the Desana's rebuke of those who ignore them, are a way to keep people in equilibrium with their food supplies.

◎ KUIKURU

SOME 300 KUIKURU survive in a single group near the Kuluene River, a tributary of the Xingu in central Brazil's rain forest. They are famous for slash-and-burn, shifting agriculture, practiced amid a large forest tract near their one village. Before 1900 and the coming of iron tools, Kuikuru farmers cleared their gardens with stone axes and the sharp-toothed jaws of piranhas. Their material culture was of the most simple kind, marked by skill in making feather ornaments and baskets. Like other Brazilian groups, they clustered their thatched houses in a circle, with the men's house a major center of ceremonial activity.

Now, as then, Kuikuru farmers begin clearing land at the end of the rainy season. They let felled trees and other vegetation dry for a while; then, just before the rains come, they fire the debris in piles atop the fields. As rain falls, wood ash washes into the soil and fertilizes it. The Kuikuru plant at least 11 varieties of manioc, a tropical root crop that is poisonous unless pounded and boiled before being eaten. Although they harvest about four or five tons of manioc an acre, they lose more than half the crop to peccaries and ants.

Most other slash-and-burn farmers must move their villages regularly, but the Kuikuru have so much land within a comfortable four-mile walking radius that they never have to leave their long-established traditional settlement. Under ideal conditions, each man spends only about three and a half hours a day working to feed his family; about two hours go to farming and an hour or so to fishing. Kuikuru men spend the rest of the day dancing, wrestling, and gossiping. Today, with modern agricultural methods and fertilizers slowly coming into use, many people are choosing to leave the traditional village and settle on small family holdings nearby. Nevertheless, the Kuikuru have shown that the simplest methods of manioc cultivation can provide enough food for people to remain in the same village permanently.

Over time, social tensions and factions develop in the community, but the Kuikuru find strength in traditional religious beliefs. They seek the help of their shamans, who play important roles in a society where secular and spiritual worlds are deeply intertwined. The shamans defuse quarrels that could lead to violence. They also investigate accusations of sorcery, attempting to identify the perpetrator of evil spells so they can neutralize the magic. The Kuikuru believe in a creation god—Kanassa—and he is said to have trapped a king vulture, the master of fire, and thereby brought fire and life to the people.

◈ MUNDURUCÚ

IN 1770 A Mundurucú war party traveled more than 400 miles from the group's homeland on Brazil's upper Tapajós River to attack Portuguese settlements along the Amazon. Afterward, the Portuguese promptly engaged their services as mercenaries to help them fight other hostile Indians. At home, the Mundurucú lived on gently rolling grasslands away from the river. But by 1920 many of them had moved closer to the riverside forest, where they tapped rubber trees during the slack months of the agricultural year to satisfy a burgeoning demand from the distant industrial world.

Today, the Mundurucú number only about 1,250, their earlier population reduced by disease, maltreatment, and the abuses of gold and rubber hunters. They are mainly subsistence farmers and rubber traders. Between September and late May, the people cultivate manioc and other crops, but both hunting and fishing are important throughout the year in a climate where dried fish lasts just two weeks.

Traditionally, Mundurucú warriors lived in the village men's house and were responsible for guarding their community. Their society was a violent one that made raids on enemies during the dry summer months, primarily for the purpose of obtaining trophy heads. Although hostile in their behavior toward outsiders, the Mundurucú repressed aggressions closer to home; they placed a high premium on cooperation and social harmony between neighboring villages for joint hunting and fishing expeditions.

The people have a simple material culture, making much use of cotton thread, basketry, and poor-quality clay vessels. To hunt, they rely on bows, reed arrows, and wooden spears, and for generations they used war clubs in raids against their enemies. The Mundurucú are famous for their featherwork, which includes aprons, capes, arm bands, and other ornaments made by attaching tropical bird feathers to netting. They are also known for body tattoos and for lines on the face that give the appearance of wings spread across their countenance.

Every village has one or two male shamans who are believed to have had supernatural powers since birth. These men cure sick people by blowing tobacco smoke on the skin, then massaging the skin while looking for the magical darts thought to have caused the illness. Shamans are feared for their powers, for they are also believed capable of causing sickness and misfortune. In extreme cases, when they are suspected of causing evil to descend on an individual or a community, they are executed. Although raids and head-hunting have ended, the Mundurucú still form an aggressive and male-dominated society in which violence is sometimes accepted social behavior—especially against women and sorcerers.

◈ NUKAK

NOT UNTIL 1988 did the Nukak of eastern Colombia come into sustained contact with Western civilization, the results of which were influenza epidemics and massacres at the hands of growing numbers of colonists. Between 1991 and 1997, intense pressure by Survival, an indigenous peoples advocacy group, led to the establishment of a tribal reserve for the remaining Indians. Now, 700 to 1,000 Nukak occupy a territory about 110 miles long by 38 miles across. They are hunters and foragers who take monkeys, peccaries, and birds, as well as insects, plant foods, and fish from the rain forest. At the same time, they manipulate such wild plant species as *chontaduro* palms, *achiote,* and plantains, growing them in small garden plots established some distance from their settlements. Because of the influence of missionaries and frontier farmers, the Nukak have started farming more systematically in recent years.

After centuries of building campsites in the forest, the Nukak have modified the rain-forest environment to their considerable advantage. Every five or six days, the people move to a different area and construct a new campsite, and each time they do this, they disturb the ground and leave behind seeds from plants they collect and consume. Those seeds eventually sprout and grow.

The Nukak live in a well-defined world. Like other groups, including Fuegians in the far south, they identify three geographic and social facets of their world: the area habitually used by each band; a carefully delineated wider area around their homeland; and both areas in relation to those of other indigenous people in the region.

◈ SARAMAKA

DESCENDANTS OF escaped African slaves, the Saramaka live in the deep forests of Suriname. They are one of several such groups who survived not only the era of slavery but also armed aggression and other efforts to root them out of territory ceded by England to the Netherlands in 1667. Effective raiders of European-owned slave plantations, their numbers grew as other escaped slaves sought sanctuary among them.

Saramaka society, since its very foundation, has been dependent upon manufactured goods and food staples brought from Europe, a situation that was addressed by an 18th-century agreement with the Dutch. In 1762 a treaty granted unconditional freedom to the people and required the Dutch Crown to pay them tribute every year. Representatives of the Crown subsequently brought boats up the winding rivers into Saramaka territory, carrying axes, pots, guns, thread, needles, cloth, and other manufactured items needed by the people. In return, the Saramaka stopped making raids on the Dutch plantations along the coast.

In 1863, after all the slaves on the coast had been emancipated, the Dutch ceased sending tribute upriver and allowed Saramaka men to venture freely into areas controlled by Europeans. Saramaka also traveled to neighboring French Guiana, where they were able to find work and earn money to buy goods that they eventually took back to their villages.

In the 19th century, nearly every able-bodied man spent about half his adulthood living and working outside of Saramaka territory, either in Suriname or French Guiana. Men worked for periods that lasted as long as several years, and this form of migrant labor helped the Saramaka and their villages to remain semiautonomous. Today, the tradition continues, but the much sought-after goods now include outboard motors, gasoline, chain saws, and a wide variety of foods.

When men eventually return to their home villages, they usually give about half their wealth to their wives, children, aunts, sisters, and various other dependents. The other half is kept in storage to be used during periods of unemployment or in times of special need. If a dependent becomes ill or marries, for example, the associated expenses are paid for with accumulated goods.

The Saramaka supplement their economy through swidden horticulture, with the men responsible for cutting and burning trees to clear fields and the women having the tasks of planting and harvesting. Most local food items come from the women's gardens, where they plant rice and other staple foods. Men also engage in hunting and fishing, and when a man kills an animal or makes a large catch of fish, his kill or catch is always redistributed along kinship lines within the village.

Because Saramaka society is matrilineal, each person receives his or her identity through the mother's line. Fathers play significant roles in bringing up children, but legally the most important connections are on the mother's side of the family; these include her sisters, parents, and grandparents. At the same time, polygamy is widely practiced, so men have several wives. Every man and every woman has a separate house. People have houses in their own villages, which means their mothers' villages, and often women have houses in their husbands' villages as well.

In a legal sense, matrilineal groups strongly resemble corporations. If a man commits a crime, for example, his relatives are held responsible, too. If that crime involves murder, the matrilineal descendants of the murderer are thought to be visited forever by the vengeance-seeking ghost of the victim.

Over the years, the Saramaka have developed a rich polytheistic religious tradition involving sky, earth, water, and forest gods. They also believe in the *Akaa,* a person's most important spirit. The Saramaka say that when an individual is born, the Akaa comes from the world of the ancestors to accompany the person throughout life; later, it travels with him or her to the *(Continued on page 96)*

FOLLOWING PAGES:
A descendant of escaped African slaves untangles a fishing net on the banks of Suriname's Tapanahoni River. All South American countries now strive to forge common identities from ancient and modern cultural diversity.

PAGES 94-95:
On Colombia's frontier, Yagua children wait to dance for important government visitors and their armed bodyguards. Many South American groups use their dances and traditional culture as a way of earning money for basic commodities.

land of the dead. There are two kinds of Akaas—good and bad. The "bad" one, as in much of the New World African theology, is not all bad, however. For one thing, it helps protect a person's body from other evil spirits that may try to take up residence there. It also causes the individual to have dreams—which may end in a nightmare if the spirit suddenly leaves the body. The good Akaa, on the other hand, is loyal and requires beauty and purity. But it is very timid: At the first sign of a problem, the good Akaa departs, possibly causing sickness. If a person's Akaas are out of balance, he or she is sure to become ill.

◈ SHUAR (Jívaro)

THE SOUTHERN LOWLANDS and lower uplands of eastern Ecuador and neighboring Peru are home to the Shuar, or Jívaro. The 20,000 Untsuri Shuar are the most numerous group, and they live across the Macuma River from their traditional enemies, the Achuar.

Killing, warfare, and other violence permeated all aspects of traditional Shuar society, which placed a high premium on acquiring individual power. From youth, every Shuar was prepared to face conflict. Everyone had potential enemies, with the more successful individuals linked to higher potentials for violence. Their objectives were simple: Kill all the members of an enemy household and decapitate them to make *tsantsas*, shrunken heads. The grim trophies not only proved that revenge had been taken but also provided the victor with powerful magic, thereby preventing the dead man's soul from wreaking vengeance in this life or the next.

Today, most Shuar killings involve feuds between members of the same group, and these usually arise from accusations of sorcery, competition over women, or quarrels over crop damage caused by pigs. First, a member of a neighbor's family is assassinated. Then a blood feud begins, resulting in another killing. Feuds can last for generations.

Until recently, these hunters and root-crop cultivators lived in small, autonomous groups that were in a constant state of political disequilibrium from all the feuding, shifting alliances, and warfare. Political power lay in the hands of talented individuals who were expert hunters, good warriors, or shamans. Qualities of physical strength and supernatural knowledge, the courage to protect and avenge family members, and the ability to endure the hardships of war were highly valued in this bellicose society. Lacking a formal political structure, the culture counted personal power and influence above everything else. Kinship ties held society together in loose, ever changing alliances that gave people the moral obligation to avenge the death of a relative. Revenge has long been a driving force in Shuar society.

Contact with European colonists, missionaries, and the Ecuadoran government led the Shuar to form a federation that would help them protect their land and their rights against government-sponsored white colonists. Since 1961, the federation has set up permanent centers and associations with communal ownership of the surrounding land. It also gives these entities loans to start cattle cooperatives. The people now govern themselves with a complex mix of traditional and modern political organization.

Head-hunting has long since been outlawed by the government, and although Shuar culture still places a premium on power and revenge, killing is not as widespread as it used to be. Now, nonviolent means such as "strong speaking" are often used to resolve conflicts.

◈ TAPIRAPÉ

UNTIL THE EARLY 20th century, the Tapirapé of central Brazil had virtually no contact with Europeans. They were forest farmers living in isolated villages between the Araguaia and Xingu Rivers, and their fate offers an interesting example of the impact of exotic diseases on such communities.

Around 1900, there were five Tapirapé villages, each with a population of 200 to 300 people. Within a decade, one village had disbanded after enemy raids and another had been depopulated by an epidemic, possibly malaria. The first Brazilians arrived in 1910. Although the Tapirapé had only sporadic contact with outsiders in the next few decades, many of them succumbed to new diseases such as influenza, smallpox, and yellow fever. By 1932, another village had been abandoned, and seven years later the last two merged into a single settlement that still survives.

In the 1940s, Dominican friars began meeting families at a Tapirapé River port during the annual dry season, when the people worked the river for turtles and fish. The Dominicans would bestow gifts of salt, tools, and other exotic goods. Eventually, Catholic missionaries settled among the Tapirapé, helping the few who remained to preserve their customs and ceremonies; even so, the society was changing profoundly.

Today, there is an oversupply of men, which means that many men have no women to perform tasks that women have traditionally done for them. To solve this problem, men make convenient social marriages with very young girls, whose mothers then do all the domestic work. The Tapirapé now sell some crops for cash and are slowly being integrated into Brazilian society, but they live at the margins of a rapidly industrializing state. Families in cities and towns survive under conditions of extreme poverty.

◈ XIKRÍN (Kayapó)

FEW BRAZILIAN GROUPS still follow their traditional lifeways, for the expanding frontier of industrial civilization has spread deep into the Amazonian rain forest. The Xikrín are among the ones who do. The northernmost group of Kayapó Indians, the Xikrín are farmers, hunters, and foragers living along the Rio Catete in a homeland rich with Brazil nuts. Their material culture is very simple, except for featherwork and basketry, and the people wear few clothes—the men a penis cover; the women, short skirts. The people cultivate manioc and maize within a day's journey of settlements made up of thatched houses set in a circle around a central open space. Men and boys hunt and search for land turtles while the women gather wild plants, including the heart of the babassú palm. The most important house in a settlement is the men's dwelling: Inside, young boys receive instruction, and preparations take place for major ceremonies that may, for example, celebrate the first maize harvest or honor fish poisons. Only single men reside there; the married men live with their wives' families.

At night, Xikrín communities often gather for orations and discourses, which are important as a way to deliver instructions for the next day, to air and resolve disputes, and to enhance individual prestige. Little is known of Xikrín traditional religion, but shamans play a major role in mediating between the living and supernatural worlds, as they do in many other South American groups.

Throughout the first half of the 20th century, contacts with Brazilian rubber interests, nut gatherers, and mahogany loggers were sporadic and hostile. But in the early 1960s, younger members of the tribe elected to live near the mouth of the Rio Cateté in the hope of becoming more closely integrated into Brazilian society. The rest of the community moved farther upriver to keep clear of the intruders. Since then, Xikrín society has been under siege: The downriver village became a rest stop for nut collectors, who used the threat of firearms to obtain women and to get help in their search for nut trees; also, infectious diseases decimated the Indian population.

After years of being exploited, the downstream Xikrín realized the true market value of both their resources and their labor, as well as the extent of their exploitation. They reunited with the traditional group back at the original upstream village and welcomed a Catholic mission among them, which has helped control social and commercial relationships with outsiders. In 1998, the Xikrín entered into an agreement with the Brazilian government and the World Bank for a sustainable mahogany-logging project. But their traditional culture remains under threat from the inexorable forces of the global economy.

◉ Yanomami

Of all the surviving indigenous South American groups, the Yanomami are among the most numerous. Some 20,000 of them occupy an area of rain forest in the upper Orinoco highlands of southeastern Venezuela and north-central Brazil. They are also one of the best known groups, thanks to many years of anthropological research.

The studies of anthropologist Napoleon Chagnon, in particular, have made the Yanomami famous for their alleged fierceness and violent behavior. Recently, however, controversy has engulfed the research of Chagnon and other anthropologists who have worked with him. Critics have accused them of inciting violence among the people, using inappropriate research methods, and even deliberately inoculating the Yanomami with measles vaccine. While many allegations are blatantly false, and the extent of violence among the Yanomami may be exaggerated, there is no question that aggressive, violent behaviors—from wife abuse to raiding—are commonplace in this society. For all his controversial research, Chagnon's enormous database on Yanomami culture and society is of potentially great value as a study of people under siege from the outside world. Only future, carefully controlled field research will establish if the people are as violent as a generation of undergraduates has been led to believe.

The Yanomami are farmers, subsisting on plantains, sweet potatoes, and other carbohydrate-rich crops, as well as game and wild plant foods. Each village is some distance from its neighbors, and each specializes in different products, such as hallucinogenic drugs, arrow points, or cotton hammocks. Communities are not self-sufficient, meaning that they must depend on one another, mingling to trade and feast. Still, everyone distrusts everyone else in a volatile environment where violence and warfare can always erupt. It is largely up to the village headmen to not let things get out of control.

Many disputes are settled by aggressive chest-pounding duels or by slapping one's sides. Two or more men may engage in club fights, or there can be a formal war between neighboring villages. The ultimate level of violence involves trickery. On rare occasions, a village may invite its enemies over for a friendly feast, then try to kill them as soon as they have let their guard down. Only by resisting ferociously or moving away as far as possible can a weaker community without allies protect itself against enemies.

In villages occupying the lower lying areas, where populations are larger and fertile land is in shorter supply, behavior is especially aggressive and violence more frequent. Headmen in these communities must be very astute, as well as expert at persuading people to help prepare for feasts and other communal activities. Above all, they must be willing to intervene in the volatile interpersonal disputes and attempt to control the outcomes. Leadership in such an egalitarian society of aggressive individuals only comes from respect and bravery in war.

Sometimes headmen are also shamans, expert in the summoning of *hekura* spirits that cure and cause evil. The hekura arrive in the hallucinogenic snuff ingested by nearly all men in many villages, but shamans have a particular ability to dispatch evil hekura darts at their enemies. As a result, many men go through the long period of fasting and rigorous training to become shamans. In this society, where males dominate and there is a shortage of women, origin myths proclaim that fierce, warlike men arrived on Earth before women. Thus, they are superior to them.

ANDES

AYMARA • KALLAWAYA • MAPUCHE • OTAVALEÑOS • Q'EROS • QUECHUA

AYMARA

SIX CENTURIES AGO, the Aymara paid tribute to the Inca Empire as they farmed along the shores of Lake Titicaca in highland Bolivia. They grew staple foods such as potatoes, other root crops, maize, and quinoa. They also herded llamas on the semiarid Altiplano, or high plain, that surrounds the lake. Skilled fisherfolk, the Aymara developed *totora*-reed canoes and rafts for use on Lake Titicaca. The people are famous for these craft, which are still in use, and for distinctive homespun clothing that copies colonial Spanish garments. Men wear conical woolen hats with earflaps, the women derbies with wool wimples for cold days.

After the Spanish conquest, most Aymara were put to work on large estates and held in virtual serfdom. Finally, in 1953, agrarian reform laws abolished labor without pay and provided for land distribution among former estate workers. Most Aymara communities now have difficulty achieving self-sufficiency because of overpopulation, poor soils, and a harsh climate. People live in single-roomed houses with thatched roofs and clay sleeping platforms.

A thousand years ago, many of the villages around Lake Titicaca grew potatoes in raised, irrigated fields; these fields were highly productive because the water in them provided some measure of protection against frost damage. But these fields fell into disuse some centuries ago, and farmers began to depend more and more on dry-agriculture methods practiced on exposed hillsides. Evidence for the huge raised field systems has been discovered by archaeologists working at the site of the ancient city of Tiwanaku, the capital of a great Andean empire that predated the Inca and may have been founded by the Aymara's ancestors.

With the cooperation of local communities, teams of scholars working on both the Bolivian and Peruvian sides of Lake Titicaca have re-created the raised fields and cut canals. On the Peruvian side, more than 2,000 acres have been rehabilitated so far, and while crop yields do fluctuate because of frosts, the surrounding canal water does serve as a heat sink, retaining solar radiation.

The experiment has proved that this farming method is quite effective and that such fields can be created and maintained by a small group of people. Much modern agriculture on the Altiplano operates on an industrial scale, but the Aymara and their neighbors do not possess the capital to support large operations. Now that some land has been turned over to them, the Aymara are again turning to ancient, and frequently ignored, indigenous agricultural methods to regain their self-sufficiency.

KALLAWAYA

LIVING IN THE Peruvian Andes northwest of Lake Titicaca, the Kallawaya are highland village farmers who cultivate maize, potatoes, quinoa, and other crops in a series of environments "stacked" one above the other on the slopes of Mount Kaata.

The Kallawaya's *ayllu*, an ancient social unit based on kinship and communal ownership of land, is so deeply tied to Mount Kaata that it treats the peak as a metaphorical human body, whose parts are kept in order by the continued existence of ayllu members. The diviners of Ayllu Kaata are responsible for ritually pumping energy into the 13 earth shrines distributed up the mountain. In this way, the mountain "eats" produce from every climatic zone and is thus able to feed its inhabitants in turn. The shamans who act as diviners obtain their powers from ancestors whose mummified remains were once paraded around the fields during fertility rituals.

The Kallawaya are renowned for their curing powers and abilities as coca diviners. At least a fifth of village men and women are involved in divination, serving visitors who come from hundreds of miles around to seek help.

The most powerful diviner is also responsible for the New Earth ceremony. During this important rite, blood and fat are poured into the earth shrines, nourishing Mount Kaata so that it will continue making its resources available to people, crops, and animals.

Like many other Andean groups, the Kallawaya rely on their rituals to sustain them and bring order to their lives. For these people, rituals help maintain and regulate everything that is part of human existence, including the environment, subsistence activities, and interpersonal and intercommunity relations.

◈ MAPUCHE

"PEOPLE OF THE LAND," the Mapuche are one of the surviving groups of Araucanian Indians who once occupied the fertile valleys and coastal areas of central and southern Chile. Araucanians spoke a common language and fiercely resisted the Spaniards, but the Mapuche resisted the most strongly and were never completely subdued. Many retreated to isolated settlements when newcomers tried to force them to work on large estates.

Today, more than 1.5 million Mapuche live in southern Chile, inhabiting rural villages and towns or major urban centers like Santiago, where many are impoverished. For much of the year, rural Mapuche still dwell in comparative isolation in small communities, coming together now and then for formal gatherings in which they honor returning travelers, debate important affairs, or simply enjoy a fiesta. These events are always marked by feasting, drinking, oratory, and, above all, singing.

Mapuche singing has profound social meaning, with every song bearing a message and subtle nuances. Some are prayers and supplications; others air grievances or are courting songs. Chiefs and shamans have their own more formal compositions, while other singers may improvise in their efforts to convey a message or let off steam. Women, in particular, use songs to express their feelings, even to air marital problems, since this is a socially acceptable way to do so. This tradition also fills a vital educational role in a society where skills are passed orally from one generation to the next. The songs often have a high poetic quality and help develop the personalities of young and old alike.

◈ OTAVALEÑOS

THE VOLCANO-SURROUNDED homeland of the Otavaleños lies two hours north of Quito in highland Ecuador. In 1455, Inca armies entered the region, bringing with them the llama and the Quechua language, and before long the Otavaleños, who had woven cotton for generations, were also weaving wool and speaking the new tongue.   *(Continued on page 104)*

Women of Otavalo, Ecuador, wash the family laundry and long wool skeins in a mountain stream near their town (above). Later, Otavaleño weavers will turn the fine skeins into blankets, as well as ponchos and other clothing sold to both locals and tourists.

FOLLOWING PAGES: Mimicking Spanish conquistadores, revelers in Tarabuco, Bolivia, wear woolen hats shaped like steel helmets. Although Spanish cultural influences are strong throughout South America, indigenous cultural traditions and religious beliefs still flourish.

PAGES 102-103: Melding Christianity with ancient Andean beliefs, a Chipaya family honors a dead family member and other ancestors at a windswept cemetery on November 1, the eve of the Day of the Dead.

Celebrants in Cuzco, Peru, reenact the Inca's sun festival, a time when people offered thanks for the harvest and prayed for new crops.

Otavaleño weavers traditionally used back-strap looms that required them to lean backward to create the necessary tension. When the Spanish came into contact with Otavaleño regions in the mid-16th century, they introduced treadle looms and sheep's wool, and they encouraged the raising of cash crops, which supplanted the cultivation of maize, potatoes, and quinoa by digging stick and foot plow. Otavaleño weavers prospered until the 19th century, when the industrial revolution introduced cheap mass-produced textiles. Even then, the people persisted with their ancient hand-weaving methods and became famous throughout Ecuador for fine workmanship. The Otavaleños also kept their traditional values and culture, as well as a strong ethnic identity. Although they are now Catholics, they have maintained many traditional religious beliefs that are closely tied to agriculture and the seasons.

Because of their famous textiles, the Otavaleños of today are among the most prosperous of all Indian groups in South America. On Poncho Plaza in the town of Otavalo, the handicraft market developed by the Indians in the 1960s and 1970s is a popular and colorful destination for tourists.

Many Otavaleños still dress in traditional costumes. Men put on fedora hats, ponchos, white shirts, and calf-length cotton pants, and they wear their hair in a long braid, or *shimba,* that reaches to the waist. The braid is never cut off and is such a strong cultural tradition that men serving in the Ecuadoran army are permitted to retain it. Women wear white blouses, blue skirts, shawls, and jewelry, including gold and coral necklaces. Proud and traditional, as well as entrepreneurial, Otavaleños value their clothing as an important symbol of their ethnic identity.

◈ Q'EROS

AMONG THE MOST isolated of all Andean groups, the Q'eros of Peru live on the eastern, Amazon side of the mountains, in rugged terrain that roads cannot penetrate. The people spend much of each year in small hamlets of thatched houses, tucked in the upper gorges that extend down from high pastures. Some 2,600 feet below—about a three-hour walk—lies their ceremonial center. Its 56 houses, deserted most of the year, all have doors facing the rising sun. A Catholic chapel and a schoolhouse also form part of this complex, for the Q'eros' traditional beliefs are now melded with Catholic doctrine.

The homeland of the Q'eros climbs from wooded foothills at 6,000 feet above sea level to a dry, tundra-like landscape at 15,500 feet, and within about 20 miles these people exploit the entire range of Andean mountain environments. They offer a classic example of how highland farmers live vertically rather than horizontally. At the highest elevations, people herd alpacas and llamas, whose wool is used in the making of textiles. Operating their traditional back-strap looms, weavers fashion woolen hats, ponchos, and skirts for members of their community.

Below the highest elevations, some locations allow the cultivation of potatoes, *ullucu,* and other tubers. At

8,700 feet and lower, the Q'eros combine the growing of tubers with more temperate crops such as maize, squash, chili peppers, and sweet potatoes. Until they could obtain European farming implements, people cultivated with the *chaquitaclla,* which was essentially a digging stick that a farmer drove into the soil with one of his feet. Far below all the fields lies the *sacha-sacha,* a place where the Q'eros never venture. It is the land of endless trees: the Amazonian rain forest.

Life is hard for the Q'eros, who have developed a deep distrust of outsiders over the years. For centuries they were exploited by the powerful, far-reaching Inca state. Then the Spanish arrived in their homeland, establishing several haciendas (now abandoned) and treating the people poorly. For many generations, the Q'eros have traded llama wool and potatoes with the Lake Titicaca region to the south, dealing with itinerant merchants known as *runa,* trusted people from the outside world. Today, the Q'eros continue to welcome the merchants, who bring iron tools and additional industrial commodities, but they greet other foreigners with evasion and suspicion.

◎ QUECHUA

HIGHLAND PERU'S Quechua lived under Spanish rule from the 1500s to the 1800s. In the pre-Spanish times, the Inca Empire imposed a degree of cultural uniformity and the Quechua language on the Andean highlands. But after the Spanish conquest, the Quechuan-speaking peoples broke up into many small groups, which were distinguished as much by their locations as by cultural differences. Today, they still share a common language—it is the most widely spoken native language in South America—and they are predominantly peasant farmers or workers on large haciendas and industrial farms. Many villagers have moved to larger highland towns, looking for work and living in poverty.

In Peru's highlands, the practice of agriculture has long been limited to mountain valleys and steep hillsides: Maize and quinoa are raised at lower elevations; potatoes are cultivated in terraced gardens higher up. Plows are now common, but farmers in many communities continue to use the traditional foot plow to prepare their small fields. All Quechua groups are also expert weavers who still use back-strap looms and a simple weaving technology to produce the blankets, ponchos, and other garments worn by men and women in the cold mountain environment. Many Quechua dwell on small farmsteads or in village settlements, often grouped around a plaza and a Catholic church, their houses built of mud brick or timber, with thatched roofs.

While the Quechua have adopted Catholicism, Peru's official religion, they maintain strong traditional spiritual beliefs that govern their view of the world. They envisage the cosmos as a layered entity. An upper world—often called Hanaqpacha—is a place of abundance where the spirits of people who led exemplary lives dwell, along with the pantheon of Quechua spirits, the Christian God, and Christ. Next is Kaypacha, the world of the living, and it comprises the Earth, humans, plants, animals, and the spirits of good and evil. Then there is Ukhupacha, the Inner World inhabited by diminutive people.

In Quechua belief, gods and the lives of humans are intertwined. The former intervene constantly in daily life, meting out reward and punishment in the guise of fortune and misfortune. The greatest of these is the creator-god Roal, once known as Viracocha; from his mountain home, he keeps an eye on humanity while governing the forces of nature and keeping them in balance. Pachamama is a female deity who resides in the bowels of the Earth. She presides over agriculture and is closely linked with women. Her greatest ceremonies come at the time of planting in August and September, when she receives the seed that will become the next harvest.

In a society where agriculture permeates every part of life, it is not surprising that traditional beliefs still flourish despite four centuries of vigorous missionization.

CENTRAL SOUTH AMERICA

GUARANÍ • KADIWÉU • MATACO • TUPINAMBÁ

◎ GUARANÍ

IN PRE-SPANISH TIMES, the Guaraní migrated into what is now Paraguay, arriving as part of the great population movements that took people speaking a common Tupí-Guaraní language southward from the lower Amazon region. Like other groups, these former tropical farmers sought their own form of Holy Grail, the Land of the Grandfather, a mythic sky god. They had sporadic contacts with the Inca civilization of the Andes and were subjugated by the Spanish who hoped to find silver and gold on their lands. In time, Guaraní shamans spearheaded a strong revivalist movement based on Christian belief in the Redeemer, inciting the people to rise against their oppressors before traveling to a "land without evil."

Revivalism is just a memory now, but the Guaraní legacy is still powerful in Paraguay: Today, more than a million Paraguayans speak Guaraní, most of them living around Asunción, the capital. Nevertheless, while cultural nationalism glorifies the Guaraní (Tupí-Guaraní) language

masters and slaves, the latter being individuals captured from other groups and their descendants. Despite frequent protests, the "slaves" still submit to their "masters" and are expected to provide economic services and food for no compensation; as the generations pass, however, the gap between slaver and enslaved continues to narrow.

The Kadiwéu remain a male-dominated society, which widely practiced abortion and infanticide—because sons were preferred—as late as the 1930s. For abortions, they either used a concoction of bitter roots or pounded on the mother's belly until the fetus died. Many newborn daughters were killed by asphyxiation or by breaking their necks, then buried under the beds where their parents slept.

◈ MATACO

SINCE 1628 THE Mataco Indians of northwest Argentina's arid Gran Chaco have been in contact with Europeans. They resisted attempts at colonization and conversion, and many were massacred, others forced onto reservations. Today, about 8,000 much Hispanicized Mataco survive, many of them working in the lumber business or serving as migrant laborers on large sugar plantations.

The traditional Mataco culture combined cultivation of maize and beans with the gathering of cactus fruit and other wild plants in the thorny brush. Men hunted

and heritage, no Paraguayan peasants retain the traditional culture of their ancestors. They do build thatched houses in the ancient manner and grow maté, a Paraguayan tea that was a major product of their remote predecessors, but they were Hispanicized centuries ago. Out in the countryside, people continue to be largely self-sufficient, growing a few cash crops and living at the subsistence level. Such cash as they generate is used to finance community fiestas, which here, as elsewhere in Spanish South America, play an important role in rural life and the acquisition of individual prestige.

◈ KADIWÉU

THE KADIWÉU are the only surviving group of the lordly Mbayá, who once dominated an area extending from Paraguay into the Mato Grosso and much farther afield. These people believed that they had a divine right to raid and enslave their neighbors—not only the Indian communities but also Portuguese and Spanish ones. Primarily hunters and foragers, the Kadiwéu demanded tribute in agricultural produce from their victims.

Kadiwéu hunting relied heavily on bolas, two or three balls attached to thongs and used to ensnare guanacos and other game. Always on the move, the people had a simple, portable material culture that had little use for textiles. They clothed themselves in hides, with featherwork and tattoos distinguishing between different kin groups.

Today, the Kadiwéu are peaceful farmers, having reached an accommodation with the authorities, but their social organization still reflects an ethnic division between

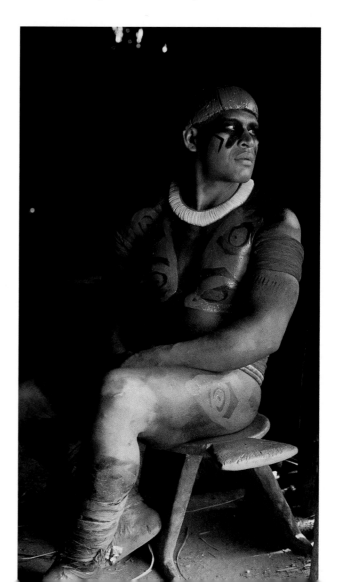

guanacos and also took large numbers of river fish during the seasonal runs. Reflecting their mobile lifestyle, most groups lived in simple brush huts; now, however, many people have become sedentary farmers, living in wattle-and-daub houses on small individual holdings. Today, even though Catholicism is widespread, shamans continue to be important in the more traditional communities: For many people, they are still intermediaries for the spirits.

The Mataco try as much as possible to remain isolated from larger society. They place a high premium on social values and reciprocity, as seen in the frequent sharing of food throughout the community and in their justice system, which punishes offenses committed against the community. Theft of field crops, especially tobacco, is treated as an offense against everyone. In small villages, people know each other so well they can even recognize footprints, which offer clues to the identity of a thief. When caught, offenders usually are punished by being expected to pay for what was taken. The punishment suits the crime, while also serving as a lesson in communal ethics.

Homicide may result from jealousy and marital disputes. If someone commits murder, the relatives of the deceased don war paint and visit the killer in his village, threatening him with their spears and gripping his chest as the women and children take to the forest. Usually, the punishment is again economic, requiring payment in, say, goats, which are then distributed among the relatives of the victim. In addition to avenging killings by asking for "blood-money," the deceased's relatives may begin a formal feud, thereby widening the conflict, or take a scalp from a member of a hostile tribe. In every case, homicide is seen as an offense against the community as a whole.

Even as the Mataco are slowly assimilated into wider Argentinian society, they strive to maintain traditional values. Their distinctive legal practices offer a measure of protection against a rapidly changing world where the individual matters more than the community.

◉ TUPINAMBÁ

WHEN THE PORTUGUESE arrived in Brazil in the early 16th century, the Tupinambá occupied more than 2,000 miles of the coast, from Ceará in the north to Porto Alegre in the south. This group had settled in their homeland some centuries earlier, after a messianic migration from the north in search of the idyllic Land of the Grandfather, their mythical sky god. The people dwelled in large

palisaded villages, supporting themselves by cultivating five varieties of manioc and fishing in both rivers and coastal waters. Each Tupinambá group waged wars against its neighbors in a constant ebb and flow of blood feuds and revenge killings. Among the Portuguese, the Tupinambá soon acquired a reputation as fierce warriors, headhunters, and cannibals, but, in fact, the people placed a high premium on social harmony within their own communities.

Following years of wars with the Portuguese, many Tupinambá captives were placed on sugar plantations and forced to do work they considered beneath their dignity as warriors. Still, even though they were subdued, the Tupinambá held on to their traditional culture. In the 17th century, another powerful messianic movement arose, again causing them to believe that when they reached the Land of the Grandfather, they would achieve immortality, regain their youth, and live at ease. But this time, the Tupinambá did not migrate from their villages. In many communities, they simply stopped working, thinking that the digging sticks used to cultivate fields would do the work by themselves. These beliefs have now been submerged in Catholicism, and the surviving Tupinambá have become peasant farmers.

PATAGONIA

In Brazil, a Waurá wrestler with girded biceps and elaborate body paint rests while waiting for his turn in the lists. Strength and endurance serve competitors well in traditional wrestling bouts, commonplace before the relentless onslaught of Western civilization.

◉ FUEGIANS

SPANISH EXPLORER Ferdinand Magellan first encountered the Fuegian Indians in 1520, when he passed through the strait later named after him and observed numerous campfires on the beaches at night—from whence came "the land of fire" (Tierra del Fuego). Botanist Charles Darwin immortalized the people as "wretched savages" in his account of the 19th-century voyage of H.M.S. *Beagle*. The Yámana (Yahgan) of the coast, and eventually the Selknam (Ona) of the interior, two of the Fuegian groups, came into sustained contact with Christian missionaries after 1875 but were not studied by anthropologists until the 1920s.

The Selknam lived in western Tierra del Fuego. In the more open areas, they hunted small burrowing rodents known as cururos, llama-like guanacos, and wild fowl. They also took guanacos in forested regions and captured sea mammals along the coast. To support their needs, Selknam groups required large hunting territories, within which people were constantly on the move, living in smoke-filled shelters made from timber poles and guanaco skins. The groups were very sensitive about territorial encroachments, so much so that incursions sometimes led to fighting and blood feuds. In matters of life and death, the people looked to their shamans, who controlled health and disease, weather and war; they could even predict the discovery of stranded whales, an ability that engendered great respect and fear.

Yámana groups inhabited the windswept archipelago along the Beagle Channel and traveled long distances in search of food. They effectively lived in bark canoes, which the women paddled fearlessly over open water. Women collected mussels and fished, while the men took sea mammals. Unlike the relatively tall Selknam, the Yámana were short of stature, the men standing just over five feet. For protection against the constant cold and wet, people smeared their bodies with fish oil, wearing almost no clothing year-round.

The traditional Fuegian cultures disappeared as people perished from smallpox and other diseases, from malnutrition, and even from bounty-hunting European settlers. Of those who survived, many married Spanish immigrants. Today, a few native Selknam can be found working as ranch hands and laborers, but full-blooded Yámana are, to all intents and purposes, extinct.

Poverty-ridden barrios in Buenos Aires, Argentina, bred the alluring strains of the tango. This popular dance music combined the rhythms of South American Indians and African slaves with the music of Spanish colonists.

Mesoamerica and the Caribbean

ESOAMERICA AND the lands lying in and around the Caribbean are geographical neighbors, with each region sharing at least part of its history and culture with the other. Each area, however, has also experienced a long and complex past quite separate from the other, and this has resulted in fundamental differences between the two.

Anthropologists recognize Mesoamerica as a distinct region whose peoples, although ethnically diverse, have shared significant cultural characteristics across varied terrains and a broad expanse of time. Beginning in the semidesert landscapes of north-central Mexico, Mesoamerica reaches south and east toward the tropical terrain of upper Central America, where it then stretches through Guatemala, Belize, and portions of Honduras, El Salvador, and Nicaragua.

The lands of lower Central America, from Costa Rica through the Isthmus of Panama, are not considered part of Mesoamerica; they were once occupied by a patchwork of chiefdoms having more in common with indigenous peoples of South America than with their neighbors to the north. Along with the West Indies, the eastern and northern shores of Central and South America may be said to be part of the Caribbean cultural region.

A young Maya of eastern Yucatán stands near a temple built by his forefathers some 600 years earlier.

In the late 15th century, when Europeans began arriving in the Western Hemisphere, Mesoamerica was dominated by the Aztec. This New World empire reached from Mexico's central plateau to Guatemala and the lowlands of the Yucatán Peninsula, where the Maya dwelled amid the magnificent remains of their ancient civilization. But within decades of the European arrival, Spanish conquistadores had, for the most part, taken control of the region. In 1521, Hernán Cortés conquered the Aztec at Tenochtitlán, now the site of Mexico City. In 1524, Pedro de Alvarado seized the Guatemalan strongholds of the Quiché, Cakchiquel, and Mam peoples after defeating the highland Maya in battle. In 1526, Francisco de Montejo began the conquest of the Yucatan's lowland Maya, an undertaking that continued into the 1540s, when the last of the major groups were officially conquered by his son, also named Francisco.

The Maya by no means disappeared after the conquest. Neither did the Aztec (Nahuatl speakers), Zapotec, Mixtec, and virtually all of the other indigenous populations. Their way of life, however, was profoundly changed and their numbers decimated by war and disease. Native peoples were congregated into European-style villages and towns and "converted" to Roman Catholicism. They were introduced to new livestock, fruits, and grains; given metal implements such as hoes, plows, and saws; and taught how to craft new products of fiber, clay, wood, leather, and metal. In short, they were forced to conform to a new economic system.

To meet their growing labor needs, the Spanish and later colonial powers also turned to Africans, who were forcibly brought to the New World. In Central America, fruit plantations along the Caribbean coastal plain, as well as construction of the Panama Railroad and early work on the Panama Canal in the mid- to late 19th century, created an enormous demand for labor; several thousand more blacks arrived, along with groups of Chinese. Today, a large number of people in both Mesoamerica and the lands rimming the Caribbean are of mixed background—mostly European-Amerindian, but also European-African or Amerindian-African. Spanish is the dominant language, though English is used along much of the Caribbean coast and is the official language of Belize (formerly British Honduras). Many indigenous peoples speak only their own languages, while some use Spanish as a second language.

Cuisine, religion, festivals, and arts also reflect both a European and an indigenous influence. Beans, maize, chilies, jicamas, guavas, and other local staples are augmented by wheat, citrus fruits, pork, beef, and chicken introduced from Europe. In religion, the phenomenon of "folk Catholicism" fuses traditional native cosmology with Catholic practices. There are numerous religious festivals, many of which honor saints, and masks, dancing, music, and street theater are a vital part of these celebrations.

To the east, extending through the Caribbean Sea from the northern coast of South America to the southern tip of Florida are the isles of the West Indies, including the Lesser Antilles, the Greater Antilles, and the Bahamas. The Spanish controlled all these islands from 1492, when Columbus arrived, until the 1620s, when northern Europeans finally established permanent settlements. Although African slavery had been introduced by the Spanish, the slave trade was expanded significantly in the French and English colonies as the plantation economy took hold and millions of Africans were

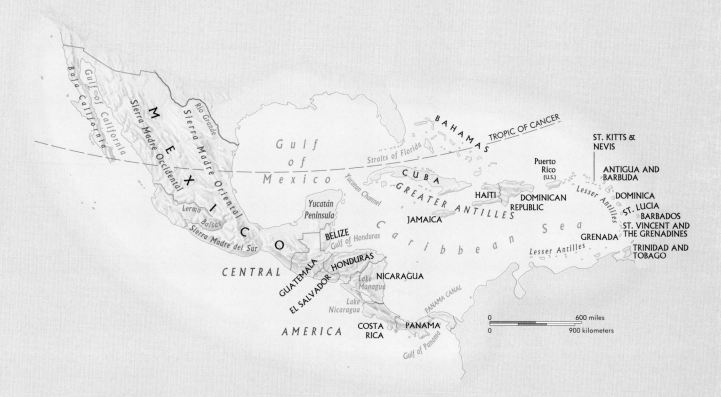

brought across the Atlantic in bondage. For much of the 17th and 18th centuries, the islands were marked by wars and piracy carried out by the dominant colonial powers of France, England, Spain, Denmark, and the Netherlands. The 19th century brought emancipation of the enormous slave population, followed by the arrival of immigrant labor from India and elsewhere.

The ethnic composition of the West Indies is difficult to describe, because culture, ethnicity, class, and race have combined in many ways through the generations and do not fall into easy groupings. Whites and blacks are about equal in number, and a slightly smaller percentage is of mixed ancestry. Across national lines, there is much that is shared by people of African descent. Similarly, people from one island might celebrate cultural traditions regardless of their European, Asian, or African origins.

A linguistically diverse region, West Indian lands include colonial languages, tongues brought by waves of immigration, and Creole forms such as Haitian Kreyol and Aruban Papiamento. The Creole and patois languages are derived from a "mother" tongue but incorporate influences from other languages to create a new tongue altogether. European languages were adopted and transformed by Africans to produce unique local forms with their own complex grammars and vocabularies.

Throughout the Caribbean, Roman Catholicism, Protestantism, Hinduism, Islam, and syncretic religions like Santeria, Vodou, Orisha, and Spiritual Baptism are all thriving. So is the music, which blends European, African, and native traditions and instruments. Some forms, such as calypso and reggae, have had an enormous impact on other musical styles around the world.

Following Pages: After a hard day's work, youths of Todos Santos Cuchumatán, in western Guatemala, array themselves in front of the local store. Their colorful outfits, typical of this town, reflect the continuing tradition of highland Maya weaving.

CLOCKWISE FROM TOP:
ZAPOTEC FIESTA-GOERS,
MIXTEC FARMER, AND
CARIB SHOPPER

MESOAMERICA AND THE CARIBBEAN

MESOAMERICA

THE CARIBBEAN

MESOAMERICA
GARIFUNA • HIGHLAND MAYA • LOWLAND MAYA
• HUICHOL • MIXTEC • NAHUA • OTOMÍ
• TARASCANS • ZAPOTEC

GARIFUNA

ALSO KNOWN AS Black Caribs, the Garifuna are descended from African slaves and the Carib Indians who once gave them refuge on St. Vincent Island in the Lesser Antilles. This group is now spread throughout parts of Mesoamerica (primarily Belize, Honduras, Guatemala, and Nicaragua), and a significant population resides in the United States.

The genesis of the Black Carib population can be traced to French and English policy in the 17th and 18th centuries. Initially, the island of St. Vincent was set aside as a refuge for Carib Indians, who later sold land to French settlers in exchange for arms. The Caribs also were joined by Maroons, African slaves who had escaped from neighboring islands or been shipwrecked, and these two groups intermarried.

In 1763, the Treaty of Paris transferred control of St. Vincent from the French to the English, without recognizing Carib land rights, and more settlers moved in. The island switched hands again, then again. As the English sought more land for sugar plantations, local resistance grew until both sides were engaged in war. The Black Caribs won the war in the sense that their lands were preserved by the terms of a 1773 treaty with the English. But that treaty also acknowledged the King of England as the people's ruler and was later used to justify their deportation. In 1795, another outbreak of hostilities led to the demise of Black Carib sovereignty and to the group's removal to Roatán Island off the Honduran coast. From there, they settled in mainland areas of Central America, where they came to be known as the Garifuna.

Today, the Garifuna thrive mainly in small towns and villages, but many have migrated to large U.S. cities. Their language is a derivation of several Indian, African, and European languages and dialects, including Arawak, Yoruba, Swahili, Bantu, Spanish, English, and French. It is distinct from others in Central America in that many words are gender marked, with men and women using different words for the same things.

Over the years, the Garifuna have developed a unique musical style that owes much to the group's various roots. The music builds from a foundation of two or three *garaon* drums: The *primera* (first) or heart drum improvises against the counter-rhythmic *segunda* (second) or shadow drum; a steady bass drum called the *tercera* (third) holds the ensemble together. Sometimes several guitar strings or wires (snares) are stretched across a drumhead to create the buzzing sound traditional in some West African music. From time to time, turtle-shell percussion, claves, bottle percussion, and a variety of shakers and scrapers are also used.

✸ HIGHLAND MAYA

THE TZOTZIL, QUICHÉ, and Cakchiquel, along with 15 or so other highland Maya groups, occupy their ancestral lands in southeastern Mexico and adjacent Guatemala. Each of these groups may be defined by its own distinctive version of the greater Mayan language family, made up of some 30 related tongues used in both the highlands and the lowlands. From the lofty, volcano-studded mountain ranges along the Pacific coast to the shores of the Yucatán Peninsula, five million Maya speak at least one of these languages.

The highland Maya known as the Tzotzil (literally, "people of the bat") live with their neighbors in Chamula, Zinacantan, Tenejapa, Oxchuc, and other towns lying in a region centered by the colonial city of San Cristóbal de Las Casas—the commercial focus of Ladino, or non-Indian, culture in Mexico's Chiapas state. Primarily maize farmers, these Maya maintain a relatively isolated existence that warily mixes the demands of national bureaucracy with an adherence to traditional customs and beliefs dating back 2,000 years or more. Their cosmology is dominated by

sacred geography, with features such as mountains and water bodies receiving special devotion, and their rituals may be a blend of Maya and Christian religious practices.

Highland Maya women of Chiapas and Guatemala are particularly noted for their traditional weavings, skillfully made with back-strap looms; distinct from town to town, weaving patterns often incorporate ancient Maya concepts of time and the cosmos. A written account of creation and the gods and heroes of sacred myth is incorporated in the famed *Popol Vuh,* or *Book of Council.* Produced by ancestors of today's Quiché people, near the Guatemalan town of Chichicastenango, it is perhaps the most notable surviving work of ancient American literature.

Generations of highland Maya have been scorned by the local Ladinos as barriers to development and commerce, and they have suffered unusual degrees of oppression and negligence by their national governments. In recent decades, military repression of the Guatemalan Maya, punctuated by torture and executions, fostered mass movements of refugees to camps in Mexico. But many people have since returned under a truce—a situation resulting in part from the leadership of Rigoberta Menchú, a Quiché woman who in 1992 received the Nobel Peace Prize.

In Mexico, the Zapatista revolutionary movement, which began in San Cristóbal de Las Casas, has spread to many of the Maya towns. It demands immediate action by the local and national governments to alleviate poverty and end the long-standing indifference toward the Maya, whose traditional culture has endured to a remarkable degree.

☀ LOWLAND MAYA

THE LANDS OCCUPIED by the Yucatec, Lacandon, and other speakers of lowland Maya languages reach from Mexico's state of Tabasco east to the Caribbean Sea, and from the highlands and piedmont of Guatemala to the northern shores of the Yucatán Peninsula. Except for the Yucatán's Puuc, or hill area, and Belize's Maya Mountains, the northern Maya lowlands consist of a vast slab of limestone, which is still emerging from the sea.

Lowland Maya mainly speak Yucatec or close relatives such as Lacandon or Itzá, often mixed to varying degrees with Spanish. For subsistence, the people depend largely on the raising of maize, beans, squash, and chili peppers in *milpas,* fields selectively cleared, burned, and planted when the rainy season begins in early June.

During the Classic period, from A.D. 250 to 900, Maya architects designed great stone palaces, temples, and public buildings. They were part of a cosmopolitan society also known for painting, sculpture, astronomy, and a complex writing system. Many traditions of lowland Maya life have survived, from house types to ancestral beliefs in the significance of the cardinal directions and in supernatural figures connected to landscapes and rain. The lowland groups associate numbers with gender: four for male,

representing the corners of the milpa; three for female, alluding to the number of stones in the traditional hearth. Towns usually feature a mix of dwellings, including rounded rectangular houses with walls of stone or bound poles sealed with mud and topped with palm thatch. In addition, they may have *mamposteria,* flat-roofed cement structures topped with tanks for conserving rainwater.

In 1847, the northern Maya began a general uprising against mestizos and whites. Known as the Caste War of Yucatán, this sporadic conflict was later spurred by a local religious movement based on an oracle in the form of a "Talking Cross." Hostilities finally ended in 1902, when the Mexican army occupied Chan-Santa Cruz, the Maya capital of the rebellion.

Modern times have seen important changes in the lives of the northern Maya. In the mid-20th century, for example, collapse of the international demand for Yucatán's sisal fiber eliminated an important source of local employment and income. This, in turn, prompted even more movement of rural people to the urban centers of Mérida, Campeche, and the coastal resorts dominated by Cancún, where age-old cultural traditions are fast disappearing.

☀ HUICHOL

THE TRADITIONAL HOME of the Huichol lies in the Sierra Madre Occidental, a rugged landscape where the Mexican states of Nayarit, Jalisco, Zacatecas, and Durango come together. Partly because of their relative isolation from the colonial Spanish capital and other main European settlements of the central plateau, the Huichol and their immediate neighbors—among them the Tepehuans and Cora—have succeeded more than most in resisting changes that came in the wake of the Spanish conquest.

In fundamental ways, modern Huichol culture differs very little from its pre-Hispanic form; this is particularly true in terms of worldview and religion, despite the Catholic appearance of the latter. The leaders of family lineages customarily lead rites held in family shrines, while native priests, officiating from sacred seats, customarily oversee community rituals on special occasions. These rites and rituals involve the nearly one hundred supernaturals in the complex Huichol pantheon, among them the messenger god who has the form of a winged deer and acts as an intermediary between people and the supernatural world.

The Huichol may be best known for religious objects: Some items include featherwork, beads, and woven string; others are made from painted stone disks and gourds. "Prayer arrows," dangling feathers affixed to shafts, help shamans send messages to the gods. *Ojos de Dios,* or "eyes of God," are made of colored yarn stretched between cruciform sticks, and these items are used to keep away the souls of the dead and ward off malevolent spirits. Perhaps the most remarkable form of Huichol art are the *tablas,* "paintings" made by pressing colored yarn into beeswax coating on

boards. Tablas range from geometrical to pictorial and depict supernatural animals and other beings.

The creativity exhibited in religious art extends to Huichol handicraft and clothing, including men's trousers, shirts, and capes, as well as shoulder bags, earrings, and other adornments. Each item displays an intricate geometry of subtle forms and colors.

✳ MIXTEC

IN THE NAHUATL language of the Aztec, Mixtec means "cloud people," an apt label, for most of the Mixtec live in the mountains of Mexico's western state of Oaxaca; others occupy lower areas such as the hot, humid coastal region to the south. To the east, centered in the valley of Oaxaca, live the Zapotec, the other great people of the region. The intertwined histories of the Zapotec and Mixtec reach deep into the past, particularly at the famed archaeological site of Monte Albán, the ancient mountaintop capital and ceremonial center.

Archaeological evidence indicates that the Zapotec flourished at Monte Albán from about A.D. 250 to 750, when the neighboring Mixtec invaded the valley and took over the city. In the centuries before the Spanish conquest, the Mixtec achieved greatness in their own right through art and craftsmanship—mainly gold jewelry, turquoise-inlay work, and deerskin codices (books). These books held pictographic histories and royal genealogies, particularly relative to the life and exploits of the king and culture hero Eight Deer Jaguar Claw. *(Continued on page 124)*

Reminders of the past: The 800-year-old ruins of Tulum (above), a Maya trading port, serve as a backdrop for today's Maya, who still fish the lagoon inside the barrier reef off Yucatán.

FOLLOWING PAGES: At dawn, Tarascan Indians set out across Lake Pátzcuaro with their distinctive winglike nets. The lake lies in the highlands of western Mexico, where the people's ancestors flourished just prior to Spanish arrival.

PAGES 122-23: In Mexico's Oaxaca state, a homecoming in the mountains celebrates the *quinceañera*, or 15th birthday, of a Trique girl. She dresses in modern finery, while most of her family wear traditional handwoven *huipils* that recall an ancient Mesoamerican tradition.

Modern Mixtec still occupy the lands where their ancestors once dwelled—highland and coastal regions in western Oaxaca and adjacent areas of Guerrero and Puebla. Their lives, like those of other traditional Mesoamerican peoples, revolve around the cultivation of maize, chilies, beans, and squash, as well as the raising of livestock.

The Mixtec and Zapotec vary somewhat in terms of their language, culture, and crafts. Stylistic differences are evident primarily in their pottery, basketry, and woven or embroidered *huipils,* the traditional blouses or tunics worn by women in the region.

☀ NAHUA

THE NAHUA OF Mexico's central highlands are defined mainly by languages that are closely related dialects descended from Nahuatl, which was spoken by the Mexica, or Aztec, when Spanish conquistador Hernán Cortés entered their imperial capital, Tenochtitlán (now Mexico City), in 1519. Nahuatl speakers may also converse in Spanish, but use of this language varies greatly according to location in rural and urban areas. Today's 1.5 million Nahua live in and around Mexico City and throughout most of the central plateau, an area more or less equal to the main part of the Aztec Empire under Moctezuma II.

The various groups of Nahua share the fundamental Mesoamerican subsistence pattern of cultivating maize, beans, chili peppers, tomatoes, and squash in the rich volcanic soils of their heartland, but to do this, they rely on the European-style plow drawn by draft animals. In steep mountain areas where the soil can be poor or indifferent, farmers burn the fields before planting. They also rotate maize and bean crops to help increase fertility. Other major crops include maguey (which is the source of the fermented drink known as pulque), sugarcane, rice, and coffee.

A typical Nahua town surrounds a church and plaza, the latter often serving as a site for the local market. The church also functions as the center point for dividing the settlement into four parts, or barrios, each of which bears a Nahuatl name—a settlement pattern that dates from the centuries before the Spanish conquest. A good example of this ancient pattern can be seen in the town plan of Milpa Alta, just south of Mexico City.

Perhaps the best known of all Nahua population centers, the Milpa Alta area is famed for its geometrical weavings of *quexquemitls* (triangular capes) and other garments made on Aztec back-strap looms. Additional household industries and crafts include adobe bricks; maguey-fiber ropes; and numerous items fashioned for the tourist trade. Among the most popular Nahua objects are pottery, copies of ancient figurines, and the remarkable lacquered boxes, chests, and gourds from the town of Olinalá, in Guerrero.

☀ OTOMÍ

A GROUP KNOWN as the Otomí occupy an area of central Mexico lying just to the northwest of Nahua lands. Like most of their close neighbors, the Otomí are highland people who seldom dwell in an area having an elevation of less than 3,000 feet above mean sea level. The language they speak is distinct from Nahuatl and other Uto-Aztecan tongues used in adjacent areas, and it is more closely related to those of the Mixtec and Zapotec peoples living to the south.

The ways of Otomí farmers vary according to their landscapes and crops. The more acculturated groups grow wheat, barley, and coffee, while more traditional farmers mix crops of maize, beans, and squash in the same field, often using the ancient Mesoamerican digging stick—or a modern version tipped with iron—for the actual planting. Otomí settlements range from compact towns to dispersed settlements, and house types include plank constructions thatched with grass or maguey leaves, and adobe houses with flat or slanted roofs.

Well-known for creating a variety of items sold to both locals and tourists, Otomí craftspeople produce pottery, stone metates (maize grinders), baskets, and woven clothing and bags. Some Otomí, particularly women in the town of San Pablito, in Puebla state, are noted for their manufacture of *amate,* paper made from the bark of the fig tree *(amatl);* theirs is a tradition that dates back more than a thousand years. In pre-Hispanic times, amate was used in rituals or sometimes as the pages of screenfold books called codices, which were filled with hieroglyphic texts and illustrations to record important events and divination practices. Some modern Otomí make cutouts of supernatural figures from this special paper and include them in rituals connected with water and agricultural fertility. Dark paper cutouts of Otomí deities, mounted on lighter background sheets, have become a popular form of folk art in central Mexico.

☀ TARASCANS (Purépecha)

A HIGHLAND REGION in western Mexico is home to the Tarascan people, most of whom live in Michoacán state. Often called a "land of fire and water" because of its volcanoes and lakes, Michoacán is where the Paricutín volcano was born in 1943. From deep new crevices in a farmer's field, Paricutín quickly built a 400-foot-high cone and destroyed two villages with its lava flows.

The Tarascan language, relatively homogeneous over the people's territory, is apparently unrelated to other linguistic groups in Mesoamerica. But it may have tenuous ties to language families in both North and South America, which suggests a very early presence on the Mesoamerican landscape. While modern Tarascans generally share in the traditional Mesoamerican ways of maize farming, potterymaking, and weaving, other circumstances attending their possible origins and cultural history make them unique in the area.

The story of Tarascan culture in pre-Hispanic times derives mainly from the archaeology of Tzintzuntzan, the ancient regional capital on the shores of Lake Pátzcuaro, and from various chronicles that were set down during the time of the Spanish conquest. After studying illustrations of the unusual clothing used in the Tarascan area around the time of the conquest, art historian Patricia Anawalt suggests that the people originated far to the south, in the region of present-day Ecuador. They eventually came north to Mexico by way of the Pacific coast, a well-known ancient route of trade.

Today, each Tarascan village specializes in one or two kinds of handicraft, a practice that may have begun in the mid-16th century with Vasco de Quiroga, first bishop of Michoacán. The bishop not only organized social and religious life in the villages but also strengthened the occupational specialization so common in pre-Hispanic times by introducing new products and techniques. Among the distinctive output of present-day Tarascan craftspeople, one finds featherwork "paintings," guitars, and lacquer-work gourd and wood products, including elaborate masks worn in the traditional dances that form an essential part of native Mesoamerican religion. Tarascans are also notable for their work with copper, bronze, and other alloys—a tradition that appears to date back to at least A.D. 1000, when knowledge of metallurgy first appeared in the region.

☀ ZAPOTEC

TODAY'S ZAPOTEC population, largest of the indigenous groups in Mexico's state of Oaxaca, occupies most of the eastern portion of that state, as well as parts of neighboring ones. The varied lands of this region range from the drier, flat landscapes of the Isthmus of Tehuantepec to the high ridges and deep canyons of the Sierra Madre del Sur; the major valleys of Oaxaca—Zaachila, Tlacolula, and Etla—lie within the Sierra Madre.

During the Classic period, between about A.D. 250 and 750, ancestors of the modern-day Zapotec built some of the largest and most important regional centers of ancient Mesoamerica. The greatest of these, Monte Albán, occupies an artificially flattened mountaintop overlooking today's city of Oaxaca. On that summit, a grand series of palaces, plazas, pyramid-temples, and other structures, including a great pentagonal observatory, were constructed over the ruins left by settlers who had occupied the site as far back as 1000 B.C.

The modern history of Oaxaca is distinguished by the career of the revered Benito Juárez (1806-1872), a full-blooded Zapotec born in Guelatao, a town in the Sierra. He rose to the governorship of Oaxaca and, ultimately, to the presidency of Mexico in the mid-19th century.

Modern Zapotec share the ways and belief systems of many of their Mesoamerican neighbors: They practice Catholicism while continuing to acknowledge a pantheon of supernatural beings associated with sacred geography and with storms, rain, and other elements of the natural world. They have also maintained their ancient belief in animal guardians, companion spirits that individuals acquire at birth.

Through the years, economic activities have included the Zapotec's highly regarded traditional weavings and ceramics, with the wares of different settlements distinct as to shape and color (red or black). The people are also known for music, as well as for cultivating their language arts—a practice that has given rise to a group of locally famous speechmakers.

THE CARIBBEAN
AFRICAN-CARIBBEAN ● AMERINDIANS ● EAST INDIANS ● EURO-CARIBBEAN

☀ AFRICAN-CARIBBEAN

AFRICANS HAVE HAD a significant impact on the shaping of the Caribbean ever since the 16th century. From across vast stretches of the African continent, slavers brought millions of people with diverse backgrounds to the New World. That experience, as well as contact with other African cultures and Europeans, has created a unique culture in the West Indies. To be sure, there are numerous variations between islands: Jamaicans, for example, differ in many ways from Guadeloupeans. Nevertheless, a unique and coherent African-Caribbean culture transcends national boundaries in important ways.

Approximately 36 million people live in the Caribbean region, and more than half of these individuals have some African ancestry. They descend from people who either brought with them or later developed unique family structures, religions, cuisines, musical forms, dances, and festivals. They even had credit associations known as susus—revolving credit arrangements whereby participants pooled their money and then withdrew individual lump sums when needed. African peoples also adopted and transformed traditions that they encountered in the New World, thereby producing new forms of culture. Among their contributions are the syncretic religions of Vodou, Santeria, and Rastafarianism; musical forms including calypso, reggae, rumba, and zouk; and festivals such as Carnival, Jonkonnu, and Crop-Over.

In almost every part of the Caribbean, Africans rebelled against their enslavement. In some cases, communities of escaped slaves, called Maroons, established themselves in difficult landscapes and held off repeated attempts by the colonial forces to root them out. In other cases, organized rebellions were attempted; the most notable success was the 1804 overthrow of the French in Haiti.

In Maroon societies, and in the rest of the Caribbean, aspects of African language were preserved to greater or lesser degrees. Much of what is spoken in the Caribbean today, whether it is the Kreyol of Haiti, the Patois of Jamaica, or the language of Papiamento in the Dutch Antilles, owes some portion of its vocabulary and syntax to African languages such as Yoruba and KiKongo.

✺ AMERINDIANS

WHEN COLUMBUS arrived in the New World, he encountered three distinct native peoples: The Ciboney, or Siboney, had settlements on Cuba and Hispaniola; the Arawak controlled the Bahamas, Trinidad, and much of the Greater Antilles; and the Caribs were settled mostly in the Virgin Islands and along the Lesser Antilles. Some Carib groups lived on the South American mainland, from the Amazon River northward to the Guianas and the sea that would be named for them.

The Caribs occupied small autonomous settlements, grew staple foods such as cassava and other root crops, and hunted in nearby areas with their blowguns or bows and arrows. Although much of their history has been lost, the people were reputedly fierce warriors whose numbers were decimated by war, disease, and the brutal conditions of slavery in the early decades of European colonization. For the most part, divisions between the Carib groups ran along linguistic lines, but the languages they spoke seem to have been mutually understandable.

The Arawak, often described by the Spanish as gentle and hospitable, had a way of life that was technologically simple yet ingenious. They and the Caribs both practiced *conuco,* a kind of ecologically sound farming method that involved burning a small patch of land to enrich the soil. Farmers then formed mounds of earth where they planted manioc and other crops that had high yields but a low environmental impact. Because they lived in a tropical climate, the Arawak usually felt the need to construct only simple shelters. The people also were known for creating elaborate stone sculptures, painting their bodies, and making jewelry.

According to accounts of contemporaries, both the Arawak and the Caribs were more centrally organized than the Ciboney. The Arawak had complex, intertwining forms of religion and government: Shamans were responsible for controlling *zemis,* good and evil spirits that they sometimes captured and housed in icons made of gold; caciques, or local chiefs, ruled semiautonomous provinces within the larger territory of an island. Carib organization was less centralized, with villages remaining largely independent

In Panama's San Blas Islands, a Cuna woman works a sugarcane press. Traditional Cuna clothing incorporates *molas,* panels with colorful, intricate designs made from a reverse-appliqué process.

of one another. Although European settlers considered Caribs to be savages who ate human flesh, most scholars today say that this image was exaggerated to justify the people's conquest. This is not to say that cannibalism was not part of the culture; it was very likely practiced in ritual situations following battles. The bravest enemy warriors were tortured and killed, and parts of their bodies were ceremonially consumed.

While no "pure" native populations are left, several Caribbean communities preserve their age-old traditions and celebrate native ancestry in such venues as the Santa Rosa Carib Festival in northern Trinidad. A concerted effort is also under way to remember contributions to Caribbean life made by people such as the Taino, a subgroup of the Arawak in Puerto Rico.

✹ EAST INDIANS

IN 1838, SLAVERY ended in the British West Indies. But the plantation economy still required workers, and planters were often unwilling or unable to pay fair wages to former slaves, the islands' only source of manpower. Besides, many Africans were understandably loath to work for their former masters. In an attempt to undercut African labor power, planters asked the colonial government to help find cheap labor in other parts of the empire. Various solutions were tried—including the importation of European workers, free Africans, and Chinese laborers—before the English found their greatest success in indentured workers from India.

Between 1838 and 1917, more than half a million people were brought from the Indian subcontinent to colonies in South America and the Caribbean. The vast majority came to Guyana (formerly British Guiana) and Trinidad, with many others going to Guadeloupe, Jamaica, Suriname, Martinique, French Guiana, and Grenada. Smaller numbers landed in Belize, St. Vincent, St. Kitts, and St. Croix. Today, descendants of people from India and its former lands make up a significant portion of the Caribbean population.

The Indian presence has had a profound impact on what many people understand as Caribbean culture, with regional cuisine, dance, music, festivals, politics, enterprise, art, and religion all holding Indian elements. These forms, though, are not "purely" Indian: Through the years a "creolization" has occurred, resulting in something unique to the region. A fine example of Caribbean Indian culture can be found in Trinidad's annual Hosay Festival, which commemorates the deaths of the Prophet Muhammad's grandsons Hassan and Husain. Known as the Muharram Festival by Shiite Muslims, it is called Hosay in Trinidad and is celebrated with a parade of large floats, or *taziya*, in the shape of elaborate mosques. The floats are accompanied by *tassa* drummers—groups of men with sticks, beating medium-size drums slung over their shoulders.

Indo-Caribbean culture has also produced "chutney" music, a fast-tempo, modernized version of folk tunes and other musical forms; it has itself become mixed with African-derived calypso and *soca* (soul meeting calypso) to produce a highly popular dance music called soca-chutney.

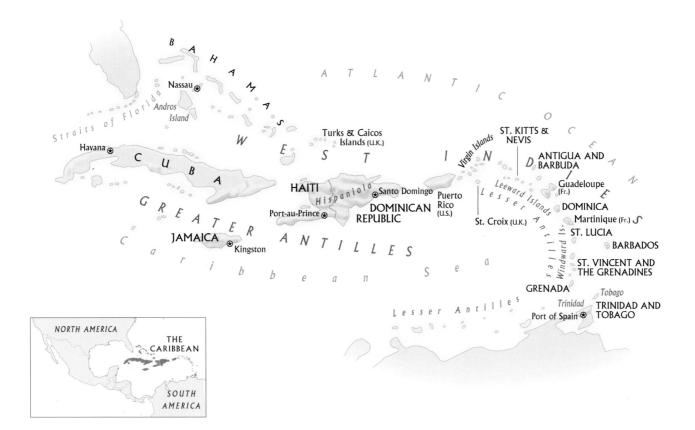

Finally, Indian cooking has greatly influenced the cuisines of Trinidad and Guyana with such mainstays as roti—flat bread filled with a stew of curried potatoes, chickpeas, and shrimp, goat, or chicken; "doubles"—curried chickpeas served between two pieces of flat bread; and *pholouri*—deep-fried balls of yellow split-pea batter served with a mango chutney, just to name a few. Hindi words pepper local languages, especially when it comes to food: Spinach is *bhaji*, potato is *aloo*, long string beans are known as *bodi*, and chickpeas are *channa*. Sometimes overlooked when considering Caribbean culture, Indian cultural forms have evolved into a major element of the region's ethnic mix.

☀ EURO-CARIBBEAN

THE PERMANENT EUROPEAN presence in the Caribbean began with the arrival of Columbus in 1492 and continued as the Spanish Empire sent colonists to extract mineral wealth from the region. Because islands without precious metals were of little interest, early colonists moved fairly rapidly from one place to another in search of riches, all the while enslaving local populations and unknowingly subjecting them to diseases brought from Europe.

With the arrival of other European powers through the 16th and 17th centuries, and the subsequent growth of plantation economies, additional labor was needed. But landowners did not turn immediately to African slavery as the solution; instead, they looked to European sources for workers. For a while, they relied on indentured servants: Some had been kidnapped and brought to the New World, while many others left their homelands to escape religious persecution, war, or even prison sentences. These early white laborers often suffered harsh treatment, succumbed to disease, and were eventually replaced by Africans.

As African slavery began to dominate the islands, white servitude declined. Even so, poor whites were not viewed kindly, and for a time local governments considered many of them to be persona non grata: idlers, thieves, and ne'er-do-wells. Owners and overseers, on the other hand, continued to do well.

Through the years, both the elite and far-from-elite classes of Europeans have had a significant effect on the Caribbean region. They brought holidays and festivals— New Year's and Carnival, for example—as well as masked balls and various cuisines, musical forms, and dances. Like the people who brought them, many of these customs, activities, and traditions have been radically transformed to emerge as uniquely Caribbean.

Wearing smiles and sprayed-on dye, Hindus in San Juan, Puerto Rico, gather during Phagwa, a springtime festival celebrating rebirth. Both Hinduism and Islam remain important to Caribbean people of Indian descent.

I N 1491, THE YEAR before Christopher Columbus set foot in the Western Hemisphere, millions of people of great cultural, linguistic, and ethnic diversity were already living in North America. They spoke hundreds of languages and had a range of political systems, family structures, art forms, spiritual beliefs, and adaptations to local environments. The marked variation of physical traits bespoke many peoples, many ethnicities.

In the southeastern and midwestern regions of what is now the United States, streams teemed with fish, forests held abundant game, and the climate provided the long growing season needed for agriculture. Out of these favorable conditions arose the most highly developed Native American civilization north of Mexico: the prehistoric Mississippian tradition. This very complex, class-structured society featured populous towns with temple mounds where elaborate ceremonies were held.

To the north, Iroquoian speakers of the Saint Lawrence lowlands dwelled in fortified villages supported by intensive horticulture, fishing, and hunting. The more severe climate of northern Algonquian speakers generally precluded farming—they hunted, gathered, and fished—but it was perfect for white birch trees, from which people built wigwams and highly maneuverable canoes.

NORTH AMERICA

Cree girls, considered members of Canada's First Nations, relax in the cooling waters of Quebec's Lake Opemisca.

In the vast boreal forest of the Alaskan and Canadian subarctic lived a number of related tribes who spoke languages of the Northern Athapaskan family. They were probably descendants of Paleo-Indians who crossed the Bering land bridge and began spreading south and east perhaps 20,000 years ago. Unlike their Inuit and Eskimo neighbors, groups such as the Koyukon and Kutchin, or Gwichin, saw their extreme environment as a dark and dangerous place, so they developed taboos and rituals to appease numerous forest spirits. Northern Athapaskans were also very adaptable, and their cultures easily incorporated useful customs from other groups. Thus, the Sarsi and Sekani absorbed the horse culture of the Great Plains and became almost indistinguishable from the neighboring Blackfeet, while the Eyak took on the appearance of a northwest coast tribe. Still other groups wandered thousands of miles into the American Southwest.

Athapaskans migrated from Canada sometime before European arrival, adapted to a new landscape and new neighbors, and became the Navajo and six Apache tribes. The Kiowa-Apache and other groups mingled with Plains tribes, living in tepees and sharing their customs, while the Navajo and Western Apache incorporated farming and ceremonies from the Pueblo. Called Pueblo by the Spanish, for their compact villages of multistoried houses, Puebloan peoples have been living in the Southwest since 500 B.C.

On the Great Plains, drought and population pressures caused significant population shifts long before white settlers began displacing tribes. Around A.D. 1300, the agricultural Pawnee moved into Nebraska from east Texas; by 1400, the Mandan had left eastern prairies for the upper Missouri Valley. Both groups lived in villages made possible by agriculture near rivers, while groups such as the Siouan tribes were bison-hunting nomads who carried their belongings on dog-pulled travois. Horses would transform their lives: The Lakota and other Sioux got their first horses between 1750 and 1770, after which they reached the height of their powers, riding freely across vast grasslands.

Far from the grasslands are the lush cedar forests and salmon-streaked waters of the continent's northwest coast, a region whose rich resource base enabled people to develop complex societies and elaborate ceremonies. California, south along the coast, offered a benign climate and a plentiful supply of wild foods. Home to the greatest concentration of divergent and unrelated languages, California was probably settled over a long period by peoples who spoke different languages and who, over generations, developed a wide array of dialects that distinguished their home villages and ethnicity.

By the late 19th century, most tribes in the United States had been isolated on reservations. Children were removed from communities to hasten assimilation into white culture; forced to attend boarding schools, they were forbidden to speak their own languages, a situation that led to the loss of most Native American tongues. Canadian Indians, designated "First Nations," did not experience such wholesale removals and great reductions in tribal land, because competition for resources was not as intense. Established in 1876, the Canadian reserve system—so called because land was "reserved" as hunting grounds—continues to administer Indian affairs, but now the First Nations also face economic pressures to exploit their oil and mineral resources.

In 1990, more than half the Native Americans in the U.S. were living in urban areas. The government has recognized 556 Indian tribes, and about 200 groups are petitioning

for
federal
recognition.
Contemporary
Native Americans
are not only preserving
their cultures but also reshap-
ing them in ways that make them
more meaningful to their peoples.
Groups such as the Makah of Washington State, who recently conducted
their first whale hunt in generations,
are re-creating their cultural heritage,
while tribes such as the Hopi maintain
ceremonies in an unbroken tradition.
In 1978, Native Americans in the Southwest created the American Indian Language Development Institute, a major
force for the continuing vitality of tribal
languages. Many Plains tribes have
revived the Sun Dance, an elaborate ritual
in which dancers endure physical suffering to
ensure blessings for their people. Today, Native
Americans are still under considerable pressure to
assimilate, yet they continue to celebrate individual tribal
identities and their pan-tribal ethnic identity as American Indians.

Many immigrants or their progeny also celebrate their heritage and hold
fast to beliefs and traditions brought from other continents. Among the millions of arrivals
over the years were Amish from Switzerland, France, and Germany; Hutterites from
Moravia; and Old Believers from Russia—groups who sought separate ethnic identities
based on religious beliefs. Descendants of these pacifistic, agrarian peoples still favor plain
garb and reject "worldly" practices, eschewing telephones, electric lights, and mechanized vehicles. During the slave trade, more than nine million Africans were brought to
the New World against their will; many of their descendants are rediscovering the ancient
cultures of their ancestors. Between 1820 and 1924, many Asians came to work on rail-
roads and farms in the West, followed later by large groups from the Philippines, India,
and Korea. Recent decades have seen the arrival of millions more from Asia, Eastern
Europe, and elsewhere in the Americas, almost all of them drawn by the promise of a
better life in North America, a land that is still home to many peoples, many ethnicities.

Following Pages: A Navajo woman holds corn and bunches of *cota*, a wild plant used to make medicine, dye, and a beverage. Sacred to the Navajo, corn provides both physical and spiritual sustenance because its pollen, the people believe, has the power to bless and protect.

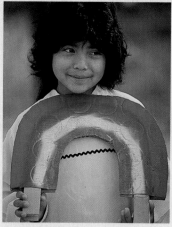

CLOCKWISE FROM TOP LEFT: ONONDAGA CHIEF, HOPI GIRL, AND TOHONO O'ODHAM DANCER

SOUTHEAST
CHEROKEE • SEMINOLE

CHEROKEE

FOR CENTURIES the Appalachian highlands in North Carolina and Tennessee were home to the Cherokee, largest tribe in the southeastern United States. Then, white settlers pushed across the Appalachians, taking over the fertile farmland of the Cherokee and other Indian groups in the region and forcing their removal to Indian Territory (now Oklahoma).

The Cherokee, who with the Chickasaw, Choctaw, Creek, and Seminole were known as the Five Civilized Tribes, had adapted to white culture and owned houses, farms, livestock, and slaves. By the 1820s, thousands of the people had learned to read and write their own language, using a syllabary devised by a Cherokee named Sequoyah, the only man in history known to have created a writing system single-handedly. His phonetic system comprised 85 symbols, each of which signified a sound in the Cherokee language. Tribal doctors recorded their medical beliefs and practices with Sequoyah's invention, and as a result more is known today about traditional Cherokee medicine than about the healing practices of any other southeastern tribe.

In 1838 President Andrew Jackson enforced the Indian Removal Act of 1830, evicting 18,000 Cherokee from their homes even though the law had said the people must give their consent—and the Supreme Court had affirmed their rights to remain. Under conditions so brutal that 4,000 died, the Cherokee were marched westward; over the next decade, 60,000 Native Americans would walk the "Trail of Tears" to Oklahoma. Some Cherokee managed to elude capture by hiding in North Carolina's mountains, and eventually their right to remain in the east was recognized by the federal and state governments. In 1889 they became known as the Eastern Band of Cherokee Indians. Members of this band still tell the story of Cherokee removal in their revered outdoor drama, *Unto These Hills*.

When the majority of Cherokee arrived in Oklahoma in 1839, they adopted a new constitution and established schools, churches, and businesses. They also began printing their own newspaper and periodical. Soon, the Cherokee had a higher literacy rate than their white neighbors.

In 1984 the Eastern Band of North Carolina and the Cherokee Nation of Oklahoma met in council for the first time in nearly 150 years; since then, they have met every two years. Both groups have elected women as principal chiefs, evidence that women play important roles in Cherokee society. Both have also striven to keep their culture strong through the continued use of their own language and by participation in such age-old activities as the stickball game. Traditional basketmaking, long a vital part of the identity of Cherokee women, is still carried out in North Carolina, where, in 1996, the Eastern Band used their nontraditional casino profits to buy farmland encompassing Kituhwa, the Cherokee origin place and sacred burial ground.

✸ SEMINOLE

OF PRIMARILY CREEK descent, the Seminole tribe came into being because of European settlement and subsequent warfare. In the 1700s, after the English and their Creek allies had all but destroyed the Apalachee and Timucua tribes of Spanish-held northern Florida, some Creek began moving into the region from Alabama and Georgia. They became the Seminole, from the Muskogee word *simanóli,* meaning "runaway" or, more appropriately, "frontiersman," which refers to the tribe's move to a new homeland, away from encroaching planters.

Border friction between white slaveholders and the Seminole intensified, though, because the latter treated African Americans as equals, giving haven to runaway slaves, intermarrying with them, and heeding their advice in council. By the 1830s, when President Andrew Jackson signed an act to relocate the Seminole to Oklahoma, small bands were waging fierce guerrilla warfare in what came to be considered the longest and least successful Indian war in United States history. Determined to preserve their freedom, the Seminole managed to carry on even after Osceola, their most famous leader, was captured under a flag of truce in 1837 and died in captivity the following year. From 3,000 to 4,000 Seminole were forcibly marched to Oklahoma; a few hundred escaped, however, by fleeing south into the sloughs and saw grass of the Everglades, eluding pursuers who in time gave up looking for them.

In clothing of Plains design, a Cherokee elder teaches his grandson a traditional dance. Feathered back bustles typify powwow regalia worn for the Fancy Dance, noted for its whirling style and fast tempo.

By the early 1900s, Florida's Seminole were trading alligator hides and egret feathers for cotton cloth, pots, and metal tools from non-Indians; in 1928, they started selling their crafts along the recently built Tamiami Trail, which linked Tampa to Miami via the Everglades. Over the next three decades, as increasing numbers of tourists began to flock to Miami, non-Indian entrepreneurs invited the tribe to create and work in Seminole "villages." Alligator wrestling, popularized at this time, and the machine-sewn patchwork clothing women began to make around 1900 have continued to promote a strong sense of tribal identity.

In 1957 the Seminole Tribe of Florida received federal recognition. Four years later, the Miccosukee broke from the Seminole to form their own tribe; more conservative in social and religious values, they continue to follow the political leadership of their medicine men and council. Today, both tribes attract European and American visitors to their re-created villages, where museums tell the history of their people. They also operate successful ecotourism enterprises that take visitors through the Everglades in airboats and swamp buggies. In contrast, most Oklahoma Seminole rely on jobs in the oil industry or work in construction, manufacturing, retailing, and agriculture.

NORTHEAST
CHIPPEWA • IROQUOIS

✿ CHIPPEWA (Ojibwa)

ONE OF NORTH AMERICA'S largest Indian groups, the Chippewa live on reservations or reserves in Michigan, Wisconsin, Minnesota, North Dakota, Montana, and the Canadian provinces of Ontario, Manitoba, and Saskatchewan. They once spoke an Algonquian language and dwelled in dome-shaped wigwams covered with birch bark, but because wild plants and game in their region did not support large villages, they formed widely scattered, autonomous bands of a hundred or so people. In the fall, hunters traveled as far as a hundred miles to track moose, woodland caribou, and bears—animals with which people also tried, through prayer and ceremonies, to establish spiritual connections central to their religion.

Joining other families in maple groves near rivers and lakes, the Chippewa marked the end of winter with sugar-making activities. From there, they proceeded to summer villages, where they spent the warm months tanning hides and building the birch-bark canoes for which they were famous. At summer's end, families harvested corn, squash, and perhaps wild rice, a seed-bearing grass that grows along the muddy shores of some streams and marshes. Wild rice often made survival possible in regions where a short growing season made agriculture unreliable.

The Chippewa performed the ceremonies of the Midewiwin (Great Medicine Society), a secret group of men and women healers whose primary purpose during the rituals was healing the sick and initiating new members who had served long, demanding apprenticeships. Today, the Chippewa continue to carry out the two- to five-day ceremonies, as well as traditional forms of hunting, fishing, sugar mapling, wild-rice gathering, and beadworking—all very important markers of their ethnicity.

✿ IROQUOIS

NOW LIVING ON reservations and reserves in upstate New York and Canada, the Iroquois are best known for the powerful league formed by five Iroquoian-speaking tribes to peacefully resolve conflicts. The league, which gave fair representation to each group, was established sometime between A.D. 1400 and 1600, after a long history of bloody intertribal feuding. Within the member tribes—Mohawk, Oneida, Onondaga, Cayuga, and Seneca (and later, the Tuscarora)—clan mothers chose sachems to represent their family lineages on the basis of their integrity, wisdom, vision, and oratorical ability. The 49 sachems composed the governing council of the league, also served on their separate tribal councils, and settled disputes through diplomacy and ceremonies.

Inspired by the Iroquois model that put values of unity, democracy, and liberty into action, Benjamin Franklin and other leaders of the American Colonies sought the help of the Iroquois in establishing a fair and democratic colonial union. Their meeting in 1754 produced the Albany Plan of

Union, a precursor of the Articles of Confederation. Today, ideals espoused by the Iroquois League continue to guide such organizations as the United Nations.

The Iroquois call themselves the Haudenosaunee—People of the Longhouse—in reference to their traditional homes. Accommodating as many as a dozen families, each bark-covered dwelling was as long as 200 feet, with a width of 25 feet; families had separate apartments but shared a fire with others. Iroquois settlements held between 30 to 150 longhouses and were protected by palisades.

Large numbers of Iroquois now pursue urban lifestyles, holding jobs in industry, education, and other fields, but they continue returning to the reservations for ceremonies. They also still play lacrosse. The Iroquois version of this Native American game was the basis for today's sport, and it is a mainstay of ethnic identity, promoting the health, strength, and community spirit that binds Iroquois nations together. To control land claims, counter environmental pollution, and keep traditions alive, the people have revitalized the Six Nations Iroquois Confederacy, as it is known today. The confederacy actively participates in international forums related to the rights of indigenous peoples and even issues its own passports, which are honored by many nations.

PLAINS

BLACKFEET • CHEYENNE • CROW • LAKOTA SIOUX • MANDAN

BLACKFEET

AMONG THE westernmost Algonquian-speaking peoples are the Blackfeet tribes: The Southern Piegan have a reservation in northern Montana, and the Northern Piegan, Blood, and Blackfeet proper live on reserves in southern Alberta. Once dependent upon the bison for food, shelter, and tools, the Blackfeet saw their way of life transformed when they acquired horses in the mid-1700s. Families following bison had used dogs to carry tepees and other belongings, but dogs were easily distracted by rabbits and drawn into fights. Plus, they could carry only about 75 pounds, which meant women had to carry large loads, and the old and the infirm who could not walk had to be left behind.

After they obtained horses and guns, the Blackfeet became fierce warriors who were known for raids far from home. Extending their hunting and raiding territory, they eventually forced the Shoshoni, who lacked guns, southward and westward into the Rocky Mountains, and they drove the Kutenai westward across the Canadian Rockies.

Today, like many other tribes, the Blackfeet are sharing their land through "edu-tourism." In the form of tribally run tours, edu-tourism allows visitors to see some of the most beautiful wilderness in the West, and it may also help bring down the extremely high unemployment rates found on reservations. Such programs enable people to work as guides near their homes, telling tourists what they want them to know about their cultures. In Montana, Blackfeet Historical Site tours take visitors to centuries-old places, teaching them about the significance of sacred sites and how to travel with a spirit of respect. The Blackfeet themselves still smudge their bodies with (Continued on page 144)

FOLLOWING PAGES: Powwow dancers get ready in Oklahoma, a state that has fostered development of so many styles of powwow singing, dancing, and costumes that people often call it "the cradle of powwowing." **PAGES 142-43:** In Rocky Boy, Montana, a Sioux from South Dakota prepares for the Traditional Dance while his wife adjusts her eagle feather. Traditional dancers, known for their air of dignity, represent a distinct style of powwow dancing and dress.

sweet grass and pine boughs for purification before going into the mountains, and they leave tobacco offerings to the trees and animals that they find along their way. They also continue to hold an annual Sun Dance, take ritual sweat baths, and maintain sacred medicine bundles.

✸ CHEYENNE

AROUND A.D. 1700, the ancestors of the Algonquian-speaking Cheyenne moved onto the northern prairies from the eastern woodlands, where they had long been gatherers of wild rice. By 1800, they had moved farther west onto the Great Plains, becoming nomadic bison hunters who depended upon animals they killed during the summer to get them through the long winter.

Cheyenne warrior societies, such as the Dog Soldiers, enforced strict control over hunters and, together with the Council of Forty-four, provided order for the physical and spiritual survival of their people. The council head was the Sweet Medicine chief, who protected the sacred sweet grass bundle; just below him were four subchiefs representing supernatural beings. The next level of power was vested in 39 chiefs known for their generosity and wisdom in settling disputes. If, for example, the council decided that a case of murder threatened tribal welfare, they banished the accused person, along with those who chose to accompany him or her, for at least five years. While their decisions today often conflict with those of the officially recognized tribal government, the Southern and Northern Cheyenne chiefs, religious leaders, and military society members continue to operate as the traditional tribal government authority.

The Northern Cheyenne Reservation is in southeastern Montana. The Oklahoma reservation of the Southern

Cheyenne was eradicated by the federal government, but this group formed the Cheyenne-Arapaho Tribes of Oklahoma, an organization with its own tribally elected business council and president. Both the Northern and Southern Cheyenne teach their language and culture in their schools, and many continue to perform traditional ceremonies, some of which have been revived—the Sacred Arrows and Sun Dance, for example. Women participate in the War Mothers Association, honoring Cheyenne veterans from all wars; for those skilled at working with porcupine quills, there is the Quillwork Society, whose members have sacred rights to use particular quill and beadwork designs.

Today the Northern Cheyenne and 50 other tribes participate in the InterTribal Bison Cooperative. By purchasing bison, which are indigenous to the plains, and learning to manage their herds, the tribes are helping to restore the ecological balance that was disturbed when cattle ranching led to overgrazing; they are also gaining needed income from bison meat, a leaner source of protein than beef. Restoring bison to the plains helps accomplish two other important goals: reestablishing connections to the Creator and reviving ancient traditions.

✸ CROW

IN THE STRUGGLE for control of the northern plains, the Crow were such fierce enemies of the Lakota Sioux that they served as scouts for Lt. Col. George Custer in his 1876 campaign against Sitting Bull on Crow lands near the Little Bighorn River. Even so, the Sioux defeated Custer, whose name was subsequently used in the battlefield designation. In 1991, following lengthy Congressional hearings, the site was renamed Little Bighorn Battlefield National Monument,

and a memorial for Indian warriors was commissioned to correct a one-sided view of history. After two centuries of animosity, people from both native nations met in 1995 for reconciliation ceremonies at the battlefield, along with other tribes and representatives of the Seventh Cavalry.

Historic accounts of the Crow record their tall, striking appearance, noble bearing, and horsemanship. The men placed elaborately ornamented blankets and saddles on the backs of their horses, and women used beadwork on trade cloth to create collars that adorned the animals' necks and chests. Women also painted designs on the hide coverings of tepees, cone-shaped dwellings that they made even larger after they acquired horses to carry heavier loads.

Today's Crow, whose reservation is in south-central Montana, retain their unique vision of themselves. They continue to perform the traditional Sun Dance in summer; medicine men conduct healing ceremonies throughout the year; and a majority of children and adults still speak the old language. At the Crow Fair each August, people renew their kinship and social ties while celebrating with parades, feasts, rodeos, giveaways, and powwow singing and dancing. For competitions, Crow artists use vivid colors and both geometric and flower designs to decorate horse-riding gear and dance clothing. Also called "the Tepee Capital of the World," the fair boasts as many as 1,500 tepees pitched near the banks of the Little Bighorn.

✿ LAKOTA SIOUX

EVEN THOUGH the image of a Lakota warrior galloping across the plains of South Dakota still captivates non-Indians, this nomadic horse culture lasted only a short while. Not until after about 1750 did the Sioux acquire horses through raiding and trading.

As eastern tribes headed west, away from white settlers, native groups displaced others in a domino effect. By the late 1700s, Lakota tribes, the westernmost group of Sioux, had moved from eastern prairies onto the western High Plains, where they used strategy and horsemanship to develop warfare into an art.

Horses also transformed the bison hunt, because men no longer had to stampede entire herds over cliffs; instead, riders could bring down several bison with rifles or bows and arrows. The Lakota considered the bison a sacred gift from the Creator, and through the Sun Dance, their annual ritual of sacrifice and thanksgiving, they honored it for the food, shelter, tools, and fuel it provided. By 1875, the bison was nearing extinction because of overhunting by whites, who took the hide and left the carcass to rot.

Extermination was encouraged by the military, who believed the end of the bison would help bring the Indians under their control. They continued pursuing the Sioux until 1876, when the Sioux and their Cheyenne allies defeated Custer at the Battle of the Little Bighorn, the greatest Indian victory in a losing war.

Now living on reservations in Minnesota, North and South Dakota, Nebraska, and Montana, the Sioux comprise 14 tribes grouped into three divisions on the basis of dialect and cultural traditions: The eastern tribes are Dakota or Santee Sioux; the central tribes, Nakota or Yankton; and the western tribes, Lakota or Teton. For all of them, pipe smoking remains an essential marker of Sioux identity, and in Pipestone, Minnesota, both Sioux and Ojibwa artists continue carving dusty-red catlinite into the traditional T-shaped calumets. Highly prized, pipes are smoked to bring a spiritual dimension to human affairs, for as the smoke rises, it carries the smoker's prayers to the spirit world.

Today, mounted Lakota warriors embody pan-Indian identity for all Native Americans, many of whom travel great distances to participate in annual powwows featuring Plains-style dancers. These gatherings are also opportunities for sharing spiritual values based on respect for the Earth. Prominent Lakota author and lawyer Vine Deloria, Jr., for example, continues to raise public awareness about the dependence of human survival on the land's well-being.

On the Pine Ridge Indian Reservation of South Dakota, Lakota Sioux brothers (opposite) try to keep cool in the heat of summer. The Sweat Lodge Ceremony at the reservation remains an important aspect of Lakota traditional religion, which people still follow under the leadership of medicine men. **ABOVE:** Blackfeet on recently broken mustangs gallop across a Browning, Montana, ranch. In the 1990s, the Blackfeet began breeding their own herd to replace the original mustangs lost when they settled on their Montana reservation. Two centuries earlier, the Spanish mustangs—prized for their quickness and maneuverability in buffalo-hunting—had transformed the lives of the Blackfeet and other Plains people.

🏵 MANDAN

NOT ALL PLAINS people became nomadic after they had acquired horses: The Mandan of the upper Missouri River continued to live in fixed settlements rather than change their way of life to follow bison. They retained their agricultural lifestyle and simply went on summer and autumn bison hunts in the neighboring countryside.

Each Mandan village featured a formal town plan with a central plaza, where ceremonies and competitive games were held. Surrounding the plaza were dome-shaped earth lodges for families. Partly subterranean, lodges were snug in winter and cool in summer; their slightly flattened roofs also served as porches and proved ideal for relaxing at the end of the day. In addition, women used the roofs for drying corn and as storage areas.

In the rich soil near the Missouri, women raised corn, tobacco, sunflowers, pumpkins, beans, and squashes. But rich soil was not all that was needed for growing crops; the Mandan also invoked divine assistance through elaborate agricultural rituals. Playing important roles in ceremonies of renewal were sacred ceremonial bundles considered vital to the people's continued existence. The owner of the sacred corn bundle, for example, was responsible for calling the spirits of the corn back from the south before seeds were distributed to women for planting.

Traditional Mandan culture was illustrated in paintings by George Catlin and Karl Bodmer and also described in the journals of explorers Lewis and Clark, who spent the winter of 1804-1805 with the Mandan. As portrayed, the people lived in settled villages, and this made them especially susceptible to European-introduced diseases such as smallpox, which killed more than 800 in 1837.

Today, the Mandan share North Dakota's Fort Berthold Indian Reservation with the Arikara and Hidatsa; known as the Three Affiliated Tribes, all look to a single tribal government, although each tribe maintains its separate ethnic identity. The Mandan strive to keep their culture alive with language classes and with traditional religious ceremonies, beadwork and quillwork, and powwows.

PLATEAU AND GREAT BASIN

PLATEAU AND GREAT BASIN
NEZ PERCÉ • NORTHERN PAIUTE

🏵 NEZ PERCÉ

NOW RESIDING ON a reservation in north-central Idaho, the Nez Percé are best known for a leader named Chief Joseph, whose valiant attempt to lead 200 to 300 warriors and their families to sanctuary in Canada is one of the most heroic—and tragic—feats of American history. Forced to relocate in 1855, when Oregon settlers wanted their land, the Nez Percé again were pressured to move eight years later, after gold was discovered on their reservation. Tempers flared dramatically in 1877, but when the Army refused to negotiate with Chief Joseph, he and his people pushed north in a 15-week, 1,700-mile trek over the steep Bitterroot Range. Seeing his people cold and starving, Joseph stopped and delivered his legendary surrender pronouncement: "My heart is sick and sad. From where the sun now stands, I will fight no more forever."

The Nez Percé homeland—where Washington, Oregon, and Idaho meet and the Clearwater, Salmon, and Snake Rivers flow—provided the people with grassy valleys and forested mountains. In the spring, summer, and autumn, men hunted and fished while women gathered camas bulbs, roots, and berries. After the autumn bison hunt on Montana's eastern plains, the Nez Percé would return to winter camps in the sheltered valleys of their homeland.

The most renowned horsemen of their area, the Nez Percé carefully worked to improve the bloodlines of their herds. Men prized Appaloosas for their endurance and distinctive speckled markings, and women fashioned elaborately beaded horse trappings such as collars, bridles, and saddles. Although the people were forced to give up their 1,100 horses when they surrendered in 1877, today's tribe now has a few Appaloosas; they were a gift from a New Mexico Appaloosa breeder who donated ten mares to the tribally sponsored Chief Joseph Foundation in 1991.

The Nez Percé are very proud of their heritage. In 1988, they began the Cultural Resources Program as a means of preserving their language, history, and arts, and every July descendants of Chief Joseph's band travel to Oregon to celebrate Chief Joseph Days in a town named for the chief.

✿ NORTHERN PAIUTE

THE HOMELAND OF the Northern Paiute once encompassed more than 70,000 square miles of Nevada, southern Oregon, western Idaho, and eastern California. It was part of the Great Basin, the only area in North America where nearly all groups spoke languages from the same language family; such uniformity came about probably because this resource-poor region never attracted a large, diverse population.

Today, Northern Paiute tribes have reservations in Nevada, California, and Oregon. Descendants of a cultural tradition that stretches back more than 10,000 years, the Northern Paiute have survived by developing an intimate knowledge of their environment. With limited precipitation and no rivers that drain to the ocean, the Great Basin forced its early inhabitants to establish an even more delicate balance with their surroundings than did people in more hospitable areas. Resources and terrain still vary widely here, from the freshwater marshland of western Nevada to the deserts and salt flats that make up the major portion of the region.

The rugged environment supported small groups who could get by on intermittent harvests of roots, seeds, and berries. Seminomadic family groups survived by gathering a wide variety of plants that ripened at different times of year, and by supplementing this activity with hunting and fishing. Groups with relatively richer, more specialized environments were able to remain for a season or part of a season in one location, while other groups had to follow a more nomadic or generalized seasonal routine, relying on an immense range of plants and animals. Each family belonged to a flexible camp group, which expanded and contracted according to the changing seasons and availability of resources. In autumn, groups came together to harvest piñon seeds and to undertake communal activities such as rabbit and antelope hunts.

Although each tribe has its own government today, not all groups have been able to develop viable tribal businesses. Some individuals raise cattle and grow hay and grain, while others make a living through wage work in a variety of jobs. In the 1980s, to preserve an important part of their heritage, some Northern Paiute tribes began conducting classes in traditional basketmaking, a highly developed art form that had been necessary for survival.

Most of the people now participate in some branch of Christianity; even so, some individuals retain aspects of their heritage through Paiute songs, stories, and prayers, and a few traditional healers continue to practice. The Ghost Dance Movement, which originated with two late 19th-century prophets who envisioned a revival of native culture, has come and gone. But since the 1930s, people have adopted a number of other tribes' religious movements and activities: the Native American Church, the Sweat Lodge, and the Sun Dance, for example. Because so few of their own traditions have survived, many young Northern Paiute join in these pan-Indian rituals as a way to establish their ethnic identity.

SOUTHWEST AND FAR WEST

CHIRICAHUA APACHE ● HOPI ● NAVAJO ● POMO ● TOHONO O'ODHAM

SOUTHWEST AND FAR WEST

CHIRICAHUA APACHE

SOUTHERN ARIZONA, western New Mexico, and northern Mexico were considered the homeland of the Chiricahua Apache—last Indians in the United States to lay down their arms. The people surrendered in 1886, and for the next 27 years they were treated as prisoners of war and shuffled between prison sites in Florida, Alabama, and Oklahoma. When they finally were freed in 1913, most chose to join the Mescalero and Lipan Apache on their reservation in south-central New Mexico. Today, many of their traditions are maintained by the Chiricahua Apache Prisoners-of-War Descendants, whose ancestors include Cochise, Geronimo, and warriors who rode with the famous chiefs.

The Chiricahua and Mescalero are two of six Apache tribes; the others are the Kiowa-Apache and Lipan, who lived on the southern plains, the Jicarilla of northern New Mexico, and the Western Apache of east-central Arizona. All Apache speak Athapaskan, as do their Navajo cousins and more distant relatives in northwestern Canada.

In the past, the Chiricahua lived in bands made up of several extended families. They were seminomadic hunters and gatherers, moving frequently to avail themselves of plants that grew at different elevations and matured in different seasons. But as settlement by whites cut off access to traditional food-gathering locations, raiding became increasingly important for obtaining food. This activity was significantly different from warfare, which was intended to avenge the deaths of individuals.

Today, Apache Crown Dancers continue to perform nighttime sacred ceremonies: Wearing painted, wooden-slat headdresses and holding wooden swords aloft, they embody mountain spirits. Together with a medicine man and singers and drummers, they evoke supernatural power to cure and protect. The Chiricahua also continue the Sunrise Ceremony for girls reaching puberty, infusing them with the White-Painted Woman's powers to ensure long life, vitality, prosperity, and a good disposition. During the elaborate, four-day ritual, singers recount tribal history from the creation of the universe to the present.

HOPI

FOR THE HOPI occupying 13 villages on and around three mesas in northern Arizona, each year centers around the arrival and departure of the *katsinam,* spirit beings who carry prayers to Hopi deities. The people believe that katsinam live among them from roughly January to June, then for the next six months dwell in the spirit world atop San Francisco Mountain. These beings are not worshiped; instead, they are respected as powerful spirits who help bring rain and other blessings.

The word *katsina* (singular) refers to the incorporeal spirit and to the dancer who brings this spirit to life. As a baby, a Hopi girl receives the first of many katsina carvings representing spirits as real beings who will bestow upon

her the gift of reproduction. Such carvings are sacred and made exclusively for the Hopi—as opposed to the carved kachina figures that went on sale to the public in the 1930s.

The Hopi are also known for their distinctive basketry, jewelry, and pottery. The art of pottery-making was revived around 1900 when Nampeyo (circa 1860-1942), a Hopi-Tewa, began to copy fine prehistoric ware that had been found at nearby Sikyatki, an abandoned Anasazi pueblo. Developing a style based on the ancient pottery, as well as Hopi-Tewa ceramic traditions, Nampeyo painted stylized birds and katsinam in black, orange, and white designs on cream, white, or dark red backgrounds.

In the Hopi world, corn is life, tended with almost the same depth of care that people give their children. To grow this crop in an environment that receives just a few inches of rain or snow each year is an act of faith requiring deep commitment—and the help of katsinam. These beings are considered masters of the art of raising corn and other plants, and songs and ceremonies with katsina dancers evoke the reverential attitude that the Hopi believe is necessary for growing corn. The rituals renew the people's faith, as well as their aspiration to ideals of compassion and cooperation.

Today, the Hopi continue their ceremonies, including the well-known Snake Dance, and tourists from around the world come to watch. Although most outsiders are respectful, some push aside members of the Hopi audience, disregard signs that prohibit photography, and dress inappropriately. The Hopi, who believe that every person can contribute spiritual energy and heartfelt prayers, are struggling with whether to exclude visitors from rituals.

NAVAJO

SPRAWLING ACROSS parts of Arizona, New Mexico, and Utah, the Navajo reservation is home to a group of people who speak Athapaskan, like their Apache cousins and distant relatives in northwestern Canada. By A.D. 1400, small bands of Athapaskans had begun to arrive in the Southwest, and sometime later, the Navajo separated from the rest, moving into the Four Corners area and settling on land that could not support the agricultural towns of their Pueblo neighbors.

The Navajo thrived, however, and by the early 1800s they counted their wealth in horses and flocks of sheep. As pastoralists and farmers, they lived in isolated family groups surrounded by grazing land, and they built earth-covered, domed dwellings known as hogans. Most Navajo live in houses today, but some still use hogans as homes. The structures are also settings for ceremonies.

Navajo ceremonies often focus on the physical, mental, and spiritual healing of persons who become ill after failing to maintain proper relations with supernatural powers. The many songs, prayers, rites, and sandpaintings in a ceremony must be precisely replicated for it to be effective. Each chant, or ceremony, is a ritual drama that tells the story of a hero or heroine who overcame great obstacles to receive healing.

For some ceremonies, the chanter and his helpers make a sandpainting from 12 to 20 feet in diameter on a hogan floor. After its completion, the painting is blessed, and the patient sits on it to absorb healing power. The power of the Holy People, who created the ceremony with its sandpainting designs, penetrates the person's body and restores a state of well-being, harmony, and health. Unlike the sandpaintings that are applied to a board and sold as art, ceremonial works are sacred and ephemeral and can include crushed flowers, pollen, and cornmeal.

Today, a major part of Navajo ethnic identity centers on the Long Walk, an event people still talk about as if it had happened just yesterday. In 1863, after burning Navajo fields and property, the military forced nearly everyone to walk to Bosque Redondo, New Mexico, where many died of starvation and disease. Five years passed before the Navajo signed a treaty that established a reservation and allowed them to go home.

Long before trading posts were built in the late 1800s, Navajo women had created a market for their magnificent blankets far beyond the Southwest. Then, in an effort to increase the commercial value of Navajo weaving, traders introduced non-Navajo designs, such as geometric motifs from Plains beadwork and hooked elements from Persian rugs. Today, women no longer weave rugs as a career, but most still practice the art because knowing how to weave is a vital part of Navajo ethnicity.

In 1969 the Navajo opened the first tribal college in the United States. Now known as Diné Community College (from the Navajo name for themselves, which means "the people"), it integrates typical college classes with Navajo culture and language courses.

✹ POMO

WHEN THE SPANISH came to California in 1769, some 300,000 native people were already living there and speaking scores of mutually unintelligible languages that differentiated into an unknown number of dialects. Although there are a few other places in the world where as many languages are spoken within a small geographical area, California is the only place in North America where this level of diversity is known to have occurred.

As different ethnic groups moved into the area, they discovered an abundance of natural resources and a relatively mild climate. Each group found its own territory, and with time, isolation from each other led to variations in speech and dialect. The Pomo, for example, speak seven distinct and mutually unintelligible languages of the Hokan language stock—more appropriately called the Pomoan family of languages. The most divergent of these differ more from one another than English does from Icelandic.

The Northern Pomo lived north of San Francisco in the Russian River Valley area, where their territory had 22 miles of coastline. As did other California *(Continued on page 154)*

Having received the blessing of sacred pollen, which invests her with healing powers, an Apache girl nears the end of her Sunrise Ceremony. The puberty (or coming-of-age) ceremony celebrates longevity, physical strength, good temperament, and prosperity; it also promotes the well-being of her people. ***FOLLOWING PAGES:*** Apache Mountain Spirit dancers encircle a bonfire. Only seen at night, these masked dancers play a vital role in the ceremonial life of nearly all Apache tribes, including the Chiricahua, Mescalero, and Western Apache. ***PAGES 152-53:*** A Navajo weaver teaches her centuries-old craft. Although few women make a living from this demanding art form, most of them still know how to weave because Navajo consider it an essential part of their identity.

Indians, they formed tribelets, small autonomous groups occupying a territory that was recognized by neighboring communities. The rocky coast provided crustaceans, sea mammals, and fish, while streams held plenty of trout and salmon. In summer and fall, the Pomo relied on temporary shelters when they were gathering wild plants and hunting game, but the dependability of their food supply allowed them to live in permanent camps with substantial houses for the rest of the year. Acorns, which they ground into flour to make gruel or bread, were a staple of their diet.

Known for weaving baskets that are considered to be among the finest in the world, California Indians have revitalized this once dying art as an essential part of their tribal identities. Learning to weave also means learning the songs and cultural knowledge related to the making and use of baskets. Traditionally, Pomo women made feathered, twined, and coiled baskets—some of them as small as pearls—while men wove bird traps, fishing weirs, and the baby baskets that were begun immediately after the birth of a child. Basketmaking requires dedication and desire, the same traits California Indians are using to revitalize their cultures.

❂ TOHONO O'ODHAM

IN THE SONORAN DESERT of southern Arizona and northern Mexico, where drought is an ever present threat, the Tohono O'odham once divided the year between summer villages near their fields and winter villages near permanent springs in mountain foothills. Their reliance on mesquite beans led the Spanish to call them Papago (Bean People), but in 1986 they became officially known as the Tohono O'odham (Desert People) Nation, their name for themselves. Today they dwell on three southern Arizona reservations.

In the intense summer heat, these people harvest the crimson fruit of the giant saguaro cactus, such a symbol of their culture that its harvest traditionally marks the start of the year. Resembling kiwi fruit in taste, the saguaro fruit is boiled into syrup, candy, and jam. The Keeper of the Smoke, who is the village headman and ceremonial leader, oversees the fermentation of the juice produced from the fruit, a three-day process that occurs in the "rain house."

At night, while the juice ferments, men and women dance to the singing of rain songs, and on the third day, the headman partakes of the wine as he recites ritual orations describing the desolation of the desert without rain. The ceremony is intended to bring rains up from the Gulf of California, thus ensuring the well-being of crops planted after the festival. By saturating his body with saguaro wine, the headman simulates the rain's saturation of cracked and dusty land. As if in answer to a prayer, a desert landscape can change in minutes when lightning rips the sky and rain fills dry washes with rushing torrents.

The Tohono O'odham are a contemporary people who are using income from their casinos to build and staff their own college, as well as a nursing home where tribal elders can be cared for by those who speak their own language. Casino profits have also provided scholarships for higher education. The work of tribal members helps preserve the O'odham language—one of the few Native American languages predicted to survive into future generations.

NORTHWEST COAST
KWAKIUTL • TLINGIT

❂ KWAKIUTL

THE 30 OR SO KWAKIUTL tribes occupying the area around the Queen Charlotte Strait in British Columbia exploited a shore environment so rich in marine life that they were able to follow a settled village lifestyle usually enjoyed only by agriculturalists.

Residing in their permanent villages, the Kwakiutl developed an extensive ceremonial and artistic life that included the carving of totem poles to represent clan figures. The poles had become a well-established art form long before Europeans arrived on the Pacific coast, but they were much easier to carve—and began to increase in number—after the Kwakiutl acquired the iron and steel blades introduced by the newcomers.

Members of the Kwakiutl aristocracy demonstrated the degree of their greatness by the amount of wealth they gave away at potlatches. These events, which included much singing, speech-giving, and dancing, validated a person's social status as he or she distributed extensive property to vast numbers of guests. Because potlatches were required for membership in secret religious societies, wealthy people were also initiates who learned to conduct the societies' enthralling dance-dramas. Commoners composed most of the audiences for these dramas and were usually spellbound by the performers' apparent ability to influence supernatural powers; such magic, in turn, reinforced the status of the aristocrats.

The most terrifying ceremonial performance was the *Hamatsa*, or Cannibal Dance. For the Kwakiutl, who avoided contact with the dead, the concept of eating human flesh was both disgusting and awe-inspiring. The bodies of the dancers supposedly were inhabited by cannibal spirits, and as the performers flung themselves around in a frenzy, they screamed and pretended to eat human flesh. Hidden attendants made strange howling sounds just offstage, and carved bird monsters swooped over the anxious audience. Eventually, certain rites pacified the cannibal spirits, and the dancers vanished in puffs of smoke.

The Kwakiutl, like other tribes in the region, once built specialized canoes for whaling, sealing, fishing, freight transport, river travel, racing, and war; by 1900, however, canoemaking and seagoing travel were all but forgotten. Then, in the 1980s a Haida Indian carved a 50-foot-long canoe. His craft inspired the Kwakiutl to make similar canoes and organize paddling events, such as the 1989 "Paddle to Seattle," which included participants from several groups along the northwest coast. Bringing back the great canoes led to the revival of potlatches and the songs, dances, and prayers associated with them, instilling a sense of cultural pride in young and old alike.

A Tlinglit carver creates a totem pole for the Sealaska Corporation, largest of 13 regional native corporations. Today, museums house many of the oldest poles, hoping to preserve the carvings that record clan and tribal history.

⬡ TLINGIT

SHARING CUSTOMS and a common language rather than a political agenda, various Tlingit tribes dwell on reservations and reserves in British Columbia, the Yukon Territory, and Alaska's southeastern panhandle. Here, mountains rise almost directly from the sea, isolating the mist-shrouded land. The 80-mile-wide archipelago off the fjord-carved coast is also mountainous, and its islands, like the mainland, are covered by dense forests.

In the past, when the fishing season had ended and stores of salmon and other food had been set aside for winter, families moved from their summer fishing camps to permanent winter villages. Plentiful resources from the ocean, rivers, and land—sea mammals, shellfish, fish, deer, bears, sheep, and mountain goats—enabled people to obtain enough food to see them through winter, the time for potlatching. If a person had amassed enough wealth to validate an inherited clan leader position, he or she hosted a potlatch, a massive feast and giveaway for another clan. The size of the gathering and the value of the gifts were thought to reflect the clan leader's status. By accepting gifts, guests confirmed the host's right to the inherited privileges and tacitly agreed to reciprocate. Potlatches not only served to circulate material wealth but also helped to establish alliances between clans.

Freed from having to engage in constant economic activity in order to survive, the Tlingit developed complex ceremonies within a class-conscious society headed by high-ranking individuals. Commoners made up the majority of the people, while slaves, usually women and children captured from other tribes, were forced to perform menial labor for their masters. Each clan had several crests that members displayed on totem poles, canoes, dishes, hats, and Chilkat blankets worn by high-ranking individuals.

Today, Tlingit women still weave Chilkat blankets from cedar bark and mountain goat's wool, with designs based on clan crests that men painted on wooden boards. Recently, weavers resurrected the technique for making ravenstail robes, an ancient art that had been replaced by the curvilinear designs of Chilkat weaving. Woodcarving has also experienced a revitalization in the form of bas reliefs, transformation masks, portrait masks, house posts, and totem poles. Although artists sell much of their work, many of them dedicate a significant part of their time to carving items for ceremonial use in their villages.

A Haida boy holds a paddle symbolizing his people's seagoing heritage. The giant cedars that once provided material for paddles, canoes, and totem poles now face a serious threat from loggers.

E UROPE HAS WITNESSED over the course of many millennia an astonishing florescence of settlement and cultural development. From an area that—including the European part of Russia—is less than half the size of North America, streams of influential ideas, technologies, political and legal structures, and other products of human endeavor have poured forth into the rest of the world. Europe and the remarkably diverse Europeans have engendered and nurtured many of the ideals that inform and inspire modern society and culture.

Today, some geographers question whether Europe should still be called a continent, attached as it is to Asia in the fashion of a large peninsula. Nevertheless, the traditional division that separates the two is a line that runs south along the Ural Mountains and Ural River to the Caspian Sea before jogging west along the Caucasus Mountains to the Black Sea. More bodies of water provide other boundaries, and within them are a number of major islands, including Great Britain, Ireland, and Iceland.

After Asia, Europe has the world's largest and densest population: On just 7 percent of Earth's land live more than three-quarters of a billion people, representing over a hundred distinct ethnic groups and speaking some fifty different languages.

EUROPE

A Hungarian Magyar proudly wears a *szür*, a felt cape traditionally worn by herdsmen.

Europe's peopling by modern humans began only about 40,000 years ago, nearly 200,000 years after the continent's occupation by Neandertals and perhaps 700,000 years after the arrival of *Homo erectus*, who may have been the ancestor of both groups. Neandertals disappeared mysteriously about 30,000 years ago, and all subsequent populations in Europe have belonged to the subspecies *Homo sapiens sapiens*.

During Europe's Ice Age, Cro-Magnon hunters of western Europe gathered regularly for ceremonial purposes, bringing with them an increasingly advanced tool technology and an aesthetic sense represented by shell and amber ornaments and by small, exquisite carvings of people and animals. On their caves in northern Spain and southern France they rendered dramatic and graceful images of horses, bulls, reindeer, and other animals that figured prominently in their Stone Age culture.

The migrations that gave way to most European ethnic groups of today are believed to have begun some 5,000 years ago with Indo-European pastoralists from Central Asia. They carried with them the beginnings of the Indo-European language family, which in Europe survives in eight main branches, ranging from the Italic family—including modern Italian, French, Spanish, Portuguese, and Romanian—to the Thraco-Illyrian, with Albanian the lone modern representative. Not all European languages are Indo-European, however. Finnish, Hungarian, and Estonian fall into the Uralic family originating in the area of the Ural Mountains, while the Basque language of the Pyrenees is related to no other and predates the Indo-Europeans.

Hunter-gatherers had already made the transition to agriculture when peoples from the Middle East and Egypt arrived on the island of Crete. Accomplished seafarers, they spread the influence of the Minoan civilization through the Mediterranean world. But by 1450 B.C. the balance of power had shifted to mainland Greece and the Mycenaeans. The ancient Greeks, especially those of the fifth century B.C., left a legacy of excellence in art and architecture, mathematics and scientific achievement, and philosophical and political thought, bequeathing the democratic ideals that still shape European thinking.

Romans helped filter this legacy through their widespread empire, which in the second century A.D. stretched from the British Isles to Iran. By the fourth century, they had adopted Christianity as the state religion, and the empire's decline did not end the faith's influence. As ethnic groups moved into areas that would become their homelands, leaders often embraced Christianity on behalf of their people. A split in the 11th century produced the distinction between Roman Catholicism and Eastern Orthodoxy that persists today, with southern and western Europe generally following the former and Orthodoxy taking hold in the east. The effects of the Reformation of the 16th century endure in the Protestantism of most northern European groups. Between the 12th and 20th centuries, Ottoman Turks conquered and controlled parts of Europe, and wholesale conversions to Islam took place; today, however, Islam survives on the continent mainly in Albania, among Bosnia's Muslims, and in the small European nub of Turkey. Followers of Judaism once formed significant populations throughout Europe, but their numbers were reduced tragically during the Holocaust.

As Europe began to move from the feudal model of the Middle Ages to that of centralized authority in the second millennium, the concept of nationalism began to

A commonly accepted division between Asia and Europe—here marked by a red dotted line—is formed by the Ural Mountains, Ural River, Caspian Sea, Caucasus Mountains, and the Black Sea with its outlets, the Bosporus and the Dardanelles.

replace provincial allegiances. Nationalism became imbued with the notion of a common language and religion and thus helped create the modern states that formed toward the end of the millennium. It also led to the spread of empires around the globe as rising powers emphasized their own cultures and promoted their own interests over those of other peoples. The dawn of the industrial revolution in the 18th century further aided Europe's domination of the world economy while it turned Europeans into urban workers. In the 20th century, industrial might and nationalistic fervor fueled two World Wars and other upheavals. Borders were redrawn and millions of people were forced to relocate. Massive migrations occurred as people sought to avoid conflict, escape persecution, or find better economic opportunities.

The current trend toward unity and cooperation, typified by the European Union formed in 1993, demonstrates the pragmatic nature of cultures and nationalities to work past divisions that have separated them. At the same time, Europeans are indicating renewed interest in their own languages, music, and other aspects of cultural identity. Religion, becoming less important in a secular world, nevertheless shows the ability to divide, as seen in the disheartening cases of Northern Ireland and the former Yugoslavia.

Following Pages: In the Sicilian hill town of Palazzolo Acreide, a large crowd and a downpour of confetti greet a statue of St. Paul on the patron saint's feast day.

CLOCKWISE FROM TOP LEFT:
DANISH SHIPBUILDER, RUSSIAN
ORTHODOX NUN, IRISH TEENAGER,
AND ROMANIAN GYPSY

EUROPE

NORTHERN EUROPE

WESTERN EUROPE

SOUTHERN EUROPE

CENTRAL EUROPE

EASTERN EUROPE

NORTHERN EUROPE

CORNISH • FAROESE • FINNS • ICELANDERS
• IRISH • NORTHERN ISLANDERS • SAMI
• SCANDINAVIANS • SCOTS • WELSH

CORNISH

DESCENDANTS OF ONE of the three Brythonic kingdoms (the others were Wales and Strathclyde, now southern Scotland), the Cornish reside in Cornwall, at the southwestern tip of Great Britain. For generations, they spoke a language that was closely related to Welsh and a cousin to Irish and other Gaelic languages; today, however, they speak English almost exclusively, while retaining certain words and phrases that mark the distinct Cornish English dialect.

At present, about 500,000 people live in Cornwall, but because the British government does not officially recognize the Cornish as an ethnic group, no one knows for certain how many residents claim specific Cornish ancestry. Recent developments in a solidarity movement have pushed the identity issue forward, and many people are now asserting the uniqueness of their culture and history. They hope that Cornwall will eventually see the establishment of its own regional government—like Scotland and Wales, which have independent parliaments.

Cornwall has long been known not only for the skill of its miners but also for a ubiquitous stuffed pastry dubbed the Cornish pasty. In fact, the histories of the two are deeply intertwined: Miners were said to offer corners of the pasty to the "knockers," mine-spirits who could prove troublesome if unappeased. Cornish miners emigrating to the American West brought this tradition with them, and around mines from Colorado to Montana it is still common to hear stories about the "tommyknockers." Although the last Cornish mine closed in 1998, storytelling and other traditions that are associated with mining persist in today's culture.

FAROESE

THE FAROESE WAY of life centers on small villages spread out among the North Atlantic's 18 Faroe Islands. Intensely proud of their beautiful homeland, the people are primarily fishermen who exploit rich Gulf Stream waters surrounding their archipelago. The Faroese have enormous boating skills, and these are frequently exhibited at festivals where wooden boats are raced; the events recall a time when large groups worked together to hunt whales from such vessels. But the sea is not the only focus here: Sheep herding is also a feature of Faroese life, with twice as many sheep as people occupying the islands.

The 45,000 Faroese are scattered across the islands, dwelling in and among towns that may have as few as 500 inhabitants. People often gather for religious holidays observed by the Lutheran Church, which continues to be an active force in the culture. Chain dances where people

form circles, hold hands, and sing catchy, rhyming songs were first known in the Middle Ages and are still popular here, even among residents who drive modern vehicles and carry cellular phones. Because of their geographic isolation and small numbers, the people are untroubled by most urban problems, but the collapse of the fishing industry in the 1990s created a recession and encouraged emigration. Though the Faroes have recovered, their heavy dependence on fishing leaves them vulnerable.

With a history much like that of Iceland—these islands were settled in the ninth century by Norwegian Vikings and people of Celtic origin—the Faroe Islanders speak a language very similar to Icelandic. But unlike Iceland, the Faroe Islands are part of the Danish kingdom. A movement to break free of Denmark continues to grow in popularity, mostly because of differing attitudes toward European unity; Denmark is a member of the European Union while the islands are not. The Faroes, however, already enjoy a high degree of autonomy, and they would find it difficult to survive without financial subsidies from Denmark.

FINNS

UNTIL 1809, FINLAND was part of the Swedish kingdom and had been for more than 500 years, a fact that causes some people to think of it as a Scandinavian country. Further, about 20 percent of the population in southern Finland, especially in the Åland Islands, is of Swedish descent. But while Finns may resemble Scandinavians,

with light skin, hair, and eyes, their culture is actually very distinct from that of Scandinavia.

The people speak a Finno-Ugric language, which has more in common with Hungarian than with Swedish, and this suggests that they may have originated in eastern Europe or Siberia. The *Kalevala*, an epic poem about a mythical hero who not only brings music and prosperity to Finland but also rescues the sun and moon, is considered the national story. It has elements that are thought to be more than 3,000 years old. Composed in Finnish, the poem is sung and performed on national holidays as a way of celebrating the distinct Finnish identity. The *Kalevala* was based on folktales collected in Karelia, an eastern section of Finland where the tradition of singing complex poems lasted well into the 19th century. A large part of this region now lies within Russia's borders, and its people follow the Russian Orthodox religion.

Like other northern Europeans, Finns celebrate their past while embracing the future and absorbing diverse cultural influences. Politically, Finland was annexed by tsarist Russia in 1809 and was for many years influenced by Russian culture, architecture, and political thought. Even so, it became an independent republic in 1917 and later observed strict neutrality during the Cold War. Today's Finns see themselves as bridging the cultures of Western and Eastern Europe; some adhere to the Eastern Orthodox faith, but more than 90 percent practice Evangelical Lutheranism, the dominant faith in Scandinavia.

Though Finns are typically known for their reserved personal style, they are today's number-one users of cellular phones, and their main recreational activities are mambo dancing, winter sports, *pesäpallo* (a form of baseball), and relaxing in saunas, which they invented. Several designers and architects enjoy world renown, and the design style often associated with Scandinavia actually finds it origin in Finnish aesthetics of austerity, beauty, and practicality.

ICELANDERS

LITTLE MORE THAN a quarter of a million people live on the volcanic island of Iceland, first settled by Norwegian Vikings in A.D. 874 and included in the Scandinavian kingdoms until its people declared independence in 1944. Because of that long connection, Icelanders are similar to Scandinavians in more ways than just physical type: They enjoy a high standard of living, have socialized health care, eat the same kinds of food, and are Lutheran.

A number of early settlers, however, were Celtic slaves who had been captured in Scotland and Ireland, and their contribution to the gene pool means Icelanders are as likely to be brown haired as blond. After a thousand years of intermarriage, Scandinavians and Celts have become one people—a tightly knit culture in which almost everyone is related to everyone else by blood, if only distantly, and family names do not exist.

The language of Iceland, a form of archaic Norwegian, is very different from the ones of modern Scandinavia. It is considered a main distinguishing ethnic marker, with the government pursuing an aggressive policy of language purity and even maintaining a list of approved names for newborns. Iceland's people are also distinguished by a love of writing and storytelling that led to their creation of the Icelandic sagas, a medieval body of literature that continues to be read and cherished. One of the most literate peoples in the world, Icelanders most often give books as birthday and Christmas presents.

While rooted in the past, Iceland is also very modern. More than half the population resides in Reykjavík, the capital city, where high technology, tourism, music, and fashion have overtaken fishing and farming. Living on a geologically active volcanic island, where natural hot springs abut huge glaciers, Icelanders have pioneered the use of geothermal energy to produce electricity for industry and to provide heat and light for their homes.

Although they have high-quality public education through the university level, Icelanders often go abroad for specialized education, which also contributes to the international influences on the country's population. Wherever they go, though, Icelanders remain attached to their "little nation." Today, Iceland's cultural influences come primarily from Europe and the Americas, befitting a nation that sits astride the Mid-Atlantic Ridge, where the European and North American tectonic plates meet.

IRISH

IN THE REPUBLIC of Ireland, the Irish number somewhat less than four million, but it is impossible to know just how many Irish live and work throughout the British Isles and abroad. In terms of global Irish culture, it is probably equally impossible to quantify how many people worldwide claim some degree of Irish ancestry.

In the modern era, after a long period as a colony of England, Ireland asserted its independence with the Easter Rebellion of 1916. This eventually led to creation of the Irish Free State, in 1921. Ratification of the Free State meant an independent Ireland, but it also ensured British sovereignty in Northern Ireland. In 1949, the Republic of Ireland that we know today was born.

Following the tragic potato famine of 1846-1851, some two million Irish emigrated to England and America to seek employment. Even in more recent years Irish workers continued to emigrate and pursue their fortunes abroad, but today many expatriates have come home to participate in a wide-ranging economic revival. Growth in personal computing, telecommunications, and other high-technology industries has increased opportunities for professional employment. In addition, Ireland's expanding infrastructure, spurred by its inclusion in the European Union, has brought about a marked increase in skilled tradesmen.

Ireland's cultural traditions remain firmly ensconced in its people, more than 90 percent of whom are Roman Catholic, with minority populations of various Protestant denominations. The Irish, and the rest of the world, revere the legacy of intellectual centers such as Trinity College in Dublin, where the most famous medieval Gospel book, the *Book of Kells*, resides. Literature, music, and theater are staples of Irish life, along with soccer, Gaelic football, and hurling—an exuberant relative of field hockey. Like their English neighbors, the Irish have an appreciation for life in the public house. At the pub, friends gather for snooker, darts, and other games while debating James Joyce or the finer points of Irish politics—all, of course, accompanied by a pint of Guinness or Murphy's stout.

The principal language of Ireland is English, but Irish is still very important in the contemporary culture. Irish, or Irish Gaelic, is spoken by a large part of the population, especially in the north and west, and cities, towns, and roads bear Irish names, as do many organizations and businesses. Learned either traditionally or in schools, Irish Gaelic is used professionally, informally, and artistically.

NORTHERN ISLANDERS

INHABITANTS OF the Orkney and Shetland Islands—called Orcadians and Shetlanders, or Northern Islanders—share a culture that is a product of their special history. Because both groups of people have long been buffeted by political disputes between Norway and Scotland, their culture has evolved to reflect Scandinavian as well as Scottish

influences. The islands were originally occupied by a non-Celtic people known as Picts, but in the ninth century A.D. they were seized by the Vikings, who would eventually overtake and largely replace the local population, leaving a lasting Nordic imprint.

The Orkneys and Shetlands remained part of the Norwegian kingdom until they were ceded to Scotland in 1469, the year Princess Margaret of Norway married Scotland's James III. From that point, Scottish and British cultural influences slowly began to replace aspects of the Scandinavian legacy. Orcadians for a time were bilingual in English and an old Scandinavian dialect known as Norn, but beginning in the 18th century, fewer and fewer people spoke the old language. The Shetlanders, on the other hand, continued to speak it into the 20th century, and indeed their association with their Scandinavian cultural side continues to be strong.

In summer, Northern Islanders enjoy long, sunny days perfect for outdoor festivals such as St. Magnus Fair. This August festival is a way for Orcadians to commemorate one of the most important Norwegian earls of the Orkneys and Shetlands. When winter comes, short days are followed by long nights still filled with tales told around evening fires. Orcadians tell stories of trolls and giants not unlike those of Norwegian folktales. In the Shetlands, a high point of the winter season is the Up Helly Aa, a January fire festival that reenacts a famous Viking battle and ends when the revelers set a Viking boat afire.

For Northern Islanders, their religion is another link to the past: Unlike the Scots and English, Shetlanders are followers of Lutheranism, the state religion of Norway. In this important way, they differentiate themselves from other citizens of the United Kingdom. But *(Continued on page 172)*

In Athenry, County Galway, site of a Norman castle and an annual medieval festival, the past is ever present and not forgotten. Here, the Macnas theater group (above) celebrates Ireland's pre-Christian religious traditions. Near England's border with Scotland, a farmer (right) shears one of his sheep. Many neighboring farms have disappeared in the wake of lower wool prices and the frustrating subsidy policies of recent years.

FOLLOWING PAGES:

In Sweden, one generation passes to the next the tradition of St. Lucia. Girls wear crowns of candles and flowing white gowns as they bring gifts of light, song, and refreshments to family members each December 13.

PAGES 170-71:

Reindeer and the Sami people of Europe's northern reaches have persevered through life together for thousands of years.

like their fellow citizens in the U.K., they do speak English; they sprinkle it, though, with Norn words having to do with fishing and animal husbandry, the basis of daily life.

During the reign of Queen Victoria, the British Crown helped popularize Orcadian and Shetland handicraft. The queen favored fine lace from the Shetlands, and Prince Albert liked Orcadian banded-pattern sweaters.

SAMI (Saami)

MOST LIKELY THE longest inhabitants of the Scandinavian peninsula, the Sami are a non-Germanic ethnic group living in northern Norway and Sweden, as well as in northern Finland and northwestern Russia (the Kola Peninsula, in particular). The Sami were traditionally nomadic pastoralists and occasional hunters heavily dependent on their reindeer herds—likely the inspiration for Santa's reindeer. They practiced a shamanistic religion that saw power in natural features such as rocks and mountains. But because of their nomadic way of life, they were discriminated against by Scandinavians who called them Lapps, a derogatory name.

The Sami are well adapted for living north of the Arctic Circle. To get from place to place, for example, they rely on skis—which they invented as a means for accompanying their sleds. Traditionally, they used every part of a reindeer for survival; animal skins were made into clothing or draped around poles to create a transportable dwelling similar to a tepee. Their brightly colored ceremonial costumes, worn with up-turned boots, include jackets, skirts, and hats ornately decorated with strips of colored material.

Although they follow a way of life that shares customs with other Arctic groups, the Sami are genetically different. Some researchers place their origin in the Alps, while others say ancient Siberia. In any case, they most likely came to northern Europe thousands of years ago, following reindeer herds as the polar ice cap receded. The people speak a Finno-Ugric language like Finnish, but the two tongues are not mutually intelligible. In fact, there are three main dialects of Sami, and these developed probably through the isolation of the different bands in the hard-to-cross terrain of northern Scandinavia. Today, Sami is a vibrant, living language that continues to be taught in schools and is a distinguishing ethnic marker of the people who speak it. The vocabulary reflects a particular way of life, and at least one word—tundra—is used worldwide.

More than a thousand years of close cultural ties with Scandinavians and other Europeans have created considerable variation within the Sami, only 10 percent of whom still live exclusively off the reindeer herds; many instead subsist as farmers and fishermen or live in villages, working as miners and loggers. But changes in their traditional lifestyle have not weakened the Sami's sense of who they are, and today this group is reasserting its unique identity. Sweden, Norway, and Finland once tried to limit claims of Sami identity to the people who still practice

reindeer herding. But all of the people who speak the Sami language or who had Sami parents and grandparents, regardless of occupation, consider themselves to be Sami. They also are demanding political autonomy for northern areas of the Scandinavian peninsula that have traditionally been their home. To secure their rights and ensure the continuance of their culture, the Sami have organized a representative body—the Sami Parliament—in Norway, Sweden, and Finland.

SCANDINAVIANS

ALTHOUGH DANES, Swedes, and Norwegians reside in separate countries and speak their own languages, they are all Scandinavians. They typically have light skin, hair, and eyes, but the primary basis for their common identity is the mutual understandability of their languages. While their speech may exhibit considerable local variation, these differences do not follow strictly national boundaries: There is, for example, more linguistic variation within the scattered fishing villages of Norway than between Norwegians in Oslo and Danes in Copenhagen; a Swede can watch Norwegian television and read a Danish newspaper with only a bit of extra attention.

Identity is also based on a shared history. During the last 800 years, the kingdoms of Denmark, Sweden, and Norway were united in various combinations that, among other things, resulted in the development of similar religious and political systems. Lutheranism was the state religion in all three countries until Sweden dropped its official status in 2000. Kings and queens still function as formal heads of state, and in each country the dominant political system is social democracy—meaning that heavy taxes support a number of essential societal functions, from health care to child support, and contribute to a relatively high standard of living. Generally well-educated, Scandinavians live in modern houses, have access to health care, and often enjoy short workdays and mandatory vacations. Their Western, capitalist, industrialized economy emphasizes natural resources such as timber, minerals, and oil, as well as service industries such as tourism and retail.

This high standard of living accompanies a flourishing culture. Paintings by Edvard Munch are known around the world, and the writings of Hans Christian Andersen and Henrik Ibsen continue to be cherished. Traditional crafts, including painted and carved wooden bowls and finely made woolen knitwear, are still valued, while the decorative Scandinavian glass of recent years has become extremely fashionable. In Sweden and Norway, but less so in Denmark, there is great interest in winter sports and outdoor activities. Many Scandinavians spend a large part of the summer in country cottages, a tradition reaching back to an agrarian past when herds were taken to the hills during the summer.

Scandinavian food also has roots in the agrarian past, though urban centers are full of international restaurants and fast-food chains. Accompanied by strong alcoholic drinks such as aquavit and vodka, the main diet includes whitefish and marine mammals, often pickled, along with vegetables such as cabbage and peas. Both breakfast and lunch may be open-faced sandwiches of sliced meat and cheese on freshly baked bread, spread with butter. The people have been heavy coffee drinkers for centuries.

Today, the homogeneity of Scandinavians in Denmark, Norway, and Sweden is increasingly challenged. With its enviable standard of living and governmental supports, Scandinavia has become a favorite destination of emigrants from poorer countries. Now its capitals and large cities have distinct ethnic populations from Eastern Europe, the Middle East, and Southeast Asia, and these immigrants will undoubtedly create changes in Scandinavian culture.

The European Union (EU) is another force having an impact on Scandinavia. Norway remains outside the EU, but Denmark and Sweden have joined even though they both reject Europe's common currency. Despite differences in foreign policy, all three of the countries participate with Iceland and Finland in the Nordic Council, an advisory body, and in the Nordic Council of Ministers, which seeks to ensure economic, scientific, and cultural cooperation among the five nations.

For the traditional Festival of the Horse, a young boy on the Orkney Island of South Ronaldsay displays the handiwork of his mother: a colorful costume complete with small horselike ears.

SCOTS

SCOTLAND'S POPULATION of more than five million is largely concentrated in major urban centers such as Edinburgh, Glasgow, Dundee, and Aberdeen. Scots are also found beyond the Scottish border, living and working elsewhere in the United Kingdom and in many other parts of the world. Most people are members of the Church of Scotland, which is Presbyterian, while other Christian denominations mingle with followers of less prominent faiths.

For much of its history, Scotland has been viewed by its English neighbors as a rugged, untamed land filled with rugged, untamed people. And like widely held views of the American West, this conception has some measure of truth and a goodly portion of fancy. The latter stems from English prejudice against Scotland's warring clans. These groups wore tartans, plaid woolens of various colored patterns that served the important political function of identifying one's clan affiliation. Worn less and less frequently, though still preferred for formal wear, kilts continue to be symbols of Scottish ethnicity and the time of independence before 1707, when England and Scotland united under one king.

Known as the birthplace of golf, Scotland is perhaps equally famous for its poets, military heroes, whisky, and national dish. Called haggis, this dish is a pudding made from a mixture of organ meats and oatmeal, stuffed and boiled within a sheep's stomach. Haggis originated in Scotland's agrarian past, when the herding of sheep was a mainstay of the economy.

While many Scots continue to ranch and farm, the modern economy increasingly revolves around such high-technology endeavors as semiconductor production, software design, genetics, and environmental science. The recent appearance of the world's first cloned sheep, called Dolly, bears ample testimony to Scotland's ability to blend cutting-edge science with traditional occupations. These new industries happily coexist with long-standing work in petroleum production, shipbuilding, and the making of malt whisky known to the world as Scotch.

But if Scotch is a drink, the name "Scots" means a people and their language. Scots English, known from the 18th century as Broad Scots, is a Germanic dialect akin to English. Although it was the language of the great Scottish poet Robert Burns (1759-1796), it was largely abandoned in the latter part of the 19th century—banned in schools and discouraged everywhere else—so that Scots could compete in the dominant English economy. Scots English enjoys only limited use today and is principally observed in dialects such as Glasgow Patter and the Broad Buchan of the northeast coastal region. Scots Gaelic, a Celtic language that had nearly disappeared by 1970, has recently experienced a resurgence. There are now Scots Gaelic development programs, theater groups, and television programs, and the language is taught in some schools. The new popularity of bagpipe music, played by an instrument perfected in 18th-century Scotland, is another sign of the survival of Scottish ethnicity.

Scotland's greatest heroes—William Wallace, Robert the Bruce, and Bonnie Prince Charlie—all fought for independence. Today, after the 1997 referendum to convene a new parliament, a measure of that independence has been realized. The Scottish Parliament first met in 1999 and has administrative authority over internal finance, education, transportation, the environment, and other important areas.

WELSH

THE POPULATION in Wales currently stands at nearly three million, but countless Welsh and people of Welsh descent live throughout the world. Ever since the decline in the coal and steel industries after World War II, the majority of citizens have dwelled in or near urban centers such as Cardiff, the capital. Nearly all are Protestants, with the Methodist Church foremost.

Although many people now enjoy city ways, life in smaller villages remains an important touchstone to cultural identity. Nowhere is this more apparent than in the annual *eisteddfodau*, or "chairing" festivals, where towns choose poetry champions who are crowned and raised aloft on chairs or thrones. The festivals have expanded in recent years to cover the breadth of Welsh cultural life and now include music in all forms, as well as dancing, drama, and arts and crafts. Winners hope to compete in the Royal National Eisteddfod of Wales, Europe's largest folk festival, and to this day, only Welsh may be spoken on the poetry stage.

Currently, Welsh is spoken by at least 500,000 people in Wales alone. Contrary to popular belief, Welsh is not a Gaelic language, like Irish, but a language of British origin; both, however, are subgroups of the same Celtic language family. A living tongue, Welsh is learned at home and in schools, and it is used in any circumstance, whether professional, artistic, or informal. "Wales" itself is not a Welsh word; in fact, it comes from the Anglo-Saxon *wæl*, meaning "foreigner" or "slave." The country's name in Welsh is Cymru (KUM-ree), from which Cambria, another name for Wales, survives in some English usage today. For most Welsh, English is the language of everyday use.

Issues of language use have become more prominent since 1998, when the Government of Wales Act was passed by the British Parliament. This act established the National Assembly for Wales, which exercises administrative authority over such important concerns as transportation, education, housing, and the environment. Wales still retains representation in the British Parliament as well. The advent of the National Assembly has accompanied a gradual transformation in the Welsh economy. While Wales maintains an agrarian base—it is Europe's most important sheep-raising center—the modern economy revolves around many high-technology enterprises. These include software design, precision manufacturing in aerospace and hydrodynamics, and the development of sustainable environmental strategies, all of which contribute to a Wales at ease with its past and its future.

WESTERN EUROPE
BASQUES • BRETONS • CATALANS • DUTCH
• FRISIANS

BASQUES

IN THEIR PYRENEES stronghold straddling the French-Spanish border, the Basques developed one of the most enigmatic cultures in Europe. Many scholars consider them the oldest ethnic group on the continent, saying that they lived in the area before Indo-European peoples arrived more than 3,000 years ago. Some suggest they are descendants of Upper Paleolithic Cro-Magnons who occupied the region about 30,000 years ago.

The Basque language, Euskera, occupies its own family and is not related to any other language spoken in Europe; scholars have even looked for its roots in the Russian Caucasus and in North Africa as well. It is an extremely complex tongue, and a Basque tradition holds that the devil spent seven years trying to learn it but finally gave up. Nevertheless, Euskera has lent itself to a vast oral tradition kept alive by storytellers and spontaneous versifiers called *bertsolariak*. Most Basques are bilingual in French or Spanish, and sometimes in both.

Although the overwhelming majority of people are Roman Catholics, a millennium has passed since the Basques were a unified community. Today, they occupy three provinces in France and four in Spain—a homeland that includes the Pyrenees, their foothills, and the coastal plain along the Bay of Biscay. An intensely independent people, the Basques managed to maintain some autonomy even when dominated by foreign powers. Under the 1939-1975 regime of Spain's Francisco Franco, however, Basque language and culture were vigorously suppressed, giving rise to the ETA, a strong and sometimes violent independence movement that endorses terrorist acts.

Traditionally, Basques worked as fishermen, farmers, and shepherds. Noted mariners, some even crewed for Columbus and Magellan. Many people now work in the area's large industrial sector, and while only 20 percent of Basques continue to farm, the *baserria*, or farmstead, remains a fixture in rural areas. Large, three-storied stone dwellings include livestock on the bottom floor, an extended family on the middle level, and storage for hay on the top. One child within each baserria is designated the heir, who will receive the landholding at the time of marriage. Males are favored, but females may also inherit.

In the past, other siblings typically left the farm, sometimes settling for a religious life; many also emigrated. A village comprises 10 or 12 farmsteads, a church, a school, taverns, a town hall, and a handball court, often an extension of the church wall. A number of fast-paced ball games, including jai alai, originated in Basque country.

BRETONS

JUST A LOOK at a map showing Brittany, a peninsula jutting into the English Channel and the Atlantic Ocean, gives a hint that this region's population stands apart from other ethnic groups in France. The Bretons are a Celtic people, with ties to the British Isles dating back to migrations that occurred between the third and fifth centuries A.D. Over the years, numerous invasions thwarted their attempts to remain independent, and in the early 16th century their land was annexed to France. Provisions for some autonomy, however, and distance from the (Continued on page 180)

Muscles straining and manhood at stake, a Basque furniture mover hoists a 350-pound boulder. The lifting competition evolved from rock-clearing chores on farms in the Basque region of France and Spain.
FOLLOWING PAGES:
Amid a labyrinth of vines, women collect grapes destined to become one of Portugal's fine wines.

Women provide much of the workforce involved in Portuguese viticulture.
PAGES 178-79:
Red-shirted *castellers* lend their arms to create a human castle in Barcelona, capital of Spain's Catalonia region. This popular Catalan activity dates from the 18th century.

On a winter's evening in the Netherlands province of Friesland, skaters eagerly take to the ice. Hard freezes turn the country's canals into rinks, allowing Frisians and other Netherlanders to pursue this beloved sport.

state administration in Paris served to isolate and insulate the Bretons, preventing their assimilation into the French nation until well into the 19th century.

With some 2,100 miles of coastline, including islands, Brittany has a distinct maritime orientation and a regional cuisine in which seafood figures prominently. The economy has long been based on fish and crustaceans and, until recently, algae-gathering. Brittany also relies on its strong agricultural base. For generations, Bretons have worked the lands of the interior, planting vegetable crops and raising livestock on farmsteads marked by dense hedges. Today, mechanization of farming has made Brittany the premier agricultural region of France, complemented by large food-processing and agricultural-machinery industries.

The traditional rural scene was composed of scattered homesteads—rectangular granite buildings with roofs of thatch or slate and chimneys at their gabled ends—as well as small villages and larger settlements called *plous*. The largest plous were subdivided into *treviòu*. This system survives in the many place-names beginning with "Plou-" or "Tre-," especially in northwestern Brittany.

The Breton tongue, today spoken by just over half a million residents, belongs to the Brythonic branch of Celtic languages, making it closely related to Welsh and the now extinct Cornish tongue. Despite the decline in their spoken language, Bretons avidly foster their Celtic heritage and enjoy its many traditions, particularly folk music—which features a small bagpipe called a *biniou*—and dance. They routinely invite Celts from the British Isles to their festivals.

Most Bretons are Roman Catholics, with their regional celebrations tending to be religious in nature. They show much devotion to hundreds of local saints, make pilgrimages to the region's nine cathedrals, and participate in festivals called *pardons*. These feature large processions, as well as traditional music and dancing, and they take on a secular atmosphere once religious devotions have been completed.

CATALANS

LIKE THEIR BASQUE neighbors to the west, Catalans retain a strong sense of identity and autonomy despite their long-standing incorporation into the national structures of France and Spain. These people reside in the *Països Catalans*, the "Catalan countries," which historically included the Catalonia region of northeastern Spain, as well as Valencia, the Balearic Islands, the independent state of Andorra, and the French province of Pyrénées-Orientales. Now numbering about nine or ten million, they are speakers of Catalan, a Romance language with ties to the Provençal language of southern France.

Spanish Catalonia has long been an area of strategic importance. Union with Aragon in the 12th century and with Castile and León in the 15th century widened the region's political sphere but subjugated Catalan interests. The people later experienced repression of their language and culture under Francisco Franco's dictatorship (1939-1975). Finally, in 1979, regional autonomy for Catalonia was established and the Catalan language was allowed to flourish again, fueling the cultural pride that has led to a renaissance of Catalan music and literature, especially poetry.

Catalans are overwhelmingly Roman Catholic, with the cycles of the church year defining cultural observances. Each village and town honors its patron saint at an annual festival where processions typically feature huge papier-mâché representations of ritual figures: "bigheads" (capgrosses) and giants, some 15 feet tall. All of Catalonia reveres St. George (Sant Jordi). On his feast day in April, which is also the official opening of the book-publishing season, Catalans distribute his symbols of roses and books to their loved ones. Another feature of these celebrations is the sardana, the traditional dance whose stately cadences reflect the highly regarded concept of seny, a kind of refined good sense and self-realization.

Economically, the region depends on a strong base of industry and tourism—seen at such places as Costa Brava, where hundreds of thousands of Europeans, including Catalan families, vacation each year. Only 10 percent of the approximately six million Spanish Catalans currently farm, while 25 percent reside and work in cosmopolitan Barcelona, the Catalonian capital.

DUTCH

SOME 16 MILLION Dutch inhabit the Netherlands, "lowlands" at the southeastern edge of the North Sea. The people speak Dutch, a Germanic language related to English, and though regional dialects abound, these are mutually understood and tempered by media influence. Dutch schoolchildren learn English as well, with many people, especially younger urbanites, quite fluent in it.

The Dutch are descendants of German, Frisian, and Frankish tribes who entered the area in pre-Roman times. Long tied to the fortunes of the Frankish and Habsburg empires, the Netherlands came into its own with the development of cities and subsequent involvement in commerce, trade, and colonial expansion. In the 17th century, the Netherlands was an international center of trade and culture, its golden age splendidly documented in the paintings of Rembrandt, Vermeer, and Frans Hals.

The Dutch are vigilant stewards of the land, much of which has been reclaimed from a former North Sea inlet, the Zuider Zee (now the IJsselmeer). In this densely populated country, people ameliorate their cramped urban living situations by using railroad right-of-ways, creating garden plots and building leisure-time sheds or cottages beside the tracks. Despite their renown for growing tulips and for other kinds of horticulture and agriculture, only 4 percent still farm. Many people now work in the petrochemical, food-processing, and electronics industries.

Modest and reserved in public, the Dutch place much emphasis on a gezellig, or cozy, family life. The nuclear family (gezin) has long been the ideal, with families tending to be small and children generally receiving much care and attention. A birthday is a major occasion, celebrated all day by the family and with colleagues, friends, and neighbors. (The queen's birthday is a national holiday enthusiastically observed by local communities.) People take fierce pride in their homes and gardens, and an evening stroll reveals the old practice of schmeren: the opening of curtains and letting passersby get an often lingering glimpse of the respectable gezellig gezin within. The ubiquitous bicycle serves many transportation needs in urban and rural areas in a country that boasts 6,200 miles of bike trails.

Though noted for their racial and ethnic tolerance and for neutrality in war, the Dutch traditionally divide along lines of religion. Currently, more than a third of the people are Roman Catholics, and about a quarter are Protestants spread among six groups, the largest being the Dutch Reformed Church. Religious affiliation forms the basis of verzuiling, a "pillarization" of society into separate groups with their own schools, newspapers, political parties, labor unions, and other organizations at the local and national levels. While divisions have weakened—and were always moderated by the Dutch emphasis on mutual respect— verzuiling significantly influences rural communities, as do the opinions and preachings of pastors and priests.

FRISIANS

THOUGH ONLY about 700,000 strong, the Frisians are a noticeable ethnic and linguistic minority in the Friesland region of the Netherlands. Their distinctive flag, one of the oldest in Europe, bears seven red water lilies symbolizing their water-oriented existence in a region that is largely below sea level and includes several barrier islands in the North Sea. Since the early days of settlement, around 400 B.C., the Frisians have battled the sea, constructing and constantly maintaining a system of dikes (the "golden hoop") for protection against frequent storms and flooding. Laws specific to Frisian life were codified by Charlemagne into the Lex Frisionum in A.D. 801-802. Among them is buorreplicht (neighbor's duty), requiring that neighbors assist one another in a crisis.

The Frisian language belongs to the West Germanic family and is related to English and Dutch. Although most Frisians speak Dutch in the community and use their own language only at home, Frisian pride permeates the province. With its 11 cities, Friesland has remained fairly independent of the rest of the country throughout its history, and a modern independence movement persists.

Historically, trade was important in Friesland. Today, most Frisians participate in agriculture, growing crops or dairying, as well as breeding their prized milk cows. The typical "head-neck-body" house, a fixture in the countryside, consists of living quarters attached to a large barn by a passage containing a kitchen, milk cellar, and churning area.

Frisians enjoy outdoor recreation, including walking the mudflats at low tide and participating in local contests of *fierljeppen,* pole-vaulting across canals. In years of hard freeze, the famous 125-mile Elfsteden skating race takes place through Friesland's cities.

The Franks Christianized the Frisians in the seventh and eighth centuries, and 85 percent of the people are now Calvinists of either the Reformed or Dutch Reformed sects. Lingering pre-Christian beliefs, called *byleauwe,* include tales of "white ladies" who lead a subterranean existence and come out at night to kidnap travelers.

SOUTHERN EUROPE
ALBANIANS • CRETANS • SICILIANS

✹ ALBANIANS

FOR SOME ETHNIC groups religious identity is paramount; Albanians, however, are fond of saying that they are, above all else, Albanian. Ethnically, they are a homogenous group probably descended from ancient Illyrians who controlled the Balkan area and parts of Greece in the 13th century B.C. Conquered by Romans a thousand years later, Albania was part of the Roman and Byzantine Empires before Ottoman Turks took control in the 14th century. Russia defeated the Turks in the late 19th century, and as the weakened empire came apart, Albania lost most of its territory to neighboring countries. Now, just as many Albanians live in Bosnia, Macedonia, and Greece as in present-day Albania, whose population stands at more than three million.

The Albanian language, one of the nine original Indo-European languages, is written in the Latin alphabet. Although Albanian was proscribed during Ottoman rule, it has made a strong comeback since the late 19th century. Its speakers make up two groups—Ghegs in the north and Tosks in the south—and the main distinction between them has to do with certain aspects of pronunciation.

The religious lives of Albanians are difficult to discern at the present time. Before the communist takeover in 1946, about 70 percent of the people were Muslim (a reflection of Ottoman rule); 20 percent were Eastern Orthodox; and the rest were Catholic. From 1967 until independence in 1990, Albania was an officially atheist state. Today, many people are drawn to Evangelical Christian groups; there is also the suggestion of a resurgence of Catholicism. Albanians historically have been tolerant of other religions, and in the era before communism the clergy of all faiths, in short supply nationwide, were respected and consulted by members of different faiths. During World War II, Albania not only sheltered its own Jews but also took in those of neighboring countries, meaning that at war's end its Jewish population was larger than the one it had at the beginning.

Albanians are a very polite and formal people with extremely elaborate forms of greeting and social interaction. Great respect is shown for elders, especially older men, to the point that boys and young men will kiss their hands. A person's pledged word is his bond, and a pledge sealed with a handshake or embrace is the most binding of contracts. Traditionally, slights to a family's honor and transgressions such as theft and murder were answered with a blood feud. Since World War II and the communist era, women have gained status in this male-oriented country.

About 35 percent of Albanians live in urban areas, 65 percent in rural. Despite valuable mineral resources and strong agriculture, Albania's transition to a market economy has been very shaky, though not for lack of effort by its residents. Political repression continues to occur, even in the wake of democratic elections. Outside Albania, in the Kosovo region of Serbia, Muslim Albanians have been persecuted, killed, or forced out of their communities.

In cuisine, as in other aspects of Albanian life, the Turkish influence is strong. Bread is the main staple and lamb is the main meat. Greek influence is seen in a

multilayered stuffed pastry called *lakror*. The Mediterranean climate in the southern reaches of the country assures an abundant supply of fruits and nuts. One of the most prized products is a three-star brandy named for George Kastrioti (1405-1468), the national folk hero known as Skanderbeg.

CRETANS

THE ISLAND OF Crete witnessed Europe's first advanced civilization: the ancient Minoans. But after the Minoan culture disappeared around 1450 B.C., the island and its people experienced domination by mainland Greeks, Romans, Byzantines, and Turks. Venetian rule from A.D. 1204 until 1669, when Crete was conquered by the Ottoman Empire, had a lasting effect on the culture.

Numbering about half a million, the Cretans speak a variant of Greek that shows a connection to ancient times and more recently to Italian and Turkish occupation. Although used for written Cretan, the Greek alphabet does not cover all the sounds of the spoken language.

Rural Cretans divide themselves into mountain dwellers and plains dwellers, both of which are organized into groups related through the male line. These groups continue to feud about such transgressions as the stealing of brides, the raiding of animals, or the insulting of a member's manhood or family, and they will try to avenge the death of a close kinsman. The patronage of political leaders often supports feuding groups. In general, mountain dwellers are known for their political independence and resistance to authority. Herders look down on agriculturalists, who are perceived as less manly. Among the crops raised by the agriculturalists are olives, grapes, and other fruit such as bananas, pears, and oranges. Tomatoes are grown in huge greenhouses on the fertile Messara plain.

Though Cretans are overwhelmingly Greek Orthodox, they are, as a whole, critical of the clergy and may consult informal practitioners, especially ones who can deal with the "evil eye," an important form of social control. Some refuse to acknowledge the Gregorian calendar and are known as Old Calendrists for celebrating feast days according to the older, Julian one. At funerals and later memorials for the deceased, women are expected to keen, or wail their grief in improvised verses. Cretans generally value the ability to improvise and hold contests during which competitors duel with assonant verses called *mantinades*.

SICILIANS

SOME FIVE MILLION people inhabit Sicily, the Mediterranean's largest and most populous island. The Sicels, who settled the island in prehistoric times, came under the domination of many powers, including the Greeks, Romans, Carthaginians, Byzantine Greeks, North African Muslims, Normans, Angevin French, and Spanish. The 11th-century Norman Conquest gave the culture a unique flavor, as European influences blended with Arabic and Byzantine aspects.

Elderly women of Crete visit on a village street, their black garb contrasting with the sunny hues of buildings on the Mediterranean island. Their appearance suggests widowhood, a status they will likely mark by dress for the rest of their lives.

An Albanian shepherd watches over a settlement of his ethnic group in northern Macedonia. Driven by poor economic prospects in their homeland, several thousand Albanians have emigrated to neighboring countries.

Some linguists classify the Sicilian language as a dialect of southern Italy, although it is not mutually intelligible with standard Italian. Essentially a Romance language that is related to Latin, Sicilian contains many borrowings from Arabic and shows a lot of regional variation. Most young Sicilians speak Italian as well.

Sicilians of the rugged, sparsely populated interior are mainly farmers who once also herded sheep and goats. Their towns always have a piazza, or plaza, with government buildings, shops, and a church situated around it and a main street where locals can see and be seen during traditional Sunday strolls. Most Sicilians live in the coastal towns and are employed in fishing, the service sector, and industry. Some leave to pursue work elsewhere in Europe, their wages forming an important part of Sicily's economy.

A notorious fact of Sicilian life is the existence and power of the Mafia, known locally as the Cosa Nostra, meaning "our thing." Rising from lawless conditions that developed during many years of foreign domination, the families of organized crime in recent decades have been involved in the international drug trade, as well as bogus government contracts and extortion from small businesses. Conviction of Mafiosi remains difficult, however, because Cosa Nostra members observe a strict code of silence.

Almost all Sicilians are Roman Catholics who show special devotion to the Virgin Mary and St. Joseph. Each town also has a patron saint whom it honors on an annual feast day. When a person dies, relatives wear black for a period determined by their relationship to the deceased. Widows may observe mourning for the rest of their lives.

Sicilian artists are noted for puppetry and for brightly painted farm carts. Artistry can be seen, too, in rather ornate pastries. Besides sweets, the people enjoy a traditional diet that includes bread, pasta, olive oil, and tomato sauce.

CENTRAL EUROPE
BOSNIAN MUSLIMS • CROATS • CZECHS • MAGYARS • SERBS • SLOVAKS • SLOVENES

BOSNIAN MUSLIMS

OF ALL THE countries that once formed Yugoslavia, Bosnia and Herzegovina (or simply Bosnia) is probably the most unusual. Distinctions there tend to be made on the basis of religion and culture, not ethnicity. About 44 percent of the total population are Muslims, 31 percent are Serbs who follow the Eastern Orthodox religion, and 17 percent are Roman Catholic Croats. All of Bosnia's people speak what was known before the breakup of Yugoslavia as a Serbo-Croatian language.

By the seventh century A.D., south Slavic peoples had populated the area that is now Bosnia. During the long occupation by Ottoman Turks, from 1328 to 1878, many Bosnians converted to Islam from Christianity (in particular from a heretical sect called the Bogomils) because doing so was often a way to obtain economic or social advantage with Turkish officials. Bosnian Muslims were landowners and merchants then but tend to be urban dwellers now. The Turks strongly influenced other aspects of Bosnian culture, including architecture, cuisine, music, poetry, and dance.

Typically forgoing orthodoxy or fundamentalism, Bosnian Muslims mostly follow the Sunni form of Islam, although Sufism, or Islamic mysticism, is also practiced. Muslims observe the month-long fast of Ramadan, which ends with a three-day feast known as Bajram (Id al-Fitr elsewhere). Bosnian Muslim women do not wear the all-enveloping coverings called chadors, but some wear raincoats and scarves for public occasions. During the oil shortages of the 1970s, Yugoslav President Josip Broz Tito highlighted the religion of Bosnia's Muslims to obtain favorable terms from Saudi Arabia and other oil-producing countries; then, as fundamentalism took hold in the Middle East, Tito backed away from this approach, fearing its potential divisiveness in Yugoslavia.

With the breakup of the former Yugoslav federation in 1991, a great deal of religious and ethnic hatred has been released, much of it directed toward Bosnian Muslims. War broke out in 1992, as Serbs vigorously pursued a policy of "ethnic cleansing"—raping and murdering Muslims and forcing them from their towns—with the goal of forming a "greater Serbia."

Intervention by the UN and NATO, along with the Dayton Peace Accords signed in 1995, has brought about some semblance of stability, but in general, much of Bosnia remains in ruins. In the once beautiful city of Sarajevo, where many people were rendered homeless, residents are trying to rebuild their lives and their city. The Muslims have been effectively isolated, though, by a Croat alliance with Croatia and a Serb alliance with Serbia. At least 40 percent of the population is unemployed, and many young Bosnians of all faiths are leaving in pursuit of a better future.

CROATS

IN THE SEVENTH century A.D., a south Slavic group known as the Croats settled in the Dalmatian region of the Adriatic coast; in the northern area of present-day Croatia; and in parts of Bosnia and Herzegovina. A Croatian state began to form in the ninth century and endured until the early twelfth century. Strategically situated at a crossroads for Western and Eastern Europe and for Western and Eastern Christianity, the Croats sustained years of domination by Hungarians, Austrians, Italians, French, and the Turks; they were, however, more successful in containing the expansion of the Turks than others whose territories fell to

the invaders. In the 19th and early 20th centuries, Croats resisted joining forces with other south Slavs, preferring their independence, and only reluctantly did they decide to become part of the newly created Yugoslavia following World War I, all the while remaining suspicious of Serbian expansion and control.

During the era of President Josip Broz Tito, Croatian nationalism was thwarted. But after Tito died in 1980 and communism began to wane, Croats voted for independence in 1991; they did so despite aggression from Serbs, who controlled the government and the army even though they made up only about 12 percent of Croatia's population. Following years of fighting, peace has been restored. Nevertheless, the country must contend with significant unemployment, currently around 20 percent.

The Croatian language, which is spoken by about 3.5 million people inside Croatia and by just as many outside perhaps, belongs to the South Slavic family and has three major dialects. It is written in the Roman alphabet and contains a number of loanwords, mainly from Latin and German.

Almost 80 percent of Croatia's people are members of the Roman Catholic Church, and about 11 percent are Eastern Orthodox who also adhere to the teachings of the pope. Catholicism has largely defined the country's culture, as it has in other parts of the former Yugoslavia, though it was suppressed during the communist era. While Carnival and Easter are important religious holidays, Croatians also look forward to the celebration of Badnjak, or Christmas Eve, and the traditional lighting of the yule log.

The country is made up of 115 communes (opcina)—carryovers from socialism—and each comprises several villages and a local government. A majority of people work in the service sector, about 35 percent in industry, and only 20 percent in agriculture. Croatians build their lives around family and a gregarious café-type culture, with much socializing in public places and homes.

CZECHS

IN DESCRIBING THE modern Czech people, it is inevitable that they be compared with Slovaks, the ethnic group with whom they were politically united from 1918 to 1993 (except during World War II). Ethnically, the Czechs are an amalgam of Celtic, Germanic, and Slavic peoples who accepted Christianity in the ninth century. In 1085, they formed the kingdom of Bohemia, which was centered in Prague, and by the 14th century this kingdom oversaw the greatest expression of political and cultural development in central Europe. In 1526, a vacant Bohemian throne was filled by an Austrian Habsburg, whose house would then control the kingdom until the end of World War I, when the Czechoslovak Republic was created.

Adolph Hitler annexed the republic's provinces of Bohemia and Moravia 20 years later, and Slovakia became a Nazi puppet state. After World War II, communists controlled a reunited Czechoslovakia until the "Velvet Revolution" under dissident playwright and political activist Václav Havel ushered in democracy. Leaders of the Czechs and Slovaks disbanded the union in 1993, and since then Czechs have fared better than Slovaks at effecting economic and social progress.

In general, the Czechs have made a rapid transition to a market economy, with a long history of industrialization translating into highly regarded ceramics, glassware, and textiles. Agriculture is also heavily mechanized, and farms are very productive. The Plzen area, 50 miles southwest of Prague, is known worldwide for its beer production.

Over the years, Czechs have been far more urbanized than Slovaks, and today many live in small towns and in the largest cities of Prague and Brno. People may also have *chaty*, or country homes, which they visit on weekends and holidays. Although about 60 percent of the population is Roman Catholic, adherence to Catholic practice often tends to be quite relaxed. Evangelical Lutherans make up about 20 percent of the population.

Most Czechs are part of small nuclear families, which may expand at some point as adult children assume the care of their aged parents. Many families make time in the middle of the day to enjoy their main meal, traditionally heavy in meats, game, and the characteristic *knedliky*, or

dumplings. Current trends, however, seem to indicate that people are trying to consume lighter, healthier meals. In terms of dress, traditional folk costumes of embroidered shirts, pants, and vests for the men and embroidered blouses, skirts, and aprons for the women are worn mostly in the more rural southern areas.

The Czech language, like Slovak, is part of a cluster of Slavic tongues written in the Roman, rather than the Cyrillic, alphabet. Though Czech and Slovak are mutually intelligible, they are actually two distinct languages. Czech makes a distinction between formal or written communication and everyday speech.

According to a common saying, "every Czech is a musician," and while folk songs and classical music remain popular, rock has entrenched itself in the Czech culture—especially in Prague—and continues to be the medium of political protest.

MAGYARS (Hungarians)

HUNGARY'S MAGYARS stand out amid the mostly Slavic peoples who live around them. As a result of population shifts occurring after World War II, Magyars now make up more than 97 percent of Hungary's population, establishing their country as one of the most ethnically homogeneous in the area.

Magyars first settled the Carpathian basin in the ninth century A.D. and were descended from a tribal people with origins in the forests between the Volga River and Ural Mountains. Their language, also called Magyar, is today spoken by some 15 million people; it belongs to the Ugric branch of the Finno-Ugric family and is distantly related to Finnish and Estonian. Used interchangeably with Magyar, the name "Hungarian" probably derives from the Turkic words *on ogur*, or ten arrows, a reference perhaps to the number of Magyar tribes.

In A.D. 1000, pagan Magyars embraced Christianity under King Stephen I, who gained legitimacy for a Hungarian monarchy. About 62 percent of Hungary's people are now Roman Catholic and 25 percent are Protestant. Centuries of invasion and domination by the Turks, who forced massive conversions to Islam, and by the Austrian Habsburgs ended in the late 1800s when Hungary entered a joint monarchy with Austria. World War I undid that alliance and greatly reduced Hungary's territory. The post-World War II era saw the development of a communist state, which in 1956 crushed a popular pro-democracy revolution quickly and harshly, causing hundreds of thousands of Magyars to leave the country. The communist regime ended with the declaration of a republic in 1989, although some socioeconomic changes had begun in the 1970s.

In the past 50 years, the Hungarian population has shifted from rural to urban, and even in areas where agriculture is predominant, many households derive income from both industry and farming. More than three-fourths of the women work outside their homes, and one in four workers of both sexes commutes a considerable distance. Holding down more than one job is not unusual here, as people try to make ends meet or to afford a more comfortable lifestyle. Families tend to be smaller than in the past, with many couples eventually opting for divorce. A quarter of all families live below the poverty line, and the suicide rate is one of the highest in the world.

Although Magyars are becoming more secular, they continue to celebrate significant days of the liturgical year, as well as many benchmarks in the agricultural calendar. As with other expressions of traditional culture, the distinct Hungarian folk music—based on a pentatonic (five-note) scale—is in decline. Composers Béla Bartók and Zoltán Kodály preserved the best examples of this music form in the early 20th century. Hand kissing, a formal gesture still practiced by older men, has been replaced with the verbal greeting *"Csókolom—I kiss it"* by the younger generation.

SERBS

ABOUT 6.5 MILLION Serbs form the ethnic majority in Serbia, one of the two republics (the other is Montenegro) that constitute the new, self-proclaimed Federal Republic of Yugoslavia. In addition, there are Serb minorities in Croatia and in Bosnia and Herzegovina. Serbs speak Serbian, a South Slavic language related to Croatian but written in the Cyrillic alphabet.

Most people belong to the Serbian Orthodox Church, a self-governing body that has wielded a great deal of political power throughout the republic's history. In recent ethnic conflicts in the region, Serbian Orthodoxy has been drawn even further into the cause of Serbian nationalism.

During the sixth century A.D., Serbs and their flocks moved from the Carpathian Mountains into the Balkan Peninsula and occupied an area that stood to the east of the territory of the Croats, another south Slavic people. Within three centuries, the Serbs had established a state that would expand into a powerful kingdom by the mid-1300s. But internal struggles weakened Serbia to the point that Ottoman Turks were able to conquer the region and hold it for more than 400 years. During this time many Serbs fled west into the Dinaric Alps. A strong sense of nationalism nevertheless prevailed and led to several revolts by rival Serbian families, eventually forcing the Turks to grant autonomy to the Serbs in the early 19th century. Interfamily rivalries remained a theme of Serbian history into the 20th century.

Following World War I, the Serbs saw an opportunity for a greater Serb kingdom, but what came about was a more inclusive state—the former Yugoslavia—uniting the south Slavs. It fell to communism at the end of the Second World War. Under Josip Broz Tito, Yugoslavia withdrew from the Soviet alliance and forged a brand of communism that allowed more worker control and a greater degree of prosperity. President Tito's death in 1980 and communism's decline set the stage for the dissolution of the Yugoslav federation in the last decade of the 20th century.

Serbian nationalism and long-harbored animosities against other groups, such as the Croats and Muslims, engendered aggression in Croatia and Bosnia. In Serbia, violence ensued against Albanian Muslims who formed the majority population in the autonomous province of Kosovo. The conflicts took tens of thousands of lives, led to large-scale movements of peoples, and brought worldwide sanctions against the Serbs and their leader Slobodan Milošević. His ouster in 2000 and the presence of UN and NATO overseers have offered some hope of less conflict for the Serbs, their compatriots, and their neighbors.

Before World War II, most Serbs obtained their living through agriculture, but today many families have a mixed economic base involving farming and industry. As a result, some of the tasks once performed exclusively by men have been taken over by women. The *zadruga*—extended family household composed of several generations in the male line—continues to survive in Serbia, though not in most other south Slavic communities; it is seen more often in rural areas than in urban ones.

Also important is the *vamilija*, or lineage traced from a common male ancestor. Vamilija members share a last name and venerate the same patron saint, whose annual feast day is one of the most important celebrations for the family. In this strongly male-dominated society, being heirless in the male line is considered a tragedy. A man without an heir can bring in a son-in-law to inherit his land and possessions, but such a step is almost always regarded as an unfortunate compromise.

Serbs have long been known for their grand tradition of oral epic poetry, which is often accompanied in recital by a single-stringed instrument called a *gusle*. The people like to socialize outside the home, and in cities and towns they frequent sidewalk cafés for coffee and conversation. On a daily basis, their diet generally consists of bread and a hearty stew made with a lard base. Lamb appears on festive occasions such as Easter.

FOLLOWING PAGES: Czech musicians in a Prague pub let loose with a tune celebrating a national antihero, the Good Soldier Schweik, a literary character created to mock the era of Austrian domination. Czechs have long expressed dissidence through the arts, and for their first president in the post-communist era, they elected playwright/activist Václav Havel. *PAGES 190-91:* Formidable foes in any time, Cossacks pose during a celebration commemorating their heyday as the warrior defenders of Russia. Poet Alexander Pushkin viewed the Cossacks as "eternally on horseback, eternally ready to fight, eternally on guard."

🌑 SLOVAKS

A SLAVIC PEOPLE, Slovaks first inhabited the area between the Carpathian Mountains and the Danube River around the fifth century A.D. As residents of the former Czechoslovakia, they occupied the easternmost third of the country. The Slovak language—like Czech, a closely related tongue—belongs to the West Slavic group and is distinctive for its inflection and large number of vowel-less words.

After a period of hegemony by the Moravian Empire, named for the Morava River Valley, the Slovaks endured a series of invasions by the Magyars, or Hungarians, who controlled Slovakia from A.D. 907 to the end of World War I. The Magyars themselves were incorporated into the Austro-Hungarian Empire in the 16th century. Through a "Magyarization" program, they tried to suppress Slovak language and culture, and as a result, Slovak expatriates joined with their Czech counterparts at the end of World War I to press for the creation of Czechoslovakia. Except for the years from 1939 to 1945, this union persisted, albeit under communist control following World War II. In 1989, the "Velvet Revolution" led by Václav Havel overthrew the communist regime, and three years later the Czech and Slovak republics became separate entities.

Slovaks traditionally have been a more rural people than the Czechs. Their hamlets and villages still contain many of the simple one- and two-room homesteads that, slightly expanded, would often house three generations of a Slovak family. Rural families typically farmed, growing rye, wheat, corn, potatoes, sugar beets, and wine grapes. The steel, chemical, and aluminum industries established during the communist years have declined following the dismantling of the socialist state.

Much socializing takes place along gender lines, with men gathering in bars at night and women visiting at home. This is especially common in rural areas, as is adherence to pre-Christian beliefs and to superstitions about such things as the giving of flowers; cut flowers, for example, should be presented to one's host in an odd number; even-numbered bouquets are only appropriate at funerals. About 60 percent of Slovaks are Roman Catholics, who practice a much more observant form of Catholicism than their Czech neighbors, while about 6 percent are Lutherans. A once sizable Jewish population was annihilated during the Holocaust.

Slovaks are a rather formal people, with ritualized greetings that include using a person's professional credentials in a form of address. Like Czechs, many are avid musicians who enjoy both vocal and instrumental forms of folk music. Folk dancing is a favorite activity as well. It is quite common to see traditional folk dress at festivals and on occasions such as marriage. For men, this means dark woolen suits, blouses, and knitted caps; for women, full skirts, aprons, and scarves. Celebrations are also good times for enjoying the traditional *bryndzové halusky,* potato dumplings served with sheep's cheese.

🌑 SLOVENES

TOGETHER WITH CROATS, the Slovenes provided a catalyst for the independence movement leading to the 1991 dissolution of the former Yugoslavia. In many respects, the Slovenes have emerged from the country's breakup in a stronger position than the other ethnic groups who lived there. These people have long had a western orientation and a higher standard of living, and since independence that difference has only been enhanced.

Almost two million Slovenes inhabit the northwestern corner of the former Yugoslavia. Their new nation, Slovenia, is quite hilly and contains a sizable area of limestone karst; both geologic realities make the country unsuitable for large-scale agriculture and to some extent reliant on grain imports. Nevertheless, wheat, rye, oats, barley, and potatoes are grown, and livestock is raised. Forestry, industry, and tourism are also major economic activities. Today, about 50 percent of the Slovenes live in urban areas, the largest and most populated being Ljubljana, the capital.

Slovenes are a Slavic people who have inhabited the area for more than 13 centuries. They speak Slovene, an old South Slavic language having many dialects and subdialects. After joining a Slavic union in the seventh century, the Slovenes came under Frankish rule in the late eighth and early ninth centuries and were heavily converted to Christianity. For much of Slovenia's history, though, the people were under German control and influence, then Austrian and Austro-Hungarian rule until World War I, when Yugoslavia—"land of the south Slavs"—was created. Communists took over after World War II, but Yugoslavia managed to forge significant regional autonomy.

During the communist era, the Roman Catholic Church fared better in Slovenia than it did in other areas of Yugoslavia. Today, its members make up more than 70 percent of the population, while 5 percent or less of the country's people are Serbian Orthodox or Protestants. For centuries, Catholicism has been inextricably intertwined with Slovenian culture. And while regular attendance at Mass has dropped off, the church continues to influence cultural celebrations and the recognition of most life-cycle events. Slovenes enthusiastically celebrate the pre-Lenten Carnival season, called *pust,* combining Christian and pre-Christian elements. Both children and adults don costumes at this time, and children go door-to-door in search of treats from neighbors.

Music and dancing—both folk and modern—play a very large role in Slovene culture. Choral music is quite popular and is supported by hundreds of different singing groups. For numbers of people, entertainment involves family activities and the visiting of friends, and it is not unusual for city dwellers to spend weekends out in the country, helping relatives with their agricultural chores and relaxing together afterward. Many urban families also have small country cottages of their own.

Potatoes are frequently featured in Slovenian cuisine, as are breads and pastries. *Potica,* a festive bread that can be made with either a sweet or salty filling, appears during holidays, especially at Christmas and Easter. So, too, do copious amounts of alcoholic beverages. In recent years, alcohol consumption has risen by 25 percent, and alcohol abuse is a recognized problem for many Slovenes, regardless of age or gender.

EASTERN EUROPE
JEWS • ROMA • RUSSIANS • UKRAINIANS

JEWS

NEARLY ALL OF the Jews in Europe belong to one of two traditions based on distinctions of geography, language, and culture. The Ashkenazic Jews, or Ashkenazim, and the Sephardic Jews, or Sephardim, share a belief in the primacy of the Babylonian Talmud and in some basic tenets and practices of Judaism. Beyond these commonalities, however, lie a host of significant differences.

In the strictest sense of the term, Ashkenazic Jews are people who have lived, or had ancestors who lived, in the German-speaking areas of Europe, particularly in the Rhineland. Since pre-Roman times, Ashkenazim have resided throughout northern, central, and eastern Europe and been united by the Yiddish language. Yiddish is an amalgamation of Middle German with Hebrew and Aramaic terms, as well as Slavic influences, written in Hebrew characters. As a lingua franca, it united Jews among widely scattered communities, and it served as a language for imparting religious instruction, mainly to women and unschooled men. Hebrew was reserved for educated males. A strong Yiddish press fostered a vast body of both religious and secular literature. Over the centuries, a rich Yiddish folklore developed, with regional variations reflecting, for example, the differences between communities in Russia and Hungary.

As part of the worldwide Jewish diaspora, Europe's Ashkenazim kept alive the traditional belief in a Jewry someday reunited in Israel. They occupied several economic niches, including those of the middleman and merchant. But increasing persecution and forced resettlement changed the nature of Europe's Jewish communities, culminating in the catastrophic genocide undertaken by the Nazis in World War II. After the war, the largest populations of Ashkenazic Jews were found in Russia, Belarus, and Ukraine. The Ashkenazim now account for 80 percent of the Jewish population worldwide, with large emigrant communities in Israel, the Americas, Australia, and South Africa.

The community of Sephardic Jews developed in the Iberian Peninsula, where Jewish settlements existed in Roman times. ("Sepharad" refers to a place of exile mentioned in the Old Testament Book of Obadiah.) Large populations flourished in southern Spain and in Portugal. After the Moorish conquest in 711, the Sephardim entered a cultural and economic golden age, which diminished with increasing persecutions and ended when Jews were expelled from Spain in 1492 and Portugal in 1497. Some Sephardim remained, however, nominally converting to Christianity but nonetheless continuing to experience discrimination. The several waves of Sephardic diaspora established communities on the Balkan Peninsula and in Italy, northern Europe, North Africa, and the New World. Another population shift followed World War II, with settlement taking place in Israel, the United States, France, and Spain. Today, France, Italy, and Spain have significant Sephardic populations.

The early Sephardim spoke Ladino, sometimes called Judeo-Spanish, a dialect of Castilian Spanish with influences from Hebrew, Turkish, and other languages. At first written in Hebrew characters, Ladino later used the Latin alphabet. As was the case with Yiddish, a vast body of religious and secular Ladino literature developed along with a fertile oral tradition, which included the typical Iberian form of ballad known as the *romancero*. While some people continue to speak Ladino, most Sephardic Jews now use the language of the country in which they reside.

Sephardim differ religiously from Ashkenazim in their orientation toward Jewish traditions of ancient Babylonia; Ashkenazic Jews follow those of Palestine. In general, the two groups differ in their interpretation of some religious laws, in the extent to which they adhere to certain dietary restrictions, and on the details of their prayer services. Today, Jews who follow the Sephardic traditions may call themselves Sephardim even if their ancestry does not trace back to the Iberian Peninsula.

ROMA (Gypsies)

THE ROMA ARE known by a number of names, many of which—"Gitanes" in France, "Czigany" in Hungary, and "Zigeuner" in Germany—are variations of "Gypsy," a term that erroneously ascribed their origins to Egypt. In fact, the Roma have been linguistically traced to northwest India: They speak Romany, an Indic language from which comes the word "Roma," meaning "man" or "people."

One theory ties the group's 11th-century diaspora from India to their recruitment as troops who drove out Islamic invaders, pursuing them over the centuries into the Byzantine Empire and southeastern Europe. Today, the Roma are a minority in every country in Europe, and their worldwide population is estimated at 8 to 12 million. Exact numbers are unknown; for one reason, a long history of discrimination has made them reluctant to admit their heritage. Targeted by Nazis, more than half a million died in World War II. Communist regimes also suppressed their culture, but the collapse of communism did not stop the repression. A rise in nationalism led to more violence. In 1971 the first World Romani Congress established a much-needed forum through which the people can address their struggle against racism and loss of cultural identity.

The Roma have long existed at the margins of other societies, partly to avoid discrimination and partly because of their migratory lifestyle. For centuries, families traveled in brightly painted, horse-drawn caravans, plying trades consistent with this kind of nomadism. They were horse traders, peddlers, metalsmiths, musicians, fortune-tellers, and carnival workers. In recent decades, some countries encouraged or forced permanent settlement, especially in Eastern Europe, where the Roma were put to work in state-run industries. With the fall of socialism, many of the settled Roma have lost their livelihoods.

Over the years, the people have embraced a number of faiths, often depending on the dominant local tradition. But while they observe many rituals of mainstream religion, they sometimes add their own practices. For example, followers of Roman Catholicism gather near France's Rhône Delta each May to honor Black Sarah, their patron saint, even though she is not recognized by the church. Recently, many Roma have been drawn to Pentecostalism.

The Roma are organized into clans that are usually based on occupation, each with a chief or head. Clan

Fifty years of wedded bliss reside in the kiss of a Crimean couple, who celebrate their golden anniversary in the city of Sevastopol', Ukraine.

Residents of the Crimea, a large Black Sea peninsula, include Russian pensioners who revel in the region's pleasant climate.

members, or large groups of Roma in general, will travel long distances together, but now they frequently do so in mobile homes and RVs. Music and dance are integral parts of their culture and have influenced aspects of other European cultures. In recent years, Roma musical rhythms have enjoyed a surge of worldwide popularity.

Marimé, the Roma code of ritual purity, is a remnant of the people's origins in India and incorporates a number of taboos regarding social relationships and food. As a result, traditional Roma society is a closed one shunning out-of-group marriages and other contacts with *gadjés,* non-Roma peoples who, as a group, are deemed unpure. Ideally, marriages were arranged and occurred at an early age, but such arrangements are becoming less common.

While birthrates for other European ethnic groups are declining, the Roma one is rising dramatically. Some demographers even speculate that by 2060 Slovakia's Roma population will outnumber the country's Slovaks.

RUSSIANS

LARGEST ETHNIC group in Europe, the Russians developed from ancient Slavic tribes who had settled in the area north of the Black Sea by the first millennium A.D. By the ninth century, when Vikings established a dynasty in the state of Kievan Rus, a number of tribes inhabited the area from the Black Sea to the Baltic.

Official conversion to Eastern Orthodox Christianity occurred in A.D. 988, linking Russians to the Byzantine Empire. Mongol occupation from the mid-13th to the late 15th centuries, however, sealed off the people from the cultural changes coming to Western Europe. These would not be felt until the early 18th century, when Tsar Peter the Great (1672-1725) modernized and westernized the culture and enlarged Russia's territory, a trend that continued under Catherine the Great (1729-1796). As the tsars expanded Russia's boundaries, the original Slavic tribes assimilated groups with Finnish, Turkish, Siberian, and Baltic origins to form the present-day Russian people, who number about 120 million. In the post-Soviet era, ethnic strife has led to violence in some parts of Russia, notably in Chechnya, a region in the Caucasus Mountains.

The Russian language belongs to the East Slavic group of Indo-European tongues. An old form of Russian known as Old Church Slavonic survives through the Russian Orthodox Church. Until the tenth century, Russian did not have a written form, but then the monks Cyril and Methodius constructed a hybrid alphabet from the Latin, Greek, and Hebrew alphabets. Today, a number of other Slavic languages also use the Cyrillic alphabet.

Though officially condemned during the Soviet era, when perhaps up to 85 percent of churches were closed and their property confiscated, the Russian Orthodox Church survived and has been experiencing a resurgence of participation and elevation of status as a cherished cultural institution. Western proselytizers have also had significant influence in present-day Russia, as evidenced by growing numbers of Baptists, Jehovah's Witnesses, and Seventh-Day Adventists.

Russians have traditionally been rural people. For centuries, many of them were serfs, but even after their emancipation in 1861, serfs saw little improvement in their condition. During the Soviet era from 1917 to 1991, the central government endeavored to hold all property and organized large collective and state farms. This did not deter food production on private plots, though, and people sold their surplus produce to alleviate shortages caused by a poor distribution system.

As the society and economy continue to adjust to the post-Soviet era, some situations have changed dramatically while others remain virtually the same. A warm, effusive people by nature, Russians of the Soviet era had become guarded in their public lives and thus led a dual existence, which has since eased. Shoppers' lives have also eased: The long lines for food and consumer goods have disappeared. One aspect that has not changed, however, is the housing shortage. After marriage, a young couple typically resides with the groom's parents until housing becomes available— sometimes a very long wait. Children continue to be highly valued, and parents will commit much of a family's time and resources to them. Unfortunately, the standard of living for most people is austere, and alcoholism and domestic abuse remain serious social issues.

Russians have a rich folk culture that is often expressed in music and decorative arts. *Byliny* are traditional epic songs, some dating back more than a thousand years. Songs are frequently accompanied by a balalaika, a three-stringed, triangular guitar. Also popular among all levels of Russian society are classical music, literature, and chess.

A typical Russian meal has four courses and often includes borscht, a red beet-and-meat soup served with sour cream. Among other traditional fare are *ikra* (caviar) and blini (small, filled pancakes). Sweetened hot tea, vodka, and brandy are typical beverages. Russians celebrate the feast days of the Orthodox liturgical year, as well as life-cycle rituals such as weddings and graduations.

UKRAINIANS

UKRAINIANS ARE an amalgam of Slavic tribes who settled the vast grassy plains, or steppelands, west of the Black Sea. By medieval times, the area around Kiev in the north had gained supremacy, and a union known as Kievan Rus dominated the region between the 9th and 13th centuries. At that time, the people were known as Ruthens. A Ukrainian republic did not exist until the fall of tsarist Russia in 1918; it was short-lived, however, and another was not formed until the end of the First World War, when Soviet leaders made Ukraine a socialist state. In 1991, Ukraine became an independent nation.

Today, approximately 37 million Ukrainians make up about three-fourths of the country's population. They speak Ukrainian, a language that belongs to the East Slavic group and is written in the Cyrillic alphabet. Since the end of the Soviet era, this language, along with other aspects of ethnic identity, has flourished while Russian influences and language use have declined in Ukraine.

Blessed with rich soils, Ukraine was regarded as the "breadbasket of Europe" until the 1986 nuclear meltdown at Chornobyl' rendered some agricultural lands radioactive for many years to come. People continue to farm on lands that were unaffected, growing grains, fruits, and vegetables, and raising livestock. Ukrainian farmers live in villages that tend to be large, often holding more than a thousand residents. Until the 18th century, it was not uncommon for three generations to live together; since then, however, the nuclear family has been the norm in both rural and urban areas, which contain about two-thirds of the country's people. Industry is centered in the east and includes the mining of coal and other mineral resources.

Most people follow a branch of the Eastern Orthodox faith. Because of their proximity to the Near East, Ukrainians became Christians early on, although the prince of Kievan Rus did not officially adopt the religion on behalf of the state until A.D. 988. Of the many Christian holy days celebrated by Ukrainians, Easter remains foremost, surpassing Christmas. Pre-Christian beliefs continue to influence observances of life passages, especially death, but weddings exhibit the fullest expression of Ukrainian life-cycle recognition.

Ukrainians are an effusive people who often greet others exuberantly with hugs, vigorous handshakes, or triple kisses. They entertain readily, frequently turning routine events into parties, at which toasting is a common form of recognition. In Ukrainian rituals, food plays an important role, as can be seen in the variety of breads used to commemorate different occasions. Traditionally, a dinner is not considered complete unless borscht, a red beet-and-meat soup, is served.

At least one form of Ukrainian folk art elicits worldwide recognition: the *pysanky*, or decorated Easter egg. The art dates to pre-Christian times, but it readily became infused with Christian symbols and meanings. Elaborate embroidery applied to clothing and to everyday textiles is another typical form of folk art. Ukrainians are also enthusiastic dancers and singers, known especially for their unique New Year's carols.

A Roma, or Gypsy, moves to her own beat in Arles, France. Gypsies throughout Europe have carried with them their unique musical rhythms in the thousand-year diaspora from their homeland in India.

Africa is the birthplace of humankind, an ancient land where our hominid, or humanlike, ancestors lived more than four million years ago. Extraordinarily diverse in its geography and cultures, this immense continent measures about 5,000 miles north to south and 4,600 miles east to west—from the Horn of Africa to the tip of Senegal—and over the millennia it has given rise to a rich mix of peoples now inhabiting deserts and rain forests, mountains and valleys.

Even within similar geographic areas, one finds a wide range of social and political organizations. The Nuer of Sudan, for example, have no indigenous leadership roles, while the Zulu of southern Africa are known for their once heavily militarized kingdom. Societies such as the Asante and Yoruba in the west and the Buganda, Bunyoro, and Tutsi in the east maintained large states, while numerous others, like southern Africa's Shona and Tswana, composed smaller states or kingdoms. The Mbuti and Efe Pygmies of central Africa and the San of the Kalahari Desert continue to live by hunting and gathering and have a fluid political organization without any recognized political authority.

The languages spoken by Africa's many peoples can be grouped into a few general families, such as Bantu or Nilo-Saharan, but just

SUB-SAHARAN AFRICA

Wearing a headdress of beads, shells, and ostrich feathers, a painted Masai warrior presents a striking image.

one group may include several different tongues. European languages are also spoken throughout Africa because of the long colonial period, which lasted until the 1960s. French is spoken in the former French and Belgian colonies of western and central Africa; English is heard in the west, east, and south; and Portuguese is spoken in the former Portuguese-occupied areas of Angola, Mozambique, and Guinea-Bissau.

Although African societies vary considerably in the ways they organize their families and social lives, some general patterns can be found. Marriage, for example, is usually considered a union of groups rather than individuals, and that union is symbolized and made legal by the transfer of bridewealth from the groom's family to the bride's. In many societies, a man must first pay a certain amount of money to the bride's father to set the marriage in process; later, he must make childwealth payments for rights in his offspring. Most Africans permit polygamy, the marriage of a man to more than one woman, although one area in Nigeria once permitted polyandry, the marriage of a woman to more than one man. Among the Lese of the Democratic Republic of the Congo, and in some other societies of western and central Africa, an infertile wife may marry another woman. In a woman-to-woman marriage, the other wife reproduces with the husband, helping to make sure that he does not abandon the infertile wife for lack of children.

The vast majority of African societies reckon descent unilineally, either through the mother in matrilineal societies or through the father in patrilineal societies. In both cases, however, the men have most of the authority. In matrilineal societies, one traces descent through the mother's brother and is subject to his authority, not the mother's. A small number of African societies reckon descent in the same way that most Americans do: bilaterally, but with a bias toward the male side of the family.

Some African societies are well known for art that is both useful and aesthetic. Styles vary greatly, but the most common products are figurines used in sacrifice and worship, generally with oversize heads in relation to the body, and masks worn in ritual performances. Among the Dan of Liberia, masks hide the faces of secret-society members and protect the identity of judges involved in settling disputes. The Akan of Ghana rely on wooden figures to facilitate childbirth. Africans also produce an enormous amount of "tourist art," much of which is distributed in Europe and North America; despite the name, this art is often of the same style and quality as art not created for export.

African people practice many religions, including Islam, Christianity, Judaism, and Hinduism. In western Africa, Islam now has numerous adherents. This is especially true among the Hausa of Nigeria and other societies that have engaged in trade with northern Africa, where Muslim Hamitic-speaking peoples have long been distinguished both culturally and religiously from the sub-Saharan societies.

The economies of Africa are also diverse, as disparate as hunting and gathering in the central African rain forest; diamond and gold mining in southern Africa; and large-scale farming in western Africa. Often, the differences between the urban and rural areas are quite dramatic. Some families occupy cable-ready high-rise apartments and perhaps hold positions as engineers, teachers, doctors, lawyers, or software developers. But many of their countrymen dwell in thatched-roof huts, with no plumbing, electricity, or, in some cases, access to cities; they may spend their lives as pastoralists or hunters or farmers who

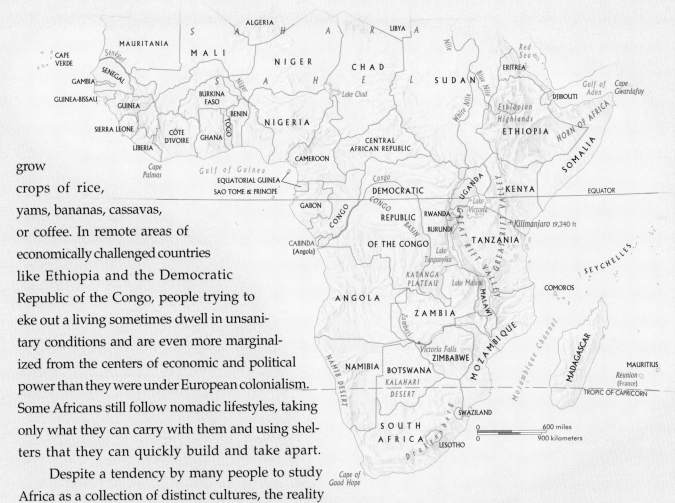

grow
crops of rice,
yams, bananas, cassavas,
or coffee. In remote areas of
economically challenged countries
like Ethiopia and the Democratic
Republic of the Congo, people trying to
eke out a living sometimes dwell in unsanitary conditions and are even more marginalized from the centers of economic and political power than they were under European colonialism. Some Africans still follow nomadic lifestyles, taking only what they can carry with them and using shelters that they can quickly build and take apart.

Despite a tendency by many people to study Africa as a collection of distinct cultures, the reality is that various groups have had long, extensive contacts with one another, with much cultural exchange. Neighboring societies may have borrowed elements of each other's rituals over the years, in a manner so subtle and inconspicuous that trying to determine the precise origins of a particular ritual becomes an impossible task. The continent's "distinct cultures" are, in fact, composed of many threads.

In Africa, the rich cultural pluralism allows alternative beliefs and practices to coexist. Here, major religions of the world are practiced alongside indigenous religions, and a range of medical treatments are made available to everyone; different illnesses may be treated with therapies that are religious in nature, indigenous or traditional, or even based on Western medicine. A spectacular example of how cultures can coexist, work together, and even borrow elements from one another can be seen in the hometown of Felix Houphouet-Boigny, a former president of Côte d'Ivoire and a devout Roman Catholic. It is an extra-large replica of St. Peter's Basilica in Vatican City. Engineered by Lebanese architects and built by French and Israeli contractors, the European-style structure incorporates Greek columns, Italian marble, and French stained glass. In 1990, the basilica was consecrated by Pope John Paul II amid traditional dancing performed by the Baule society of Côte d'Ivoire.

Following Pages: Masters of exploiting a harsh terrain, San families in southern Africa's Kalahari Desert survive by sharing food within an intricate social network.

SUB-SAHARAN AFRICA

CLOCKWISE FROM TOP LEFT: EAST AFRICAN GIRLS, ETHIOPIAN PRIEST, MASAI DANCERS, AND BUSHMAN HERDER

WEST AFRICA

CENTRAL AFRICA

EAST AFRICA

SOUTHERN AFRICA

WEST AFRICA

ASANTE • BAMBARA • DOGON • FANG • HAUSA • WOLOF • YORUBA

ASANTE (Ashanti)

NEARLY 1.5 MILLION Asante dwell in southern Ghana. They speak the Asante language, which is part of the Akan cluster of Twi languages, and are perhaps best known for their colorful, geometrically designed Kente cloth.

The mighty Asante kingdom emerged in the forests of central Ghana in the late 17th century, after the union of several smaller states. At that time, the Golden Stool—symbol of Asante statehood—appeared. This sacred relic is said to have descended from the heavens in answer to the prayers of Okomfe Anokye, a legendary priest and adviser; it came to rest on the knees of Osei Tutu, who ascended to power as the first Ashantehene or Asante ruler. Treated with the reverence given to a king, the Golden Stool travels with a retinue and occupies its own palace. It has never been sat upon.

In the early Asante economy, the people depended on the gold-and-slave trade that developed between them and the Manding and Hausa, as well as with Europeans who came to their shores. By acting as middlemen in the slave trade, they received firearms, which were used to increase their already dominant power, and various luxury goods that were incorporated into symbols of status and political office. The Asante turned to the surrounding forest for another economically important item: kola nuts. These were sought after for gifts and used as a mild stimulant among the Muslim peoples to the north.

Today, the Asante are primarily farmers, growing cocoa for export and planting yams, plantains, and other produce for local consumption. They also include master stool makers and accomplished carvers, jewelers, metalsmiths, and weavers. Originally worn by rulers, the famous Kente cloth is now donned by commoners and has become an important cultural symbol for many African Americans.

Most of the Asante reside in south-central Ghana's Asante region, which is centered around Kumasi—second largest city in the country, after Accra. Villages include the extended families of clans that descend from common female ancestors traced along the maternal lines.

The population is made up of Christians, Muslims, and animists, but Asante maintain customs and beliefs in the spirit world that are common to everyone.

BAMBARA

MALI'S LARGEST ethnic group, the Bambara are approximately three million strong. They are especially concentrated in the western part of the country and along the Niger River. The Bambara speak Bamana, a Manding language widely used in Mali, particularly in the areas of business and trade. Bamana belongs to the larger Niger-Congo language family, which also includes Bantu tongues such as Swahili and Zulu.

During the 1700s, there were two Bambara kingdoms: Segu and Karta. Aggressive Muslim groups overthrew these kingdoms in the 1800s, but many Bambara remained wary of Islam until the arrival of the French as a colonial power. As resistance to French colonialism grew, so did Islam, and today nearly 80 percent of Bambara peoples are Muslim.

The Bambara are farmers who produce large quantities of sorghum and groundnuts; their main crop, however, is millet. They also grow maize, cassava, tobacco, and numerous other plants in private gardens. Environmental hardships such as drought frequently make farming difficult, so people may keep livestock to supplement their diet. Often they trust their neighbors, the Fulani herdsmen, to look after their domestic animals. This arrangement lets the Bambara focus on farming during the short rainy season that lasts from June to September. Both men and women share the farming duties, although the division of labor allows women to leave the fields earlier to prepare meals for their families.

Bambara villages are collections of different family units, usually all from one lineage or extended family, and each household, or *gwa*, has the responsibility of providing for all of its members and helping them with their farming duties. The members of each gwa work together every day except Monday, which is usually considered market day. In general, Bambara dwellings are larger than the homes of most other West African groups and may house 60 or more people.

For the Bambara, marriage carries heavy expenses, but many men are prepared to sacrifice a great deal because they view it as an investment. The return on that investment

Harvesting millet in southern Mali, Bambara farmers—like other people in arid regions—must work intensively to take advantage of the land's very brief fertile period.

is the eventual arrival of many children, who then help with the farming and contribute to the growth of a family's fortunes. Many Bambara women give birth to eight or more children. All adults marry, and it is not unusual for widows in their 70s or 80s to have suitors, for marriage enhances a person's reputation.

Although most Bambara are Muslims, old beliefs and rituals persist. In many areas, traditional male religious societies perform ceremonies to honor ancestors and promote the fertility of both the land and the people. Each society has its own distinctive masks, carved in wood and often depicting animals.

DOGON

NOW INHABITING the Bandiagara cliffs region of south-central Mali, as well as parts of Burkina Faso, the Dogon are thought to be descended from the first inhabitants of the Niger River Valley. From there, the Dogon probably migrated to Burkina Faso between the 13th and 15th centuries. Then, around 1490, they fled the onslaught of Mossi people and found a haven among the cliffs of southern Mali.

Numbering about 250,000, contemporary populations speak a Voltaic language also known as Dogon. These people live in a stratified society, with each individual's status determined by his position within important sub-groups, such as his clan, village, male lineage, and age set. Each subgroup has a hierarchy based on age and rules of descent, meaning that individuals who enjoy high status in their families are the people most likely to occupy important positions in society.

The Dogon build their dwellings into and atop the dramatic cliffs of their homeland, as well as on the land below. Family homes are made of stone or adobe and are arranged around a courtyard open to domestic animals. Often set above the corners of this courtyard are thick-walled, fortress-like towers where millet and wheat are stored; such towers have also been used in defensive efforts against attackers.

Because the Dogon are an agricultural people, the land is of great importance in their lives and in their religious views and practices. The Lebe cult, for example, is dedicated to agricultural renewal; its altars contain clumps of earth to encourage the land's continued fertility. Perhaps the most significant agricultural rite is called the *bulu,* which takes place before the rains come and the planting begins.

Dogon religion involves the worship of ancestors, as well as spirits the people encountered as they moved across the landscape of West Africa. In this respect, the most important institution is the Awa society, which carries out rituals enabling the deceased to leave the world of the living for the world of the dead. Many ceremonies are public, and these include funerary rites known as *bago bundo,* with masks and dancing, and the *dama* ceremony to mark the end of mourning. The society's most important

responsibility is the planning of the *sigui* ceremonies held every 60 years, when the star Sirius appears between two mountain peaks. At such times, the functions of deceased members are passed on to novices. All rites and ceremonies involve masking traditions and are performed by males who know how to personify supernatural beings and speak their special language *(sigi so).*

The Dogon's carved masks and wooden figurative art—usually in red, black, and white, with spirals and checkerboard patterns—have drawn the attention of artists and collectors around the world.

FANG

AN ESTIMATED one million Fang dwell within the rain forests of northwest Gabon, Equatorial Guinea, and southern Cameroon. These people have not occupied their territory for very long, having migrated from the northeast only a couple of centuries ago. Although the Fang were feared at first by Europeans on the coast, they later traded ivory and forest products with them; they did not, however, take part in the widespread slave trade.

The Fang rely on swidden cultivation, or slash-and-burn agricultural techniques to create temporary plots. There they grow crops such as manioc and plantains, rotating them to help preserve the fertility of the land and to prevent severe erosion of the soil. Today, many Fang cultivate cash crops of cocoa and coffee, while still others make a living by working in cities.

Outside of Africa, the Fang are perhaps best known for their wooden reliquary figures, the stylized carvings meant to embody aesthetic and social values of opposition and vitality. Contrasting features in Fang art reflect the idea that through opposition will come strength, growth, and energy; from antagonism or difference comes new life. Perhaps the simplest example of this concept is the joining of men and women to produce children. The principle of dichotomies also extends to architecture: Entering a Fang village, one sees straight rows of houses flanking a central courtyard or plaza, creating a square of houses. Clan members who build opposite each other often say that "it is better to shout insults to your brother across the court than to whisper them to his ear as your neighbor." They believe conflict, a form of opposition, is resolved in the open but festers in secret.

HAUSA

THE HISTORY OF the Hausa, who inhabit northern Nigeria and southern Niger, is marked by the rise of powerful kingdoms built on lucrative trade markets. Living along caravan routes that reached to the Middle East, the Hausa became expert traders, even though the majority of the people were, and remain, settled farmers.

Hausa origin myths hold that heroic Bayajidda rescued the queen of Daura and her people from a powerful serpent. As a reward, the queen married Bayajidda and gave birth

to seven sons, each of whom founded a Hausa kingdom. Allied politically, all of the kingdoms specialized in economic and military activities that were based on their locations and natural resources. These substates were known, for example, as chiefs of indigo, slaves, markets, government, war, and so forth. Constant military vigilance was required to fend off such aggressive neighbors as the Akan and Songhay.

From at least the 11th century, the history of the region has been intimately tied to Islam and the Fulani ethnic group, which seized power from the Hausa in the early 1800s through a series of jihads, or holy wars. In many areas, intermarriage has since blurred the distinctions between Hausa and Fulani, and both peoples are generally considered one group in contemporary Nigeria. Together they form the largest ethnic group in the country and the most numerous Muslim group in sub-Saharan Africa.

Political leadership in the early Hausa states was based on ancestry, with individuals who could trace their relations back to Bayajidda considered royal. When Islam arrived, many Hausa rulers embraced the religion and combined it with traditional ways. Rulers also welcomed praise singers known as *maroka*, who were, in part, historians of lineage; these people rose in status as they were granted access to important personages—a privilege that in turn benefited the people with whom the maroka associated.

In the early 20th century, the British colonized the region, and during that period the Hausa became part of Nigeria. Today, the people are still traders and farmers; they are also well known for their production of indigo-dyed cloth. The Hausa language, related to Arabic, Berber, and Hebrew, is widely spoken throughout Africa as a common language of trade.

WOLOF

NEIGHBORS TO the Mandika and the Fulani, the 2.5 million Wolof are the dominant ethnic group of coastal Senegal. Their history dates from about the 12th or 13th century and is preserved in the art of the griots, or oral praise singers.

After the fall of the Ghana Empire in the 11th century, the ancestors of today's Wolof no longer felt protected in their old territory and migrated westward from Mali to the Atlantic coast. By the 15th century, they had established a powerful presence in what is now the Wolof homeland. The Portuguese also established a presence on the African continent around that time, building a fort on Gorée Island, off the coast of Dakar; that fort would be used in the Atlantic slave trade. Islam arrived in the 15th century as well, having been brought to Senegal by Mauretanian imams. Today, the majority of Wolof are Muslims, with many of the men belonging to Muslim brotherhoods, each with its own unique features.

The traditional Wolof political system involved the rule of powerful headmen from elite *(Continued on page 212)*

Colorful Kente cloth adorns an Asante dancer in Ghana. Invented and named for past rulers, Ghana's textile designs reflect and preserve aspects of the country's rich history.

FOLLOWING PAGES: Women's voluntary associations, such as this group in Côte d'Ivoire, play major roles in promoting progressive political causes throughout the sub-Saharan region. They foster gender solidarity, encourage the economic independence of women, and help many young females prepare for adult responsibilities.

PAGES 210-11: Steeped in a complex cosmology, a Dogon fortune-teller divines meaning from patterns and figures in the sand.

lineages. These headmen acted as a sort of parliament, electing a supreme ruler from a pool of candidates. Slavery was a part of Wolof society, and the people were themselves involved in the slave trade. In West Africa, there were two types of enslaved people: those born into a household and those who were captured in war or purchased.

In today's world, the Wolof people are well known for their rich musical tradition. They have developed an enormously sophisticated body of percussion instruments and harps, the most famous of which may be the *tama,* or talking drum; its resonance can be altered by pressing strings that attach the drumhead to the drum. Also important is the *xalam,* a five-string "guitar." Some contemporary Wolof musicians—Youssou N'Dour and Baaba Maal, for example—have established international reputations and made popular recordings that are widely available.

The Wolof are known for their spicy stews, too. Sorghum and millet are the staple crops, but tomatoes, peanuts, beans, and peppers are important fare as well. So are fish and rice. All of these ingredients can be found in the stews and other dishes that are characteristic of Wolof cooking.

YORUBA

ONE OF THE largest groups in Africa, the Yoruba-speaking people are spread primarily through southwestern Nigeria and the neighboring countries of Benin and Togo. While some of the Yoruba make their homes in grasslands and forests, members of this group have also been city dwellers for centuries and are therefore among the most urbanized people on the continent.

In the past, Yoruba city-states were governed by a king, or *oba,* and a supreme council. Ancient city-states frequently went to war, and in the mid-18th century the Oyo kingdom became dominant, providing a cohesive identity among the Yoruba that continues to this day.

Religion has always been very important in Yoruba society, with traditional beliefs still exercising a major influence on daily life even though both Christianity and Islam are now widespread. Olorun is the high god, but he has no specific shrines. People consider him relatively inactive in human affairs and instead seek help from traditional deities known as *orisha,* which are said to number 401. The Yoruba believe that when they die they enter the ancestors' realm, from which they continue to influence earthly affairs. In rare instances, they may even become orisha like Shango, the thunder god who had been a celebrated king. Yoruba spiritual beliefs have had an enormous influence on such New World religions as Cuba's Santería, Trinidad's Orisha, and Brazil's Candomblé.

Along with their skills in woodcarving, weaving, potterymaking, and metalwork, the Yoruba are famous for something else: their high incidence of twinning. With 45 births in 1,000 producing twins, the rate is four times that of the United States or Great Britain. This biological phenomenon has yielded a special status for twins in the Yoruba cosmology; they are known as thunder children, because the first twins were believed to be the children of Shango. Twins are considered both a burden and a blessing: Twice as much trouble to raise, they also bring twice as much good fortune to parents who give them proper care.

CENTRAL AFRICA

EFE • KONGO • MANGBETU • TUTSI AND HUTU

EFE

THE CENTRAL AFRICAN rain forest is home to the Efe, one of several hunter-gatherer groups popularly known as Pygmies, a term increasingly viewed in the region as a pejorative. With a total population of nearly 200,000, these groups also include the Mbuti, the Sua, and the Aka.

Numbering about 3,000 today, the Efe—like their immediate neighbors, the Mbuti—are almost exclusively hunter-gatherers. They are all shorter than their farmer neighbors, the Lese. Although some Efe men may reach a height of five feet, the vast majority of both men and women never exceed four feet ten inches. The reason why they developed short stature is not known exactly, but many researchers believe that their shortness is an adaptation for the tropical rain forest environment. Smaller individuals have more surface area in proportion to volume and are better able than larger ones to dissipate body heat in the hot and humid forest.

The Efe live in camps of between four and twenty people, whose quickly built huts are occupied for only a few months before the camp moves on to a new hunting territory. Unlike the Mbuti, who use nets, the Efe hunt exclusively with bows and arrows, usually for monkeys and small African antelopes known as duikers. But the Efe cannot survive by eating only what they find in the rain forest. For carbohydrates they depend on cassava, rice, peanuts, potatoes, and yams collected from their farmer neighbors, with whom they engage in long-term, hereditary exchange partnerships; the two converse in mutually understandable dialects of the same Sudanic tongue.

Ideally, a Lese farmer inherits the son of his father's Efe trading partner as his own partner (as one inherits wealth or property). Nearly everyone has a partner, and often it is said that a "true man" must have a partner. The Efe give their partners meat, honey, and other forest foods in return for cultivated foods and metal. Farmers sometimes marry Efe women, and their children are considered by both groups to be members of the farmer group. It is taboo, however, for Efe men to marry farmer women. This means that, over time, the height of the farmer group has decreased while the height of the Efe has remained the same.

Art, practicality, tradition, and religion come together in a West African funeral: Anointed with schnapps and sheep's blood, this carved casket bears the body of a Ghana fishing chief.

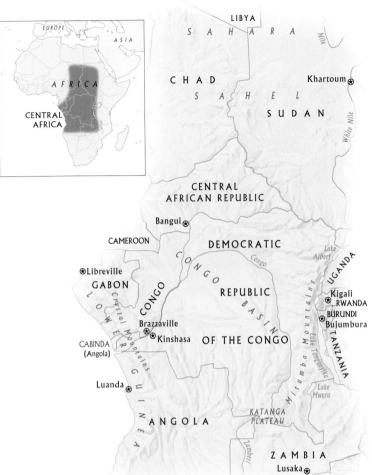

Because they have a somewhat nomadic lifestyle, the Efe do not possess property or wealth that they cannot move. Artistically, they are perhaps best known for their distinctive bark cloth paintings, simple black geometric designs that are common to nearly all Pygmy groups—even the ones who occupy very different territories and speak mutually unintelligible languages.

KONGO

MORE THAN TWO million Kongo live in the southwest part of the Democratic Republic of the Congo, in northwestern Angola, and in southern Congo. These people reckon descent through the maternal line, believing they descend from 12 female ancestors who assisted the founders of the ancient kingdom of Kongo. In 1482, Portuguese explorers first encountered this kingdom. They saw a vibrant and complex political and economic organization of chiefs, governors, and judiciary, with a strong military and a system for collecting taxes. Though the Portuguese had limited success converting the people to Christianity, they still retained respect for them and later agreed to help them when the Kongo were plundered by the Jaga in the 16th century. Even so, the Kongo never fully recovered, and in 1885 they became colonial subjects of Belgium.

Over the years, the Kongo have occasionally gained power in national politics, especially in 1960 when Joseph

213

Central African Pygmies live in hemispherical huts made from leaves and sticks. In times of harmony, entrances face those of other huts, but in times of conflict, people reposition them so they face away from each other.

Kasavubu, a Kongo, became the first head of state of the newly independent Republic of Congo. The economy of the ancient kingdom depended on taxes, tribute, and proceeds from the slave trade, but now the Kongo subsist primarily through agriculture and fishing. The people maintain a conventional division of labor in which women toil in fields of cassava, beans, and squash, while men tend orchards of palm oil trees.

Kongo live in cities and in the countryside, but in the Democratic Republic of the Congo many of them live in independent religious communities, some of which derive from the religion of the prophet Simon Kimbangu (1889-1951). Like South Africa's Isaiah Shembe, a Zulu Zionist, the Kongo prophet developed a syncretic religion based on Christianity and native beliefs. Eventually, Kimbangu became so powerful that the Belgian colonial government sentenced him to life in prison, where he died a martyr in the eyes of his many followers. With a current membership of more than three million, Kimbangu's church was the first one in Africa to be admitted to the World Council of Churches.

MANGBETU

APPROXIMATELY 50,000 Mangbetu live in the northern part of the Democratic Republic of the Congo. Like their neighbors, the Efe and the Azande, they speak a Sudanic, tonal language. The Mangbetu and other Sudanic-speaking populations in central Africa most likely originated in the Sudan, from which they either migrated or were displaced into the Congo basin.

Until the late 19th century, when slave traders and European colonial powers began to dominate central Africa, the Mangbetu people formed a vibrant group of kingdoms. Leadership positions were hereditary, and social organization was founded on the smallest societal unit—the house. More than just a rectangular, physical structure made of mud and sticks, a "house" was also a concept that might refer to whole villages and groups of villages. Houses of varying size could incorporate nonlineage members such as wives, sisters' children, slaves, and even non-Mangbetu people.

The Mangbetu are one of the most physically distinctive groups in central Africa, with some of their women having a conical head shape. During much of the 20th century, high-status families would bind the heads of infant girls so that they became elongated as the craniums hardened. This procedure is seldom practiced today, but for the Mangbetu a conical head is still a sign of great beauty and status, reflecting the right to authority and political power. A unique, elaborate hairstyle emphasizes the distinctive shape of the head.

Mangbetu artistic traditions have spread throughout the northern Democratic Republic of the Congo, making this group one of the most artistically influential societies in central Africa. Mangbetu are known for their decorated harps, trumpets, knives, pots, and boxes—many of which bear elongated head sculptures.

TUTSI AND HUTU

ALONG WITH THE Hutu and the Twa (Pygmies), the Tutsi people—sometimes called Watutsi—occupy the nations of Rwanda and Burundi. While the Hutu and the Tutsi have lived side by side for several centuries, their relationship has been marked by hostility and occasional outbreaks of intense violence. The 1.5 million Tutsi, a minority in both countries, have long ruled the Hutu, who now number approximately 9.5 million. The Twa constitute only about one percent of the total population of Rwanda and Burundi.

Even though the Tutsi and Hutu groups intermarry and thus blend their physical features, the Tutsi generally remain taller and thinner than the Hutu; they also maintain cultural boundaries. In both Rwanda and Burundi, the Tutsi and the Hutu speak different dialects of the same Bantu language—Kinyarwanda in Rwanda and Kirundi in Burundi.

The Tutsi, who have traditionally been cattle herders, began as early as the 15th century to incorporate the Twa hunter-gatherers and the Hutu farmers into their society as subordinates. They established a complex and hierarchical political system headed by a king, or *mwami,* who was considered to be a divine figure. Even the German and Belgian colonists who took control of the area in the 19th and early 20th centuries called the Tutsi "lords" and the Hutu "vassals."

Anthropologists have often described the former kingdom of Rwanda as having a caste system, and some scholars marveled at how Tutsi leaders kept communities from fragmenting. The integration of the two peoples into a single social system was achieved primarily through a patron-client relationship. Since cattle were the key to social power and prestige, the dominant Tutsi needed to retain control over the distribution of their livestock, and they achieved this through a process called *ubuhake.* A Tutsi cattle owner or patron permitted his less well-off client—a Hutu or perhaps another Tutsi—to use his cattle in return for the client's labor and cultivated goods. As a result of this system, most Hutu and Tutsi families, including their extended families, have long been linked in some way.

During the colonial years, the powerful Tutsi received greater access to European resources, including education, and this situation fueled resentment among the Hutu. Following independence in 1962, two separate countries emerged from what had been Ruanda-Urundi, or Belgian East Africa; the Hutu seized power, and some of the worst violence of the 20th century ensued. Military campaigns on both sides resulted in the deaths of thousands.

In 1994, civil war erupted after Rwanda's Hutu president, Juvénal Habyarimana, was killed; the conflict left thousands dead and created one of the largest groups of refugees in the history of the African continent. The Tutsi took back power in Rwanda, and the country then became enmeshed in the complex politics of the civil war in neighboring Zaire (now the Democratic Republic of the Congo). Many Hutu and Tutsi have stood trial before the United Nations for crimes of genocide.

EAST AFRICA
AMHARA • BETA ISRAEL • KIKUYU • MALAGASY
• MASAI • SOMALI • SWAHILI

AMHARA

MORE THAN 12 million Amhara live in the highlands of Ethiopia. For most of their history these people have been farmers and part-time pastoralists, but they have also been the most powerful ethnic group in Ethiopia. Amhara kings fought for power in Ethiopia throughout the 18th and 19th centuries, and in 1889 Menelik II declared himself emperor of an area that was about the same size as today's country. Except for its 1935-to-1941 occupation by Italy, when Emperor Haile Selassie (1892-1975) was forced into exile, Ethiopia was the only African nation to escape European domination in the 20th century.

Like many other residents of the highlands, the Amhara maintain religious traditions that derived from extensive and early contacts between Ethiopia and the Near East. Some groups follow Islam, but perhaps the most distinctive aspect of Amhara religion is Coptic Christianity, which had been widely practiced in Egypt until the Arab conquest in the seventh century A.D. The Ethiopian Orthodox Church would eventually emerge from early Greek and Coptic influences.

According to linguists, the Amharic language is from the Afro-Asiatic group of languages spoken mostly in parts of Mediterranean Africa; these tongues are also spoken by certain peoples of West and central Africa, as well as small numbers in the Horn of Africa. Some linguists suggest that Amharic is most closely related to Hebrew.

The Amhara economy is based primarily on cultivation of maize, wheat, sorghum, and a cereal grass called teff. In the past, land ownership was bestowed as a gift from the emperor in return for loyalty and military service, and new landowners would then become patrons to client farmers.

Throughout history, the social organization of the Amhara kingdom has been patriarchal, with women having little authority or potential to own much property. To some extent, the status of a woman is tied to the kind of marriage she has. The most common form of marriage, called *serat*, is a civil union not bound by religious restrictions. In such a union, a woman is more likely to be able to seek divorce or to air a dispute with the help of a mediator; she may also claim part of her husband's wealth if they divorce. A smaller number of people marry in the Ethiopian Church, a process called *qurban*, and this kind of marriage cannot be dissolved even if a partner is an Ethiopian priest. Finally, the form of marriage in which women have the lowest status is called *damoz*; it occurs often, despite being illegal in Ethiopia. In this arrangement, women are paid to become short-term wives or sexual partners, sometimes for just a few weeks.

In the 20th century, the Amhara expanded militarily and became the political elite of Ethiopia. People who did not speak Amharic—the language of the elite—were soon at a severe disadvantage in everyday life and before the law. By the middle of the century, after Amharic had become the national language, neighboring groups declared they would no longer be dominated by the Amhara. One of the central forces behind the rebellion was the growth of Oromo nationalism; although the Oromo have far greater numbers, they were long subordinate to the Amhara. The country continues to struggle for the national integration of its different ethnic groups, and in this respect Ethiopia shares much with the rest of sub-Saharan Africa.

BETA ISRAEL (Falasha)

OUTSIDERS HAVE OFTEN referred to the African Jews of Ethiopia as Falasha, meaning "moved" or "gone into exile" in the ancient Ge'ez language. Today, the community considers the word derogatory and prefers Beta Israel, a Hebrew term for "House of Israel." For millennia, this ethnic group from northwestern Ethiopia has practiced a form of Judaism, but now only a few thousand of its people remain in Africa, where they are concentrated in Addis Ababa, Ethiopia's capital city. Since the 1980s, most Beta Israel have migrated to Israel—many in a series of airlifts dubbed Operation Moses—and more than 60,000 currently reside there.

Although the origins of Judaism in Ethiopia remain a mystery, it is likely that the community's roots go back 2,500 years. Until relatively recent times, the Beta Israel were cut off from the rest of the Jewish world. This isolation left them unaware of the presence of other Jews and without access to important Jewish scripture, such as the Talmud. Furthermore, most Ethiopian Jews had no idea that many other Jews

were white. Despite this situation, the Beta Israel have always considered themselves to be exiles from the land of Israel, followers of Moses, and one of the lost tribes. Some trace the group's history to the biblical parting of the Red Sea, claiming that the Jews of Ethiopia were those who did not cross before the waters returned and so had to escape from Egypt by heading south.

Some scholars have suggested that the Beta Israel descend from a people who spoke Agaw, a Cushitic language, and were converted roughly 2,000 years ago by Jews from southern Arabia (present-day Yemen). In the second century A.D., the Ethiopian kingdom of Aksum arose, and when it adopted Christianity as its official religion in the fourth century, the Beta Israel were forced to relocate to the mountainous region around Lake Tana. During the 13th century, the people numbered in the hundreds of thousands and ruled a powerful state in what is today Ethiopia. But beginning around 1400, the Solomonic Dynasty of Ethiopia gradually subdued the Beta Israel. In the 17th century, the Ethiopian emperor finally defeated the Jewish state and seized the people's lands. Most Beta Israel eventually gave up their Agaw language and adopted the Tigrinya or Amharic language of their neighbors.

The religious life of the Beta Israel is based on the Torah (the Bible's first five books), on oral interpretations of the Torah as passed down from generation to generation, and on the community's own holy writings. Members of the community strictly adhere to the kosher diet, observe the Saturday Sabbath as a day of rest, and celebrate all the festivals mentioned in the Torah, as well as those of their own tradition. The timing of holidays is determined by a religious lunar calendar used only by the Beta Israel.

For century upon century, the Ethiopian Jews have grouped their Sabbaths into seven-week cycles. The seventh Sabbath, called Legata Sanbat, is considered particularly holy and includes special prayers, festivities, and a sanctification service; at this time, priests may have their sins absolved completely. A traditional priesthood, the Kohanim, leads the community's religious life, and its importance as the repository of the group's traditions has increased during the upheavals of the past century.

KIKUYU

LARGEST ETHNIC GROUP in Kenya, the Kikuyu number about five million and live throughout modern Kenya and in parts of Tanzania and Uganda. The earliest Kikuyu arrived in what is now Kenya during the massive Bantu migrations of A.D. 1200 to 1600, and over the years this ethnic group has played an important and very visible role in the country's politics.

Kikuyu legend holds that a man named Gikuyu was the group's founder. He and his wife had nine daughters who eventually married, had their own families, and retained a dominant role in Kikuyu society—a story that helps explain the Kikuyu's nine family groupings. In fact, there are ten clans, but because the number ten is taboo, the usual practice is to count nine clans (plus one).

The Kikuyu were mainly farmers during the period of English colonization, but as the city of Nairobi grew under British rule, Kikuyu migrants made their way there. Many of the migrants had been educated at mission schools and had held municipal jobs that gave them unique exposure to colonial abuses. As a consequence, the city's Kikuyu began to organize politically in the 1920s; by the 1950s, the Kikuyu protest had solidified into a nationalist movement involving all ethnic groups. The government declared a state of emergency during the Mau Mau rebellion, arresting approximately 15,000 Africans in Nairobi, many of them Kikuyu, and sending them to detention camps. With Kenyan independence in December 1963, Nairobi became the national capital, and Jomo Kenyatta, a Kikuyu, soon became the first president of the Republic of Kenya.

The British once banned the Kikuyu language, often known as Gikuyu, but today many schools teach it to children, following a policy of teaching the local language first, then Swahili and English. With respect to their children, many Kikuyu continue to name them after important family members, alternating between families of the father and the mother. All Kikuyu recognize a supreme deity called Ngai, who habitually dwells invisibly in the sky but periodically manifests himself within an enormous cloud on Mount Kenya. When the people see clouds on the mountaintop, they know that Ngai is present.

MALAGASY

THE TERM "MALAGASY" denotes the language and identity of a complex and diverse group of people who live on Madagascar, the fourth largest island in the world. As many as 20 different ethnic groups—including the Merina, Betsimisaraka, Betsileo, Sakalava, and Antandroy—occupy the island. But while their 14 million members claim particular cultural affiliations, these people tend to also say they are Malagasy and to speak Malagasy, the national language. Despite their many differences, most Malagasy communities have similar religious beliefs, bilateral kinship systems, and irrigated rice-farming economies. Perhaps the most salient ethnic division is not between particular groups but between the central highlands people, mainly of Indonesian descent, and the coastal people of black African descent; today, these two regions are engaged in a fierce political, social, and economic competition.

Although Madagascar's native inhabitants are known to be descendants of people who *(Continued on page 222)*

A wedding in Africa may call for the ritual seclusion of the bride. Confined to her mother's house, this recently circumcised Masai woman and her best friend will miss most of the celebration associated with the sacred event.
FOLLOWING PAGES: Six species of the distinctive baobab tree grow on Madagascar. For the island's Malagasy people, the baobab's gourdlike fruit provides a good source of concentrated vitamin C.
PAGES 220-21: Despite massive migrations to urban centers such as Nairobi, Kenya, many Kikuyu women continue to work on large farms, like this tea plantation hugging the fertile slopes of Mount Kenya.

In Madagascar, a market's offerings include bread, bananas, and baskets of rice. The amount and variety of food available in an African market give a good indication of the richness and diversity of the local cuisine.

came from islands off the coast of eastern Africa or from the Indonesian archipelago, the specific migrations that led to the current population have not yet been precisely identified by scholars. The Malagasy language, which shares many linguistic features with Indonesian tongues, is classified by scientists as either Malayo-Polynesian or Austronesian. French, the language of colonists who occupied Madagascar and its close neighbor Mauritius, is a secondary national language spoken by about a quarter of the population—mainly city and town dwellers.

Like other Malagasy, the large Merina ethnic group divides its society into elites, commoners, and descendants of slaves. For the most part, people of higher status are wealthier and more influential than people of lower status. This social hierarchy is evident not only in politics, where the elites hold the most power, but also in such small-scale activities as eating the evening meal; the people eating last are the youngest family members and more distant relatives from commoner or slave kinship groups. Although the French abolished slavery on the islands of southern Africa in 1897, the Malagasy people retain extensive genealogical memories of slave ancestry. Still, even though their kinship systems have hierarchies based on lineages of varying status, there is some freedom in kinship affiliation. People can choose to reckon descent through either the father or the mother's brother, a process that occasionally becomes confusing. Many people descend from different Malagasy ethnic groups, as well as from Indians, Chinese, Arabs, and other non-Malagasy Africans.

Perhaps the culture's most distinctive aspect—the one that has stimulated the most anthropological research—is the burial tomb. The Malagasy take great care to protect and honor the dead because they, like many other African peoples, believe ancestors continue to influence everyday life. Often they build elaborate wood, stone, or concrete tombs that remain partly above the ground. Relatives can thus enter a tomb to adorn it or to offer sacrifices and prayers. They may also practice what anthropologists sometimes call secondary funerals: Certain Malagasy groups in central Madagascar will place a deceased relative in a tomb, then remove the body a short time later either for reburial in a larger tomb or to change the way the body had been wrapped and positioned. The Malagasy believe that failure to properly care for the dead during and after burial can harm the living.

MASAI

THE MORE THAN 200,000 Masai, pastoralists living near the Rift Valley of Kenya and Tanzania, are among the most easily recognizable people in East Africa. Tall, with dark skin, Masai men wear colorful toga-like garments and jewelry, and they often carry spears as symbols of their manhood. Very few of them escape the attention of the annual swarms of tourists in East Africa. Nevertheless, the people appear to have profited little from the safari business that goes on all around them. Some marketing efforts include photographs of Masai in native costumes and even offer visits to their households.

Unlike most African pastoralists, who rely on crops as well as animals, the Masai do not practice agriculture. They depend on cattle for subsistence, consuming the milk, blood, and meat of their animals. The Masai are one of the few African societies who struggle, usually with success, to practice pastoralism exclusively, even in the context of East Africa's extensive tourist industry. Often moving their cattle to available grasslands and water, they see themselves ideally as nomadic; however, in the 1970s they began privatizing herds into ranches, a process that has increased inequality among the people.

Each Masai settlement contains a cattle enclosure and homesteads consisting of houses made of mud and wood. Some of the residences are occupied by youths, others by warriors, and still others by elders. Among the more distinctive aspects of Masai society is the age-set kinship system, which defines relations among men and also between men and women. Age sets are groups of people born into the same generation. Members share the same life events, such as circumcision and marriage, and remain in the same groups for life. The age sets group men into three main categories—uncircumcised, circumcised, and elders—and these are divided into smaller categories having to do with property ownership, marriage, parentage, and so on. In Masai society, elders have great power, for they make most of the important decisions regarding the physical layout of villages; the production, sale, and distribution of livestock; and marriage choices. Women, by comparison, are grouped into only two categories: circumcised and uncircumcised.

The Masai of different territories employ numerous rituals to initiate men and women into age sets, but all of the rites involve recognition of changing status. In some areas, rituals incorporating a man into the set of elders may take up to 15 years to complete. They involve various sacrifices of oxen and the consuming of certain foods. One ceremony, called *e unoto*, is held years after the last member of an age set has been circumcised; it is intended to signal passage into the stage of true adulthood. Preceding e unoto is the "ox of the earplugs" ritual in which adult men and their mothers accuse each other of incest, then slaughter oxen that the men feed to their mothers as a sign they now can care for them. At this time, men still wear their hair in braids, but at the close of e unoto they cut their hair to signal their new status.

SOMALI

EAST AFRICA'S entire Horn area is home to the Somali people, the majority of which live in the country of Somalia and in the breakaway nation known as Somaliland. In 1991, after escalating civil conflict, northwestern Somalia declared independence and became Somaliland, but it still awaits diplomatic recognition from the international community. Somali are the principal inhabitants of the Ogadēn region of southeastern Ethiopia; they can also be found in Djibouti and in northeastern Kenya.

According to archaeological and historical evidence, Somali have been living in the Horn of Africa for nearly 3,000 years. In some local genealogical accounts, certain Somali clans have been traced to the Arabian Peninsula and associated with the Sharifs, the family of the Prophet Muhammad. But linguistic, cultural, and historical evidence indicates the Somali came originally from the southern highlands of what is now Ethiopia and are a Cushite people with ties to a broad range of Cushite ethnic groups. Part of an ancient region known as Nubia, Cush gave rise to a group of languages that eventually defined numerous peoples in northern and northeastern Africa; the Somali tongue is a member of the Eastern Cushite language family.

Claims to an Arab origin may arise not only from trade relationships and marriage alliances with Arab colonies on the Somali coast but also from a desire for stronger ties to the heart of Islam. The Somali people had accepted Islam by the 1400s, and according to some historians they may have done so as early as the 1100s. In recent years, the Borana's "Ayaana" possession religion, emphasizing fertility, has been growing among the Somali. At the same time, Islamic fundamentalism has been gaining ground over the traditional Sufi mystical orders.

As with many African groups, the Somali people were never a unified or corporate political body before the arrival of various European powers. Instead of establishing a political system that encompassed all the people, they relied on clan federations that provided a broad, loose identity. These were traditionally nomadic, even though they maintained boundaries for the herding area of each clan and subclan. Somali clans did resist invasions into recognized settlements and herding areas; however, actual borders were somewhat vague, and military clashes were common among the clans themselves. During the colonial era, the British, French, and Italians established territories, or Somalilands, roughly following the geographical areas of the clan federations. Britain and Italy, in 1960, combined their territories into a unified, independent nation known as the Somali Democratic Republic. The French territory remained separate and in 1977 gained independence under the name Djibouti.

As a nomadic, pastoral people, the Somali center their economic culture around camels, with a few cattle, goats, and sheep raised in the more fertile areas. The women and young children care for sheep and goats while the young men and boys are responsible for herding the highly esteemed camels. In a land where rainfall averages less than four inches a year, Somali lives are consumed with finding water and grazing land for their livestock. The diet once consisted almost entirely of cow's milk and milk products, but for most people it now includes maize meal and rice.

SWAHILI

ALTHOUGH THE WORD "Swahili" usually refers to an East African lingua franca, it is also the name for a large mercantile civilization on the East African coast and on islands such as Zanzibar and Lamu. The word is widely thought to have come from the Arabic *sawahil*, meaning "coast," thus making the Swahili the "people of the coast."

Descendants of Arab and Persian traders who, over the years, intermarried with East Africans, the Swahili are merchants with a long history as brokers between East Africa and Middle Eastern, European, and central African countries. They also frequently served as middlemen between Africa and Asia during the slave trade. Today, the extensive interaction between Africans and Arabs is reflected in the art and architecture: Because Swahili art is Islamic art, the human body is never depicted. Instead, the people create elaborate carvings or paint intricate designs, and these can be seen decorating doors, chests, furniture, house walls, and even boats known as dhows.

The Swahili language—the national language of both Tanzania and Kenya—is a mixture of Bantu grammar and Arabic vocabulary. As evidence of the Swahili's success as long-distance traders, variants of the language are spoken today throughout Uganda, Rwanda, Burundi, and the eastern portion of the Democratic Republic of the Congo. There is also an extensive literature in Swahili, dating back to the mid-17th century.

About 500,000 Swahili live on East Africa's coast and nearby islands, but some Swahili traders live on islands as far south as Mozambique and as far north as Somalia. Because the Swahili are spread out over such a large area, they have significant ethnic or cultural differences, with many groups claiming different origins. Moreover, while the Swahili consider themselves a unique civilization, they are almost always integrated politically and socially into other ethnic communities. Even so, the people who consider themselves to be Swahili do share many beliefs, traditions, and attributes. Most of them are Muslim. They are wealthier, in general, than many of their African neighbors, residing in stone houses with the distinctive, carved wooden doors that are markers of wealth. The people eat Swahili cuisine, wear Swahili styles, and use a Swahili system of naming.

Both men and women place a high value on a good physical appearance, which they believe can symbolize inner purity. Swahili men wear amulets that contain Koranic verses. Women, who use the reddish dye henna to create intricate designs on their hands, also adorn their bodies with jewelry, cosmetics, interesting hairstyles, and various aromatics.

SOUTHERN AFRICA
AFRIKANERS • SAN • SHONA • TSWANA • ZULU

AFRIKANERS

IN 1652, DUTCH farmers arrived at the Cape of Good Hope near the southern tip of Africa. They initially called themselves Boers, literally "peasant" or "farmer" in Dutch, but in time they developed a distinctive South African identity and a Dutch dialect with many loanwords from English and local African languages. They began to see themselves as Africans, or Afrikaners, the term used today by their Afrikaans-speaking descendants.

The history of the Afrikaners is both heroic and tragic. On the one hand, their struggle for religious and economic freedom in a sometimes inhospitable land illustrates their bravery and endurance. On the other hand, the struggle entailed countless violent clashes with native Africans who had been dispossessed of their lands after the Boer arrival. The expansion of the Boers in South Africa was motivated in part by a deep-seated religious conviction that Africans, or Kaffirs—Afrikaans for "heathen"—were descended from the biblical Ham and created by God to serve whites. Today,

approximately three million Afrikaners live in South Africa, which has a total population of about forty million.

Working for the Dutch East India Company, the settlers of 1652 set up a trading post on the southwest coast of South Africa. But soon the company released many of the increasing number of workers to settle the land, grow food for its fleets, and expand eastward. In 1795, the Dutch East India Company ended its rule of the Cape colony, and the Boers found themselves in direct opposition to the British.

The British colonized all of the Cape settlements, outlawed slavery, and gave native black Africans many civil rights previously denied them by the Boers. In 1835, feeling threatened by both Africans and the British, the Boers began their Great Trek into the Transvaal, where gold and diamonds would eventually be found. Neither the Boers (they called themselves Voortrekkers) nor any of the local African societies they encountered along the way would ever be the same. From that point on, the history of native South Africans would be inextricably tied to the history of white expansion.

In 1899, President Paul Kruger of the South African Republic declared war on the British, who wanted to stop the rise of Afrikaner power and get control of the gold. Thus began the Boer War, a bloody conflict won by the British in 1902. The victors would maintain control of South African politics until 1948, when Afrikaners won the legislature on a nationalist platform that advocated increased segregation between blacks and whites. During the Boer War, many Afrikaners had lost their land and become impoverished; they had also been forced to travel from their farms to the cities, where they often competed with black South Africans for employment.

Once in control, the Afrikaner government designed a system of apartheid, or separateness, which divided the people racially, geographically, socially, economically, and politically. The people were grouped into four categories: White, Bantu (all-black Africans), Colored (people of mixed race), and Asian (Indians and Pakistanis); all were separate and unequal. Beginning in the early 1990s, South Africans began to dismantle the apartheid system, but the legacy of differential access to economic and political resources remains. Many white South Africans, especially those descended from Boers, have continued to farm.

Today, the ethnic identity of Afrikaners is characterized by the Afrikaans language; membership in the Dutch Reformed Church; the celebration of holidays remembering early historical struggles; and contemporary class and political relations within South Africa, particularly with non-Afrikaner whites. Afrikaner identity continues to be defined by a long-standing, ambivalent relationship with South Africans of British descent. Over time, stereotypes have developed: Afrikaners see themselves as nationalist whites who are poor, rural, and Christian; they view non-Afrikaners as social liberals who are wealthy, urban, and Jewish.

While proud of their European heritage, Afrikaners (above) see themselves as Africans. In South Africa, identity remains a highly contested matter.

FOLLOWING PAGES:
Seasonal changes such as floods and droughts often affect the lives and economies of African peoples. Here a woman carries her child across Botswana's swollen Okavango River.

PAGES 228-29: An enduring tradition in many African societies, masking hides the faces of lawmakers, judges, and otherwise recognizable people who at times must conceal their identities. Images on the masks may represent ancestors or spirits.

Contrary to popular belief, African women often act as family breadwinners. Many, such as this group carrying woven fishing traps used in the Okavango River, not only fish and hunt but also control their local markets.

SAN (Bushmen)

AFTER THE PYGMIES of central Africa, the San-speaking peoples of southern Africa are the most well-known hunter-gatherers in the world. Often referred to collectively and pejoratively as "Bushmen," they call themselves the Zhun/twasi: "the real people." They live in small camps composed of loosely organized kinship groups with no formal system of leadership.

The San name applies to a large group of people who have been living in remote desert regions of Botswana, Namibia, and Angola for perhaps thousands of years, but they are nonetheless ethnically and, to some extent, linguistically diverse. The San in the western Kalahari, for example, have a very different history from people in the desert's eastern part. Some San have lived closely with Bantu pastoralists for several hundred years and were much affected by the wars and population movements that followed the rise of the Zulu empire in the early 1800s; other San have remained relatively isolated from other ethnic groups.

In the European and American media, the San have been depicted as living in total isolation, or as they might have lived long before the advent of agriculture 10,000 years ago. Such commercially successful films as *The Gods Must be Crazy* have perpetuated the false image of these people as living fossils. In fact, the San have interacted with neighboring societies for hundreds of years, and archaeological evidence strongly suggests they were engaging in regional trade as far back as A.D. 500. Today, the San maintain relationships with cattle herders such as the Herero and the Tswana. They pay taxes and have even served in the South African and Namibian armies, despite the fact that the South African government has resettled San-speaking peoples on a number of occasions.

Compared with their neighbors, the San are a peaceful and egalitarian society in which sharing is highly valued but private property and individualism are disdained. They are known for their skills as hunters of small mammals, and they occasionally can bring down an elephant or a giraffe by using poisoned arrows. Once the arrow finds its mark, the hunter follows the wounded animal, sometimes for several days, until it collapses. This is one reason why the San have been enlisted by military forces as trackers. In a remarkably inhospitable environment, the people can collect enough food and water to survive. But they must travel often to find resources, and sometimes the only available water is what they can squeeze out of deep roots.

The San also have a rich medical knowledge that they have incorporated into a series of rituals. During the medicine trance rituals, audiences dance and clap, and ill people who have come to be cured watch as healers go into a trance state. The healers may administer medicines, derived from local plants or roots, and touch the patients to draw the sickness out of them and into their own bodies.

SHONA

LIKE MANY AFRICAN ethnic groups, the Shona are actually a collection of peoples speaking such mutually intelligible languages as Korekore, Ndau, and Karanga. The Shona language itself—among the most widely spoken tongues in southern Africa—is in the Bantu family. About nine million Shona live in Zimbabwe and southern Mozambique, the majority of them residing in Zimbabwe.

Many contemporary archaeologists believe that Great Zimbabwe, the ruins of which make up one of Africa's most formidable archaeological sites, was built by Shona ancestors. The rich artistic tradition of these people has continued into the 21st century, with intricate wooden headrests perhaps their best known creations.

The Shona are primarily an agricultural group. Maize is their main crop, but the people grow millet, sorghum, rice, peanuts, and a variety of tubers, too. They also raise cattle, sheep, and chickens; the cattle work, though, is taboo for women and therefore done exclusively by men. Women may supplement their income by selling pottery and hand-woven baskets that serve primarily as utilitarian objects.

In their traditional political organization, Shona people still live mostly in villages that typically accommodate one or more interrelated families and consist of clustered mud-and-wattle huts, granaries, and common cattle kraals. Although villages have often been quite distant from each other, they were once part of central states with hereditary kings who made large-scale decisions for the territory, such as waging war. These policies were financed by substantial tributes from the surrounding settlements. Local decision-making was left to elders residing within each village, a policy that has been changed somewhat because of centralized decision-making in the nation-states where today's Shona live.

In Shona traditional religion, a major role is played by the *vadzimu,* or ancestor spirits. They represent the essence of the Shona way of life and embody the ideals and values of greatest importance, such as preserving and maintaining harmonious social networks. Vadzimu may be recently departed ancestors or heroes from the past. They will offer protection if it is merited, but they will disappear if Shona values are not upheld.

TSWANA

THE TSWANA PEOPLE constitute most of the population in Botswana—"land of the Tswana." Twice as many, however, are in northeastern South Africa, where they inhabit what was known as Bophuthatswana—"the place of gathering of the Tswana"—during the time of apartheid. Tswana also live in neighboring Namibia and Zimbabwe.

A southern Bantu people, the Tswana are closely related to the Sotho of Lesotho and South Africa. Both groups speak mutually intelligible languages, have agricultural economies, share certain customs, and trace their descent from a common ancestor known as Mogale. The meaning of "Tswana," essentially an invention of European colonists who encountered the group, is not known, but the name is believed to derive from a Xhosa word. The people themselves have no common name; instead, they use the various names of their eight constituent subgroups.

During the second half of the 19th century, the Ngwato subgroup's Chief Khama III converted to Christianity while still a boy. He attended a missionary school and recognized the growing European interest in the area. By the 1880s, most Tswana were at least nominal Christians.

Traditionally, the Tswana have included ancestors along with the living as members of their society; they call the ancestor spirits dwelling among them and possessing metaphysical powers the *Badimo.* But European settlers did not understand the powerful role of social networks among the Tswana, including their ongoing relationships with ancestors. Having Victorian notions of privacy and individualism, the Europeans did not comprehend the subtlety of Tswana life, where prestige and power are gained by obtaining followers and allies. In this way of life, a person is nothing if he is not part of a larger group. Through a highly developed system of clientage, men gained rights over others in Tswana society, a connection that was once known as "eating" another.

Since gaining independence from Britain in 1966, the Tswana of Botswana have maintained a stable, democratic government, one of the few African peoples to do so.

ZULU

PERHAPS BEST KNOWN for having one of the most powerful state and military organizations in 19th-century Africa, the Zulu remain a vital political and cultural force in present-day South Africa.

Under Shaka (circa 1787-1828), its founder, the Zulu empire became the most dominating polity in sub-Saharan Africa. Shaka's military actions led to political consolidation elsewhere, with new kingdoms arising and, in the process, stimulating large population movements into frontier territories. But behind the florescence of the Zulu and other African kingdoms, such as the Swazi and Sotho, were oppression and the ejection of many people from their homelands. And the political intrigue in some societies rivaled the best fictional thrillers: Shaka, for example, was assassinated by his half-brother Dingane, who was deposed within 12 years by Mpande, another brother.

Though dominant over other African societies, the Zulu eventually found themselves in conflict with the Boers, Dutch colonists who escaped British oppression in western Cape Colony by trekking east to occupy Zululand. Dingane agreed to let the Boers into Zululand in early 1838 but then changed his mind and sent his men to murder dozens of men, women, and children. On December 16, 1838, the Boers retaliated against Dingane in a fight so bloody it became known as the Battle of Blood River. Thousands of Zulu were killed while not a single Boer soldier died.

The Zulu nation has long been defined as several hundred clans held together by their loyalty to the king, who owned all land. Men demonstrated their allegiance by fighting for the king's regiments and chiefs; in the time of

Shaka, a man was called *isihlangu senkosi,* meaning "the war-shield of the king." Today, the Zulu remain a stratified society that values political power. Indeed, the Zulu chief has played an important role in South African national politics and civil rights.

Now numbering more than three million, the Zulu generally live in the Natal region of eastern South Africa and speak a language that contains the clicking sounds common to Bantu languages in South Africa, Swaziland, Botswana, and Lesotho. Many contemporary Zulu live in cities or near the gold mines where they work, but a large number live in the countryside, herding cattle and growing corn and other vegetables. They are well known in Africa for their artistic beadwork, basketry, and circular houses.

Zulu men and women are easily recognized by their distinctive traditional dress. Men tie a beaded belt over a goatskin apron and wear certain clothing for rituals and other special occasions. When a man wears a red-and-white cloth, for example, he is letting people know he is courting a young woman. Because the Zulu identify themselves as a warrior people, rituals often call for men to carry cowhide shields with small vertical slits running through the middle; various shields and spear designs distinguish different regiments. Zulu women make elaborate and multicolored beaded necklaces, with colors representing different ideas; blue, for example, means fidelity, and white means purity.

Zulu society is patrilineal. Descent is thus reckoned through the male line, and after marriage women almost always travel to the homes of their husbands, where they will then dwell. Marriages continue to be conducted with the exchange of *lobola,* or bridewealth—goods given by the groom's kin to the bride's kin. Although cattle are preferred, money and other goods are being given more and more. On the surface, the practice appears to be a sort of bride "purchase," but like other societies that have bridewealth customs, the Zulu consider it more of an entitlement to domestic and sexual rights. Bridewealth also makes the marriage legal, and so women are able to hold their husbands responsible for their actions.

Believing in a single creator called Nkulunkulu (in-GOO-loon-koo-loo), the Zulu look to a spiritual world inhabited by ancestors who intervene in everyday life. These ancestors are known as shades and appear in dreams, omens, and other phenomena. They are not considered distant from the living, and they may even be called the living dead. Many Zulu are Christian, but many follow the faith first revealed by Isaiah Shembe, a Zulu prophet who brought Christian and Zulu beliefs and practices together in a religion he called Zionism.

In a land of great visual and historical contrasts, these Zulu men of South Africa may live and work in cities and wear Western-style clothing, but on ritual occasions they don the garb of their 19th-century warrior ancestors.

THE HISTORY AND CULTURES of North Africa have long been influenced by those of the Middle East, a region rich in ethnic groups and ancient traditions. Encompassing the Near Eastern civilizations of antiquity, the Middle East was also the birthplace of Judaism, Christianity, and Islam, all of which trace their roots to the biblical Abraham. Today, religion remains a key defining factor for ethnicity, more so even than language, region of origin, or class; still, religious differences between groups are often diminished by a shared past and similar traditions.

Around 8,000 to 10,000 years ago, the Tigris and Euphrates Rivers in Mesopotamia and the Nile in Egypt gave rise to the world's earliest agriculture. Cultivation of crops in turn helped lead to the first civilizations, in Sumeria and Egypt. But despite the presence of these major rivers and a few other fertile areas, much of the Middle East and North Africa is arid, with some of the most hostile deserts in the world. Nomadic herding has been the means of subsistence for generations, and human life has centered around oases scattered through the deserts. On the Arabian Peninsula, domestication of the camel between 3000 and 1000 B.C. offered a way to travel in these otherwise inhospitable lands, opening new routes for trade and expansion across the peninsula and the Sahara.

NORTH AFRICA AND THE MIDDLE EAST

In Morocco a potential bride attends an annual festival where marriageable Berber women meet would-be grooms.

Four major cultural groups with ancient roots still predominate in the Middle East: Arabs, Turks, Persians, and Jews. While Turks, Persians, and Jews are dominant in Turkey, Iran, and Israel, respectively, Arabs are spread throughout the region and all across North Africa. The word "Arab" comes from the Semitic-speaking A'raab people, who by 900 to 800 B.C. had established trade and pastoral networks between Syria and the Arabian Peninsula. They are related to speakers of such other Semitic languages as Hebrew and Aramaic. Over time, some Arab groups became sedentary, while others continued as nomads. The settled Arabs called the nomadic Arabs "Bedu," from which the word "Bedouin" comes. Today, Arabs are quite diverse, with their own cultural differences, but they continue to be unified by a common language—Arabic—spoken in many dialects from Morocco into East Africa, throughout the eastern Mediterranean, and into the Persian Gulf region.

Because Bedouin were the ancestors of modern Arabs, these people are regarded by other Arabs as true and original representatives of their culture and language. Even in the 21st century, a few Bedouin continue to travel the deserts of the Arabian Peninsula, Egypt, and Libya by camel, living in tents and tending their herds as they have for centuries. But pressures from modern governments and the relatively recent phenomenon of national boundaries are making huge incursions into the Bedouin's nomadic way of life, and at most only 10 percent of them remain nomads.

Arabic and Hebrew are Semitic languages spoken by Arabs and Jews. Although these two groups share common religious roots, relations between them have been strained to the point of war on a number of occasions since the mid-20th century, when the state of Israel was created as a Jewish nation by the partitioning of Palestine. Today, Israel's population is roughly 80 percent Jewish, while Islam is the major religion of most other Middle Eastern and North African nations. Islam itself is split into two sects, the Sunnis and Shiites, each of which holds different beliefs concerning the successor to Muhammad, the Prophet of Islam. Most Shiites reside in Iran and southern Iraq, while Sunnis predominate in the rest of the region.

Ancient traditions straining against modern trends introduced from the West have created friction between cultures in recent decades, resulting in the pan-Islamic movement that has swept the region; a return to orthodox practices has also been occurring in Israel. As more people have chosen to follow traditional religious customs and centuries-old habits, and as ethnic and religious pride has swelled, tensions have grown between different ethnic and religious groups. Still, common customs unite the various peoples in their day-to-day lives, even down to the foods they eat. Central Asian and Mediterranean influences flavor the cuisine, and bread—flat or in loaves—is a staple so important that in Egypt it is called *aish*, "life" in Arabic. Rice dishes with herbs, beans, fruits, or nuts abound everywhere, except in North Africa, where couscous takes the place of rice. Yogurt salads and kebabs made of lamb, beef, or chicken are widely eaten, as are lamb or chicken stews with vegetables or fruits. And meze, a plate of appetizers featuring eggplant, bean dips, olives, and pickles, often starts a meal in the countries of the eastern Mediterranean. Rice pudding, halvah (a sesame-based confection), deep-fried honey-soaked pastries, or European-style pastries frequently bring a meal to its end.

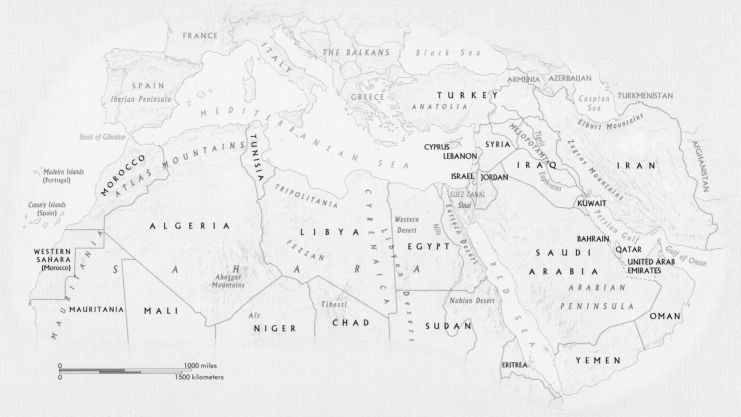

Some customs have to do with rites of passage. For example, most groups bury their recently deceased loved ones within specified periods of time; they also observe prescribed periods of mourning. Marriage, too, follows shared customs. Though "love matches" are becoming more prevalent, arranged marriages occur among all religious communities, with a first-cousin marriage traditionally deemed an ideal match. In either case, whole families are involved in the negotiations concerning bride price (the amount of money the groom should give the bride's family); the marriage contract; the time of the marriage; and the future residence of the couple, traditionally the family home of the groom. Marriages are celebrated for several days, even a week, by Jews, Christians, and Muslims. Among Arab Muslims and Coptic Christians in Egypt, the bride and women from both sides of the family come together for a day or more to decorate their hands and feet with geometric and floral henna designs. These gatherings allow women to become better acquainted before the marriage.

Among adherents of all three Abrahamic religions, women are expected to dress modestly. In Saudi Arabia and Iran, veiling is mandatory but with a wide range of interpretation. A Muslim woman in Saudi Arabia must be completely covered, including her face, hands, and feet. In Iran, a scarf covering the hair and a loose coat are deemed sufficient. Most Christians and Jews in the Middle East wear Western-style clothing, though Orthodox Jewish women also cover their hair and wear long dresses.

In an area of the world where invasions and political uncertainty have been consistent realities, such long-cherished traditions and the ethnic identities that engender them offer constancy and comfort in the face of change. Commonly held customs help to keep communities intact from one generation to the next.

237

Following Pages: Her hands and arms adorned with elaborate but temporary henna designs, a bejeweled Omani bride follows the tradition of *lailat al henna,* celebrating with her female friends and relatives on the night before the wedding.

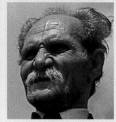

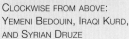

CLOCKWISE FROM ABOVE:
YEMENI BEDOUIN, IRAQI KURD,
AND SYRIAN DRUZE

NORTH AFRICA

THE MIDDLE EAST

NORTH AFRICA
ARABS • BERBERS • COPTS

ARABS

UNTIL THE ADVENT of Islam, Arabs and their culture remained almost entirely on the Arabian Peninsula. But the revelations of God to the Prophet Muhammad, himself an Arab, resulted in a cultural and economic flourishing in seventh-century Arabia. This, in turn, led to a spectacular spreading and mixing of cultures, as Arabs traveled throughout the Middle East, North Africa, and Spain, and into central and southern Asia. The result today is an incredibly diverse culture, where both nomadic Bedouin and long-time urban dwellers call themselves Arabs.

Despite their diversity, Arabs throughout the world share cultural ideas and practices, including a common faith (more than 90 percent are Muslims) and language (Arabic), traditional gender roles, male-oriented inheritance laws, and ritualized ideas of honor, hospitality, and generosity.

Classical Arabic is the sacred language of Muslims, because it is believed to be the language in which God revealed the Koran to Muhammad. Well-educated Arabs and religious scholars speak and read classical Arabic, and its use in radio and television has increased its comprehension among less educated listeners. Every Arab, however, speaks at least one of the many colloquial forms, which may be quite different from one another. Moroccan Arabic, for example, is almost incomprehensible to an Arab of the eastern Mediterranean or the Persian Gulf area. In recent times, movies and television soap operas, often produced in Cairo but widely distributed, have helped familiarize Arabs with other dialects.

As with all Muslims, Arab Muslims are enjoined to make the pilgrimage to Mecca, in Saudi Arabia, before they die. The most important rite of passage next to birth, marriage, and death, the journey is a spiritual and religious event, a return to the birthplace of Muhammad. Muslims believe that if they die on the pilgrimage, they will immediately go to heaven.

The Bedouin, believed to be ancestral to other Arab groups, are considered the culture's purest representatives, although they now make up less than 10 percent of the modern Arab population. Living in Libya, Egypt, Lebanon, Jordan, Syria, Israel, Iraq, and throughout the Arabian Peninsula, they are distinct from other Arabs because of their nomadic, pastoral lifestyle and their more extensive kinship networks, which provide them with community support and the basic necessities for survival. Such networks traditionally served to ensure the safety of families and to protect their property. As contemporary Middle Eastern governments have encouraged the Bedouin to settle, large family networks and the nomadic lifestyle have been diminishing. Nevertheless, the Bedouin continue to be hailed by other Arabs as "ideal" Arabs, especially because of their rich oral poetic tradition, their herding lifestyle, and their traditional code of honor.

While poetry and literature are very important for all Arabs, the Bedouin are masters at oral verse, an emotional and evocative form of poetry that is recited from memory in classical Arabic. These people believe displays of unchecked emotions weaken the group's solidarity, so they use poetry to express such strong feelings as sadness, love, and anger. Among other Arabs, poetry is also a way to convey feelings that might be difficult to express in everyday life.

Another important feature of the Arab world is the honor code, which dictates certain behaviors among family members to preserve a family's reputation and help its members in times of need. For men, honorable behavior means supporting their families economically and defending the reputations of relatives, particularly women. For women, honorable behavior translates into being loving mothers and wives, running efficient and generous households, and acting in modest and respectable ways.

Arab families are very close, and home life is seen as the reward for hard work. While the life of a family remains quite private, Arab hospitality is famous: The people are generally quick to invite strangers to join them for a meal. Their hospitality and generosity are sincerely offered; as a result, friendships are intense, with sincerity and kindness expected in return.

BERBERS

A DIVERSE GROUP some 15 million strong, Berbers comprise the indigenous peoples of northwest Africa. They include the Irifiyen, Imazighen, and Shleuh of Morocco; the Kabyles of Algeria; and the Tuareg of Algeria, Libya, Mali, and Niger. All speak dialects of Berber, a language of the Afro-Asiatic family.

Though scholars are uncertain about the Berbers' exact origins, they think members of this group probably came from the Near East and settled in northwest Africa around 3000 B.C. Over the millennia, Berber territories were invaded by Carthaginians, Romans, Vandals, Turks, Arabs, and Europeans, but against all these foreign powers the Berber culture remained distinct. The Arabs exerted the greatest influence on their culture, and in the early eighth century, Berbers were the main force behind the Arab conquest of the Iberian Peninsula. Later, in the eleventh and twelfth centuries, two great Berber empires arose and dominated much of Morocco, Algeria, Tunisia, and southern Spain. Berber traders once connected the Mediterranean markets to those of West Africa, and even today some Berber tribes still link trade between North and West Africa.

Most Berbers today are sedentary agriculturists who also tend small herds of goats and sheep. A few tribes, such as the Tuareg of Mali and the Imazighen of central Morocco, are seminomadic, herding sheep and using camels for mobility. The majority of Berbers trace their ancestry through their fathers, and men govern tribal affairs. There is a strong division of labor, with the men managing lands and herds and the women performing

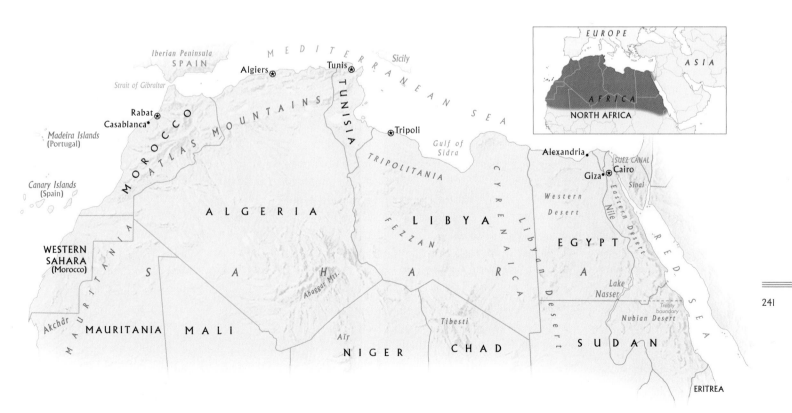

housework. Among the Tuareg, though, women inherit and own property, control the herds, cultivate land, and bring in the harvest. Tuareg men herd, tend the gardens, and conduct the direct activity of trade.

In urban areas, the distinction between Arabs and Berbers is diminishing, but Berber dialects, tribal customs, and traditional handicraft—handwoven carpets, silver jewelry, leather, and pottery, for example—continue to prevail in such remote areas as the mountains and valleys of Morocco's interior. A persistent custom is the local tribal council, which is composed of clan heads representing extended families.

Berber religious beliefs and practices are derived from Islam and are no different from the orthodox ones of other Sunni Muslims. There is a strong emphasis, however, on *baraka*, the belief in the special blessings from God, and on marabouts, individuals who are considered holy. Even in death, marabouts are thought to act as spiritual intermediaries and to bestow God's blessings upon the living. These individuals once played key political, religious, and economic roles, and they are still honored at numerous shrines throughout northwestern Africa.

Protected from a winter storm by a handwoven wool *djellaba*, a Berber man (below) wends his way along a path in the Ait Bou Guemmez valley of Morocco's Atlas Mountains. In Egypt, Coptic Christians gather for midnight Mass in Wadi el Natrun's Anba Bishoy Monastery (opposite). While their religious roots date back nearly 2,000 years, Copts trace their ethnic roots to the time of the pharaohs.

PAGES 244-45:

Distinctive hats shield Yemeni women from the sun as they gather clover for their cattle in Wadi Hadhramaut. Typical of Yemeni architecture, the family compound behind them incorporates defensive walls and mimics the colors and shapes of its environment.

PAGES 246-47:

Inside a comfortably outfitted tent, a Bedouin woman carefully adjusts her veil as a companion watches. Saudi Arabia's veiling practices remain more conservative than those of other Middle Eastern countries, but these women can express their own styles through the use of colorful, fashionable fabrics.

COPTS

DESCENDING FROM PEOPLE who did not convert to Islam after the Arabs' seventh-century conquest of Egypt, Copts are Christians who also consider themselves descendants of pharaonic Egyptians. Most of Egypt's approximately six million Copts—less than 10 percent of the population—reside in Cairo and in several villages in the southern part of the country.

Except for religion, Coptic and Muslim Egyptians share many cultural customs and usually are impossible to distinguish from one another by their dress styles, occupations, or even cuisines. Some Copts do choose to tattoo a small cross on the inner side of the wrist as a way to show that they are Christians. With respect to cuisine, Muslims are prohibited from eating pork, but Copts are not. Nevertheless, pork is not part of the Coptic diet.

The Coptic community is wary of conflicts that can arise from religious differences, especially in light of recent clashes with ultraconservative Muslims. As a result, Copts try to keep a low profile, thereby protecting the privacy of their families and their community.

Because religion is at the heart of their identity, many Copts strive to live honorable lives incorporating long-established sacred practices. Their center of worship, the Coptic Church, has its own patriarch, or pope, who is selected by the community and believed to be divinely ordained and in possession of the holy power to bestow blessings. The church's sacred texts and liturgy use only the Coptic language, which is based on ancient Egyptian, with a strong Greek influence. In their everyday affairs, Copts speak Arabic, as do other Egyptians.

Coptic monasticism dates from the fourth century A.D., and monasteries still form an important component of the church, drawing membership from the community. While monks cannot marry, priests are expected to be married before joining the priesthood. People believe that priests who are married and have their own families can better understand and support the families in their community.

As with minorities around the world, Copts place a high premium on education; many of their members are highly educated and employed in most white-collar professions. For 500 years, up until the 19th century, the Copts served as financial inspectors for the government bureaucracy. Their schools have established a reputation for excellence, and some Egyptian Muslims send their children to them to receive a broader education.

THE MIDDLE EAST
DRUZE ● JEWS ● KURDS ● MARONITES ● PERSIANS ● QASHQAI ● TURKS ● ZOROASTRIANS

DRUZE

FOLLOWERS OF a secret gnostic religion, the Druze are an Arab minority with between half a million and one million members. Most live in Syria, Lebanon, and Israel, where they strongly support the government; some even serve in the Israeli Army, among the very few non-Jews who do so.

An offshoot of Islam, the Druze religion originated in the 11th century and was closed to converts just three decades after its inception. Since then, the Druze have been isolated socially, and often geographically, a situation that has helped create a distinct culture. Centuries of persecution have shaped fearless warriors and forged solidarity among community members. But not *(Continued on page 248)*

every member shares in the secrets of the religion. The community is divided between the *ëuqqal,* who are initiated into the esoteric mystical teachings, and the *juhhal,* who live the Druze way but are kept ignorant of deeper knowledge. Some basic beliefs, though, are known to the outside world: The Druze say that there is one, omnipresent God; a messiah will return one day to lead them; and a dying Druze's soul reincarnates in a Druze about to be born.

Druze marry only each other, a practice that is central to the survival of a people who do not accept converts and who want to protect their traditions from outside influences. Husbands and wives are legally equal and have the same access to divorce, which can be initiated only within specific and clearly spelled-out circumstances. Druze women hold more political and religious power than women in many other Middle Eastern societies. They can also become ëuqqal and embark on the path to religious knowledge.

Many Druze continue to wear traditional clothing. A woman's attire consists of a blue or black dress, a white head scarf, and red slipper-styled shoes. A juhhal man puts on a checkered Arab head scarf, or kaffiyeh, and a ëuqqal man wears a white turban.

All Druze villages are built in the mountains, preferably toward the summits, near sacred shrines. While they are closed communities, they are nonetheless very hospitable: Nearly every village has a guest house intended exclusively for visitors. Most Druze are agriculturists, cultivating fruit and olive trees and growing eggplants, cauliflowers, wheat, chickpeas, potatoes, tomatoes, cucumbers, and herbs. Their everyday cuisine is largely vegetarian, with the eating of meat, such as lamb, reserved for festive occasions. Although pork is not prohibited, Druze rarely consume it.

✿ JEWS

THE MORE THAN five million Jews who live in the Middle East and North Africa share the same religion and have the sacred language of Hebrew in common; even so, members of this group are as diverse as the peoples they have dwelled among for over two millennia. Until the state of Israel was formally established in 1948, almost all Jews also held in common the feeling of living in exile. Destruction of the First and Second Temples of Jerusalem—in the sixth century B.C. and first century A.D.—was followed by great dispersions of Jews from the city and the surrounding region. They went to what is now Iraq, as well as Yemen, Egypt, Ethiopia, Turkey, Iran, and Central Asia. Some Diaspora Jews settled among the Berbers of northwestern Africa.

In the 20th century, tensions between Zionists and Arab nationalists, along with the realization of a homeland, led many Jews to move to Israel. As a result, the old Jewish communities of North Africa and the Middle East, once numbering in the thousands, were reduced to a few hundred as Israel's cities and towns grew to include representatives from every Jewish group in the world. These groups are often placed in two categories: Sephardim—Jews from the Middle East, North Africa, and Western Europe—and Ashkenazim—Jews from central and Eastern Europe. In the United States, Orthodox Jews are usually Sephardim, while the more numerous Conservative and Reform congregations belong to the Ashkenazic tradition.

Because they have a homeland, Jews no longer suffer as exiles, but their cultural diversity has become apparent

In Israel, Hasidic students (opposite) engage in a lively debate, a vibrant and highly valued aspect of social life. People view the art of debate, which has deep roots in Talmudic tradition, as a creative way to find solutions.
PAGES 250-51: Kurdish women, active and highly visible in the public life of their people, gather for a wedding in Iraq; one carries a weapon in case feuding clans disrupt the celebration.
PAGES 252-53: During the

Muslim festival of Ramazan, people in Cizre, Turkey, take the holiday to the cemetery, where they remember their ancestors. Many people may also stop for picnics at their ancestors' graves, a common custom throughout the Middle East
PAGES 254-55: Cast and crew prepare to shoot a scene for an Iranian film. To communicate psychological themes, the filmmaker draws heavily from Iran's traditional symbols and cultures.

during their resettlement in Israel. The country faces the enormous task of integrating the many languages, customs, occupational classes, and religious interpretations that have developed over the centuries. All Jews follow the same religious laws and offer up their prayers, but the words and styles may vary; the differences are especially obvious between the Sephardic and Ashkenazic traditions. Given the many Jews from the Arab world, Arabic is widely spoken, along with Hebrew, Persian, Turkish, Kurdish, Russian, and other Asian languages. Some African languages are also in the mix. Jews from Eastern Europe may speak Yiddish, a hybrid of Hebrew and Medieval German. People from the eastern Mediterranean may speak Ladino, a form of Spanish retained by 15th-century Jewish refugees from Spain.

Like Muslims and Christians, many Jews believe in pilgrimages and in mystics and holy people—saints—who can intercede in earthly affairs. And in several areas of the Middle East and North Africa, Jews and Muslims make pilgrimages to the same holy sites.

Some Jewish laws also have features in common with those of the surrounding Muslim majority in the Middle East and North Africa. Laws pertaining to inheritance, residence, and marriage, for example, have traditionally favored the father's side of the family, even though one major definition of Jewishness is birth by a Jewish mother. With immigration and urbanization, however, fewer Jews are following the practice of residing with the groom's family, and new families are setting up smaller, separate households.

✿ KURDS

RESIDING FOR MORE than 2,000 years in contiguous mountain regions of Turkey, Syria, Iraq, Iran, and Armenia, the Kurds have remained reasonably autonomous, despite the fact that they have rarely enjoyed self-governance over the territory they call Kurdistan, "land of the Kurds." Some

scholars believe these people are descended from Medes, an ancient Iranian group who settled in southwest Asia more than 2,700 years ago.

Today, some 20 million Kurds live in Turkey, Iraq, Iran, Syria, Europe, and the United States. Because of their long, isolated existence in mountainous areas, Kurds have been able to retain their own language—Kurdish, which is most closely related to Persian—as well as their own social organization and oral traditions. Almost all Kurds are Muslims, but a small minority known as the Yazidi practice a unique religion that blends Zoroastrianism, Manichaeanism, Nestorian Christianity, and Shiite Islam.

Though Kurdish society is patriarchal and only male siblings inherit property, Kurdish women nevertheless enjoy a more public life than do other rural women from surrounding Turkish, Arab, and Iranian societies. They have greater involvement in community decisions and more freedom of interaction with men. Women may also opt not to wear a veil, a choice that is much more difficult for women in some neighboring societies. A Kurdish woman traditionally wears a bright floral skirt, an embroidered jacket, and a turban or scarf on her head. A man's traditional attire consists of loose-fitting pants, a short-waisted jacket, a sash around the waist, and a turban similar in style to a woman's. While the Kurds share many of their culinary practices with Turkish, Arab, and Iranian neighbors, they are famous for their cheeses and yogurt.

Because of the Turkish, Iraqi, and Iranian policies of forced settlement, Kurds are now a settled agrarian people. Not long ago, more of them were nomadic and tribally organized, though some continue to organize themselves tribally, with loyalty building from family to lineage to clan to tribe. Other Kurdish farmers have organized instead around village leaders, who usually own the land and lease it out to farmers in exchange for (Continued on page 256)

Spinning wool for carpets, Qashqai women will weave the tales of their people into beautiful masterpieces. Their work helps keep their lifestyle independent and distinct from other Iranian peoples.

(Continued from page 249) labor or a portion of the harvest. Unlike Arab nomads, whose leaders are selected, Kurdish nomadic leaders inherit their titles. Many aspects of the Kurds' social life are changing dramatically as Iraq, Iran, and Turkey adopt policies aimed at integrating the people into mainstream culture. Some Kurds have migrated to cities and now work in urban trades.

Having been controlled by many outside forces and forced to witness the deaths of numerous members of their group, including children, Kurds have adopted a rather stoic attitude over the years. Their New Year's celebration, Nowruz, is similar to the Persian holiday, except that the Kurds not only celebrate new life and new beginnings but also ritually mourn their dead.

✤ MARONITES

CONCENTRATED IN Lebanon, the Maronite people are the only Middle Eastern Christian group to exercise significant political power in the Arab world. Their country was half Christian and half Muslim in 1932, when the last census was taken. Since then, emigration and the hardships of civil war have reduced the number of Christians to about 40 percent of the population.

As with many Christian Arabs, Maronites trace their origins to Palestine during the time of Christ. But unlike Eastern Orthodox churches, the Maronite Church falls under the jurisdiction of the Roman Catholic Church and the pope, even while it retains its own rituals and patriarch. Maronites observe the same sacraments as Catholics, though the language of the church is Arabic, not Latin. In addition, Maronites observe St. Maron's Day, celebrating the fourth-century Syrian hermit from whom their name is derived. Despite their strong group identity and religious adherence, some Maronites marry people from other religious traditions; divorce is not sanctioned by the Maronite Church.

Through their long history, Maronites have often allied themselves with the West, first with medieval Crusaders and Rome and later with the French. After World War I, the French held a mandate over Lebanon and Syria. They gave considerable political power to the Maronites, who continue to feel a special affinity for French culture and often send their children to French schools in Lebanon. Most Maronites are bilingual, using Arabic as the language of community and religion and French as the language of education. While the French influence is still strong, it has not compromised the identity of the Maronites. These people are clearly Middle Eastern, with hospitality customs, foods, and social-etiquette practices similar to those of other Arabs. They also have deep historic roots, their identity reinforced not only by Muslims who have surrounded them for centuries but also by their longtime rivalry with the Druze.

Unlike other Arab Christians, such as Palestinians who belong mainly to Eastern Orthodox churches, the Maronites are less involved in Arab nationalist movements. Many, in fact, are affluent and hold high positions in Lebanese society. Maronites are found in all occupational stations, and many own land and cultivate orchards and vineyards. Some of the people in rural areas still practice the art of silkmaking, a Maronite industry from the 19th century.

PERSIANS

THE MAJORITY population in Iran, Persians are also well represented in Afghanistan, Tajikistan, the United Arab Emirates, and Bahrain. Since the Iranian Revolution of 1979, many Persians have immigrated to Western Europe and North America.

Persians speak an Indo-European language called Farsi and are descended from waves of Eurasian pastoral nomads who arrived in southwestern Asia from 2000 to 1000 B.C. Ancient Persia was home to many different tribes, but as long ago as the sixth century B.C., these tribes were united under the Persian Empire and by the Zoroastrian religion. Only in the seventh century A.D. did invading Arabs bring Islam to the region and supplant the old religion.

Despite many foreign invasions since then, Persians have continued to maintain their distinct culture, language, and group identity. Their uniqueness is in part reinforced by their religious beliefs: They represent the single largest group of Shiite Muslims in the world, in contrast to the Sunni Muslims who dominate in the rest of the Middle East. A minority of Persians still practice Zoroastrianism, and there are small communities of Jewish, Christian, and Baha'i Persians as well. Members of all faiths observe and celebrate the Persian New Year—Nowruz—an ancient Zoroastrian rite of spring and rebirth that begins with a thorough cleaning of the house and the setting of an altar rich with items that symbolize good luck and abundance. Beginning on the first day of spring and continuing for 13 days, the holiday is a time when families visit each other. On the 13th day, families go on picnics and spend time outdoors while ridding their homes of any bad luck from the past year.

A Persian family is dominated by the father, who tends to be formal and disciplinarian, while the mother often plays the role of peacemaker and intermediary. The nuclear family is the most important domestic group, but extended families often choose to live near one another. Drawing artistic and poetic inspiration from their past, contemporary Persians have a cultural pride that runs very deep: Mystical poetry, classical Persian music, calligraphy, and miniature painting continue to be practiced in their traditional forms, although the global pop culture also exerts an influence.

Perhaps the most dramatic differences among Persians in the Middle East are found between urban residents and people who reside in rural areas. Urban Persians live in a hierarchical society based on occupation and social class, while rural Persians occupy tightly knit villages and have a farming lifestyle. Whether urban or rural, Persians have formal social customs whose fluency is an important aspect of functioning correctly in their hierarchical society. One of these customs is *taroof*, the social art of deference. Though a person may be offered much—in the form of concrete items such as gifts or abstract items such as social favors and friendship—by the subtle practice of taroof, the recipient knows how much to politely accept.

QASHQAI

LARGELY NOMADIC or seminomadic, the Qashqai are famous for their political prowess. They are among the few peoples in the contemporary Middle East to organize themselves into a tribal confederacy with influence on national and local politics. Shiite Muslims, the Qashqai trace their origins to the 18th century, when several Iranian groups united under one tribal banner. An estimated 500,000 to 700,000 live in southwestern Iran, traditional Qashqai territory.

In the 1930s, the Iranian government forced the people to settle, and other periods of repression followed. But immediately after the founding of the Islamic Republic of Iran in 1979, many Qashqai made a dramatic return to their nomadic lifestyle, herding sheep and goats across the large territory between their summer and winter pastures in the Zagros Mountains. The city of Shiraz lies in the middle of this territory, and the people have many ties to it.

Qashqai women enjoy social equality and hold roles that are complementary to those of men in the tribe. Given the demands of nomadic life, every man, woman, and child participates in breaking camp, migrating, and setting up a new camp. Because of the policies of the Islamic Republic, Qashqai women now wear the veil more than in times past. Traditionally, however, women did not veil themselves unless they were going to non-Qashqai towns or into urban centers. Women's dress still retains its traditional style of bright colors, multilayered skirts, tunics, and ornate scarves. Men's attire is less colorful but consists of loose-fitting trousers, a tunic and vest, and the famous felt cap with its rounded top and side earflaps. This cap has become a symbol of Qashqai political unity.

The Qashqai are also famous for woven carpets, the designs of which often depict tribal life and lands in symbolic form. As with many ethnic groups, storytelling is a highly enjoyed and revered skill.

TURKS

FROM AS FAR away as Mongolia and China, several migratory waves of different Turkic tribes came to southwestern Asia between the 11th and 15th centuries. Each tribe created a distinct culture, identity, and way of life. Those invaders who unified—first the Seljuk Turks, in a large part of the Middle East, and later the Ottoman Turks, in Anatolia (a portion of Turkey) and the Balkans—formed an expansive Turkish culture with a common language and historical experience. Islam was everyone's religion, and Turkish was the shared identity. Other Turkic peoples, speaking related Turkic languages, diverged and forged their own identities and cultures separate from the Anatolian Turks. These groups live in Iran, Afghanistan, China, Azerbaijan, Kazakhstan, Uzbekistan, Kyrgyzstan, and Turkmenistan.

There are more than 62 million Anatolian Turks in Turkey, with an additional 1.8 million living in Europe, especially in Germany, Cyprus, and Bulgaria. Although most Turks speak Turkish, members of the large groups of emigrants now residing and working in Europe may also speak German or other European languages. A tongue unrelated to Arabic or Persian, Turkish is from the Ural-Altaic language family of Central Asia.

From the beginning of their settlement in Turkey, Turks rose in influence in the Middle East and North Africa. They ruled many Middle Eastern peoples during the time of the Ottoman Empire and integrated these groups into their culture. At their most powerful, around A.D. 1700, Ottoman Turks governed all the lands from the Persian Gulf, through the Balkans, and across North Africa to Algeria. The Ottoman Empire ended after World War I and was met by a rise in Turkish nationalism and pride under the leadership of Mustafa Kemal, or Atatürk.

A long time has passed since Turks in Turkey were nomadic or tribally organized, and today their society is a complex mix of opposites: People see their identity as both European and Middle Eastern, as secular while still devoted to Islam, and as Western while also honoring their Eastern traditions. Turks in western Turkey tend toward more cosmopolitan and Western attitudes and industries. But many Turks in the central and eastern regions of the country are closely tied to the land; they have maintained traditional customs, such as a division of labor where the women tend fields and weave rugs and the men govern public life. Turkish family relations, which are similar to those of other Middle Eastern peoples, follow marriage and inheritance practices that emphasize the father's lineage and are in accord with Islamic law.

A Turkish Islamic mystical order—the famed Mevlevi Sufis—are popularly known in the West as the whirling dervishes. While mystical Islam is expressed throughout the Middle East, in Turkey the Mevlevis uphold the philosophy that all humans can gain direct experience of the divine, and they combine this belief with the physical practice of whirling. Their aim is to achieve a trance state wherein their awareness is fully concentrated on God.

Predating Islam are traditional symbols still used in Turkey's well-known rugs; they derive from ancient Central Asian peoples who were ancestral to the Turks. Traditional styles of another sort are retained in much of the classical literature and architecture—the mid-16th century Ottoman Suleymaniye mosque in Istanbul being a famous example. Many of today's literary and visual arts have taken on a modern tone because of reforms made by Atatürk.

ZOROASTRIANS

GOOD WORDS, good deeds, and good thoughts are at the heart of the Zoroastrian faith, and this faith is at the center of being Zoroastrian. Based on the divine visions and revelations of Zoroaster, a Persian prophet of the sixth century B.C., this ancient monotheistic religion has, over the years, influenced such basic ideas in Judaism, Christianity, and Islam as the concept of good and evil, heaven and hell, and the existence of a supreme being. The wise men of the Christian Epiphany were quite probably Zoroastrian: Magi means "priest" in Avestan, the Zoroastrian sacred language and an Indo-European tongue closely related to Sanskrit.

The state religion of ancient Persia, Zoroastrianism is still practiced by followers in Iran, India, and North America. Sacred rituals and rites of passage are important for binding together the small Zoroastrian communities around the world, as is their holy book, the Avesta. Central to this religion is the belief that good and evil are at war with each other, but good will ultimately prevail. It is imperative for each Zoroastrian to aid the victory of light over darkness by practicing good words, good deeds, and good thoughts. Given this fact, Zoroastrians have the reputation among other Middle Easterners for being honest and forthright. All ritual observances revolve around fire, which has been considered the most sacred element since the time Zoroaster looked into flames and saw the divine essence. Zoroastrian temples maintain a sacred fire that must be ritually attended and never allowed to go out.

As a means of keeping the community and the religion alive, Zoroastrians traditionally have married only within their group. But with small numbers and widely dispersed communities, some are now marrying non-Zoroastrians willing to convert and learn their ways.

Affirming the conquest of life over death and good over evil, Zoroastrians wear white or colors such as purple and yellow to funerals. But to avoid polluting the sacred elements of earth and fire, they neither bury nor cremate their dead. In the past, when such practices were permitted, Zoroastrians placed their dead on a stone platform atop a mountain. On this "tower of silence," the body gradually deteriorated as it was subjected to wind, sun, and animals. Today, to balance the old way with modern life, a metal stretcher is enclosed in cement and placed in a cemetery.

With an estimated population of 220,000 to 250,000 worldwide, Zoroastrians tend to be well-educated, which is their way of being prepared for times of sudden political and social change. The majority reside in Iran as a minority group among Muslims and speak standard Persian (Farsi) and their own dialect of Persian. While Zoroastrians in Iran have been a marginalized minority group, Iranians of all faiths hold romantic ideas about them as bearers of the country's original religion and culture. In the early 11th century, groups of Zoroastrians emigrated to India. Now called Parsis, most reside in Mumbai (Bombay).

With one palm held upward and the other downward, Mevlevi Sufis unite heaven and earth in a sacred dance dating back 700 years to the time of Jalal al-Din Rumi, the Mevlevi founder.

THE ARCTIC IS THE enormous stretch of land, sea, and ice surrounding the North Pole and lying beneath two familiar constellations often called Great Bear and Little Bear. Stories about these northern stars have been told by many cultures, including the ancient Greeks, whose word for bear, *arktos,* is the root word for the region's name. In a sense, then, "Arctic" means "place of the bear." In a strict geographic sense, however, it means the area north of the Arctic Circle. A less precise but more natural boundary might be the high-latitude timberline.

This region is essentially an ecological continuum, a circumpolar rim of land broken only at the Bering Strait, at points off Greenland, Iceland, and Norway, and at a few areas in Canada and Russia. From one place to the next, climatic conditions, landforms, plants, and animals are very similar; even the human societies have many characteristics in common. The ice, snow, glacial terrain, and permafrost all influence the region's biosphere, basically made up of just three ecological zones: taiga, or boreal forest, most of which is considered subarctic; tundra; and sea.

The extreme conditions in the Arctic—with very long periods of darkness in winter, equally long periods of daylight in summer, and constant cold—impose severe limitations on human cultures.

ARCTIC

A Chukchi herdsman keeps a close watch on his reindeer during the harsh Siberian winter.

As one moves toward the Pole, organic processes such as photosynthesis, soil formation, and nutrient recycling become slower, and growing seasons get shorter. The total number of plant and animal species diminishes, while biomasses increase; this means that there are fewer species but more individuals per species. Very few species of small game animals, birds, fish, and edible plants occur in sufficient numbers, however, to be more than just a dietary adjunct or a temporary source of food. As a result, Arctic peoples have been almost completely dependent, until recently, on a limited number of species for sustenance.

The complexities of life in the Arctic lie in the rhythmic responses made by societies—animal as well as human—to the seasonal light-and-temperature extremes that cause the fluctuation from scarcity to abundance. Thus, all elements of an ecosystem are important, because all populations are limited to the number of individuals who can subsist during the leanest month of the year.

Among circumpolar peoples the very important activities of getting food, keeping warm, and moving around have produced not only similarities in material culture but also widely flexible social and familial structures, settlement patterns, and dietary practices. Living in the Arctic necessitates high mobility in response to the seasonal movements of migratory game animals; requires the portability of material culture (nearly all Arctic cultures use sleds, skin boats, oil lamps, skin clothing, and harpoons); and involves the coming together and moving apart of families and social units to accommodate dramatic population fluctuations.

For 50,000 to 60,000 years people have sporadically inhabited the Eurasian Arctic, and about 30,000 to 40,000 years ago some groups began to move into Siberia and northern North America. The Eskimo peoples of Siberia, Alaska, and Canada emerged as a distinct cultural group in the Bering Strait area about 6,000 years ago, while their predecessors seem to have traveled on to the southeast. Today, descendants of these Eskimo peoples form the primary native population of the American Arctic. Far from being the marginal, isolated remnants of Ice Age hunting groups, they have made unique, dynamic, and positive adaptations to an environment that they perceive as essentially friendly.

The native peoples of the American Arctic are frequently called Eskimos, especially in Alaska. A French corruption of an Algonquian word meaning "eaters of raw meat," the term "Eskimo" is thought to be unflattering in Canada, so the eastern Eskimos call themselves Inuit, which means "people" in their language. In Alaska, "Eskimo" is still used to refer to the Inupiat of the north and to the Yupiat, or Yupik, of both southern Alaska and eastern Siberia. This is not true of the Aleut, who live in the Aleutian Islands and speak yet another language of the Eskimo-Aleut family. This language family is made up of polysyllabic tongues that have particularly complex nuances for handling space and time. With great precision, Eskimo-Aleut speakers can tell each other the location of a thing, how to get to it, and what its attributes are in relation to its surroundings. This linguistic ability is a tremendous advantage for these people, whose lives depend on their success in finding fast-moving game in the vast, often featureless lands of the far north.

All North American Arctic peoples have been hunters, gatherers, and fishermen. West of the Bering Strait, however, the original hunter-gatherer populations of Siberia

and northern Eurasia developed animal domestication, and in recent times nearly all of them subsisted by herding reindeer. The distinctively different forms of reindeer herding among these geographically contiguous cultures, occupying essentially the same environment, have given rise to theories suggesting reindeer domestication may have had more than one origin.

Among the so-called Paleosiberian cultures of the Chukchi, Koryak, and Yukaghir, the people "tamed" their deer rather than fully domesticating them, and their use of reindeer for pulling sleds and as hunting decoys for meat suggests that the deer were used much as dogs were employed elsewhere. The Evenk and the Nenets had larger, fully domesticated deer that they milked, rode, used as pack animals, and only rarely ate. The Yakut seem to have had a history as horse and cattle breeders until they moved into the Arctic in the 13th century.

Reindeer herding probably reached the Bering Strait by about a thousand years ago, but the practice never took hold in the American Arctic. (The wild caribou of Alaska and Canada and the reindeer of the Old World are members of the same species.) At almost the same time, Norse settlers approached from the east, making the first European encounters with the Inuit of Greenland and Labrador; they, too, had a relatively limited impact. The Norse abandoned their failing Greenland colony in the 1400s, but in later centuries, other European cultures would have an enormous effect on traditional Arctic life.

263

Following Pages: A Koryak reindeer herder on Russia's Kamchatka Peninsula lassoes one of his semidomesticated deer, which he may harness for transport or spear for food.

CLOCKWISE FROM TOP LEFT:
NORTHWEST TERRITORIES
INUIT, SIBERIAN YUKAGHIR,
AND ALASKAN ESKIMO

ARCTIC
ALASKAN ESKIMOS • ALEUT • CHUKCHI AND KORYAK
• EVENK • INUIT • NENETS • YAKUT • YUKAGHIR

☸ ALASKAN ESKIMOS

OF ALL THE ESKIMO populations today, the Alaskans are the most numerous and most diverse, dwelling in a variety of environments from the Arctic tundra of the North Slope to the forested seacoasts of the south. Several thousand years ago, Alaska's Eskimos split into the northern Inupiat and the southern Yupiat, or Yupik, peoples.

In the north, the interior Eskimos were mainly caribou hunters, while the coastal groups had diverse economies alternating between sea-mammal hunting, fishing, and inland hunting. Because of these seasonal subsistence activities, social organization was flexible, often bilateral, with ties relating individuals to the families of both their mothers and fathers maximizing territorial connections. The nuclear family—father, mother, children, and perhaps an older relative—was the basic social unit during most of the year. The larger, extended family band met and lived together during times of abundance in the spring or fall.

Non-kin extensions of social ties, such as wife exchanges and trading partnerships, were also important. Belying the notions of popular fiction, wife exchange was considered an economic necessity: The tasks of both men and women were essential for survival, and men often had to be away hunting for weeks at a time. Partnerships established between interior and coastal villages were beneficial in that they assured fairness in trading, access to each other's territory in times of need, and availability of products not found in one's home environment.

Infanticide (abandonment of newborns, especially females) and senilicide (voluntary suicide by the elderly) were practiced by all Eskimo groups in times of extreme hardship; such acts were never common, however, and they were always occasions of great sadness. The elderly were much valued for their wealth of life experiences, and children were cherished, as shown by the frequency of adoption and the complete lack of social stigma attached to an adopted child.

As culturally diverse as the Inupiat in the north, the Yupik-speaking Eskimos have long lived south of Norton Sound, scattered along the coasts of the Bering Sea and Pacific Ocean; some dwell on Siberian shores, including those of Russia's Kamchatka Peninsula, west of the Bering Strait. Because they have had access to an abundance of sea mammals and fish, Eskimo settlements and populations on Kodiak Island and elsewhere in southern Alaska have been among the largest in the circumpolar Arctic.

Today, Alaskan Eskimos are not entirely dependent on hunting and fishing. Most lead relatively settled lives in villages, where they operate their own businesses or work for wages, and if they go hunting, they may take snowmobiles instead of dogsleds and carry rifles rather than harpoons. Sometimes they supplement their incomes with sales of local art, such as soapstone and fossil-ivory carvings of animals; the Nunamiut at Anaktuvuk Pass are particularly famous for their skin masks.

In 1971 the Alaska Native Claims Settlement Act authorized a grant of 44 million acres (180,000 sq km) and a payment of 962 million dollars to Alaska natives. Village and regional corporations were established, and these entities have functioned more or less successfully to encourage economic growth. In 1990 there were about 57,000 Alaskan Eskimos.

✺ ALEUT

THE HARDY, SEAFARING Aleut originally occupied the 1,100-mile-long Aleutian archipelago, more than 70 volcanic islands stretching between North America and the Asian mainland, with the Bering Sea on the north and the North Pacific to the south. Until two centuries ago, the Aleut maintained a population of perhaps 20,000, but because of exploitation and introduced diseases, the population of today is less than 1,000 and declining. Often relocated by the United States government, the people live in scattered villages, sometimes not even in the Aleutians.

Compared with northern Alaska, the Aleutian Islands enjoy a relatively temperate climate, made less harsh by the warming influence of the Pacific's Kuroshio (Japan) Current flowing from the west. Even so, the islands are still lashed by violent winter storms, soaked by summer squalls, and blanketed by heavy fog. The continually windy and wet climate has naturally had a profound effect on the Aleut way of life. People settled in fairly permanent villages with large multifamily houses built underground, and because staying dry was as important as staying warm, they developed highly sophisticated rain parkas made of bird skin, fish skin, and sea-mammal intestine.

Surprisingly, the Bering Strait region contains Earth's greatest concentration of animal protein, but the sources of all this protein are usually deep in the water or under the ice. To get at them, the Aleut became some of the world's most capable hunters of seals, sea lions, walrus, and whales. They excelled as builders of seaworthy skin boats (called *baidarka* by Russians) and as seamen and navigators, and it was not uncommon for hunters to paddle for days on end in search of sea mammals, covering hundreds of miles in often turbulent waters.

The Aleut used nearly every part of the animals they caught—skin, bones, organs, sinews, even whiskers—for food, clothing, fuel, and tools. Excellent weavers, they made basketry items from tundra grasses and whale baleen. They also were very knowledgeable about animal and human anatomy and the principles of physiology, even practicing

Aleutian Islanders are masters of the rich offshore fishing grounds. This Aleut woman dries her catch of salmon (kings, reds, humpies, and dogs), which will provide food for the long winter.

mummification; they wrapped corpses in woven mats and placed them in caves facing the sea.

The Aleut's extraordinary seamanship, combined with a wealth of sealskin and furs in the region, made their first contact with Russian explorers and traders, in 1741, an unmitigated disaster. In the 18th and 19th centuries, the area was plundered by Russian hunters, adventurers, thieves, and princes, some of whom commissioned Aleuts to build two-, three-, and four-hole baidarka to transport missionaries and traders. The Russians wiped out many villages, and diseases further decimated the population.

During World War II, key battles protecting American territory from Japanese aggression disrupted the dwindling Aleut population, now concentrated in only a few seaside towns. One such town is Unalaska. Its population of 150 is about three-quarters Aleut, and although the people no longer hunt sea mammals, they have recently renewed their tradition of crafting skin boats.

❀ CHUKCHI AND KORYAK

ACROSS THE BERING Strait from the Alaskan Eskimos are the Chukchi and Koryak, two peoples who have been in close contact over the years. The Chukchi inhabit the farthest reaches of northeastern Siberia, and the Koryak live on the Kamchatka Peninsula to the south. Both groups descend from Paleolithic hunters and fishermen, and both are physiologically related to the Mongoloid northern Asians. They speak mutually intelligible languages from the Chukotko-Kamchatkan family.

Originally, the Chukchi and Koryak were split into coastal groups—focused on maritime hunting and fishing—and inland groups of reindeer herders. The coastal societies had more in common with each other and neighboring Eskimo groups than they did with their inland relatives. They hunted on the ice in winter and from skin boats during the summer, relying on sea mammals such as whales, seals, and walrus for their primary subsistence. Since Koryak territory impinged on the taiga, or boreal forest, to the south and west, the Koryak also availed themselves of plant resources and freshwater fishing.

The inland Chukchi and Koryak, on the other hand, maintained relatively large herds of semidomesticated reindeer, not only for food but also for transport, clothing, and shelter materials. Apparently more "tamed" than domesticated, the deer had to be recaptured and retrained each time they were needed to pull sleds. Watching over the animals were herdsmen who lived in family encampments having four or five very large skin tents made of thirty to forty reindeer hides. Because the families kept such large herds, concepts of wealth, private property, and social stratification became well developed among these people even before the first Russian contacts in the 1640s.

In both Chukchi and Koryak cultures, shamanism was highly developed, and their religious systems shared

a number of beliefs and associated rituals, including the sacred family fire and the concept of Raven as a major cultural hero. Complex fertility ceremonies held at annual reindeer slaughters and sea-mammal feasts were intended to ensure the continued availability of game.

The Chukchi now number about 15,000 and live mostly in villages established by the Soviets during the Siberian collectivization of the 1930s; only a few villages still keep reindeer herds. Among the difficulties faced by this nomadic culture as it adjusted to settled life were the pressures of industrialization and later nuclear testing, all of which—until recently—contributed to very high rates of infant mortality, alcoholism, and suicide.

These same general conditions affect the contemporary Koryak people, who were also formed into a national district by the First Congress of Kamchatka Soviets in 1930. The 9,200 Koryak counted by the 1989 census suffer the same diseases of "civilization" as their northern neighbors, and their average life span is now less than 50 years.

❀ EVENK (Tungus)

AMONG THE MOST widespread of the Siberian Arctic cultures, the Evenk number about 33,000 today and are subdivided into two parts. The Evenki group inhabits the area extending eastward from the Yenisey River to the Pacific Ocean and northward from the Amur River to the Arctic Ocean; the Even group, or Lamut, lives along the coast of the Sea of Okhotsk.

The Evenk are reindeer pastoralists who keep large herds of completely domesticated deer, which are bigger and of a more uniform color than the wild variety. For these people, reindeer domestication seems to be more closely modeled on herds kept by horsemen to the south than on dogs kept by the northeastern Siberians. Evenk reindeer are milked, ridden, and used as pack animals but, owing to their value, are not eaten except on important ceremonial occasions or if starvation is imminent.

Although herding is the primary subsistence base, the Evenk derive the bulk of their food, clothing, and shelter from hunting and trapping, the main daily activities of the men. Like the Aleut, they have a great interest in animal anatomy, not hesitating to pursue and capture unfamiliar creatures to observe their behaviors and learn about their anatomies when the animals are dissected. The Evenk's knowledge of physiology and comparative anatomy astonished early Russian ethnographers, who also noted that the people could perform complex surgical procedures with phenomenal success.

For generations, reindeer herds were communally owned by clans who traced their lineage through the male line. Each Evenk clan had a recognized territory and was responsible for redistributing stock among clan families. In the old days, two or more exogamous (out-marrying) clans formed an endogamous (in-marrying) tribe.

Shamanism was more highly developed by the Evenk than by any other Siberian group (the word "shaman" has an Evenki origin), and shamans could reputedly tell the future, predict the weather, cure or cause an illness, and assure success in hunting or herding. A shaman frequently used the agaric mushroom to induce trance states, but the mushroom's hallucinogenic powers were highly valued by other members of the society as well. Bear ceremonialism, another frequent circumpolar practice, was also common.

In the past, the Evenk lived near the taiga in winter, then moved their herds out onto the tundra in summer. Because of the area's climatic extremes, people were widely scattered in groups of only two or three families during the long Arctic "winter," which lasts about three-quarters of the year; in summer, they came together to form larger camps.

The people continued keeping their herds and trading furs with the Chinese and later Russian merchants. Then, during the Soviet period, they and other Siberian nomads were coerced into moving to permanent villages in the 1930s. Today, from 30 to 50 percent of the population still herd and hunt for a living, while the rest of the people work in industry, education, administration, and health care, or as unskilled labor.

The Evenk National Okrug (district) was created in 1930, but its relationship with the state remains uneasy. As late as 1999, this district, which was by then autonomous, refused to hand over power to the governor of Krasnoyarsk, Gen. Aleksandr Ledbed, who was a former security chief and Russian presidential hopeful.

Carefully watched by her mother, a Chukchi child (left) ventures out of her reindeer-skin *yaranga* into the Siberian winter, when temperatures may remain far below zero. The play of these Chukchi boys (top) prepares them for their serious adult roles of capturing reindeer for transport and food. Camped in his snow house in northern Canada, a young Inuit hunter (above) awaits the dawn while contemplating his role in the new territory of Nunavut, which means "our land."

FOLLOWING PAGES: Vestige of the old Soviet regime, a statue of Lenin stands in the background as Nenet women, clad in their reindeer finery, gather at a co-op in Yar Sale, Russia. The new capitalist energy boom in this area of northwestern Russia has had a significant impact on the traditionally nomadic Nenets.

☼ INUIT

THE EARLIEST recognizable Eskimo peoples came into the Bering Strait area around 6,000 years ago and over the next 2,000 years moved east toward Greenland. After about A.D. 1000, these earliest cultures began to be absorbed or replaced by groups rapidly migrating into the region from the west—sea-mammal hunters who were the ancestors of today's Inuit. The term "Inuit" encompasses not only the Greenlanders but also the Polar Eskimos and the Central Eskimos (Caribou, Iglulik, Netsilik, and Copper Eskimos).

Around A.D. 1500 the climate began to change, initiating what some scientists call the little ice age and hastening the Norse abandonment of Greenland. It also forced the Central Eskimos of what is now northern Canada to give up semi-permanent coastal villages for a new lifestyle: In summer, they fished and hunted caribou; in winter, they hunted sea mammals out on the ice. For winter encampments, they built snow houses, while their Greenland cousins—able to maintain the stable coastal subsistence of former times—still lived in partly subterranean houses of sod, driftwood, and stone. The Greenlanders also continued to hunt from their single-cockpit skin kayaks and larger open umiaks.

Skin boats were used by nearly all of the Eskimo and Siberian groups. But the Polar Eskimos were an exception. This small, isolated Inuit group, whose culture inspired the legendary image of Eskimo life, inhabited the northernmost reaches of western Greenland and Ellesmere Island, where the polar seas were frozen all year and made boats useless. Dogsleds, with the animals harnessed in a fan shape by the

A Nenet woman uses larch poles and reindeer skins to construct her family's tent. Considered the best reindeer breeders in the world, the Nenets adapted their herding practices from horse and cattle breeders to the south.

Inuit and in tandem by the Alaskans, were also used by almost every group. The Aleut didn't have them because the warmer climate of the Aleutians rendered them useless.

Inuit cosmology was similar to that of other Eskimo societies: It was directly linked to hunting and fishing, with the most common religious practices related to taboos about subsistence. Religion was animistic; that is, all things human, animal, and inanimate had souls, and all were related to each other. Fantastic ivory carvings dating from A.D. 1000 to 1300 attest to the rich spiritual life. A shaman, or *angakok,* served as a direct link to animal spirits, and he could prophesy and cure illness by sucking out objects that had intruded into souls. In Alaska, the shaman's job also included retrieving lost souls in an elaborate, village-wide, ritual. Although successful shamans could accrue a good deal of power, community leaders were chosen because of their abilities as providers. Social control was generally informal, and leaders were usually followed by consensus.

The Inuit finally were accorded full Canadian citizenship around 1960. In the 1970s, ten assembly seats were allocated to the Northwest Territories for Inuit territory, and in 1979 the first Inuit was elected to the National House of Commons. The people of the Northwest Territories voted in

1982 to create a new territory called Nunavut, and in 1993 the Nunavut Act was passed. It set aside 1.9 million square kilometers for the Inuit and authorized the government to pay them 1.1 billion dollars between 1993 and 2007. In a historic step toward self-determination, the election for the First Nunavut Legislative Assembly was held in 1999.

The story is different in Greenland, which became part of Denmark in 1953. Although complete home rule was achieved in 1979, most key administrative positions in the government are still held by Danes.

Today, hunting and fishing remain important activities, but they are abetted by modern equipment such as rifles and snowmobiles. A number of Inuit communities—Baffin Island's Cape Dorset, for example—have established arts cooperatives that attract much international interest.

☀ NENETS

ALSO KNOWN AS the Nentsy, Samoyed, and Yurak, the Nenets inhabit northwestern Siberia, from the Kanin Peninsula on the White Sea to the Yenisey River Delta. This is a region of wet tundra underlain by permafrost, combined with tundra and taiga mosaic ecosystems to the south.

Apparently, the ancestors of modern Nenets moved into this area from the south during the early centuries of the first millennium A.D., replacing or assimilating the original hunting-and-gathering population with one that relied on reindeer herding. These newcomers practiced herding techniques that seem to have been adapted from ones used by horse and cattle breeders to the south.

Like other Siberian groups, the Nenets developed a migratory lifestyle fully adjusted to tundra existence. In autumn they moved with their herds from the coast to the taiga, and in spring they went back to the tundra. The Nenets became well known as expert breeders of reindeer large enough to be ridden like horses, a fact that caused their animals to be widely sought after by other groups. By comparison, the neighboring Evenk's reindeer were so small that riders had to sit forward, above the shoulders.

Nenet contacts with the Russian Empire were hostile and fraught with uprisings, a situation that did not improve with the Sovietization of the 1930s; a millennia-long history as successful nomadic herdsmen did not yield easily to the concepts of collectivization. The area has since become the focus of the chemical and oil industries, and nuclear testing on Novaya Zemlya has posed grave dangers to the health of indigenous peoples. During the 1989 census, 34,665 Nenets were counted, more than 70 percent of whom still speak Samoyedic, a language related to Turkic. Their life expectancy is now reckoned at only 45 to 50 years.

☀ YAKUT (Sakha)

CALLING THEMSELVES the Sakha, the almost 400,000 Yakut compose the most numerous ethnic group of Siberia, and the Yakut Republic of today is the largest administrative subdivision of Russia. Although the early history of the Yakut is obscure, the people emerged as a distinct ethnic group in the early 1300s, a fact that makes them the most recently arrived indigenous group in the Siberian Arctic. By the 17th century, they had peacefully assimilated with other northern peoples, particularly the Evenk, and had organized themselves into 80 independent tribes that were themselves subdivided into numerous clans. Like the Evenk, the Yakut based their subsistence on herding, but in this case the herds were made up of horses and cattle. Because of the extreme cold, Yakut animals tend to be hardy; even so, they are rather unproductive and have to be sheltered and fed for a large part of the year.

The far northern Yakut, known as Dolgan, adapted to reindeer herding and hunting learned from neighboring peoples, often hunting the wild reindeer from the backs of either oxen or horses. The people also hunted ermine, sables, otters, and ferrets, and their culture flourished as the Russian fur trade grew in importance. Because the Yakut considered reindeer hides and furs to be personal property, great wealth could be accumulated by families with hunters and large herds. The society eventually became stratified, causing the old clan system to become nonfunctional and then fall apart. Shamans among the Yakut got paid for their services, and as shamanism developed a complex hierarchy of duties, the shamans, too, accumulated enough wealth and power to become threats to the social order.

From the 17th century on, the Yakut were best known as fur traders and blacksmiths; by the early 1800s, most had joined the Russian Orthodox Church. As in the rest of Siberia, Yakut pastoralism and agriculture were collectivized between 1930 and 1950, but in a particularly brutal manner: Thousands who resisted were arrested, killed, or forcibly deported. Yakut schools, publications, and organizations were officially banned by Joseph Stalin, who promoted the development of heavy industry in the region.

Yakut nationalism reemerged in the wake of Mikhail Gorbachev's reform policies of the 1980s, and in 1990-1991 Yakutia proclaimed its sovereignty and established its own parliament. Despite political differences between Yakut and Russian leaders during the 1990s, President Boris Yeltsin in 1994 officially apologized to the people for their persecution by the Stalin regime and granted them greater control of their own resources. In 1997, with the help of the Worldwide Fund for Nature, 270,000 square miles (700,000 sq km) of Yakutia's Arctic tundra were set aside as an ecological preserve. In 2000, President Putin made the Sakha (Yakut) Republic part of the Far Eastern Federal District.

☀ YUKAGHIR (Odul)

ALTHOUGH THE Yukaghir, or Odul as they call themselves, are among the smallest of the Eurasian Arctic populations, they are extremely important to the understanding of far northern cultures. These people probably represent most

closely the ancient, original cultural adjustment to the coldest region of Arctic Siberia. The area they occupy is generally north of the Verkhoyansk Range and is known for having the most severe winters in the world. Here, all of the water surfaces are frozen for seven or eight months of the year; the January temperature averages minus 70°F, as measured at the town of Verkhoyansk; and only 70 to 80 days each year are free of frost. During the short summer season, the land becomes a vast lake-studded marsh because the meltwater from the considerable snow mass cannot percolate down into the permafrost.

The most important subsistence animals in this region are large herds of herbivores, specifically reindeer. For generations, reindeer hunting furnished virtually all of the food, clothing, and shelter items needed by the Yukaghir, who were originally a nomadic people with an unusually large inventory of hunting methods. They used tame deer as decoys, crouching behind them to infiltrate a wild herd, and employed noose-traps to catch deer along reindeer trails. From skin boats, they hunted deer at water crossings, using harpoons and compound bows. The most elaborate, large-scale communal hunts were the "drives" or "pounds" held during calving season in the spring. At these times, men stampeded a whole herd into a keyhole-shaped funnel formed by waiting hunters, who then killed as many of the animals as possible.

The Yukaghir formerly lived in extended-family bands with fewer than a hundred people, occupying conical skin tents much smaller than the Chukchi *yaranga* and somewhat resembling the Plains Indian *tipi* of North America. Their shamans, like those of other Siberian societies, were very powerful individuals, and elders and ancestors occupied places of particular prominence. At one time, the people used a pictographic writing system, the only remaining evidence of which is a love letter written on birch bark; it is now preserved in the collections of the American Museum of Natural History in New York.

To ethnologists, the Yukaghir were known as a kind, mild-mannered, and honest people whose good nature was exploited and abused by Cossacks, Russian settlers, and local priests, leading to the rapid assimilation of their native culture. Russianization brought the Yukaghir to the brink of extinction in the latter half of the 20th century. In recent years, the people have adapted to life in small permanent villages with rectangular wood houses and herds of no more than 30 to 40 domesticated reindeer. The last census counted just 1,100 Yukaghir who continue to fish, hunt, and herd reindeer; few still speak their native tongue, a language related to Chukchi and Koryak.

Her child securely swaddled in his cradle board, a Nenet mother eagerly prepares for the annual trek following the family reindeer herd to the high Arctic tundra.

CULTURES IN CRISIS

BY WADE DAVIS

Prehistoric figures dating from 6500 B.C., discovered near Amman, Jordan, embody the artistry of a vanished culture.

BARREN, STARK, AND WINDSWEPT, Easter Island is a lonely rock protruding from the depths of a dark ocean, about as far away from inhabitable land as one can venture on this vast Earth. There are no forests, and, though the volcanic soils are rich, the land is covered for the most part with grasses, sedges, and the dozens of species of exotic plants that have invaded the island since European contact. There are only two native trees, both of them small, and few other sources of fuel. The indigenous fauna boasts no creature larger than an insect. Even in the perfect light of a Polynesian evening, it is difficult to imagine a time when this hostile land was, in fact, a tropical paradise.

Certainly it showed no gentle face to the first Europeans who came ashore in the early years of the 18th century. The Dutch explorer Jacob Roggeveen, who landed on Easter Sunday, 1722, encountered a wretched people and a wasted land, a place of singular poverty and forlorn isolation. When Capt. James Cook arrived some 50 years later, he took note of the dreadful condition of the local canoes, frail and scarcely afloat, hardly the craft of a great seafaring people.

Yet in the midst of this misery, scattered about the island, were signs of an entirely different world—enormous stone statues, ceremonial icons of a lost civilization. Weighing as much as 80 tons, standing 30 feet tall, set in place as far as 6 miles from the mountain slope where they had been quarried, these astonishing megaliths could only have been produced and erected by a highly complex, hierarchical society capable of generating sufficient surplus food to feed the hundreds, if not thousands, of laborers and specialists who had been employed in the monumental effort.

For centuries the mystery of the Easter Island statues defied explanation, provoking wild speculations and impossible intrigues. As in the case of so many scientific enigmas, the solution ultimately proved to be both more wondrous and more ominous than the most sensational of theories.

DNA analysis has confirmed what James Cook himself suspected, that the original inhabitants of Easter Island were Polynesians, who arrived here during one of the greatest migrations in history. Over a thousand years, this migration spread a single way of life across a quarter of the circumference of the world, a cultural sphere that eventually encompassed ten million square miles, from Samoa and the Marquesas to Hawaii and New Zealand. Sailing in enormous outrigger canoes, constantly exposed to the elements, reading the currents and following the stars, the Polynesians moved on from island to island, virtually eating their way through the Pacific. Ironically, the exhaustion of resources they themselves left in their wake created at least one of the incentives for the seafarers to cast off again and again into the unknown.

By about A.D. 500 they had reached the volcanic redoubt we now know as Easter Island. Archaeological excavations and pollen analysis provide unequivocal evidence that the island they encountered was not desolate, as it is today, but rather lush and verdant, as it had been for many thousands of years.

For several centuries the people of Easter Island—the Rapa Nui—thrived, clearing and burning the forests, harvesting abundant crops of bananas, taro, and sweet potatoes. Unlike most Polynesians, they ate relatively little fish. Instead, for protein they depended largely on porpoises, hunted far from shore in vessels carved from the trunks of a remarkable endemic plant, the Easter Island palm. A veritable tree of life, it gave the Rapa Nui edible fruit and a sugary sap that may well have been used for honey and wine. Towering perhaps to 80 feet, it was wide at the base with a consistent girth. Once felled, it made a perfect roller for transporting large objects, such as the megalithic statues.

Scholars now believe that, by about the 13th century, rival Rapa Nui chieftains were engaged in a constant struggle to produce larger and larger versions of these monuments. As the cult of the ancestors grew, the forests fell. Pollen records suggest that grasses slowly began to displace the forest cover. By 1400 the Easter Island palm was extinct, its reproduction curtailed by imported predatory rats, which thrived on its fruit. With the end of the palm, there was no wood for canoes, and porpoise meat disappeared from the diet.

By the 15th century, the Rapa Nui, through their environmental degradation, had driven half the seabird species to extinction, all native wildlife had disappeared, and the forests were gone. Croplands eroded as wind dispersed the soil and rain leached nutrients from the earth. Food supplies plummeted, and without surplus there was nothing to support the priestly caste. The warriors rebelled and open warfare ensued between enemy clans. Each toppled the statues of the others, until every image lay flat, overgrown by grass. Without wood for shelter, the people moved underground into damp caves. Without food, came famine. The population imploded as misery and despair stalked the land. In the shadows survived a handful of wretched souls whose children would meet the Dutch in 1722 and whose grandchildren's children would encounter Cook half a century later.

O N A MAP OF THE WORLD, Easter Island appears insignificant, a mere 64 square miles of land isolated in the middle of an ocean. But when you are there, standing on the summit of Rano Raraku, most dramatic of the volcanic craters, the island appears vast, infinite, a world unto its own. For the Rapa Nui, whose memories of ancient migrations had long ago dissolved into myth, it was the entire universe. When things went wrong, as the population soared and resources were depleted, there was no escape. Even today it is haunting to envision the moment when a Rapa Nui farmer, or perhaps a ritual specialist, cut down the last specimen of the tree upon which their civilization had been built.

The story of Easter Island is a parable for our times. As we stand on our planetary island, we see only a limitless horizon and the stunning products of human ingenuity, a perspective that for centuries has been the measure of our dreams. But in recent decades we have achieved, for the first time in history, a wider perspective.

When the first astronauts circled the Earth in the 1960s, they described a small and fragile blue planet, veiled in clouds, floating, as one of them put it, in the "black vastness of space." From their vantage thousands of miles away, the Earth was revealed as a single interactive sphere of life, a living organism composed of air, water, and soil. This transcendent vision, more than any amount of scientific data, taught us that our world is a finite place that can endure our neglect for only so long. If things go wrong, we cannot simply escape into space. Like the Rapa Nui, we are trapped on a very small island in the midst of an infinite sea.

This new perspective has provoked a profound shift in consciousness that in the end may prove to be the salvation of a lonely planet. Thirty years ago, for example, biodiversity and biosphere were exotic terms, familiar only to certain scientists. Today they are part of the vocabulary of schoolchildren. The biodiversity crisis, marked by the extinction of more than a million life-forms in the past three decades alone, together with the associated loss of habitat, has emerged as one of the central issues of our times. But even as we lament the collapse of biological diversity, we pay too little heed to a parallel process of loss: the demise of the very cultural diversity so elegantly portrayed in this book. The most pessimistic biologist would not dare suggest that half of all extant species are endangered or on the edge of extinction. Yet, that may well be the fate of the world's languages and cultures.

Despite the spread of a global culture across the planet, there are indigenous peoples whose traditional ways of life are rooted in history and language, attached by myth and memory to a particular place. Though their numbers are small—perhaps some 300 million people or roughly 5 percent of the total world population—these cultures account for at least 60 percent of the world's languages and together represent over half the intellectual and spiritual legacy of humanity, a legacy that is being lost in a whirlwind of change and conflict.

The loss of languages is a clear bellwether of this unprecedented crisis. In the course of human history, something on the order of 10,000 languages have existed. While some 6,000 are still spoken today, fully half of these are not being taught to children, meaning that they are destined for extinction. Just as disturbing, only 300 of those 6,000 are spoken by more than a million people, and only 600 languages are considered by linguists to be stable and secure. Some scholars believe that, if current trends continue, in another century we may lose 97 percent of our remaining languages, with only 200 surviving.

A language is as divine and mysterious as a living creature. Just as a rare orchid is as biologically relevant as a landscape of white spruce trees, so too does each language have its unique and significant lineage, no matter how few individuals can understand its mysteries. The biological analogy is apropos. Extinction, when balanced by the birth of new species, is a normal phenomenon. But the current loss of species due to human activities has never occurred before. Languages, like species, have always evolved. A few hundred years ago, for example, as Latin was losing its dominance in the Western world, it gave rise to a score of diverse but related languages. Today, by contrast, languages are being lost at such a rate—sometimes in a generation or two—that they have no chance to leave descendants.

Every two weeks, somewhere on Earth, a language disappears. Of the roughly 150 native languages still alive in the United States, 55 are spoken by fewer than 10 individuals; 7 by a single person. Imagine how those surviving speakers feel. Enveloped in silence, isolated and alone, they are no longer capable of passing along the wisdom of their ancestors, the nuances of song, the poetics of a unique tongue that was itself an entire ecosystem of ideas and intuitions, a watershed of thought, an old-growth forest of the mind.

Throughout history, cultures have come and gone, absorbed by other more powerful societies or eliminated altogether by violence and conquest, famines, or natural disasters. But the current wave of assimilation and acculturation, in which peoples all over the Earth are being drawn away from their past, has no precedent.

To grasp fully the significance of what is at risk and what is being lost, and perhaps to find ways of ameliorating the situation, it is essential to distinguish cultural change from what is, in effect, cultural annihilation. One can lament the transformation of small town U.S.A., for example, and identify any number of causes: Technological innovations, such as television and air-conditioning, that lured families away from the front porch and the social realm of the street; or the automobile and the network of roads and interstate highways that changed the architecture of place. While it is true that all of these developments provoked profound changes in the cultural landscape, none challenged the fundamental existence of the United States as an idea, a nation, a sphere of life and inspiration.

Similarly, the arrival of digital technology in India, or even the flood of genetically modified seed crops, will not fundamentally threaten a nation and a culture that for 4,000 years has absorbed every conceivable intrusion, from the Moguls to the British. In Canada, it is recent immigrations that have impacted the country, mostly for the better, in little more than a decade. In Vancouver, once an Anglo bastion, 50 percent of schoolchildren today speak English as a second language; Toronto hospitals provide medical advice to patients speaking 80 different languages; and the streets of the city play host to peoples from some 150 nations.

Such changes are not, in and of themselves, threats to culture. The Kiowa Indians did not cease being Kiowa when they gave up the bow and arrow, any more than Americans stopped being Americans when they gave up the horse and buggy and embraced the car. The notion that small, indigenous societies are frozen in time and thus fated to slip away, reduced by circumstance to the sidelines of history as the modern world moves inexorably on, is simply wrong. No culture, however isolated, is static. Traditional cultures have survived precisely because of their ability to cope with change, the one constant in history. People disappear only when they are overwhelmed by external forces, when drastic conditions imposed on them from the outside render them incapable of adapting to new possibilities. Sadly, these are precisely the circumstances confronting most of the world's indigenous peoples today.

In the upper reaches of the Orinoco, a gold rush brings disease to the Yanomami, killing a quarter of the population in a decade, leaving the survivors hungry and destitute. In Colombia, Barasana men and women are reduced to coca-growing serfs by drug lords and their allies, the revolutionary guerrillas of the left. In Nigeria, pollutants from the oil industry so saturate the floodplain of the Niger River, homeland of the Ogoni, that the once fertile soils can no longer be farmed. A vortex of violence and war-induced famine in the Sudan claims the lives of tens of thousands of Nuer. The Efe, forest dwellers of the Congo, dwindle toward extinction as sexually transmitted diseases ravage the population. In Borneo, the nomadic Penan drift toward settlements as their forest homeland is ravaged by the unsustainable extraction of timber. These are not cultures destined to fade away. On the contrary, in virtually every instance, these peoples are being torn from their past and propelled into an uncertain future because of specific political and economic decisions made by powerful outside entities.

The ultimate tragedy, as anthropologist David Maybury-Lewis has written, is not that archaic societies are disappearing but rather that vibrant, dynamic living cultures and languages are being forced out of existence. It is not change that threatens the integrity of cultures; it is power, the crude face of domination. Genocide, the physical elimination of a people, is universally condemned by all nations. Ethnocide, the destruction of a people's way of life, is too often embraced as appropriate development policy.

If governments and institutions are the agents of cultural destruction, they can also be the agents of cultural survival. Their organizers, and we as individuals, need to remember that our modern way of life, however wondrous it seems with its technological wizardry and cities dense in intrigue, is but one cultural possibility, one model of reality. It is the consequence of only one set of choices that our particular intellectual ancestors made, albeit successfully, generations ago.

The great revelation of anthropology is the realization that there are other ways of being, morally inspired and inherently right. Whether it be the nomadic Penan in the rain forests of Borneo, the Vodoun acolytes in Haiti, the Rendille pastoralists in the searing deserts of northern Kenya, or any one of the myriad cultures celebrated in this book—all of these peoples teach us that there are other options, other possibilities, other ways of thinking and interacting with the Earth itself.

Together these cultures make up an intellectual and spiritual web of life, an "ethnosphere" if you will, that envelopes and insulates the planet. Think of the ethnosphere as the full complexity and complement of human potential, the sum total of all thoughts, beliefs, dreams, intuitions, and myths brought into being by the human imagination since the dawn of consciousness. It is humanity's great legacy, as vitally important to our future as is the biosphere upon which all life depends.

Before she died, anthropologist Margaret Mead expressed her concern that, as we drift toward a more homogeneous world, all of human potential might be reduced to a single modality, a blandly amorphous generic culture, a monochromatic world of monotony. Her greatest fear was the possibility that we might awake one day as from a dream, having forgotten that there had ever been any other options.

There is a fire burning over the Earth, taking with it plants and animals, human languages, ancient skills, and visionary wisdom. Quelling this flame, and kindling in its wake a new respect for the value and importance of both biological and cultural diversity, is one of the great challenges of our age.

ETHNIC GROUPS OF THE WORLD

THE FOLLOWING LIST contains the names of more than 5,000 traditional ethnic groups and identifies the regions of the world in which the groups maintain their greatest presence. The regions correspond to the ones included within the major chapters of the book. The names listed are those used most commonly for each group, and alternative names for a group are enclosed within parentheses. Owing to space limitations, the list does not include extinct groups, immigrant groups, or groups whose predominant identifying trait is based on nationality or bloodline; groups who have a distinct sense of ethnicity and shared culture based on religion are included. Diacritical slashes or exclamation points beginning the names of some southern African groups denote the click sounds used in their languages.

C=Central E=East N=North S=South W=West
NA=North America SA=South America

ABANYANDA — C Africa
ABAU — Melanesia
ABAYDAT — N Africa
ABEGWEIT — Northeast NA
ABELAM — Melanesia
ABENAKI — Northeast NA
ABIDA — Middle East
ABIPON — Central SA
ABITIBIWINNI — Northeast NA
ABKHAZIANS — Caucasus
ABOR (Adi) — S Asia
ABOURE — W Africa
ABRIWI — W Africa
ABRON — W Africa
ABSENTEE SHAWNEE — Plains NA
ABUKAYA — C Africa
ABUNG — SE Asia
ABURRA — Caribbean Coast SA
ABUTIA — W Africa
ACADIA — Northeast NA
ACATEC (Aguatec, Awakateko) — Mesoamerica
ACAXEE — Mesoamerica
ACEHNESE — SE Asia
ACHAGUA (Achawa) — Amazon Basin
ACHANG — E Asia
ACHAWA (Achagua) — Amazon Basin
ACHE (Guayaki) — Andes
ACHI — Mesoamerica
ACHIKOUYA — C Africa
ACHO DENE KOE — Subarctic
ACHOLI — E Africa
ACHOMAWI — Far West NA
ACHUALE — Amazon Basin
ACHUAR — Amazon Basin
ACOMA PUEBLO — Southwest NA
ACUERA — Southeast NA
ADA — W Africa
ADAMAUA — W Africa
ADANGBE — W Africa
ADI (Abor) — S Asia
ADIVASIS — S Asia
ADJA — W Africa

ADJARIANS (Ajarians) — Caucasus
ADYUMBA — C Africa
AFAR (Danakil) — E Africa
AFAWA — W Africa
AFO — W Africa
AFRICAN CARIBBEAN — Caribbean
AFRIKANERS (Boers) — S Africa
AFSHAR — C Asia
AFUSARE — W Africa
AGARIA — S Asia
AGHULS — Caucasus
AGIRYAMA — E Africa
AGMIUT — Arctic
AGNI — W Africa
AGOI — W Africa
AGTA — SE Asia
AGTO — Arctic
AGUACADIBE — Caribbean
AGUANO — Andes
AGUARUNA — Andes
AGUATEC (Acatec, Awakateko) — Mesoamerica
AGUSAN — SE Asia
AHIARIUT — Northeast NA
AHIR — S Asia
AHOUSAHT — Northwest Coast NA
AHTAHKAKOOP — Plains NA
AHTENA — Subarctic
AHTNA — Northwest Coast NA
AIGA — Melanesia
AIMAQ — C Asia
AINI — E Asia
AINU — E Asia
AIR — W Africa
AIRIMAN — Australia
AIRITUMIUT — Northeast NA
AIS — Southeast NA
AISHIHIK — Subarctic
AIT ATTA — N Africa
AIT IDRASSEN — N Africa
AIT KHEBACHE — N Africa
AIT OUMALOU — N Africa
AIT WALNZGIT — N Africa
AIT YAFELMAN — N Africa
AIVILLIRMIUT — Arctic
AIZO — W Africa

AJA — W Africa
AJABAKAN — Australia
AJABATHA — Australia
AJARIANS (Adjarians) — Caucasus
AJIE — Melanesia
AK POSSO — W Africa
AKA — C Africa
AKAN — W Africa
AKANSA (Quapaw) — Plains NA
AKAWAIO — Orinoco Basin
AKHA (Kaw, Ko) — SE Asia
AKIE — E Africa
AKLANON — SE Asia
AKLAVIK — Arctic
AKOKISA — Plains NA
AKOKO — W Africa

Children's love is like water in a basket.

ARGENTINE PROVERB

AKOSA — S Africa
AKUDNIRMIUT — Arctic
AKULIARMIUT — Arctic
AKUNA — Melanesia
AKURIO — Orinoco Basin
AKWA'ALA (Paipai) — Mesoamerica
AKWE — Amazon Basin
AKWESASNE MOHAWKS — Northeast NA
AKYEM — W Africa
AL HARABA — N Africa
AL HAWAASHIB — Middle East
AL HIBAB — Middle East
AL MAJAABRA — N Africa
AL MURAIKHAT — Middle East
AL MURRA — Middle East
AL SHALAWAH — Middle East
ALA — E Africa
ALA'NGAN — SE Asia
ALABA — E Africa
ALABAMA — Southeast NA
ALABAMA COUSHATTA — Plains NA

ALABAMA QUASSARTE — Plains NA
ALACALUF (Halakwulup) — Patagonia
ALAK — SE Asia
ALAMAMRA — N Africa
ALAND ISLANDERS — N Europe
ALAS — SE Asia
ALASKAN ESKIMOS — Arctic
ALAWA — Australia
ALAWITES — Middle East
ALBANIANS — S Europe
ALE — S Asia
ALEIQAT — Middle East
ALEUT — Arctic
ALGONKIN — Northeast NA
ALI BIN MORRAH — Middle East
ALLEGHENNY — Northeast NA
ALLENTIAC — Andes
ALOENE — SE Asia
ALORESE — SE Asia
ALSATIANS — W Europe
ALSEA — Northwest Coast NA
ALTAIANS — E Asia
ALUKU — Orinoco Basin
ALUR — E Africa
ALURA — Australia
ALUTIIQ (Pacific Eskimos) — Arctic
ALYAWARRE — Australia
AMAHUACA — Amazon Basin
AMAHUMBU — S Africa
AMALEH — C Asia
AMANAYE — Amazon Basin
AMANGU — Australia
AMARAK — Australia
AMARAKAERI — Andes
AMARAR — N Africa

AKOSA — S Africa

AMARKEN — Melanesia
AMASILI — S Africa
AMBA — E Africa
AMBAE — Melanesia
AMBERBAKEN — Melanesia
AMBO (Ovambo) — S Africa
AMBONESE — SE Asia
AMBUELLA — S Africa
AMDO — C Asia
AMERALIK — Arctic
AMERINDIANS (Amerindino) — Caribbean
AMERINDINO (Amerindians) — Caribbean
AMEYAO — Caribbean
AMHARA — E Africa
AMI — E Asia
AMIJANGAL — Australia
AMIS — E Asia
AMISH — Northeast NA
AMMASSALIMIUT — Arctic
AMNIAPE — Amazon Basin

AMOIPIRA — Central SA
AMR — Middle East
AMRAAL — S Africa
AMUESHA — Andes
AMURAG — Australia
AMUZGO — Mesoamerica
AMYU — Melanesia
ANADYR ESKIMO — Arctic
ANAIWAN — Australia
ANAKAMUTI — Australia
ANAKAZZA — N Africa
ANAMBE — Amazon Basin
ANANG — W Africa
ANARKAT — Arctic
ANATOLIAN TURKS — Middle East
ANCASH — Andes
ANDAKEREBINA — Australia
ANDALUSIANS — W Europe
ANDAMANESE — SE Asia
ANDHRAS — S Asia
ANDINGARI — Australia
ANDIS — Caucasus
ANDOA — Amazon Basin
ANDOKE — Amazon Basin
ANGAITE — Central SA
ANGARA — Andes
ANGKU — E Asia
ANGMAGSQLIK — N Europe
ANGOLARS — W Africa
ANGONI — E Africa
ANGOON — Northwest Coast NA
ANGU — Melanesia
ANIA — E Africa
//ANIKHOE — S Africa
ANISHINABE — Plains NA
ANIZAH — Middle East
ANKAZA — N Africa
ANKOLE (Banyankole, Nkole) — E Africa
ANLO — W Africa
ANMATJERA — Australia
ANMATYERR — Australia
ANOUFO — W Africa
ANTAIMORO — E Africa
ANTAISKA — E Africa
ANTAKIRINJA — Australia
ANTANDROY — E Africa
ANTIPA — Amazon Basin
ANUAK — E Africa
ANUM BOSO — W Africa
ANUTA ISLANDERS — Melanesia
APA TANI — S Asia
APACHE — Southwest NA
APALACHEE — Southeast NA
APALAI — Amazon Basin
APANYEKRA — Amazon Basin
APAPOCUVA — Central SA
APAYAO — SE Asia
APIAKA — Amazon Basin
APINAYE — Amazon Basin
APOLISTA — Amazon Basin
AQUITAINE — W Europe
ARABA — Australia
ARABAMA — Australia
ARABS — Middle East, N Africa
ARACHANE — Central SA
ARAFAH — N Africa
ARAGO — W Africa
ARAKANESE (Rohingya) — SE Asia

ARAKE — Amazon Basin
ARALWA — Australia
ARAMDA — Australia
ARANA — Central SA
ARANDA (Arrernte, Arunta) — Australia
ARAONA — Amazon Basin
ARAPAHO PLAINS — Plains NA
ARAPESH — Melanesia
ARAPIUM — Amazon Basin
ARARAIBOS — Amazon Basin
ARAUAKI — Amazon Basin
ARAVCANIAN (Pehuenche) — Andes
ARAWAK — Orinoco Basin
ARAWETE — Orinoco Basin
ARECUNA — Orinoco Basin
AREQUIPA — Andes
ARGOBBA — E Africa
ARGUNI — Melanesia
ARHUACO — Caribbean Coast SA
ARICA — Andes
ARICOBI — Amazon Basin
ARIKARA PLAINS — Plains NA
ARIKEM — Amazon Basin
ARINAGOTO — Orinoco Basin
ARMENIANS — Caucasus
ARNA — N Africa
ARNGA — Australia
AROLAND — Northeast NA
AROMA — Melanesia
AROOSTOOK MICMAC — Northeast NA
ARRERNTE (Aranda, Arunta) — Australia
ARSUK — Arctic
ARU ISLANDERS — Melanesia
ARUA — Amazon Basin
ARUNTA (Aranda, Arrernte) — Australia
ARUSHA — E Africa
ARUSI — E Africa
ARVIQUURMIUT — Arctic
ASANTE (Ashanti) — W Africa
ASHAN — Middle East
ASHANINKA — Amazon Basin
ASHANTI (Asante) — W Africa
ASHKENAZIC JEWS — Europe
ASHLUSLAY — Central SA
ASIAGMIUT — Arctic
ASMAT — Melanesia
ASSAMESE — S Asia
ASSINIBOIN PLAINS — Plains NA
ASUA — C Africa
ASURINI — Orinoco Basin
ATA SIKKA — SE Asia
ATA TANA 'AI — SE Asia
ATACAMA — Andes
ATAHUN SHOSHONE — Great Basin NA
ATAYAL — E Asia
ATHABASCA CHIPEWYAN — Plains NA
ATIE — W Africa
ATIKAMEG — Plains NA
ATJEHNESE — SE Asia

ATJINURI — Australia
ATLIN — Subarctic
ATMANIKA — Caucasus
ATNA — Arctic
ATONI — SE Asia
ATORAI — Orinoco Basin
ATROARI — Amazon Basin
ATSAHUACA — Amazon Basin
ATSI — E Asia
ATSINA — Northeast NA
ATSUGEWI — Far West NA
ATTAWAPISKAT — Northeast NA

Hunger is the teacher of many.

GREEK PROVERB

ATTIKAMEK — Northeast NA
ATUENCE — E Asia
AUANBURA — Australia
AUCA (Huaorani, Wao, Waorani) — Amazon Basin
//AU//EI (Auen) — S Africa
AUEN (//Au//ei) — S Africa
AUETI — Amazon Basin
AUGU — Melanesia
AUGUSTINE — Far West NA
AUK — Northwest Coast NA
AULAD SOLIMAN — N Africa
AULLIMINDEN — W Africa
AUSH — Patagonia
AUSHI — C Africa
AUSTRALIAN ABORIGINES — Australia
AUSTRIANS — C Europe
AUVERGNATS — W Europe
AUYANA — Melanesia
AVA — Central SA
AVARS — Caucasus
AVE — W Africa
AVERIANO — Orinoco Basin
AVEYRONNAIS — W Europe
AVIL — Middle East
AVUKAYA — C Africa
AWA — Melanesia
AWA KWAIKER (Koakir) — Andes
AWABAKAL — Australia
AWAI — Melanesia
AWAKATEKO (Acatec, Aguatec) — Mesoamerica
AWAMIR — Middle East
AWAQIR — N Africa
AWARAI — Australia
AWAZIM — Middle East
AWE — W Africa
AWEER (Kilii, Somali Boni) — E Africa
AWEIKOMA — Central SA
AWI — E Africa
AWIN — Melanesia
AWINMUL — Australia
AWISHIRI — Amazon Basin
AWLAD'ALI — N Africa
AWYU — Melanesia
AYACUCHO — Andes
AYAIDA — N Africa
AYAMARO — Melanesia
AYISENGA — S Africa
AYMARA — Andes
AYOREO (Moro) — Central SA

AZANDE (Zande) — C Africa
AZERBAIJANIS (Azeris) — Caucasus
AZERIS (Azerbaijanis) — Caucasus
AZOREANS — W Europe
BA MBENZELE — C Africa
BAADA — Australia
BABA — Melanesia
BABA CHINESE — SE Asia
BABENZELE — C Africa
BABOBO — SE Asia

BABOUTE — C Africa
BADAGA — S Asia
BADI — Australia
BADIMAIA — Australia
BADJALANG — Australia
BADJIRI — Australia
BADUI — SE Asia
BADUTU — E Africa
BAFFIN ISLANDERS — Arctic
BAFIA — W Africa
BAGA — W Africa
BAGANDA — E Africa
BAGARRA — W Africa
BAGAZ — Mesoamerica
BAGGARA ARABS — N Africa
BAGIRMI — W Africa
BAGISU (Gisu) — E Africa
BAGOBO — SE Asia
BAGU — Australia
BAHAR LU — Middle East
BAHINEMO — Melanesia
BAHNAR — SE Asia
BAHWETIG MACKINAC — Northeast NA
BAHWETIG OJIBWA — Northeast NA
BAI (Baizu) — E Asia
BAIA — C Africa
BAIALI — Australia
BAIGA — S Asia
BAIJUNGU — Australia
BAILGU — Australia
BAINOA — Caribbean
BAINOUK — W Africa
BAIT IMANI — Middle East
BAIT KATHIR — Middle East
BAIZU (Bai) — E Asia
BAJAU — SE Asia
BAKA — C Africa
BAKAIRI — Amazon Basin

BAKALAHARI — S Africa
BAKAMBA — C Africa
BAKANAMBIA — Australia
BAKELE — C Africa
BAKHTIARI — Middle East
BAKIL — Middle East
BAKO — E Africa
BAKONGO — C Africa
BAKOVI — Melanesia
BAKWE — W Africa
BALALA — S Africa
BALALI — C Africa
BALANTAK — SE Asia
BALANTE — W Africa
BALARDONG — Australia
BALE — E Africa
BALEARICS — W Europe
BALESE NDAKE — C Africa
BALGARN — Middle East
BALI — W Africa
BALI AGA — SE Asia
BALINESE — SE Asia
BALKARS — Caucasus
BALLOUK — W Africa
BALOULOU (Mongo) — C Africa
BALOUNDOU — C Africa
BALTI — S Asia
BALUA — C Africa
BALUCHI — C Africa
BAMAKOMA (Makoma) — S Africa
BAMARS (Burman) — SE Asia
BAMBARA — W Africa
BAMBUTI (Mbuti) — C Africa
BAMILEKE — W Africa
BAMOUN — W Africa
BAMU — Melanesia
BANABANS — Micronesia
BANAGAL — C Africa
BANARO — Melanesia
BANBAI — Australia
BANDA — C Africa
BANDI — W Africa
BANDJIN — Australia
BANDZA — C Africa
BANEN — W Africa
BANGALA — C Africa
BANGGAI — SE Asia
BANGGALA — Australia
BANGU — C Africa
BANHUN — W Africa
BANI — Caribbean
BANI HAJIR — Middle East
BANI HILAL — Middle East
BANI KHALID — Middle East
BANI KITAB — Middle East
BANI SHAHR — Middle East
BANI YAM — Middle East
BANIA — S Asia
BANIVA — Orinoco Basin

BANJARA — S Asia
BANKA — SE Asia
BANKS ISLANDERS — Melanesia
BANNOCK — Great Basin NA
BANTU — S Africa
BANYAK — SE Asia
BANYANKOLE (Ankole, Nkole) — E Africa
BANYORO — E Africa
BANYUA — W Africa
BANZIRI — C Africa
BAOULE — W Africa
BAPOTO — C Africa
BAQUM — Middle East
BARA — Amazon Basin
BARA — E Africa
BARABA BARABA — Australia
BARABAIG — E Africa
BARADA — Australia
BARAMA RIVER CARIBS — Orinoco Basin
BARANBINJA — Australia
BARANZAI — Middle East
BARAPARAPA — Australia
BARARA — Australia
BARASANA — Amazon Basin
BARBACOA — Caribbean
BARBARAM — Australia
BARBOCOA — Andes
BARE — Amazon Basin
BARI — Caribbean Coast SA
BARI (Beri) — E Africa
BARIBA — W Africa
BARIMAIA — Australia
BARINDJI — Australia
BARIYAH — Middle East
BARKINDJI — Australia
BARLAMOMO — Australia
BARNA — Australia
BAROK — Melanesia
BARONA — Far West NA
BARRUMBINYA — Australia
BARTANGS — C Asia
BARUNGA — Australia
BARUNGGAM — Australia
BARUNGGUAN — Australia
BARUYA — Melanesia
BASAKOMO — W Africa
BASARWA (Bushmen, San) — S Africa
BASHILANGE — C Africa
BASHILELE (Lele) — C Africa
BASHKIRS — E Europe
BASIRI — C Africa
BASKETO — E Africa
BASOGA — E Africa
BASOTHO — S Africa
BASQUES — W Europe

BASRAI — W Africa
BASSA — C Africa
BASSARI — W Africa
BASSERI — Middle East
BASUA — C Africa
BATAHIN — N Africa
BATAK — SE Asia
BATATELA — C Africa
BATEK — SE Asia
BATJALA — Australia
BATJAN — SE Asia
BATLARO — S Africa
BATLOKWA — S Africa
BATORO — E Africa
BAUL — S Asia
BAULE — W Africa
BAURE — Amazon Basin
BAVARIANS — W Europe
BAWAKI — Melanesia
BAWEANESE — SE Asia
BAYA (Gbaya) — C Africa
BAYAKA — C Africa
BAYAMO — Caribbean
BAYAQUITIRI — Caribbean
BAYEI — S Africa
BAYOT — W Africa
BE — W Africa
BEAFADA — W Africa
BEARSPAW — Plains NA
BEAUSOLEIL CHIPPEWA — Northeast NA
BEAVER — Subarctic
BEDERIAT — C Africa
BEDIK — W Africa

Flowers leave some of their fragrance in the hand that bestows them.

CHINESE PROVERB

BEDOUIN ARABS — Middle East
BEGA — E Africa
BEHERIA — N Africa
BEICO DE PAU — Amazon Basin
BEIR — E Africa
BEJA (Beni Amer) — N Africa
BELANDAS — SE Asia
BELARUSIANS (White Russians) — E Europe
BELAU — Micronesia
BELGIANS — W Europe
BELLA BELLA — Northwest Coast NA
BELLA COOLA — Northwest Coast NA
BELLE — W Africa
BELLIKAN — Caucasus
BELUBBA — E Africa

BEMBA — E Africa
BEMBE — C Africa
BEN GUIL — N Africa
BENA — E Africa
BENABENA — Melanesia
BENDE — E Africa
BENE ISRAEL — Middle East, S Asia
BENGALIS — S Asia
BENGLONG (Deang) — E Asia
BENI AMER (Beja) — N Africa
BENI ATIYAH — Middle East
BENI HAJAR — Middle East
BENI SAKHR BEDU — Middle East
BENI SUEF — N Africa
BEOTHUK — Northeast NA
BERABICHE — W Africa
BERBERI — C Africa
BERBERS (Imazighen) — N Africa
BERGAMASCO — W Europe
BERGDAMA — S Africa
BERI (Bari) — E Africa
BERIQURUK — Australia
BERRIAIT — Australia
BERSEBA — S Africa
BERSIMIS — Northeast NA

BERTA — E Africa
BESORUBE — W Africa
BETA ISRAEL (Falasha) — E Africa
BETE — W Africa
BETHANIE — S Africa
BETOI — Amazon Basin
BETSIAMITES — Northeast NA
BETSILEO — E Africa
BETSIMISARAKA — E Africa
BETTAKURUMBAS — S Asia
BEZANOZANO — E Africa
BHACA — S Africa
BHIL — S Asia
BHILALA — S Asia
BHOTA (Ngalop) — S Asia
BHOTTADA — S Asia
BHUIYA — S Asia
BHUTANESE — S Asia
BHUTIA — S Asia
BIAGAI — Melanesia
BIAK — Melanesia
BIAT — SE Asia
BIBELMEN — Australia
BICOLANO — SE Asia
BIDAWAL — Australia
BIDAYUH — SE Asia
BIDIA — Australia
BIDJANDJARA — Australia
BIDOON — Middle East
BIGAMBUL — Australia
BIHARI — S Asia
BIKALBURA — Australia
BIKINI — Micronesia
BIKOL — SE Asia
BILAAN — SE Asia
BILEN — E Africa
BILINGARA — Australia
BILLI — Middle East
BILLITON — SE Asia

DOGON STILT DANCERS RESTING ON A MUD WALL IN MALI

BILOXI — *Southeast NA*
BIMANESE — *SE Asia*
BINANDERE — *Melanesia*
BINBINGA — *Australia*
BINDAL — *Australia*
BINDJAREB — *Australia*
BINDUBI — *Australia*
BINGA — *C Africa*
BINGABURA — *Australia*
BINGONGINA — *Australia*
BINI — *W Africa*
BINIGURA — *Australia*
BINJI — *E Europe*
BINTUKUA — *Caribbean Coast SA*
BINUMARIEN — *Melanesia*
BIRA — *E Africa*
BIRDI — *Middle East*
BIRHOR — *S Asia*
BIRI — *C Africa*
BIRIA — *Australia*
BIRIFOR — *W Africa*
BIROM — *W Africa*
BIRPAI — *Australia*
BISA — *E Africa*
BISAYAH — *SE Asia*
BISIS — *Melanesia*
BISSA — *W Africa*
BISSAGO — *W Africa*
BIT — *SE Asia*
BITJARA — *Australia*
BLACK THAI (Tai Dam) — *SE Asia*
BLACKFEET — *Plains NA*
BLANG — *E Asia*
BLOOD — *Plains NA*
BLOODVEIN — *Plains NA*
BOANBURA — *Australia*
BOARDJI — *Melanesia*
BOAZI — *Melanesia*
BOBO — *W Africa*
BOERS (Afrikaners) — *S Africa*
BOFI — *C Africa*
BOHANE — *Central SA*
BOHOLANO — *SE Asia*
BOHRA — *S Asia*
BOIKEN — *Melanesia*
BOKAR — *S Asia*
BOLAANG MONGONDOW — *SE Asia*
BOLEWA — *W Africa*

If the mouth slips, it is more slippery than the foot.

GHANIAN PROVERB

BOLI — *Melanesia*
BOMA — *C Africa*
BOMBESA — *C Africa*
BOMVANA — *S Africa*
BONAN — *E Asia*
BONARI — *Orinoco Basin*
BONBARABUA — *Australia*
BONDEI — *E Africa*
BONDO — *S Asia*
BONERATE — *SE Asia*
BONGA — *C Africa*
BONGO (Bungu) — *C Africa*
BONGUE — *C Africa*
BONI (Aweer) — *E Africa*
BONO — *W Africa*
BONTOK — *SE Asia*
BOOTHROYD — *Northwest Coast NA*
BORA — *Amazon Basin*
BORAN — *E Africa*
BORO — *Amazon Basin*
BORO — *S Asia*
BORORO — *Amazon Basin*
BORUCA — *Mesoamerica*
BOSKIEN — *Melanesia*

BOSNIAN MUSLIMS — *C Europe*
BOSYEBA — *C Africa*
BOTOCUDO — *Central SA*
BOUBANGI (Mboshi) — *C Africa*
BOUGAINVILLE ISLANDERS — *Melanesia*
BOUN — *Australia*
BOUYEI — *E Asia*
BOYACA — *Caribbean*
BOYKS — *E Europe*
BOZO — *W Africa*
BRABRALUNG — *Australia*
BRAHUI — *C Asia*
BRAIAKAULUNG — *Australia*
BRAO — *SE Asia*
BRAOYA — *N Africa*
BRATAUOLUNG — *Australia*
BRETONS — *W Europe*
BRIBRI — *Mesoamerica*
BROKENHEAD OJIBWAY — *Plains NA*
BROTHERTON — *Northeast NA*
BRU — *SE Asia*
BTSISI — *SE Asia*
BUBI — *C Africa*
BUCTOUCHE — *Northeast NA*
BUDIDJARA — *Australia*
BUDU — *C Africa*
BUDUGS — *Caucasus*
BUDUMA — *W Africa*
BUGAKHOE — *S Africa*
BUGAKWE — *S Africa*
BUGANDA — *E Africa*
BUGIS — *SE Asia*
BUGLE — *Mesoamerica*
BUGULMARA — *Australia*
BUGUSU (Lhuya, Luyia) — *E Africa*
BUHA — *E Africa*
BUKIDNON — *SE Asia*
BUKITAN — *SE Asia*
BUKSA — *S Asia*
BUKULI — *E Africa*
BULALLI — *Australia*
BULGARIANS — *E Europe*

BULLOM — *W Africa*
BULUSU — *SE Asia*
BULUWAI — *Australia*
BUMBA — *C Africa*
BUMBU — *W Africa*
BUMIPUTRA (Malay) — *SE Asia*
BUNABA — *Australia*
BUNDA — *C Africa*
BUNDI — *Melanesia*
BUNGANDITJ — *Australia*
BUNGU (Bongo) — *C Africa*
BUNTAMURRA — *Australia*
BUNUN — *E Asia*
BUNURONG — *Australia*
BUNYOLE — *E Africa*
BUNYORO (Kitara, Nyoro) — *E Africa*
BURAKUMIN (Eta) — *E Asia*
BURGHER — *S Asia*
BURGUNDIANS — *W Europe*
BURIATS — *E Asia*
BURKINABE — *W Africa*

BURMAN (Bamars) — *SE Asia*
BURMESE — *SE Asia*
BURU — *SE Asia*
BURULI — *E Africa*
BURUNA — *Australia*
BURUNGI — *E Africa*
BURUSHASKI — *S Asia*
BURUSHO (Hunzakuts) — *C Asia*
BUSANSI — *W Africa*
BUSHMEN (Basarwa, San) — *S Africa*
BUTLIKH — *Caucasus*
BUTONESE — *SE Asia*
BUTUNG — *SE Asia*
BUWALLAH — *Middle East*
BUYI — *E Asia*
BVIRI — *C Africa*
BWA — *W Africa*
BWAIDOGA — *Melanesia*
BWAKA — *C Africa*
BWE — *SE Asia*
BWILE — *C Africa*
CAAPOR — *Amazon Basin*
CABAZON — *Far West NA*
CABECAR — *Mesoamerica*
CABO — *Mesoamerica*
CABRE — *Orinoco Basin*
CACHIL DEHE WINTUN — *Far West NA*
CADDO — *Plains NA*
CADDO ADAIS — *Southeast NA*
CAETE — *Central SA*
CAGA — *E Africa*
CAGABA (Kogi) — *Caribbean Coast SA*
CAHIBO — *Caribbean*
CAHTO — *Far West NA*
CAHUILLA — *Far West NA*
CAINGUA — *Central SA*
CAIRI — *Central SA*
CAIZCIMU — *Caribbean*
CAJAMARCA — *Andes*
CAJATAMBO — *Andes*
CAKCHIQUEL (Kaqchikel) — *Mesoamerica*
CALABAR — *W Africa*
CALABRESE — *S Europe*
CALAPUYA — *Northwest Coast NA*
CALAVERAS MIWOK — *Far West NA*
CALAYUA — *Orinoco Basin*
CALISTA — *Subarctic*
CALLAHUAYA — *Andes*
CALUSA — *Caribbean*
CAMACAN — *Central SA*
CAMANA — *Andes*
CAMPA — *Amazon Basin*
CAMPO (Tipai) — *Far West NA*
CANA — *Andes*
CANAMARI — *Amazon Basin*
CANARI — *Andes*
CANCHI — *Andes*
CANDOSHI — *Amazon Basin*
CANELA (Ramkokamekra) — *Amazon Basin*
CANELOS QUICHUA — *Andes*
CANICHANA — *Amazon Basin*
CANTONESE — *E Asia*
CANYON COSTANOAN — *Far West NA*
CAPANAHUA — *Amazon Basin*
CAPE VERDEANS — *W Europe*
CAPE YORK PEOPLES — *Australia*

CAPITAN GRANDE — *Far West NA*
CAQUETIO — *Caribbean Coast SA*
CARA — *Andes*
CARACA — *Caribbean Coast SA*
CARAHYABY — *Amazon Basin*
CARANGA — *Andes*
CARAVAYA — *Andes*
CARI'A — *Orinoco Basin*
CARIBOU ESKIMOS — *Arctic*
CARIBS (Galibi) — *Caribbean, Orinoco Basin*
CARIGUANO — *Orinoco Basin*
CARIJO — *Central SA*
CARIJONA — *Amazon Basin*
CARINA — *Orinoco Basin*
CARIPUNA — *Amazon Basin*
CARIRI — *Amazon Basin*
CARMEL — *Far West NA*
CAROLINE ISLANDERS — *Micronesia*
CARPATHO RUSYNS — *E Europe*
CARPATHO UKRAINIANS (Lemkos) — *C Europe*
CARRIER — *Subarctic*
CASCADE — *Northwest Coast NA*
CASHIBO — *Andes*
CASHINAHUA — *Amazon Basin*
CASHITE — *E Africa*
CASMA — *Andes*
CASTILIANS — *W Europe*
CATABA — *Plains NA*
CATALANS — *W Europe*
CATAWBA — *Southeast NA*
CATIO — *Andes*
CATUKINA — *Amazon Basin*
CAUATAMBO — *Andes*
CAUDUVEO — *Central SA*
CAVINA — *Amazon Basin*
CAVINENA — *Amazon Basin*
CAWAHIB — *Amazon Basin*
CAYABI — *Amazon Basin*
CAYAGUAYO — *Caribbean*
CAYAPA — *Andes*
CAYOOSE CREEK — *Northwest Coast NA*
CAYUGA — *Northeast NA*
CAYUISHANA — *Amazon Basin*
CAYUSE — *Plateau NA*
CAYUVAVA — *Amazon Basin*
CAZCAN — *Mesoamerica*
CEBAUN — *SE Asia*
CEBU — *SE Asia*
CENTRAL ASIAN TURKS — *Middle East*
CENTRAL ESKIMOS — *Arctic*
CENTRAL MIWOK — *Far West NA*
CENTRAL THAI — *SE Asia*
CERAM — *SE Asia*
CH'ORTI' — *Mesoamerica*
CHAAMBA — *N Africa*
CHABEANS — *Caribbean*
CHACHAPOYA — *Andes*
CHACOBO — *Amazon Basin*
CHAGGA — *E Africa*
CHAIMA — *Caribbean Coast SA*
CHAKCHIUMA — *Southeast NA*

CHAKMAS (Changma) — *SE Asia*
CHALDEANS — *C Asia*
CHAM — *SE Asia*
CHAMA — *Amazon Basin*
CHAMACOCO — *Central SA*
CHAMARS — *S Asia*
CHAMBA — *W Africa*
CHAMBRI — *Melanesia*
CHAMI — *Amazon Basin*
CHAMORROS — *Micronesia*
CHAMPAGNE — *Subarctic*
CHAMULA — *Mesoamerica*
CHANA — *Central SA*
CHANE — *Central SA*
CHANGMA (Chakmas) — *SE Asia*
CHAOBON — *SE Asia*

One meets his destiny often in the road he takes to avoid it.

FRENCH PROVERB

CHAOUIA — *N Africa*
CHAPAKURA — *Amazon Basin*
CHARA — *E Africa*
CHARCA — *Amazon Basin*
CHARIGURIQUA — *S Africa*
CHARRUA — *Central SA*
CHASTACOSTA — *Northwest Coast NA*
CHATINO — *Mesoamerica*
CHATOT — *Southeast NA*
CHAUBUNAGUNGA-MANG — *Northeast NA*
CHAUDHRI — *S Asia*
CHAVCHYVS — *Arctic*
CHAWAI — *W Africa*
CHAYAHUITA — *Andes*
CHE WONG — *SE Asia*
CHECHEHET — *Central SA*
CHECHEN — *Caucasus*
CHEHALIS — *Northwest Coast NA*
CHELAN — *Plateau NA*
CHEMAINUS — *Northwest Coast NA*
CHEMAWAWIN — *Plains NA*
CHEMEHUEVI — *Great Basin NA*
CHENCHU — *S Asia*
CHENG — *SE Asia*
CHEPARA — *Australia*
CHEREMIS (Maris) — *E Europe*
CHERO — *S Asia*
CHEROKEE — *Plains, Southeast NA*
CHESLATTA CARRIER — *Northwest Coast NA*
CHETCO — *Northwest Coast NA*
CHEWA — *E Africa*
CHEYENNE — *Plains NA*
CHEYENNE ARAPAHO — *Plains NA*
CHIBCHA — *Andes*
CHICHA — *Amazon Basin*
CHICKAHOMINY — *Southeast NA*
CHICKAMOGEE CHERO-KEE — *Southeast NA*
CHICKASAW — *Plains NA*
CHICORA SIOUX — *Southeast NA*
CHICOUTIMI — *Northeast NA*

CHIKUNDA — *E Africa*
CHILCOTIN — *Northwest Coast NA*
CHILKAT — *Subarctic*
CHILULA — *Far West NA*
CHIMAKUM — *Northwest Coast NA*
CHIMANE — *Amazon Basin*
CHIMARIKO — *Far West NA*
CHIMBU — *Melanesia*
CHIMILA — *Caribbean Coast SA*
CHIMO — *Northeast NA*
CHIMU — *Andes*
CHIN — *S Asia*
CHINANTEC — *Mesoamerica*
CHINCHA — *Andes*
CHINCHAYCOCHA — *Andes*
CHING — *E Asia*
CHINGALI — *Australia*
CHINIKI — *Plains NA*
CHINOOK — *Northwest Coast NA*
CHIPAYA (Uru) — *Andes*
CHIPEWYAN — *Subarctic*
CHIPEWYAN PRAIRIE — *Plains NA*
CHIPPEWA (Ojibwa) — *Northeast NA*
CHIPPEWA CREE — *Plains NA*
CHIQUITANO — *Central SA*
CHIQUITO — *Amazon Basin*
CHIQUIYAMI — *Andes*
CHIRICAHUA APACHE — *Southwest NA*
CHIRIGUANO (Guarayo) — *Andes*
CHIRIPA — *Central SA*
CHIRMA — *Melanesia*
CHISASIBI — *Northeast NA*
CHISHINGA — *C Africa*
CHISOS — *Plains NA*
CHITIMACHA — *Southeast NA*
CHLI (Try) — *SE Asia*
CHOCO — *Andes*
CHOCTAW — *Plains, Southeast NA*
CHOCTAW APACHE — *Southeast NA*
CHOIAH — *C Asia*
CHOINUMNI YOKUTS — *Far West NA*
CHOISEUL ISLANDERS — *Melanesia*
CHOKWE — *C Africa*
CHOL — *Mesoamerica*
CHOLON — *Andes*
CHONA — *E Asia*
CHONG — *SE Asia*
CHONO — *Patagonia*
CHONTAL — *Mesoamerica*
CHONYI — *E Africa*
CHOPI — *S Africa*
CHOQUE — *Orinoco Basin*
CHOROTE — *Central SA*
CHORTI — *Mesoamerica*
CHRAU — *SE Asia*
CHRISTMAS ISLANDERS (Kiritimati Islanders) — *Polynesia*

CHRU — *SE Asia*
CHUABO — *E Africa*
CHUANG — *E Asia*
CHUCKBUKMIUT — *Northeast NA*
CHUGACH — *Arctic*
CHUJ — *Mesoamerica*
CHUKCHANSI YOKUT — *Far West NA*
CHUKCHI — *Arctic*
CHUKOTKA — *Arctic*
CHULUPI — *Central SA*
CHUMASH — *Far West NA*
CHUPAYACHU — *Andes*
CHUUK ISLANDERS (Trukese) — *Micronesia*
CHUVAN — *Arctic*
CHUVANZY — *Arctic*
CHUVASH — *E Europe*
CINTA LARGA — *Amazon Basin*
CIPUNGU — *S Africa*
CIRCASSIANS — *Caucasus, Middle East*
CISAMA — *C Africa*
CISANJI — *S Africa*
CLACKAMAS — *Northwest Coast NA*
CLATSKANIE — *Northwest Coast NA*
CLATSOP — *Northwest Coast NA*
CO SUNG (Kuy, Lahu) — *SE Asia*
COAHUILTECAN — *Mesoamerica*
COAIQUER — *Amazon Basin*
COANI — *Orinoco Basin*
COASTAL CHUMASH — *Far West NA*
COASTAL MIWOK — *Far West NA*
COASTAL SALISH — *Northwest Coast NA*
COASTAL TSIMSHIAN — *Northwest Coast NA*
COASTAL YUKI — *Far West NA*
COCAMA — *Amazon Basin*
COCAMILLA — *Amazon Basin*
COCHAPAMPA — *Amazon Basin*
COCHIMI — *Mesoamerica*
COCHITI PUEBLO — *Southwest NA*
COCONUCO — *Andes*
COCOPAH — *Southwest NA*
COEUR D'ALENES — *Plateau NA*
COFAN — *Amazon Basin*
COHARIE — *Southeast NA*
COLLA — *Andes*
COLLAGUA — *Andes*
COLLO (Shilluk) — *C Africa*
COLORADO (Tsatchela) — *Andes*
COLUMBIA — *Plateau NA*
COLVILLE — *Northwest Coast NA*
COMANCHE — *Plains NA*
COMORIANS — *E Africa*
COMOX — *Northwest Coast NA*
CONCHO — *Mesoamerica*
CONCHUCO — *Andes*
CONHAQUE — *W Africa*
CONIBO — *Andes*
CONOY — *Northeast NA*
COOK ISLANDERS — *Polynesia*
COORG — *S Asia*
COOS — *Northwest Coast NA*

COPALIS — *Northwest Coast NA*
COPPER ESKIMOS — *Arctic*
COPTS — *N Africa*
COQUILLE — *Northwest Coast NA*
CORA — *Mesoamerica*
COREE — *Southeast NA*
CORNISH — *N Europe*
COROADO — *Central SA*
CORSICANS — *S Europe*
CORTINA WINTUN — *Far West NA*
COSTANOAN (Mutsun) — *Far West NA*
COSTANOAN ESSELEN — *Far West NA*
COTABATO MANOBO — *SE Asia*
COTE — *Plains NA*
COTO (Orejon) — *Amazon Basin*
COTOPAXI QUICHUA — *Andes*
COUCHICHING — *Northeast NA*
COUSHATTA — *Southeast NA*
COUSSARI — *Orinoco Basin*
COWESSESS — *Plains NA*
COWICHAN (Halkomelem) — *Northwest Coast NA*
COWLITZ — *Northwest Coast NA*
COYAIMA — *Amazon Basin*
CREE — *Plains NA*
CREEK — *Plains NA*
CREOLES — *Southeast NA*
CRETANS — *S Europe*
CRIMEAN TATARS — *C Asia, E Europe*
CROATS — *C Europe*
CROW — *Plains NA*
CUA — *SE Asia*
CUAUHCOMECA — *Mesoamerica*
CUBANACAN — *Caribbean*
CUBEO (Kobewa) — *Amazon Basin*
CUCIBA — *Caribbean*

Ignorance doesn't kill you, but it does make you sweat a lot.

HAITIAN PROVERB

CUICATEC — *Mesoamerica*
CUITLATEC (Teco) — *Mesoamerica*
CUIVA — *Orinoco Basin*
CULINA — *Amazon Basin*
CUMANA — *Caribbean Coast SA*
CUMANAGOTO — *Caribbean Coast SA*
CUNA (Kuna) — *Mesoamerica*
CUNIBA — *Amazon Basin*
CUPACA — *Andes*
CUPENO — *Far West NA*
CURRIPACO — *Orinoco Basin*
CURUMINACA — *Amazon Basin*
CUSCO — *Andes*
CUYAPAIPE — *Far West NA*
CYCLADES — *S Europe*
CYMRY (Welsh) — *N Europe*
CYPRIOTS — *C Europe*

CZECHS — *C Europe*
DAAROOD — *E Africa*
DABA — *W Africa*
DAFLA — *S Asia*
DAGABA (Dagarti) — *W Africa*
DAGADA — *SE Asia*
DAGAMBA (Dagomba) — *W Africa*
DAGARA (Dogara) — *W Africa*
DAGARTI (Dagaba) — *W Africa*
DAGESTANI — *Caucasus*
DAGOMBA (Dagbamba) — *W Africa*
DAGURU — *E Africa*
DAHALO — *E Africa*
DAHM — *Middle East*
DAHOMEY (Fon) — *W Africa*
DAI — *E Asia*
DAII — *Australia*
DAILU — *E Asia*
DAINA — *E Asia*
DAINGGATI — *Australia*
DAIOMONI — *Melanesia*
DAKOTA — *Plains NA*
DAKOTA TIPI — *Plains NA*
DAKWA — *C Africa*
DAL — *S Asia*
DALABON — *Australia*
DALLA — *Australia*
DALLEBURRA — *Australia*
DALLES (Ochiichagwe'babigo'ining) — *Northeast NA*
DALMATIANS — *C Europe*
DAMA — *S Africa*
DAMANI — *Middle East*
DAMARA (Herero) — *S Africa*
DAMBARA — *W Africa*
DAMERGU — *W Africa*
DAMURA — *Melanesia*
DAN — *W Africa*
DANAKIL (Afar) — *E Africa*
DANDA — *S Africa*
DANES — *N Europe*
DANGANI — *Australia*
DANGBON — *Australia*
DANGGALI — *Australia*
DANGU — *Australia*
DANI — *Melanesia*
DANI — *Amazon Basin*

DANISAN — *S Africa*
DARAB KHANI — *Middle East*
DARAMBAL — *Australia*
DARASA — *E Africa*
DARAWA — *Amazon Basin*
DARAZI — *Middle East*
DARD — *C Asia*
DARGIN — *Caucasus*
DARIA — *Mesoamerica*
DARIBI — *Melanesia*
DARKINJANG — *Australia*
DARREHSHURI — *C Asia*
DARS — *N Africa*
DARU — *Middle East*
DARUK — *Australia*
DARUSAR — *Middle East*
DARWA — *N Africa*
DARWIN — *Australia*
DATAB — *W Africa*
DAUR — *E Asia*
DAYAK — *SE Asia*
DAZA — *N Africa*
DE — *W Africa*

DEA — *Melanesia*
DEANG (Benglong) — *E Asia*
DECHERDA — *N Africa*
DEHI HAZARAS — *C Asia*
DEHWAR — *Middle East*
DELAWARE — *Plains NA*
DELAWARE MUNCIE — *Plains NA*
DENCA — *Polynesia*
DENDI — *W Africa*
DENE — *Subarctic*
DENE THA' — *Plains NA*
DEORI — *S Asia*
DERESA — *E Africa*
DERN — *Australia*
DERONG — *E Asia*
DERSIMILI — *Caucasus*
DESANA — *Amazon Basin*
DETI — *S Africa*
DEWA — *Melanesia*
DEY — *W Africa*
DHAKAR — *S Asia*
DHANKA — *S Asia*
DHODIA — *S Asia*
DHURWA — *S Asia*
DIAGUITA — *Andes*
DIAKUI — *Australia*
DIALONKE — *W Africa*
DIANBO — *E Asia*
DIANKHANKE — *W Africa*
DIBEYAT — *N Africa*
DIDA — *W Africa*
DIDI — *Caucasus*
DIDINGA — *E Africa*
DIEGUENO — *Far West NA*
DIERI — *Australia*
DIETKO — *W Africa*
DIGIL — *E Africa*
DIGIRI — *E Africa*
DIGO — *E Africa*
DIGUENO — *Mesoamerica*
DIKGALE — *S Africa*
DIMASA — *S Asia*
DINE (Navajo) — *Southwest NA*
DINKA — *E Africa*
DIOLA (Jola) — *W Africa*
DIOULA — *W Africa*
DIR — *E Africa*
DIRITYANGURA — *Australia*
DISKO — *Arctic*
DIVEHI — *S Asia*
DJABERADJABERA — *Australia*
DJAGADA — *N Africa*
DJAGARAGA — *Australia*
DJAKUNDA — *Australia*
DJALAKURU — *Australia*
DJALENDI — *Australia*
DJAMINDJUNG — *Australia*
DJANGU — *Australia*
DJANKUN — *Australia*
DJARA — *Australia*
DJARGUDI — *Australia*
DJARU — *Australia*
DJAUAN — *Australia*
DJAUI — *Australia*
DJERAIT — *Australia*
DJERIMANGA — *Australia*
DJERMA — *W Africa*
DJILAMATANG — *Australia*
DJINANG — *Australia*
DJINBA — *Australia*

DJIRINGANJ — *Australia*
DJIRU — *Australia*
DJIRUBAL — *Australia*
DJIWALI — *Australia*
DJOWEI — *Australia*
DJUKA — *Orinoco Basin*
DJUNGUN — *Australia*
DOBU — *Melanesia*
DODOS (Dodoth) — *E Africa*
DODOTH (Dodos) — *E Africa*
DOGARA (Dagara) — *W Africa*
DOGLAS — *Caribbean*
DOGON — *W Africa*
DOGORDA — *N Africa*
DOGRIB — *Subarctic*
DOKIS — *Northeast NA*
DOKO — *C Africa*
DOLGAN — *Arctic*
DOMA (Mvura, VaDema) — *S Africa*
DOMU — *Melanesia*
DONDO — *C Africa*
DONG — *E Asia*
DONGO — *E Asia*
DONGXIANG — *E Asia*
DORAZAI — *Middle East*
DORLA GOND — *S Asia*
DOROBO (Okiek) — *E Africa*
DOROBURA — *Australia*
DOROMBA — *W Africa*
DOU MENIA — *N Africa*
DOUBLA — *S Asia*
DOUKHOBORS — *Northwest Coast NA*
DOURA — *Melanesia*
DRAVIDIAN — *S Asia*
DRUKPAS — *S Asia*
DRUNG — *E Asia*
DRUZE — *Middle East*
DUALA — *C Africa*
DUAN — *SE Asia*
DUANE — *SE Asia*
DUBLA — *S Asia*
DUCIE — *Polynesia*
DUDUROA — *Australia*
DUKKALA — *N Africa*
DULONG (Qui) — *E Asia*
DUMA — *C, S Africa*
DUMU — *Melanesia*
DUNA — *Melanesia*
DUNGANS — *C Asia*
DURRANI — *C Asia*
DURUMA — *E Africa*
DUSUN — *SE Asia*
DUTCH — *W Europe*
DUULNGARI — *Australia*
DUWALA — *Australia*
DUWAMISH — *Northwest Coast NA*
DUWASIR — *Middle East*
DUZDGAH — *Middle East*
DXERIKU — *S Africa*
DYULA — *W Africa*
DYUR — *E Africa*
DZAYUL — *C Asia*
DZHEKS — *Caucasus*
E'NAPA (Panare) — *Orinoco Basin*
EABAMETOONG — *Northeast NA*
EAST GREENLANDERS — *Arctic*
EAST HUPA — *Far West NA*

EAST INDIANS — *Caribbean*
EAST SHOSHONI — *Plains NA*
EASTER ISLANDERS (Rapa Nui) — *Polynesia*
EASTERN CHEROKEE — *Southeast NA*
EASTERN CHICKAHOMINY — *Southeast NA*
EASTERN LAMOOT — *Arctic*
EASTERN PENAN — *SE Asia*
EASTERN PEQUOT — *Northeast NA*
EASTERN SHAWNEE — *Plains NA*
EBIDOSO — *Central SA*
ECHOTA CHEROKEE — *Southeast NA*
EDISTO — *Southeast NA*
EDO — *W Africa*
EFE — *C Africa*
EFIK — *W Africa*
EGBA — *W Africa*
EGEDESMINDE — *Arctic*
EHATTESHAHT — *Northwest Coast NA*
EIPO — *Melanesia*
EKAGI — *Melanesia*
EKOI (Yako) — *W Africa*
EKONDA — *C Africa*
EL ARBAA — *N Africa*
ELATO — *Micronesia*
ELEM POMO — *Far West NA*
ELIPTAMIN — *Melanesia*
ELKO TE MOAK — *Great Basin NA*
ELMOLO — *E Africa*
ELY SHOSHONE — *Great Basin NA*
EMBERA — *Mesoamerica*
EMBU — *E Africa*
EMERILLON — *Amazon Basin*
EMON — *Australia*
ENCABELLADO — *Amazon Basin*
ENDENESE — *SE Asia*
ENDO (Keiyo) — *E Africa*
ENETS — *Arctic*
ENGA — *Melanesia*
ENGGANESE — *SE Asia*
ENGLISH — *N Europe*
ENOCH CREE — *Plains NA*
ENTIAT — *Northwest Coast NA*
EORA — *Australia*
ERAWIRUNG — *Australia*
EREMA — *Melanesia*
ERI — *Australia*
ERIGPACTSA — *Amazon Basin*
ERMINESKIN — *Plains NA*
ERUKALA — *S Asia*
ESCOUMAINS — *Northeast NA*
ESELE — *C Africa*
ESHIRA — *C Africa*
ESKASONI — *Northeast NA*
ESKIMO — *Arctic*
ESMERALDA — *Andes*
ESQUIMALT — *Northwest Coast NA*
ESSELEN — *Far West NA*
ESSIPIT — *Northeast NA*
ESTONIANS — *E Europe*
ETA (Burakumin) — *E Asia*
ETCHAOTTINE — *Northwest Coast NA*
ETON — *C Africa*
ETORO — *Melanesia*
ETOWAH CHEROKEE — *Southeast NA*

COMANCHE AT RED EARTH FESTIVAL, OKLAHOMA CITY

SHEEP RAISING ON GERMANY'S LÜNEBURG HEATH

EUDEVE — *Mesoamerica*
EURO CARIBBEAN — *Caribbean*
EVEN (Lamut) — *Arctic*
EVENK (Tungus) — *Arctic*
EVENKI (Northern Tungus) — *Arctic, E Asia*
EWAMIN — *Australia*
EWE — *W Africa*
EWENKI — *E Asia*
EYAK — *Arctic*
EYLE — *E Africa*
FAJELU — *E Africa*
FAKFAK — *Melanesia*
FALASHA (Beta Israel) — *E Africa*
FALI — *W Africa*
FANG — *C, W Africa*
FANTE — *W Africa*
FANTI — *W Africa*
FAEROESE — *N Europe*
FARSI MADAN — *C Asia*
FARSIWAN — *C Asia*
FASU — *Melanesia*
FAUR — *Melanesia*
FAUSA — *W Africa*
FAWAKHIR — *N Africa*
FAWAYID — *N Africa*
FERAMIN — *Melanesia*
FERGUSSON ISLANDERS — *Melanesia*
FEZZAN — *N Africa*
FIJIANS — *Melanesia*
FILIPINOS — *SE Asia*
FINGO — *S Africa*
FINNS — *N Europe*
FIPA — *E Africa*
FLATHEAD — *Plateau NA*
FLEMISH — *W Europe*
FOI — *Melanesia*
FOKENG — *S Africa*
FOLL — *Melanesia*
FON (Dahomey) — *W Africa*
FORE — *Melanesia*
FORMOSANS (Hakka, Min) — *E Asia*
FOX — *Plains NA*
FRENCH — *W Europe*
FRISIANS — *W Europe*
FRIULIANS — *S Europe*
FUEGIANS — *Patagonia*
FUGON — *W Africa*
FUKIENS — *E Asia*
FULANI (Fulbe, Peul) — *W Africa*
FULBE (Fulani, Peul) — *W Africa*
FULNIO — *Amazon Basin*
FUMBU — *C Africa*
FUR — *N Africa*
FURIIRU — *C Africa*
FUTUNANS — *Polynesia*
FUYUGHE — *Melanesia*
G//ANA — *S Africa*
G/WI — *S Africa*
GA — *W Africa*
GA MASHPIE — *W Africa*
GAARI — *Australia*

GABADI — *Melanesia*
GABBRA — *E Africa*
GABOU — *C Africa*
GABRIELENO — *Far West NA*
GABRIELINO TONGVAH — *Far West NA*
GADABA — *S Asia*
GADABOURSIS — *E Africa*
GADDANG — *SE Asia*
GADE — *W Africa*
GADJALIVIA — *Australia*
GADJERONG — *Australia*
GADOA — *N Africa*
GADSUP — *Melanesia*
GADUDJARA — *Australia*
GAELIC SCOTS — *N Europe*
GAELS — *N Europe*
GAFERUT — *Micronesia*
GAGADJU — *Australia*
GAGAUZ — *E Europe*
GAGU — *W Africa*
GAHUKUGAMA — *Melanesia*
GAIDEMOE — *Melanesia*
GAINJ — *Melanesia*
GAIWA — *Melanesia*
GALAGO — *Australia*
GALEVA — *Melanesia*
GALIBI (Caribs) — *Orinoco Basin*
GALICIANS — *W Europe*
GALLA (Oromo) — *E Africa*
GAMBALANG — *Australia*
GAMBIER ISLANDERS — *Polynesia*
GAMIT — *S Asia*
GAMMATTI — *Australia*
GAMO — *E Africa*
GAMTA — *S Asia*
GANANWA (Mmalebogo) — *S Africa*
GANDA — *E Africa*
GANDANGARA — *Australia*
GANDJU — *Australia*
GANEANG — *Australia*
GANGULU — *Australia*
GAOSAZHU (Yuanzhumin) — *E Asia*
GAOSHAN — *E Asia*
GARADJERI — *Australia*
GARASIA — *S Asia*
GARIA — *Melanesia*
GARIA — *S Asia*
GARIFUNA — *Mesoamerica*
GARO — *S Asia*
GASIM — *Middle East*
GASPE — *Northeast NA*
GAURNA — *Australia*
GAVIOES — *Amazon Basin*
GAWA — *Melanesia*
GAWARI — *S Asia*
GAYO — *SE Asia*
GAYON — *Orinoco Basin*
GBANDE — *W Africa*
GBARI — *W Africa*

GBAYA (Baya) — *C Africa*
GBUGBLE — *W Africa*
GCOIKA — *S Africa*
GE — *W Africa*
GEAWEGAL — *Australia*
GEBUSI — *Melanesia*
GELAMAI — *Australia*
GELAO (Gelo) — *E Asia*
GELO (Gelao) — *E Asia*
GEN — *W Africa*
GENDE — *Melanesia*

To know the road ahead, ask those coming back.

INDIAN PROVERB

GEORGIANS — *Caucasus*
GERMAN SWISS — *W Europe*
GERMANS — *W Europe*
GESGAPEGIAG — *Northeast NA*
GHALJI — *C Asia*
GHAMID — *Middle East*
GHANZI — *S Africa*
GHEGS — *S Europe*
GHORBAT — *C Asia*
GHURGHUSHT PATHANS — *C Asia*
GIA — *Australia*
GIABAL — *Australia*
GIAI (Nung, Whang) — *SE Asia*
GIBE — *E Africa*
GIEN — *W Africa*
GIKUYU — *E Africa*
GILAKI — *C Asia*
GILAMBABURA — *Australia*
GILBERT ISLANDERS (Kiribati) — *Micronesia*
GILIU — *W Africa*
GIMI — *Melanesia*
GIMIRA — *E Africa*
GIMR — *N Africa*
GINOOGAMING — *Northeast NA*
GIO — *W Africa*
GIRAVARU — *S Asia*
GIRIAMA — *E Africa*
GISHU — *E Africa*
GISU (Bagisu) — *E Africa*
GITANMAAX — *Northwest Coast NA*
GITKSAN — *Northwest Coast NA*
GITLAKDAMIX — *Northwest Coast NA*
GITSEGUKLA — *Northwest Coast NA*
GITWANGAK — *Northwest Coast NA*
GITWINKSIHLKW — *Northwest Coast NA*
GITXSAN — *Northwest Coast NA*
GJELLI — *C Africa*

GLEN VOWELL — *Northwest Coast NA*
GNAU — *Melanesia*
GOA — *Australia*
GOAN — *S Asia*
GOAT — *Subarctic*
GODTHIAAB — *Arctic*
GOENG — *Australia*
GOFA — *E Africa*
GOG — *Melanesia*
GOGADA — *Australia*
GOGO — *E Africa*
GOGODALA — *Melanesia*
GOKLEN TURKOMEN — *C Asia*
GOLA — *W Africa*
GOND — *S Asia*
GONJA — *W Africa*
GOODENOUGH ISLANDERS — *Melanesia*
GOONIYANDI — *Australia*
GORENG — *Australia*
GORINDJI — *Australia*
GOROKA — *Melanesia*
GORONTALENSE (Gorontalo) — *SE Asia*
GORONTALO (Gorontalense) — *SE Asia*
GOROTIRE — *Amazon Basin*
GOROWA — *E Africa*
GOSHUTE (Gosiute) — *Great Basin NA*
GOSIUTE (Goshute) — *Great Basin NA*
GOTO — *Caribbean Coast SA*
GOUNDA — *N Africa*
GOURMANTCHE — *W Africa*
GOURO — *W Africa*
GOUROA — *N Africa*
GOWA — *S Africa*
GRASIA — *S Asia*
GREBO — *W Africa*
GREEK CYPRIOTS — *S Europe*
GREEKS — *S Europe*
GREENLANDERS — *Arctic*
GRIGUA — *S Africa*
GRINGAI — *Australia*
GROS VENTRE — *Plains NA*
GRUSI — *W Africa*
GU — *W Africa*
GUACHICHILE — *Mesoamerica*
GUADALCANAL ISLANDERS (Kaoka) — *Melanesia*
GUAHARIBO — *Orinoco Basin*
GUAHIBO — *Orinoco Basin*
GUAICA — *Orinoco Basin*
GUAIMARO — *Caribbean*
GUAIPUAVE — *Orinoco Basin*
GUAIQUERI — *Caribbean Coast SA*
GUAITACA — *Central SA*
GUAJA — *Amazon Basin*
GUAJAJARA — *Amazon Basin*
GUAJIRO (Wayuu) — *Caribbean Coast SA*
GUAMAHAYA — *Caribbean*
GUAMAR — *Mesoamerica*
GUAMBIANO — *Andes*
GUAN — *W Africa*

GUANA — *Central SA*
GUANACHAHIBE — *Caribbean*
GUANACOA — *Andes*
GUANEBUCAN — *Caribbean Coast SA*
GUANIGUANICO — *Caribbean*
GUARANI — *Central SA*
GUARATEGAYA — *Amazon Basin*
GUARAYO (Chiriguano) — *Andes*
GUAREQUENA — *Orinoco Basin*
GUARIBA (Nadobo) — *Amazon Basin*
GUARIJIO — *Mesoamerica*
GUARINE (Palenque) — *Orinoco Basin*
GUARINI — *Central SA*
GUARNA — *Australia*
GUASAVE — *Mesoamerica*
GUATO — *Central SA*
GUAYA — *Amazon Basin*
GUAYABERO — *Orinoco Basin*
GUAYAKI (Ache) — *Andes*
GUAYANA — *Central SA*
GUAYAPE — *Amazon Basin*
GUAYMI (Ngawbe) — *Mesoamerica*
GUAYTACA — *Central SA*
GUENNAKIN (Puelche) — *Central SA*
GUENOA — *Central SA*
GUERANDI — *Central SA*
GUERE — *W Africa*
GUEREN — *Amazon Basin*
GUERNO — *Australia*
GUETARE — *Mesoamerica*
GUIDAR — *W Africa*
GUIZIGA — *W Africa*
GUJAR — *S Asia*
GUJARATI — *S Asia*
GULAY — *C Africa*
GULNGAI — *Australia*
GUMUZ — *E Africa*
GUNAVIDJI — *Australia*
GUNDITJMARA — *Australia*
GUNGOROGONE — *Australia*
GUNI — *Melanesia*
GUNWINGGU — *Australia*
GURAGE — *E Africa*
GURAMA — *Australia*
GURINDJI — *Australia*
GURKHA — *S Asia*
GURMA — *W Africa*
GURMANCHE — *W Africa*
GURO — *W Africa*

HA NHI (Ha Nhy) — *SE Asia*
HADYA — *E Africa*
HADZA (Hadzabe) — *E Africa*
HADZABE (Hadza) — *E Africa*
HADZAPI — *E Africa*
HAGWILGET — *Northwest Coast NA*
HAI//OM — *S Africa*
HAIDA — *Northwest Coast NA*
HAINNA — *SE Asia*
HAISLA — *Northwest Coast NA*
HAKAVONA — *S Africa*
HAKKA (Formosans, Min) — *E Asia*
HALAKWULUP (Alacaluf) — *Patagonia*
HALALT — *Northwest Coast NA*
HALANG DOAN — *SE Asia*
HALIWA — *Southeast NA*
HALIWA SAPONI — *Southeast NA*
HALKOMELEM (COWICHAN) — *Northwest Coast NA*
HALMAHERA — *SE Asia*
HAMAR — *N Africa*
HAMBUKUSHU — *S Africa*
HAMIYAN — *N Africa*
HAN — *Subarctic*
HAN — *E Asia*
HANAMANA — *Caribbean*
HANANWA — *S Africa*
HANERAGMIUT — *Arctic*
HANI — *E Asia*
HANINGAYOGMIUT — *Arctic*
HANUNOO — *SE Asia*
HANYA — *S Africa*
HARABI — *N Africa*
HARADO — *Melanesia*
HARARI — *E Africa*
HARASIS — *Middle East*
HARB — *Middle East*
HARE — *Subarctic*
HARVAQTORMIUT — *Arctic*
HASA — *Middle East*
HASHID — *Middle East*
HASINAI — *Southeast NA*
HASSALARU — *S Asia*
HASSANAMISCO NIPMUC — *Northeast NA*
HASSANANLI — *Caucasus*
HATTADARE — *Southeast NA*

Suggestion is the art of teaching.

HUNGARIAN PROVERB

GURU — *E Africa*
GURUNG — *S Asia*
GURUNSI — *W Africa*
GURURUMBA — *Melanesia*
GUSII — *E Africa*
GUTSULS — *E Europe*
GWANDARA — *W Africa*
GWE — *E Africa*
GWICH'IN — *Subarctic*
GWINI — *Australia*
/GWOACHU — *S Africa*
GYPSIES (Roma) — *Europe*
H. RE (Hre) — *SE Asia*
HA — *E Africa*
HA NHY (Ha nhi) — *SE Asia*

HATTERAS TUSCARORA — *Southeast NA*
HAUDENOSAUNEE (Iroquois) — *Northeast NA*
HAUE — *Orinoco Basin*
HAUSA — *W Africa*
HAUSH — *Patagonia*
HAUT — *C Africa*
HAVANA — *Caribbean*
HAVASUPAI — *Southwest NA*
HAW (Ho) — *SE Asia*
HAWAIIANS (Kanaka Maoli) — *Polynesia*
HAWAWIR — *N Africa*
HAWEITAT — *N Africa*
HAWIYE — *E Africa*
HAYA — *E Africa*

HAZARA — C Asia
HEHE — E Africa
HEILTSUK — Northwest Coast NA
HELONG — SE Asia
HEMBA — C Africa
HENGA — E Africa
HENKISON — Polynesia
HENYA — Northwest Coast NA
HERERO (Damara) — S Africa
HESQUIAHT — Northwest Coast NA
HESSEQUE — S Africa
HETA (Xeta) — Central SA
HEVERO (Jebero) — Amazon Basin
HEWA — Melanesia
HEZHEN — E Asia
HIAWATHA OJIBWAY — Northeast NA
HIBITO — Andes
HIDATSA — Plains NA
HIECHWARE — S Africa
HIGHLAND MAYA — Mesoamerica
HIGHLAND SCOTS — N Europe
HIJRA — S Asia
HILIGAYNON — SE Asia
HILL VEEDAN — S Asia
HILLERI — Australia
HIMA — E Africa
HIMBA — S Africa
HITNU — Orinoco Basin
HIWI — Orinoco Basin
HIXKARYANA — Amazon Basin
HLENGWE — S Africa
HLUBI — S Africa
HMAR — S Asia
HMONG (Meo, Miao, Mong, Tai) — S, SE Asia
HO — W Africa
HO (Haw) — SE Asia
HOANYA — SE Asia
HODH — W Africa
HOH — Northwest Coast NA
HOKKIEN — E Asia
HOLIKACHUK — Subarctic
HOLOHOLO — C Africa
HOLSTEINS BORG — Arctic
HONIBO — Melanesia
HOONAH — Northwest Coast NA
HOPEWELL — Northeast NA
HOPI — Southwest NA
HOPI TEWA — Southwest NA
HORNEPAYNE — Northeast NA
HOTI — Orinoco Basin
HOTTENTOTS (Khoi, Khokhoi) — S Africa
HOULTON MALISEET — Northeast NA
HOUMA — Southeast NA
HOZAYL — Middle East
HRE (H. Re) — SE Asia
HROY — SE Asia
HTIN (T'in, Thin) — SE Asia
HU — E Asia
/HUA — S Africa
HUA — Melanesia
HUACHO — Andes
HUALAPAI — Southwest NA
HUAMBISA — Amazon Basin
HUAMBO — Andes
HUANCA — Andes
HUANCABAMBA — Andes

HUANCAVILCA — Andes
HUANUCO — Andes
HUAORANI (Auca, Wao, Waorani) — Amazon Basin
HUARAYO — Amazon Basin
HUARPE — Andes
HUASTEC (Wasteko) — Mesoamerica
HUAVE — Mesoamerica
HUAYLAS — Andes
HUBABO — Caribbean
HUCHNOM — Far West NA
HUDDAN — Middle East
HUEREO — Caribbean
HUI — E Asia
HUICHOL — Mesoamerica
HUILLICHE — Andes
HUITOTO (Witoto) — Amazon Basin
HUKWE — S Africa
HULA — Melanesia
HULI — Melanesia
HUMPTULIPS — Northwest Coast NA
HUMR — C Africa
HUMUM — Middle East
HUNGARIANS (Magyars) — C Europe
HUNGAROS — W Europe
HUNZAKUTS (Burusho) — C Asia
HUPA — Far West NA
HUPDA — Amazon Basin
HURAN POTAWATOMI — Northeast NA
HURON — Northeast NA
HURONS WENDAT — Northeast NA
HURUTHSE — S Africa
HUTAIM — Middle East
HUTTERITES — Northwest, Plains NA
HUTU — C, E Africa
HUU AY AHT — Northwest Coast NA
HWADUBA — S Africa
IADINO — Mesoamerica
IATMUL — Melanesia
IBALOI — SE Asia
IBAN — SE Asia
IBANAG — SE Asia
IBENAMA — Amazon Basin
IBIBIO — W Africa
IBN AMIR — Middle East
IBO (Igbo) — W Africa
ICA — Caribbean Coast SA
ICELANDERS — N Europe
ICHKILIK — C Asia
IDINDJI — Australia
IDOMA — W Africa
IFE ILESHA — W Africa
IFUGAO — SE Asia
IFULUK — Micronesia
IGARA — W Africa
IGBIRA — W Africa
IGBO (Ibo) — W Africa
IGIDLORSSUIT — Arctic
IGLULIK ESKIMOS — Arctic
IGNACIANO — Amazon Basin
IGNERI — Caribbean Coast SA
IGOROT (Kankanay) — SE Asia
IJAW — W Africa
IJEBU — W Africa
IJO — W Africa
IK — E Africa
IKA — W Africa
IKUNG — S Africa
ILA — S Africa
ILANON — SE Asia

ILBA — Australia
ILDAWONGGA — Australia
ILIAURA — Australia
ILLINOIS — Northeast NA
ILOCANO — SE Asia
ILONGO — SE Asia
ILONGOT — SE Asia
ILSAVEN (Shahsevan) — Caucasus
IMAKLIMUIT — Arctic
IMAZIGHEN (Berbers) — N Africa
IMRAGUEN — N Africa
INAHUKWA — Amazon Basin
INAJA — Far West NA

Air has the finest ears.

RUSSIAN PROVERB

INAN IU — Middle East
INAWONGGA — Australia
INDJIBANDI — Australia
INGALIK — Subarctic
INGANO — Amazon Basin
INGGARDA — Australia
INGILOS — Caucasus
INGUKLIMIUT — Arctic
INGURUA — Australia
INGUSH — Caucasus
ININGAI — Australia
INJIBANDI — Australia
INKJINANDI — Australia
INNU — Subarctic
INNU MAMIT INNUAT — Northeast NA
INQUA — S Africa
INUIT — Arctic
INUPIAT — Arctic
INUVIALUIT — Arctic
IONE MIWOK — Far West NA
IOWA — Plains NA
IPAI — Far West NA
IPECA — Amazon Basin
IPILI — Melanesia
IPURINA — Amazon Basin
IQUITO — Amazon Basin
IRAMBA — E Africa
IRANGI — E Africa
IRANXE — Amazon Basin
IRAQW — E Africa
IRAYA — SE Asia
IRIANESE — SE Asia
IRIFIYEN — N Africa
IRISH — N Europe
IROQUOIS (Haudenosaunee) — Northeast NA
IRUKANDII — Australia
IRULA (Irulu) — S Asia
IRULAR — S Asia
IRULU (Irula) — S Asia
ISAAQ — E Africa
ISCONAHUA — Amazon Basin
ISERTORMEEQ — Arctic
ISHAN — W Africa
ISHINDE — S Africa
ISHKASHIMI — C Asia
ISINAY — SE Asia
ISKUT — Northwest Coast NA
ISKUTEWIZAAGEGAN — Northeast NA
ISLAND TLINGIT — Subarctic
ISLETA — Plains NA
ISLETA PUEBLO — Southwest NA
ISLINGTON (Wabasseemoong) — Northeast NA
ISMAILIS — Middle East
ISNEG — SE Asia

ISOBEI — Melanesia
ISSAKS — E Africa
ISSAS — E Africa
ISUKHA — E Africa
ITA ESKIMO — Arctic
ITALIAN SWISS — W Europe
ITALIANS — S Europe
ITELMEN — Subarctic
ITENE (More) — Amazon Basin
ITENM'I — Arctic
ITESEO — E Africa
ITESO — E Africa
ITHU — Australia
ITIVIMIUT — Arctic
ITNEG — SE Asia
ITOGAPUK — Amazon Basin
ITONAMA — Amazon Basin
ITSEKIRI — W Africa
ITTU — E Africa
ITZA — Mesoamerica
IUKAGIR — Arctic
IVORI — Melanesia
IWA — E Africa
IWAIDJA — Australia
IXIL — Mesoamerica
IZHMI — N Europe
IZOCENO — Central SA
JAADWA — Australia
JAAKO — Australia
JAARA — Australia
JABURARA — Australia
JACALTEC — Mesoamerica
JACOBSHAVN — Arctic
JADGAL — Middle East
JADIRA — Australia
JADLIAURA — Australia
JAGALINGU — Australia
JAGARA — Australia
JAGUA — Caribbean
JAH HUT — SE Asia
JAHAI — SE Asia
JAHANKA — W Africa
JAIN — S Asia
JAITMATHANG — Australia
JAKALTEKO — Mesoamerica
JAKUN — SE Asia
JALANGA — Australia
JALUIT — Micronesia
JAMA — SE Asia
JAMA MAPUN — SE Asia
JAMBINA — Australia
JAMINAWA — Amazon Basin
JAMSHIDI — C Asia
JAMUL — Far West NA
JANAMBRE — Mesoamerica
JANDA — Australia
JANDRUWANTA — Australia
JANGAA — Australia
JANGGA — Australia
JANGGAL — Australia
JANGIZAI MAID — Middle East
JANGMAN — Australia
JANI KAHN — Middle East
JANJERO — E Africa
JANJULA — Australia
JANKUNDJARA — Australia
JANO — Plains NA
JAPANESE — E Asia
JARAI — SE Asia

JARALDI — Australia
JARIJARI — Australia
JARILDEKALD — Australia
JAROINGA — Australia
JAROWAIR — Australia
JARSO — E Africa
JARU — Amazon Basin
JARWAS — S Asia
JAT — C Asia
JAT — C, S Asia
JATAV — S Asia
JATHAIKANA — Australia
JAUAPERY — Orinoco Basin
JAUDJIBAIA — Australia
JAUF — Middle East
JAUNSARI — S Asia
JAURAWORKA — Australia
JAVAHE (Karaja) — Amazon Basin
JAVANESE — SE Asia
JAWABIS — N Africa
JAWONY — Australia
JAWURU — Australia
JEBERO (Hevero) — Amazon Basin
JEIDJI — Australia
JEITHI — Australia
JEKRI — W Africa
JELIENDI — Australia
JEMEZ PUEBLO — Southwest NA
JENA CHOCTAW — Southeast NA
JENU — S Asia
JERAWA — W Africa
JETENERU — Australia
JETIMARALA — Australia
JIARONG — E Asia
JIBANA — E Africa
JIBRANLI — Caucasus

JIVARO (Shuar) — Amazon Basin
JOCOME — Plains NA
JOGULA — Australia
JOKULA — Australia
JOLA (Diola) — W Africa
JONGGA — Australia
JONGN — E Africa
JOPADHOLA — E Africa
JOTIJOTA — Australia
JOVA — Mesoamerica
JU/'HOANSI (Kung) — S Africa
JUANENO — Far West NA
JUANG — S Asia
JUAT — Australia
JUHAINAH — Middle East
JUIPERA — Australia
JUKAMBAL — Australia
JUKAMBE — Australia
JUKUL — Australia
JUKUN — W Africa
JULAOLINJA — Australia
JULIANEHAAB — Arctic
JUMANOS — Mesoamerica
JUMU — Australia
JUNGGOR — Australia
JUNGKURARA — Australia
JUNIN — Andes
JUNUBA — Middle East
JUPAGALK — Australia
JUPANGATI — Australia
JUR — C Africa
JURASSIANS — W Europe
JURU — Australia
JURUNA — Amazon Basin
JUULA — W Africa
K'ICHE' (Quiche) — Mesoamerica
KA'WIARI — Amazon Basin
KAAPOR (Urubu) — Amazon Basin

PERUVIAN GIRL WITH LLAMA, CUZCO, PERU

JICAQUE (Tolupan, Torrupanes) — Mesoamerica
JICARILLA APACHE — Soutwest NA
JIE — E Africa
JIEGERA — Australia
JIJI — E Africa
JILNGALI — Australia
JIMAN — Australia
JING — E Asia
JINGPO (Kachin) — E, S, SE Asia
JINIGUDIRA — Australia
JINO — E Asia
JINWUM — Australia
JIRAJARA — Caribbean Coast SA
JIRANDALI — Australia
JIRJORONT — Australia
JITA — E Africa
JITAJITA — Australia

KABA — C Africa
KABABISH — N Africa
KABALBARA — Australia
KABARDIN — Caucasus
KABIKABI — Australia
KABISHI — Amazon Basin
KABORA — Amazon Basin
KABRE — W Africa
KABUI — S Asia
KABULA — E Africa
KABYLES — N Africa
KACHARI — S Asia
KACHI — S Asia
KACHIN (Jingpo) — E, S, SE Asia
KADAR — S Asia
KADAZAN — SE Asia
KADIWEU — Central SA
KADJERONG — Australia
KADOHADACHO — Plains NA
KADU — E Asia

KAFA — E Africa
KAFIMA — S Africa
KAFIRI — S Asia
KAGWAHIV — Amazon Basin
KAH BAY KAH NONG (Warroad Chippewa) — Plains NA
KAHKEWISTAHAW — Plains NA
KAHNAWAKE — Northeast NA
KAI — Melanesia
KAIABARA — Australia
KAIADILT — Australia
KAIBA PAIUTE — Great Basin NA
KAIGANI — Northwest Coast NA
KAIMBI — Melanesia
KAINGANG — Central SA
KAIOWA — Central SA
KAIRI — Australia
KAITITIA — Australia
KAJANG — SE Asia
KAJARS — C Asia
KAKA — C Africa
KAKADU — Australia
KAKHETIANS — Caucasus
KAKOLI — Melanesia
KAKWA — C Africa
KALAAKO — Australia
KALAALLIT — Arctic
KALABARI — W Africa
KALABRA — Melanesia
KALAGAN — SE Asia
KALAKUTS — E Europe
KALALI — Australia
KALAMAIA — Australia
KALANGA — S Africa
KALANKE — W Africa
KALAPALO — Amazon Basin
KALASHA — C Asia
KALENJIN — E Africa
KALIBAL — Australia
KALIBAMU — Australia
KALIBUGAN — SE Asia
KALINGA — SE Asia
KALISPEL — Plateau NA
KALKADUNGA — Australia
KALLAWAYA — Andes
KALMYKS (Western Mongols) — C Asia
KALO — SE Asia
KALULI — Melanesia
KAM MOU (Kammu, Khmu, Kmhmu) — SE Asia
KAMABE — E Africa
KAMANGA — E Africa
KAMAYURA — Amazon Basin
KAMBA — E Africa
KAMBATA — E Africa
KAMBURE — Australia
KAMBUWAL — Australia
KAMERAIGAL — Australia
KAMILAROI — Australia
KAMLOOPS — Northwest Coast NA
KAMMU (Kam Mou, Khmu, Kmhmu) — SE Asia
KAMOR — Australia
KAMORO — Melanesia
KAMSA — Andes
KAMSE — Middle East
KAMTANGA — E Africa
KANA — W Africa
KANAKA MAOLI (Hawaiians) — Polynesia
KANAKS — Melanesia
KANARESE — S Asia
KANBI — S Asia
KANDJU — Australia
KANDYANS — S Asia
KANEANG — Australia

288

KANEMBOU — W Africa
KANESATAKE — Northeast NA
KANG — E Asia
KANGALAS — Arctic
KANGAMIUT — Arctic
KANGATSIAK — Arctic
KANGERD — Arctic
KANGHIRYUARMIUT — Arctic
KANGHIRYUATJIAGMIUT — Arctic
KANGULU — Australia
KANICHANA — Andes
KANIDJI — Australia
KANIOK — C Africa
KANITHLUA — Northeast NA
KANJAR — S Asia
KANJOBAL (Q'anjob'al) — Mesoamerica
KANKANAY (Igorot) — SE Asia
KANNADA — S Asia
KANOLU — Australia
KANSA — Plains NA
KANUM — W Africa
KANUM ANIM — Melanesia
KANURI — W Africa
KAOKA (Guadalcanal Islanders) — Melanesia
KAPAU — Melanesia
KAPAUKU — Melanesia
KAPAWE'NO — Plains NA
KAPCHEPKENDI — E Africa
KAPECHENE — Amazon Basin
KAPINGAMARANGI — Micronesia
KAPLELACH — E Africa
KAPORE — Melanesia
KAPSIKI — W Africa
KAPU — S Asia
KAQCHIKEL (Cakchiquel) — Mesoamerica
KARABI — Middle East
KARACHAI — Caucasus
KARADJERI — Australia
KARAGO — W Africa
KARAITES — E Europe
KARAJA (Javahe) — Amazon Basin
KARAJAK — Arctic
KARAKALPAKS — C Asia
KARAKATCHANS — E Europe
KARAMAN — Australia
KARAMOJONG — E Africa
KARANGA — S Africa
KARANGURU — Australia
KARANJA — Australia
KARANKAWA — Mesoamerica
KARAWA — Australia
KARE — C Africa
KARELDI — Australia

AUSTRALIAN ABORIGINE AT A CATTLE STATION

KARELIAN IZHARS — Arctic
KAREN — SE Asia
KARENDALA — Australia
KARENGGAPA — Australia
KARIARA — Australia
KARIHONA — Orinoco Basin
KARINA — Orinoco Basin
KARINGBAL — Australia
KARINNI — SE Asia
KARIPUNA — Amazon Basin
KARMALI — S Asia
KAROK — Northwest Coast NA
KARRANGA — N Africa
KARRETIJIE — S Africa
KARTHIANS — Caucasus
KARTUDJARA — Australia
KARUNBURA — Australia
KARUWALI — Australia
KASHECHEWAN — Northeast NA
KASHIA POMO — Far West NA
KASHINAWA — Amazon Basin
KASHMIRI — S Asia
KASHUBIANS — C Europe
KASKA — Subarctic

Hope is the poor man's income.

DANISH PROVERB

KASKASKIA — Northeast NA
KASKINAMPO — Southeast NA
KASSENG — SE Asia
KASSONKE — W Africa
KASUA — Melanesia
KASUIANA — Orinoco Basin
KATALIGAMUT — Arctic
KATE — Melanesia
KATHLAMET — Northwest Coast NA
KATHODI — S Asia
KATI — Melanesia
KATO — Far West NA
KATTANG — SE Asia
KATTUNAICKENS — S Asia
KATU — SE Asia
KATUBANUT — Australia
KAUMA — E Africa
KAURAREG — Australia
KAURNA — Australia
KAVANGO — S Africa
KAVIAGMUT — Arctic
KAVINENYA — Andes
KAVIRONDO — E Africa
KAW — Plains NA
KAW (Aka, Ko) — SE Asia

KAWACATOOSE — Plains NA
KAWADJI — Australia
KAWAHIWA — Orinoco Basin
KAWAHLA — N Africa
KAWAIB — Amazon Basin
KAWAIISU — Far West NA
KAWAMBARAI — Australia
KAWCHOTTINE — Arctic
KAWEAH — Southeast NA
KAXUYANA — Amazon Basin
KAYABI — Amazon Basin
KAYAH (Red Karen) — SE Asia
KAYAKHS — SE Asia
KAYAN — SE Asia
KAYAPO (Xikrin) — Amazon Basin
KAYONG — SE Asia
KAYUVAVA — Amazon Basin
KAZAKHS (Qazaq) — C, E Asia
KAZANIS — E Europe
KEDANG — SE Asia
KEDAYAN — SE Asia
KEDE — S Africa
KEDERU — E Africa

KEE WAY WIN — Northeast NA
KEECHI — Plains NA
KEESEEKOOSE — Plains NA
KEESEEKOOWENIN — Plains NA
KEETOOWAH CHEROKEE — Plains NA
KEFA — E Africa
KEHEWIN CREE — Plains NA
KEI ISLANDERS — Melanesia
KEIADJARA — Australia
KEINJAN — Australia
KEIYO (Endo) — E Africa
KEKCHI (Q'eqchi) — Mesoamerica
KEL AIR — N Africa
KELA — Melanesia
KELABIT — SE Asia
KELE — C Africa
KELIKO — C Africa
KEMBATA — E Africa
KENAI — Arctic
KENOY — SE Asia
KENSIA — SE Asia
KENSIU — SE Asia
KENYAH — SE Asia
KEPKIRIWAT — Amazon Basin
KERABI — Melanesia
KERAKI — Melanesia
KERAMAI — Australia
KERES — Plains NA
KERES PUEBLO — Southwest NA
KEREWE — E Africa
KERINTJI — SE Asia
KET (Ostyk) — Subarctic
KETAGALAN — SE Asia
KETE — C Africa
KEWA — Melanesia
KEY — Plains NA
KGAKGA — S Africa
KGALAGADI — S Africa
KGATLA — S Africa
KHA ME (Khmer) — SE Asia

KHABYLS — N Africa
KHAKASI — C Asia
KHALKA — E Asia
KHAMSEH — Middle East
KHAN — C Asia
KHANTY — Subarctic
!KHARA — S Africa
KHARIA — S Asia
KHASI — S Asia
KHAWAR — S Asia
KHAWLAN AL AKIYA — Middle East
KHAZARA — C Asia
KHENI — S Africa
KHEVSUR — Caucasus
KHINALUGHS — Caucasus
KHIRGIS — C Asia
KHITAR — Middle East
KHMER (Kha Me) — SE Asia
KHMER LOEU — SE Asia
KHMU (Kam Mou, Kammu, Kmhmu) — SE Asia
KHOI (Hottentots, Khokhoi) — S Africa
KHOJA — C, S Asia
KHOKHOI (Hottentots, Khoi) — S Africa
KHOND — S Asia
KHORIN — E Asia
KHOWARI — S Asia
KHUA — SE Asia
KHUMI — SE Asia
KHUZE — S Africa
KIALEGEE CREEK — Plains NA
KIBENEL — Melanesia
KICKAPOO — Plains NA
KIELTAI — Plains NA
KIGA — E Africa
KIGIKTAGMIUT — Arctic
KIKAPU — Mesoamerica
KIKITARMIUT — Arctic
KIKUYU — E Africa
KIL — SE Asia
KILENGE — Melanesia
KILII (Aweer, Somali Boni) — E Africa
KILIWA (Quiligua) — Mesoamerica
KILLINERMIUT — Arctic
KILLTINHUNMIUT — Northeast NA
KILUSIKTOGMIUT — Arctic
KIMBU — E Africa
KINARAYA — SE Asia
KINCOLITH — Northwest Coast NA
KINDA — Middle East
KINGA — E Africa
KINGNAITMIUT — Arctic
KINISTIN — Plains NA
KINIYEN — Australia
KINKA — C Africa
KINTAG — SE Asia
KINUGUMINT — Arctic
KIOWA — Plains NA
KIOWA APACHE (Plains Apache) — Plains NA
KIOWIAI — Melanesia
KIPAWA — Northeast NA
KIPCHORNWONEK — E Africa
KIPSANG'ANY' — E Africa
KIPSIGIS — E Africa
KIRATIS — S Asia
KIRDI — W Africa
KIRGIZ (Qyrghyz) — E Asia
KIRIBATI (Gilbert Islanders) — Micronesia
KIRITIMATI ISLANDERS (Christmas Islanders) — Polynesia
KIRM — W Africa
KIRRAE — Australia
KISAR — SE Asia

KISPIOX — Northwest Coast NA
KISSI — W Africa
KITA — Melanesia
KITABAL — Australia
KITAMAAT — Northwest Coast NA
KITANEMUK — Far West NA
KITARA (Bunyoro, Nyoro) — E Africa
KITCISAKIK — Northeast NA
KITIGAN ZIBI ANISHIN-ABEG — Northeast NA
KITJA — Australia
KITSELAS — Northwest Coast NA
KITSUA — Andes
KITSUMKALUM — Northwest Coast NA
KIWAI — Melanesia
KLALLAM — Northwest Coast NA
KLAMANTAN — SE Asia
KLAMATH — Plateau NA
KLUANE — Arctic
KMHMU (Kam Mou, Kammu, Khmu) — SE Asia
!KO (!Xoo) — S Africa
KO (Aka, Kaw) — SE Asia
KOA — Australia
KOAKA — Melanesia
KOAKIR (Awa Kwaiker) — Andes
KOAMU — Australia
KOARA — Australia
KOARATIRA — Amazon Basin
KOASATI — Southeast NA
KOBEWA (Cubeo) — Amazon Basin
KODI — SE Asia
KOENPAL — Australia
KOFAN — Amazon Basin
KOFYAR — W Africa
KOGI (Cagaba) — Caribbean Coast SA
KOGLUKTOGMIUT — Arctic
KOHISTANI — C Asia
KOHO — SE Asia
KOIARI — Melanesia
KOINJMAL — Australia
KOITA — Melanesia
KOKAMA — Amazon Basin
KOKANGOL — Australia
KOKATJA — Australia
KOKI — E Africa
KOKNA — S Asia
KOKO — Australia
KOKOBIDIDJI — Australia
KOKOBUJUNDJI — Australia
KOKOIMUDJI — Australia
KOKOJAWA — Australia
KOKOJEKODI — Australia
KOKOJELANDJI — Australia
KOKOKULUNGGUR — Australia
KOKOMINI — Australia
KOKOPATUN — Australia
KOKOPERIA — Australia
KOKORDA — N Africa
KOKOWALANDJA — Australia
KOKOWARA — Australia
KOKRAIMORO — Amazon Basin
KOKSOAKUIUT — Northeast NA
KOL — S Asia
KOLA — C Africa
KOLAKNGAT — Australia
KOLAM — S Asia

KOLE — W Africa
KOLI — S Asia
KOLISUCH'OK — E Asia
KOM — C, W Africa
KOMBAINGHERI — Australia
KOMBE — C Africa
KOMBOBURA — Australia
KOMI — E Europe
KONAI — Melanesia
KOND — S Asia
KONDA — Melanesia
KONE — S Africa
KONEJANDI — Australia
KONGABULA — Australia
KONGALU — Australia
KONGKANDJI — Australia
KONGO — C Africa
KONIAGUI — W Africa
KONITH LUSHUAMIUT — Northeast NA
KONJO — E Africa
KONKAN — S Asia
KONKOMBA — W Africa
KONKOW — Far West NA
KONKUBURA — Australia
KONO — W Africa
KONSO — E Africa
KONYAK (Nagas) — S Asia
KOOBE — Melanesia
KOOCHICHING — Northeast NA
KOORIE — Australia
KOOTENAI (Kutenai) — Northwest Coast NA
KOPAR — Melanesia
KORA — Melanesia
KORANA — S Africa
KORANKO — W Africa
KOREANS — E Asia
KOREKORE — S Africa
KORENG — Australia
KORENGGORENG — Australia
KOREWAHE — Andes
KORIKI — Melanesia
KORINDJI — Australia
KORKU — S Asia
KORO — W Africa
KORWA — S Asia
KORYAK — Arctic
KOSRAE ISLANDERS — Micronesia
KOTA — C Africa
KOTA — S Asia

Instruction in youth is like engraving in stone.
Moroccan proverb

KOTANDJI — Australia
KOUGNI — C Africa
KOUNTA — W Africa
KOUYOU — C Africa
KOYA — S Asia
KOYUKON — Subarctic
KPANDO — W Africa
KPE — C Africa
KPELLE — W Africa
KRAHN — W Africa
KRAHO — Amazon Basin
KRAMO — Melanesia
KRAN — W Africa
KRAUATUNGALUNG — Australia
KREDA — N Africa
KREENAKAROKE — Amazon Basin
KREISH — C Africa
KRENE — Orinoco Basin
KRIASHEN TATARS — E Europe
KRIKATI — Amazon Basin
KRIM — W Africa

KRJASHEN — E Europe
KROBOB — W Africa
KROU — W Africa
KRU — W Africa
KRUAN — W Africa
KRUNG — SE Asia
KRY — SE Asia
KUA — S Asia
KUBA — C Africa
KUBACHINS — Caucasus
KUBENKRANKEIN — Amazon Basin
KUBOR — Melanesia
KUBU — SE Asia
KUERETU — Amazon Basin
KUHGILA — Middle East
KUHGALU — C Asia
KUI — SE Asia
KUIKURA — Amazon Basin
KUINMURBURA — Australia
KUITSH — Northwest Coast NA
KUJAI — Australia
KUKABRAK (Narrinyeri, Ngarrindjeri, Yaraldi) — Australia
KUKATJA — Australia
KUKPARUNGMIUT — Arctic
KUKU — C Africa
KUKURUKU — W Africa
KULA — Australia
KULAMAN — SE Asia
KULIN — Australia
KULUMALI — Australia
KUMA — Melanesia
KUMAN — E Africa
KUMBAINGGIRI — Australia
KUMBU — W Africa
KUMEYAAY — Far West NA
KUMYK — Caucasus
KUNA (Cuna) — Mesoamerica
KUNAGUASAYA — Caribbean Coast SA
KUNAMA — E Africa
KUNBI — S Asia
KUNFEL — E Africa
KUNG (Ju/'hoansi) — S Africa
KUNGADUTJI — Australia

KUNGARAKAN — Australia
KUNGGARA — Australia
KUNGGARI — Australia
KUNGKALENJA — Australia
KUNIMAIPA — Melanesia
KUNINDIRI — Australia
KUNINI — Melanesia
KUNJA — Australia
KUPANGESE — SE Asia
KUPCHAKS — C Asia
KURAMA — C Asia
KURDS — Middle East
KUREINJI — Australia
KURIA — E Africa
KURNAI — Australia
KURNANDABURI — Australia
KURRIPAKO — Orinoco Basin
KURTATCHI — Melanesia
KURUMBAS — S Asia
KURUNG — Australia

KURUYA — Orinoco Basin
KUSASE — W Africa
KUSSO — Southeast NA
KUTCHIN — Subarctic
KUTENAI (Kootenai) — Northwest Coast NA
KUTIAL — Australia
KUTJALA — Australia
KUTSWE — S Africa
KUTU — E Africa
KUTZADIKAA — Great Basin NA
KUUNGKARI — Australia
KUVALAN — SE Asia
KUVALE — S Africa
KUY (Co Sung, Lahu) — SE Asia
KUYANI — Australia
KVENS — N Europe
KWA WA AINEUK — Northwest Coast NA
KWAHU — W Africa
KWAIO — Melanesia
KWAJALEIN — Micronesia
KWAKIUTL (Kwak-waka'wakw) — Northwest Coast NA
KWAKWAKA'WAKW (Kwakiutl) — Northwest Coast NA
KWAMATWI — S Africa
KWANDU — S Africa
KWANGALI — S Africa
KWANGARE — S Africa
KWANKHWALA — C Africa
KWANTARI — Australia
KWANYAMA — S Africa
KWARANDJI — Australia
KWARE — Melanesia
KWATKWAT — Australia
KWAYHQUITLUM — Northwest Coast NA
KWENA — S Africa
KWENGO — S Africa
KWEPE — S Africa
KWERA — S Africa
KWERE — E Africa
KWIAKAH — Northwest Coast NA
KWIAMBAL — Australia
KWICKSUTAINEUK AH KWAW AH MISH — Northwest Coast NA
KWINTI — Orinoco Basin
KWISI — S Africa
KWOMA — Melanesia
KXOE (Makwengo) — S Africa
KYAKA — Melanesia
KYEREPONG — W Africa
KYUQUOT — Northwest Coast NA
LA — W Africa
LA VE — SE Asia
LA VEN — SE Asia
LA VY — SE Asia
LABBAI — S Asia
LABU — SE Asia
LABWOR — E Africa
LACANDON — Mesoamerica
LADAKHI — S Asia
LADIN — S Europe
LAGUNA PUEBLO — Southwest NA
LAGUNERO — Mesoamerica
LAHEIWAT (Safaiha) — Middle East
LAHIWAPA — Melanesia
LAHU (Co Sung, Kuy) — SE Asia
LAIA — Australia
LAIAPO — Melanesia
LAK — Melanesia
LAK — Caucasus
LAKA — C Africa

LAKA — E Asia
LAKAHIS — Melanesia
LAKALAI — Melanesia
LAKALZAP — Northwest Coast NA
LAKANDON — Mesoamerica
LAKE — Northwest Coast NA
LAKHER — SE Asia
LAKI — SE Asia
LAKMIUT — Northwest Coast NA
LAKOTA SIOUX (Teton Sioux) — Plains NA
LALA — C Africa
LALI — C Africa
LALUNDWE — C Africa
LALUNG — S Asia
LAMA — E Asia

The frog in the well knows nothing of the great ocean.
Japanese proverb

LAMAHOLOT — SE Asia
LAMBA — C Africa
LAMBADI — S Asia
LAMBAYEQUE — Andes
LAMBYA — E Africa
LAMET — SE Asia
LAMISTO — Andes
LAMOTREK — Micronesia
LAMUT (Even) — Arctic
LANDOGO (Loko) — W Africa
LANDUMA — W Africa
LANGAMAR — Melanesia
LANGI — E Africa
LANGO — E Africa
LANIMA — Australia
LANO — C Africa
LANOH — SE Asia
LAO ISAN (Thai Lao) — SE Asia
LAO LOUM — SE Asia
LAO SOUNG — SE Asia
LAO THEUNG — SE Asia
LAPPS (Sami) — N Europe
LARAGIA — Australia
LARAKIA — Australia
LARANTUKA — SE Asia
LARDIIL — Australia
LARTEH — W Africa
LASHI — E Asia
LASSIK — Far West NA
LATI — E Asia
LATJILATJI — Australia
LATVIANS — E Europe
LAVONGAI — Melanesia
LAWA (Lua) — SE Asia
LAX KW'ALAAMS — Northwest Coast NA
LAZ — Middle East
LEBE — W Africa
LEBOU — W Africa
LECO — Amazon Basin
LEGA — C Africa
LELE (Bashilele) — C Africa
LEMBU — W Africa
LEMKOS (Carpatho Ukrainans) — C Europe
LEMKS — E Europe
LENCA — Mesoamerica
LENDU — C Africa
LENGOLA — C Africa
LENGUA — Central SA
LENJE — S Africa
LEONESE — W Europe
LEPANTO (Sagada Igorot) — SE Asia
LEPCHA — S Asia
LESE — C Africa

LESU — Melanesia
LETI — SE Asia
LEU (Lue) — SE Asia
LEYA — S Africa
LEYTE — SE Asia
LEZGINS — Caucasus
LHEIT LIT'EN — Northwest Coast NA
LHOBA — E Asia
LHOMI — E Asia
LHUYA (Bugusu, Luyia) — E Africa
LI — E Asia
LIARD — Northwest Coast NA
LIBIDO — E Africa
LIKOUALA — C Africa
LILLOOET — Plateau NA
LIMBA — W Africa
LIMBANG — SE Asia
LIMBU — S Asia
LINGAYAT — S Asia
LIONESE — SE Asia
LIPAN APACHE — Southwest NA
LIPE — Andes
LISTUGUJ — Northeast NA
LISU — E, SE Asia
LISUM — SE Asia
LITHUANIANS — E Europe
LITTLE LAKE — Plateau NA
LITTLE RUSSIANS (Ukrainians) — E Europe
LITTLE SASKATCHEWAN — Plains NA
LITTLE SHUSWAP — Northwest Coast NA
LITVINS — E Europe
LO LO — SE Asia
LOBEDU — S Africa
LOBI — W Africa
LOD — C Asia
LODAGABA — W Africa
LOGAULENG — Melanesia
LOGO — C Africa
LOGOLI — E Africa
LOHARA — S Asia
LOINANG — SE Asia
LOKO (Landogo) — W Africa
LOKONO — Orinoco Basin
LOMA — W Africa
LOMAMI — C Africa
LOMWE — E Africa
LONG PLAIN — Plains NA
LORIDJA — Australia
LORITCHA — Australia
LOSSO — W Africa
LOTIGA — Australia
LOTUKO — E Africa
LOVEN — SE Asia
LOWER BRULE SIOUX — Plains NA
LOWER CHINOOK — Northwest Coast NA
LOWER CREEK — Southeast NA
LOWER ELWHA KLALLAM — Northwest Coast NA
LOWER KOOTENAY — Northwest Coast NA
LOWER MUSKOGEE CREEK — Southeast NA
LOWER NICOLA — Northwest Coast NA
LOWER SIMILKAMEEN — Northwest Coast NA

LOWER SIOUX — Plains NA
LOWER UMPQUA — Northwest Coast NA
LOWIILI — W Africa
LOWLAND MAYA — Mesoamerica
LOWLAND SCOTS — N Europe
LOWWE — E Africa
LOYALITY ISLANDERS — Melanesia
LOZI — S Africa
LU — SE Asia
LUA (Lawa) — SE Asia
LUANO — S Africa
LUAPULA — C Africa
LUBA — C Africa
LUBALE (Lwena) — S Africa
LUE (Leu) — SE Asia
LUENA — C Africa
LUFA — Melanesia
LUGAT — SE Asia
LUGBARA — E Africa
LUGSIATSIAK — Arctic
LUHYA — E Africa
LUILANG — SE Asia
LUIMBE — C Africa
LUISENO — Far West NA
LUKSHUAMIUT — Northeast NA
LULE — Central SA
LULUA — C Africa
LUMAD — SE Asia
LUMBEE — Southeast NA
LUMMI — Northwest Coast NA
LUNDA — C Africa
LUNGGA — Australia
LUNGU — C Africa
LUNTU — C Africa
LUO — E Africa
LUPACA — Andes
LUR — Middle East
LUR — C Asia
LURABUNNA — Australia
LUSHAI (Mizo) — S Asia
LUSHANGE — S Africa
LUYIA (Bugusu, Lhuya) — E Africa
LWENA (Lubale) — S Africa
LYANGALILE — E Africa
LYTTON POMO — Far West NA
MA — SE Asia
MA'AZA — N Africa
MAANYAN — SE Asia
MABINZA — C Africa
MACASSARESE — SE Asia
MACEDONIAN — S Europe
MACHIA LOWER CREEK — Southeast NA
MACHIGUENGA (Matsigenka) — Amazon Basin
MACHIS CREEK — Southeast NA
MACKINAC — Northeast NA
MACORIZE — Caribbean
MACUNA — Amazon Basin
MADA — W Africa
MADANG — SE Asia
MADAWASKA MALISEET — Northeast NA
MADEIRANS — W Europe
MADHHIJ — Middle East
MADI — E Africa
MADIRI — Melanesia
MADJANDJI — Australia
MADNGELA — Australia
MADOITJA — Australia
MADURESE — SE Asia
MADUWONGGA — Australia

289

MAE — *Melanesia*
MAFULU — *Melanesia*
MAGAR — *S Asia*
MAGATIGE — *Australia*
MAGH (Marmas) — *S Asia*
MAGNETAWAN — *Northeast NA*
MAGON — *S Africa*
MAGUANA — *Caribbean*
MAGUINDANAO — *SE Asia*
MAGUZAWA — *W Africa*
MAGYARS (Hungarians) — *C Europe*
MAHAFALY — *E Africa*
MAHAR — *S Asia*
MAHARASHTRA (Maratha) — *S Asia*
MAHEI — *E Asia*
MAHI — *W Africa*
MAHICAN (Mohican) — *Northeast NA*
MAHMERI — *SE Asia*
MAHRA — *Middle East*
MAHURA — *S Africa*
MAIA — *Australia*
MAIAWALI — *Australia*
MAID — *Middle East*
MAIDU — *Far West NA*
MAIJABI — *Australia*
MAIKUDUNU — *Australia*
MAIKULAN — *Australia*
MAILU — *Melanesia*
MAISIN — *Melanesia*
MAITHAKARI — *Australia*
MAIVA — *Melanesia*
MAJI — *E Africa*
MAJURO — *Micronesia*
MAKA — *Central SA*
MAKAA — *C Africa*
MAKAH — *Northwest Coast NA*

MAKUSHI — *Orinoco Basin*
MAKWA SAHGAIEHCAN — *Plains NA*
MAKWENGO (Kxoe) — *S Africa*
MALAGASY — *E Africa*
MALAITA ISLANDERS — *Melanesia*
MALANTJI — *Australia*
MALAY (Bumiputra) — *SE Asia*
MALAYALAM — *S Asia*
MALAYALI — *S Asia*
MALAYO — *Caribbean Coast SA*
MALECITES — *Northeast NA*
MALEKU — *Mesoamerica*
MALEKULA — *Melanesia*
MALEMIUT — *Arctic*
MALGANA — *Australia*
MALGARU — *Australia*
MALI — *Melanesia*
MALINKE (Manding) — *W Africa*
MALISEET — *Northeast NA*
MALJANGAPA — *Australia*
MALNGIN — *Australia*
MALNKANIDJI — *Australia*
MALOH — *SE Asia*
MALTESE — *S Europe*
MAM — *Mesoamerica*
MAMALELEQALA QWE QWA SOT ENOX — *Northwest Coast NA*
MAMANUA — *SE Asia*
MAMASSANI — *Middle East*
MAMBOE (Mbowe) — *S Africa*

MANDARESE — *SE Asia*
MANDARI — *C Africa*
MANDAYA — *SE Asia*
MANDE (Mandinka) — *W Africa*
MANDI — *Australia*
MANDIKA — *W Africa*
MANDING (Malinke) — *W Africa*
MANDINKA (Mande) — *W Africa*
MANDJA — *C Africa*
MANDJILDJARA — *Australia*
MANDJINDJA — *Australia*
MANDYAK — *W Africa*
MANG — *E Asia*
MANGALA — *Australia*

MARICOPA — *Southwest NA*
MARIDAN — *Australia*
MARIDJABIN — *Australia*
MARIEN — *Caribbean*
MARIJEDI — *Australia*
MARIMANINDJI — *Australia*
MARINAHUA — *Amazon Basin*
MARIND ANIM — *Melanesia*
MARING — *Melanesia*
MARINGAR — *Australia*
MARINUNGGO — *Australia*
MARIS (Cheremis) — *E Europe*

Education is an ornament in prosperity and a refuge in adversity.

GREEK PROVERB

MATTAGAMI — *Northeast NA*
MATTAPONI — *Southeast NA*
MATTOLE — *Far West NA*
MATUNTARA — *Australia*
MAU — *W Africa*
MAUE (Mawe) — *Amazon Basin*
MAUNDAN — *W Africa*
MAUNG — *Australia*
MAWE (Maue) — *Amazon Basin*
MAXAKALI — *Central SA*
MAXINJE — *C Africa*
MAY — *SE Asia*
MAYA — *Mesoamerica*
MAYAGUEZ — *Caribbean*
MAYLAYALI — *S Asia*
MAYO — *Mesoamerica*
MAYOP — *Orinoco Basin*
MAYORUNA — *Amazon Basin*
MAZAHUA — *Mesoamerica*
MAZANDARANI — *C Asia*
MAZATEC — *Mesoamerica*
MAZHI — *E Africa*
MAZIDI — *Middle East*
MBA — *E Africa*
MBAKA — *C Africa*
MBALA — *C Africa*
MBAM — *W Africa*
MBANDERU — *S Africa*
MBATA — *C Africa*
MBAY — *C Africa*
MBEERE — *E Africa*
MBEGUA — *Central SA*
MBERENZABI — *C Africa*
MBETE — *C Africa*
MBEWUM — *Australia*
MBO — *C Africa*
MBOKO — *W Africa*
MBONGGU — *Melanesia*
MBOSHI (Boubangi) — *C Africa*
MBOUM — *W Africa*
MBOWE (Mamboe) — *S Africa*
MBUDJA — *C Africa*
MBUI — *C Africa*
MBUKUSHU — *S Africa*
MBUM — *C Africa*
MBUNDA (Bamileke) — *S Africa*
MBUNDU — *S Africa*
MBUNGA — *E Africa*
MBUTI (Bambuti) — *C Africa*
MBWEI — *Melanesia*
MBWELA — *S Africa*
MBWERA — *S Africa*
MBYA — *Central SA*
MDEWAKANTON DAKOTA — *Plains NA*
ME WUK — *Far West NA*
MEANAMBU — *Melanesia*
MEDZAN — *C Africa*
MEENA — *S Asia*
MEGANIN — *N Africa*
MEGARHA — *N Africa*
MEGIAR — *Melanesia*
MEHERRIN — *Southeast NA*
MEHINAKU — *Amazon Basin*
MEHNI — *Middle East*
MEINTANGK — *Australia*
MEJBRAT — *Melanesia*
MEKEO — *Melanesia*
MEKRANOTI — *Amazon Basin*
MEKWA — *S Africa*
MELABUGAN — *SE Asia*
MELANAU — *SE Asia*
MELATES — *Caribbean*

MELOCHUNDUM TOLOWA — *Far West NA*
MELPA — *Melanesia*
MEMBERTOU — *Northeast NA*
MENDE — *W Africa*
MENDI — *Melanesia*
MENDRIO — *SE Asia*
MENDRIQ — *SE Asia*
MENGHUA — *E Asia*
MENNONITES — *Plains NA*
MENOMINEE — *Northeast NA*
MENTAWAI — *SE Asia*
MENTAWEIAN — *SE Asia*
MENTHAJANGAL — *Australia*
MENYA — *Melanesia*
MEO (Hmong, Miao, Mong, Tai) — *S, SE Asia*
MERIAM (Murray Islanders) — *Australia*
MERINA — *E Africa*
MERU — *E Africa*
MESA GRANDE — *Far West NA*
MESCALERO APACHE — *Southwest NA*
MESHKI/OSMAN TURKS (Meskhetians) — *C Asia*
MESKHETIANS (Osman/Meshki Turks) — *C Asia*
METHOW — *Northwest Coast NA*
METIS — *Subarctic*
METOAC — *Northeast NA*
METOKO — *C Africa*
MEXTITLANECA — *Mesoamerica*
MEYACH — *Melanesia*
MFENGU — *S Africa*
MIAMI — *Plains NA*
MIAN — *Australia*
MIANA — *C Asia*
MIAO (Hmong, Meo, Mong, Tai) — *S, SE Asia*
MIAWPUKEK — *Northeast NA*
MICCOSUKEE — *Southeast NA*
MICHIGAMEA — *Plains NA*
MICHIKAMAU — *Northeast NA*
MICHIPICOTEN — *Northeast NA*
MICMAC (Mikmac) — *Northeast NA*
MIDDLE SEPIK RIVER PEOPLES — *Melanesia*
MIDOB — *N Africa*
MIEN (Man, Yao) — *SE Asia*
MIJI — *S Asia*
MIJIKENDA (Nyika) — *E Africa*
MIKEA — *E Africa*
MIKIR — *S Asia*
MIKISEW CREE — *Plains NA*
MIKMAC (Micmac) — *Northeast NA*
MIKUD — *Melanesia*
MIKWOK — *Far West NA*
MILLCAYAC — *Andes*
MILPULKO — *Australia*
MILPULO — *Australia*
MIMIKA — *Melanesia*
MIMUNGKUM — *Australia*
MIN (Hakka, Formosans) — *E Asia*
MINA — *S Asia*
MINAHASA — *SE Asia*
MINANG — *Australia*
MINANGKABAU — *SE Asia*

TURKMEN FOLK DANCERS, TURKMENISTAN

MAKASSAR — *SE Asia*
MAKHANYA — *S Africa*
MAKIANESE — *SE Asia*
MAKIEWAHIN — *Melanesia*
MAKIN — *Micronesia*
MAKIRITARE (Yekuana) — *Orinoco Basin*
MAKKA — *C Africa*
MAKLEW — *Melanesia*
MAKO — *C Africa*
MAKO (Maku) — *Amazon Basin*
MAKOMA (Bamakoma) — *S Africa*
MAKONDE — *E Africa*
MAKONG — *SE Asia*
MAKOUA — *C Africa*
MAKU (Mako) — *Amazon Basin*
MAKUA — *E Africa*
MAKUNA — *Amazon Basin*

MAMBWE — *E Africa*
MAMEAN — *Mesoamerica*
MAMIKONS — *Melanesia*
MAMPRUSI — *W Africa*
MAMU — *Australia*
MAMUMBA — *W Africa*
MAN (Mien, Yao) — *SE Asia*
MANADRA — *W Africa*
MANALA — *S Africa*
MANAM — *Melanesia*
MANAO — *Amazon Basin*
MANAR — *C Asia*
MANASI — *Amazon Basin*
MANAWAN — *Northeast NA*
MANCHU — *E Asia*
MANDA — *E Africa*
MANDAK — *Melanesia*
MANDAN — *Plains NA*
MANDANDANJI — *Australia*
MANDARA — *Australia*

MANGARAI — *Australia*
MANGAREVA — *Polynesia*
MANGARIDJI — *Australia*
MANGARRAYI — *Australia*
MANGBETU — *C Africa*
MANGGARAI — *SE Asia*
MANGYAN — *SE Asia*
MANHUY — *Central SA*
MANIE — *Melanesia*
MANIEMA — *C Africa*
MANIHIKI — *Polynesia*
MANIPOS — *Andes*
MANJA — *C Africa*
MANKANYA — *W Africa*
MANMIT — *E Asia*
MANO — *W Africa*
MANOBO — *SE Asia*
MANSI — *Subarctic*
MANSIM — *Melanesia*
MANSOANKA — *W Africa*
MANTA — *Andes*
MANTIONS — *Melanesia*
MANUS — *Melanesia*
MANUVU — *SE Asia*
MANX — *N Europe*
MANYIKA — *S Africa*
MANZANITA — *Far West NA*
MAONAN — *E Asia*
MAOPITYAN — *Orinoco Basin*
MAORI — *Polynesia*
MAPOUNOU — *C Africa*
MAPPILA — *S Asia*
MAPUCHE — *Andes*
MAPUTA — *S Africa*
MAQUINDANAO — *SE Asia*
MARA — *Australia*
MARAGOTOS — *W Europe*
MARANAO — *SE Asia*
MARANGANJI — *Australia*
MARATHA (Maharashtra) — *S Asia*
MARATHI — *S Asia*
MARATI — *S Asia*
MARAURA — *Australia*
MARAWA — *Amazon Basin*
MARAZIG — *N Africa*
MARDITJALI — *Australia* — *Australia*
MARDUDJARA — *Australia*
MARDUDUNERA — *Australia*
MARIAMO — *Australia*
MARIANA ISLANDERS — *Micronesia*

MARISI — *Caribbean*
MARITHIEL — *Australia*
MARIU — *Australia*
MARIUSA — *Caribbean Coast SA*
MARIWUNDA — *Australia*
MARKA — *W Africa*
MARLGU — *Australia*
MARMAS (Magh) — *S Asia*
MARONI CARIB — *Orinoco Basin*
MARONITES — *Middle East*
MARQUESAS ISLANDERS — *Polynesia*
MARRAGO — *Australia*
MARRAKWET — *E Africa*
MARSHALLESE — *Micronesia*
MARU — *E Asia*
MARUBO — *Amazon Basin*
MARULTA — *Australia*
MARUNGU — *C Africa*
MASA'ID — *Middle East*
MASAI — *E Africa*
MASBATEMO — *SE Asia*
MASCOY — *Amazon Basin*
MASHANTUCKET PEQUOT — *Northeast NA*
MASHCO — *Amazon Basin*
MASHI — *S Africa*
MASHPEE WAMPANOAG — *Northeast NA*
MASIKORO — *E Africa*
MASSET HAIDA — *Northwest Coast NA*
MATACHEWAN — *Northeast NA*
MATACO — *Central SA*
MATAGALPA — *Mesoamerica*
MATAKAM — *W Africa*
MATAWAI — *Orinoco Basin*
MATCH C BE NASH SHE WISH POTTAWATOMI — *Northeast NA*
MATENGO — *E Africa*
MATHABATHE — *S Africa*
MATHIAS COLOMB — *Plains NA*
MATLAZINCA — *Mesoamerica*
MATSIGENKA (Matsigenka) — *Amazon Basin*

MINGAN — *Northeast NA*
MINGENDI — *Melanesia*
MINGIN — *Australia*
MINGRELIAN — *Caucasus*
MINJAMBUTA — *Australia*
MINJUNGBAL — *Australia*
MINNESOTA CHIPPEWA — *Plains NA*
MINUANE — *Central SA*
MINUNG — *Australia*

MOLET E — *S Africa*
MOLUCCANS — *SE Asia*
MOMPOX — *Caribbean Coast SA*
MON — *SE Asia*
MONACAN — *Southeast NA*
MONACHE — *Far West NA*
MONDARI — *E Africa*

Kick the world and break your foot.

MINYONG — *S Asia*
MIRI (Mishming) — *S Asia*
MIRING — *Australia*
MIRIWUNG — *Australia*
MIRNING — *Australia*
MISHARS — *E Europe*
MISHKEEGOGAMANG — *Northeast NA*
MISHMING (Miri) — *S Asia*
MISHULUNDU — *S Africa*
MISKITO (Mosquitos) — *Mesoamerica*
MISSANABE CREE — *Northeast NA*
MISSISSAUGA — *Northeast NA*
MISSISSIPPI ANISHINABE — *Plains NA*
MISSISSIPPI CHOCTAW — *Southeast NA*
MISSOURI — *Plains NA*
MISTAWASIS — *Plains NA*
MISTISSINI — *Northeast NA*
MITAKA — *Australia*
MITJAMBA — *Australia*
MITTU — *C Africa*
MIWA — *Australia*
MIWOK — *Far West NA*
MIXE — *Mesoamerica*
MIXTEC — *Mesoamerica*
MIYANMIN — *Melanesia*
MIZO (Lushai) — *S Asia*
MLABRI — *SE Asia*
MMALEBOGO (Gananwa) — *S Africa*
MMAMABOLO — *S Africa*
MNJIKANING — *Northeast NA*
MNONG — *SE Asia*
MOANDO — *Melanesia*
MOAPA PAIUTE — *Great Basin NA*
MOBA — *W Africa*
MOCHA — *E Africa*
MOCOVI — *Central SA*
MODANG — *SE Asia*
MODEKI — *Caucasus*
MODOC — *Northwest Coast NA*
MOER — *C Africa*
MOGOBOYA — *S Africa*
MOHAVE (Mojave) — *Southwest NA*
MOHAWK — *Northeast NA*
MOHEGAN — *Northeast NA*
MOHICAN (Mahican) — *Northeast NA*
MOINBA — *E Asia*
MOISIE — *Northeast NA*
MOJAVE (Mohave) — *Southwest NA*
MOJO — *Amazon Basin*
MOKEN — *SE Asia*
MOLALLA — *Northwest Coast NA*
MOLDOVANS — *E Europe*

MONETON — *Southeast NA*
MONG (Hmong, Meo, Miao, Tai) — *SE Asia*
MONGO (Baloulou) — *C Africa*
MONGOLS — *E Asia*
MONGONDOW — *SE Asia*
MONGUOR (Tu) — *E Asia*
MONI — *Melanesia*
MONO — *Far West NA*
MONOM — *SE Asia*
MONPA — *S Asia*
MONTAGNAIS — *Northeast NA*
MONTAGNARDS — *SE Asia*
MONTANA — *Plains NA*
MONTAUK — *Northeast NA*
MONTENEGRINS — *C Europe*
MOOLUKURUMBAS — *S Asia*
MOORANG (Mro, Tipura) — *S Asia*
MOOSE CREE — *Northeast NA*
MOOSOMIN — *Plains NA*
MOPAN — *Mesoamerica*
MOPNDOMISE — *S Africa*
MOQUEGUA — *Andes*
MORAORI — *Melanesia*
MORATUC — *Southeast NA*
MORDOVIANS — *E Europe*
MORDVINS — *C Asia*
MORE (Itene) — *Amazon Basin*
MORI — *SE Asia*
MORO (Ayoreo) — *Central SA*
MORONGO — *Far West NA*
MOROTAI — *SE Asia*
MOROWARI — *Australia*
MORU — *C Africa*
MOSAKAHIKEN CREE — *Plains NA*
MOSES — *Northwest Coast NA*
MOSETEN — *Amazon Basin*
MOSOPELEA — *Southeast NA*
MOSQUITOS (Miskito) — *Mesoamerica*
MOSSI — *W Africa*
MOTILONES (Yukpa) — *Caribbean Coast SA*
MOTU — *Melanesia*
MOU XOE (Museu) — *SE Asia*
MOUNDAN — *C Africa*
MOUNDANG — *W Africa*
MOUNTAIN — *Subarctic*
MOURDIA — *N Africa*
MOVIMA — *Amazon Basin*

MOWA CHOCTAW — *Southeast NA*
MOWACHAHT — *Northwest Coast NA*
MPHAHLELE — *S Africa*
MPONDO — *S Africa*
MPONDOMISE — *S Africa*
MPONGWE — *C Africa*
MRO (Moorang, Tipura) — *S Asia*
MRU — *S Asia*
MTITAMBA — *Australia*
MUCHIC — *Andes*
MUCKLESHOOT — *Northwest Coast NA*
MUDBARA — *Australia*
MUGHARBAH — *N Africa*
MUHAJIREEN (New Sindhi) — *C Asia*
MUKJARAWAINT — *Australia*
MUKLASA — *Southeast NA*
MULAM — *E Asia*
MULLUK MULLUK — *Australia*
MULTNOMAH — *Northwest Coast NA*
MULURIDJI — *Australia*
MUM — *W Africa*
MUN — *E Asia*
MUNA — *SE Asia*
MUNCIE — *Plains NA*
MUNDA — *S Asia*
MUNDU — *E Africa*
MUNDUGUMOR — *Melanesia*
MUNDURUCU — *Amazon Basin*
MUNGO — *W Africa*
MUNGOOBRA — *Australia*
MUNKIBURA — *Australia*
MUNSEE — *Northeast NA*
MUNYABORA — *Australia*
MUONG — *SE Asia*
MUR — *Polynesia*
MURA — *Amazon Basin*
MURAGAN — *Australia*
MURIAS — *S Asia*
MURIK — *Melanesia*
MURILO — *Micronesia*
MURINBATA — *Australia*
MURINGURA — *Australia*
MURMIS — *S Asia*
MURNGIN (Yolngu) — *Australia*
MURRAY ISLANDERS (Meriam) — *Australia*
MURUBURA — *Australia*
MURUNITJA — *Australia*
MURUT — *SE Asia*
MUSCOGEE CREEK — *Plains NA*
MUSCOWPETUNG — *Plains NA*
MUSEU (Mou Xoe) — *SE Asia*
MUSKODAY — *Plains NA*
MUSKOGEE CREEK — *Southeast NA*
MUSKOWEKWAN — *Plains NA*
MUSQUEAM — *Northwest Coast NA*
MUTABURA — *Australia*
MUTAIR — *Middle East*
MUTHIMUTHI — *Australia*
MUTJATI — *Australia*
MUTPURA — *Australia*
MUTSUN (Costanoan) — *Far West NA*
MUTUMUI — *Australia*
MUYU — *Melanesia*
MUYUW — *Melanesia*
MUZEINA — *Middle East*
MVURA (Doma, VaDema) — *S Africa*
MWANGA — *S Africa*

MWENYI — *S Africa*
MWERA — *E Africa*
MWILA — *S Africa*
MYENE — *C Africa*
MZAB — *N Africa*
NAATH (Nuer) — *E Africa*
NABALOI — *SE Asia*
NABESNA — *Northwest Coast NA*
NABESNA — *Arctic*
NACHO NYAK DUN — *Subarctic*
NADOBO (Guariba) — *Amazon Basin*
NAFAR — *Middle East*
NAGARWAPUNA — *Melanesia*
NAGAS (Konyak) — *S Asia*
NAGOT (Yoruba) — *W Africa*
NAGYUKTOGMIUT — *Arctic*
NAHANE — *Arctic*
NAHD — *Middle East*
NAHUA — *Mesoamerica*
NAHUATL — *Mesoamerica*
NAHUATLATO — *Mesoamerica*
NAICATCHEWENIN — *Northeast NA*
NAICHEN (Naiken, Nayaka) — *S Asia*
NAIKDA — *S Asia*
NAIKEN (Naichen, Nayaka) — *S Asia*
NAKAKO — *Australia*
NAKANAI — *Melanesia*
NAKARA — *Australia*
NAKOTA SIOUX — *Plains NA*
NALU — *W Africa*
NAMA — *S Africa*
NAMAU — *Melanesia*
NAMBE PUEBLO — *Southwest NA*
NAMBICUARA — *Amazon Basin*
NAMOLUK — *Micronesia*
NAMONUITO — *Micronesia*
NANA — *Australia*
NANAI — *Subarctic*
NANAIANS — *E Asia*
NANAIMO — *Northwest Coast NA*
NANATICOKE — *Northeast NA*
NANATICOKE LENNI LENNAPES — *Northeast NA*
NANDA — *Australia*
NANDE — *C Africa*
NANDI — *E Africa*
NANGATADJARA — *Australia*
NANGATARA — *Australia*
NANGGIKORONGO — *Australia*
NANGGUMIRI — *Australia*
NANGO — *Australia*
NANOOSE — *Northwest Coast NA*
NANOPTAIM — *Arctic*
NANSEMOND — *Southeast NA*
NANTICOKE — *Southeast NA*
NANUMBA — *W Africa*
NAPORE — *E Africa*
NARA — *E Africa*
NARAK — *Melanesia*
NARANGGA — *Australia*
NARENE — *S Africa*
NARINARI — *Australia*
NARINYERI — *Australia*
NARON — *S Africa*
NARRAGANSETT — *Northeast NA*

NARRINYERI (Kukabrak, Ngarrindjeri, Yaraldi) — *Australia*
NARUNGA — *Australia*
NASIOI — *Melanesia*
NASKAPIS — *Northeast NA*
NASS GITKSAN — *Northwest Coast NA*
NATASHQUAN — *Northeast NA*
NATCHEZ — *Plains NA*
NAUALKO — *Australia*
NAUO — *Australia*
NAURUAN — *Micronesia*
NAUSET — *Northeast NA*
NAUTHARS — *C Asia*
NAVA — *Melanesia*
NAVAJO (Dine) — *Southwest NA*
NAWAGI — *Australia*
NAWASH CHIPPEWA — *Northeast NA*
NAXI — *E Asia*
NAYAKA (Naichen, Naiken) — *S Asia*
NAYAKS — *S Asia*
NAYAR — *S Asia*
NBOMVE — *C Africa*
NDALI — *E Africa*
NDAONESE — *SE Asia*
NDAU — *S Africa*
NDEBELE — *S Africa*
NDEMBU — *C Africa*
NDENGES — *C Africa*
NDERE — *C Africa*
NDEREKO — *E Africa*
NDIBU — *C Africa*
NDJIBAND — *Australia*
NDOGO — *C Africa*
NDOMBE — *S Africa*
NDONGO — *C Africa*
NDOP — *W Africa*
NDOWE — *C Africa*
NDU — *C Africa*
NDUGA — *Melanesia*
NDUNDULU — *S Africa*

Go out from your village; don't let your village go out from you.

NDZUNDZA — *S Africa*
NEE TAHI BUHN — *Northwest Coast NA*
NEGIDAL — *Subarctic*
NEKANEET — *Plains NA*
NEMADI — *N Africa*
NEMASKA — *Northeast NA*
NENETS (Samoyed) — *Arctic*
NENTSY — *Arctic*
NENTZ — *Arctic*
NEPALI — *S Asia*
NESKONLITH — *Northwest Coast NA*
NESPELEM — *Northwest Coast NA*
NESTORIANS — *Middle East*
NETCETUMIUT — *Northeast NA*
NETSILIK ESKIMOS — *Arctic*
NEUA — *SE Asia*
NEUSIOK — *Southeast NA*
NEVA — *Amazon Basin*
NEW CALEDONIANS — *Melanesia*
NEW GEORGIA ISLANDERS — *Melanesia*

NEW SINDHI (Muhajireen) — *C Asia*
NEWAR — *S Asia*
NEZ PERCE — *Plateau NA*
NGADA — *Australia*
NGADADJARA — *Australia*
NGADI — *Australia*
NGADJU — *SE Asia*
NGADJUNMAIA — *Australia*
NGADJURI — *Australia*
NGAIAWANG — *Australia*
NGAIAWONGGA — *Australia*
NGAKU — *Australia*
NGALA — *Australia*
NGALAKAN — *Australia*
NGALEA — *Australia*
NGALIA — *Australia*
NGALIK — *Melanesia*
NGALIWURU — *Australia*
NGALONG — *S Asia*
NGALOP (Bhota) — *S Asia*
NGALUMA — *Australia*
NGAMBA — *Australia*
NGAMBWE — *S Africa*
NGAMENI — *Australia*
NGANASAN (Nia) — *Arctic*
NGANDA — *Australia*
NGANDANGARA — *Australia*
NGANDI — *Australia*
NGANGELA — *C Africa*
NGANGURUKU — *Australia*
NGAPOU — *C Africa*
NGARABAL — *Australia*
NGARALTA — *Australia*
NGARDI — *Australia*
NGARDOK — *Australia*
NGARIGO — *Australia*
NGARINJIN — *Australia*
NGARINMAN — *Australia*
NGARKAT — *Australia*
NGARLA — *Australia*
NGARLAWONGGA — *Australia*

Go out from your village; don't let your village go out from you.

NGARO — *Australia*
NGARRINDJERI (Kukabrak, Narrinyeri, Yaraldi) — *Australia*
NGATATJARA — *Australia*
NGATHOKUDI — *Australia*
NGATJARA — *Australia*
NGAUN — *Australia*
NGAWAIT — *Australia*
NGAWBE (Guaymi) — *Mesoamerica*
NGBAKA — *C Africa*
NGBANDI — *C Africa*
NGE — *SE Asia*
NGEH — *SE Asia*
NGEMBA — *Australia*
NGERE — *W Africa*
NGEWIN — *Australia*
NGGAMADI — *Australia*
NGINDO — *E Africa*
NGINTAIT — *Australia*
NGOBORINDI — *Australia*
NGOIKA — *S Africa*
NGOLIBARDU — *Australia*
NGOLOKWANGGA — *Australia*
NGOMANE — *S Africa*
NGOMBAL — *Australia*
NGONDE — *E Africa*
NGONI — *E Africa*
NGORMBUR — *Australia*

NGOUAN — SE Asia
NGUGAN — Australia
NGUGI — Australia
NGULU — E Africa
NGULUNGBARA — Australia
NGUMBO — E Africa
NGUNA — Melanesia
NGUNAWAL — Australia
NGUNDJAN — Australia
NGUNI (Xhosa) — S Africa
NGUOI KINH (Vietnamese) — SE Asia
NGURAWOLA — Australia
NGURELBAN — Australia
NGURI — Australia
NGURLU — Australia
NGURUNTA — Australia
NGWAKETSE — S Africa
NGWATO — S Africa
NHANG — E Asia
NHARO — S Africa
NHLANGWINI — S Africa
NHUON (Nyouan) — SE Asia
NI MI WIN OJIBWAS — Plains NA
NI VANUATU — Melanesia
NIA (Nganasan) — Arctic
NIABALI — Australia
NIANTIC — Northeast NA
NIASAN — SE Asia
NIBINAMIK — Northeast NA
NICICKOUSEMENECANING — Northeast NA
NICOBARESE — S Asia
NICOMEN — Northwest Coast NA
NILOTES — C Africa
NIMANBURU — Australia
NINANU — Australia
NINGEBUL — Australia
NINGERUM — Melanesia
NINGO — W Africa
NINZAM — W Africa
NIPMUC — Northeast NA
NIPPISING — Northeast NA
NIQUIRAN — Mesoamerica
NISENAN — Far West NA
NISHIS — S Asia
NISKA — Northwest Coast NA
NISQUALLY — Northwest Coast NA
NISSAN — Melanesia
NISTROVYANS — E Europe
NIUE ISLANDERS — Polynesia
NIVACLE — Central SA
NIVKH — Subarctic
NJAKINJAKI — Australia
NJAMAL — Australia
NJANGAMARDA — Australia
NJIKENA — Australia
NJININ — Australia
NJULNJUL — Australia
NJUNGA — Australia
NJUWATHAI — Australia
NKANSI — E Africa
NKOLE (Ankole, Banykole) — E Africa
NKOMI — C Africa
NKOSI — S Africa
NKOYA — S Africa
NKUMBI — S Africa
NKUTU — C Africa
NNGALIK — Melanesia
NOAHONIRMIUT — Arctic
NOALA — Australia
NOANAMA — Andes
NOARMA — N Africa
NOGAY — Caucasus
NOKON — Melanesia

NOLE — E Africa
NOMLAKI — Far West NA
NOMOI — Micronesia
NONGAIT — Australia
NONGATL — Far West NA
NONTAGNAIS — Northeast NA
NOO WHA HA — Northwest Coast NA
NOOAITCH — Northwest Coast NA
NOOKSACK — Northwest Coast NA
NOOTKA (Nuu chah nulth aht) — Northwest Coast NA
NOQUET — Northeast NA
NOR EL MUK WINTU — Far West NA
NORAGUE — Orinoco Basin
NORTHEAST ALABAMA CHEROKEE — Southeast NA
NORTHEASTERN MIAMI — Northeast NA
NORTHEASTERN PAIUTE — Great Basin NA
NORTHERN CHEROKEE — Northeast NA
NORTHERN CHEYENNE — Plains NA
NORTHERN CHICAMUNGA CHEROKEE — Plains NA
NORTHERN IRISH — N Europe
NORTHERN ISLANDERS — N Europe
NORTHERN MAIDU — Far West NA
NORTHERN MONO — Far West NA
NORTHERN PAIUTE — Plateau NA
NORTHERN PIEGAN — Plains NA
NORTHERN TEHUELCHE — Central SA
NORTHERN TEPEHUAN — Mesoamerica
NORTHERN THAI (Yuan) — SE Asia
NORTHERN TUNGUS (Evenki) — E Asia
NORTHWESTERN SHOSHONE — Great Basin NA
NORWEGIANS — N Europe
NSENGA — E Africa
NSO — W Africa
NSULA — N Africa
NTWANE — S Africa
NU — E Asia
NUBA — E Africa
NUBIANS — N Africa
NUCHATLAHT — Northwest Coast NA
NUER (Naath) — E Africa
NUGSUAK — Arctic

TUAREG WEDDING GUESTS TRAVELING TO A CEREMONY IN NIGER

NUKAK — Amazon Basin
NUKUBURA — Australia
NUKULO — C Africa
NUKUNU — Australia
NUMFOR — Melanesia
NUMIC — Great Basin NA
NUNAMIUT — Arctic
NUNATAGMIUT — Arctic
NUNENUMIUT — Northeast NA
NUNG (Giai, Whang) — SE Asia
NUNGGUBUJU — Australia
NUNUKUL — Australia
NUPE — W Africa
NURISTANIS — C Asia
NUSU — Melanesia
NUU CHAH NULTH AHT (Nootka) — Northwest Coast NA
NUVUGMIUT — Arctic
NUXALK — Northwest Coast NA
NYA HEUN — SE Asia
NYAANYADJARRA — Australia
NYAGINYAGI — Australia
NYAKYUSA — E Africa
NYALA — E Africa
NYAMAL — Australia
NYAMB — E Africa
NYAMWEZI — E Africa
NYANEKA — C Africa
NYANGA — C Africa

Who never begins, never ends.

HUNGARIAN PROVERB

NYANGAMADA — Australia
NYANGBARA — E Africa
NYANJA (Chewa) — S Africa
NYATURU — E Africa
NYEMBA — S Africa
NYENGO — S Africa
NYERI — E Africa
NYGENGO — S Africa
NYIABALI — Australia
NYIGENA — Australia
NYIHA — E Africa
NYIKA (Mijikenda) — E Africa
NYIKINA — Australia
NYINBA — S Asia
NYINING — Australia
NYOONGAH (Nyungah) — Australia
NYORO (Bunyoro, Kitara) — E Africa
NYOUAN (Nhuon) — SE Asia
NYUNGAH (Nyoongah) — Australia
NZAKARA — C Africa
NZIMA — W Africa
O'CHIESE — Plains NA

O CHI CHAK KO SIPI — Plains NA
OATCHI — W Africa
OAYCAS — Caribbean Coast SA
OBEDJIWAN — Northeast NA
OBI — SE Asia
OCAINA — Amazon Basin
OCALE — Southeast NA
OCCITANS — W Europe
OCHAPOWACE — Plains NA
OCHIICHAG-WE'BABIGO'INING (Dalles) — Northeast NA
ODANAK — Northeast NA
ODAWA — Northeast NA
ODUL (Yukaghir) — Arctic
OGADEIN — E Africa
OGAN BESEMAH — SE Asia
OGLALA SIOUX — Plains NA
OGONI — W Africa
OHEKWE — S Africa
OHINDO — C Africa
OHIO ALLEGHENNY — Northeast NA
OHLONE MUWEKMA — Far West NA
OITBI — Australia
OJIBWA (Chippewa) — Northeast NA
OJMAN — Middle East

OK — Melanesia
OKANAGAN — Northwest Coast NA
OKANESE — Plains NA
OKEBO — E Africa
OKIEK (Dorobo) — E Africa
OKINAWANS (Ryukyu Islanders) — E Asia
OKKALIGA — S Asia
OKLEWAHA SEMINOLE — Southeast NA
OLA — Australia
OLD BELIEVERS — C Asia, E Europe, Northwest Coast NA
OLKOLO — Australia
OLONGBURA — Australia
OMAGUA — Amazon Basin
OMAGUACA — Central SA
OMAHA — Plains NA
OMBILA — Australia
OMETO — E Africa
OMOTIK — E Africa
ONA (Selknam) — Patagonia
ONABASULU — Melanesia
ONDO — W Africa

ONEGAMING OJIBWAY (Sabaskong) — Northeast NA
ONEIDA (Onyota'a:ka) — Northeast NA
ONGBE — E Asia
ONGE — SE Asia
ONGKARANGO — Australia
ONGKOMI — Australia
ONGONA — S Africa
ONONDAGA — Northeast NA
ONTONAGON CHIPPEWA — Northeast NA
ONTONG JAVA ISLANDERS — Melanesia
ONYOTA'A:KA (Oneida) — Northeast NA
OPASKWAYAK CREE — Plains NA
OPATA — Mesoamerica
OPAU — Melanesia
OPAYE SHAVANTE — Central SA
OPETCHESAHT — Northwest Coast NA
OPOLYANS — E Europe
ORA — W Africa
ORAMBUL — Australia
ORANG AMBON — SE Asia
ORANG ASLI — SE Asia
ORANG BABIAN — SE Asia
ORANG DARAT — SE Asia
ORANG GLAI — SE Asia
ORANG KEPOR — SE Asia
ORANG LAUT — SE Asia
ORANG LOM — SE Asia
ORANG MALUKA SELATAN — SE Asia
ORANG MAPOR — SE Asia
ORANG MELAYU — SE Asia
ORANG RAWAS — SE Asia
ORANG TIMOR ASLI — SE Asia
ORANG UTAN — SE Asia
ORANGKANAQ — SE Asia
ORAON — S Asia
ORCADIANS — N Europe
OREJON (Coto) — Amazon Basin
OREMANO — Orinoco Basin
ORIOTS — E Asia
ORIWA — Melanesia
ORIYA — S Asia
ORMUT — Melanesia
ORNORAY — Caribbean
OROCHE — E Asia
OROCHI — Subarctic
OROCHONS — E Asia
OROIMO — Melanesia
OROK — Subarctic
OROKAIVA — Melanesia

OROKOLO — Melanesia
OROMO (Galla) — E Africa
OROMOCTO — Northeast NA
OROQEN — E Asia
OROTINA — Mesoamerica
ORU — W Africa
OSAGE — Plains NA
OSER — Melanesia
OSMAN/MESHKI TURKS (Meskhetians) — C Asia
OSOCHI — Southeast NA
OSOYOOS — Northwest Coast NA
OSPREY CHEROKEE — Northeast NA
OSSETES — Caucasus
OSTYK (Ket) — Subarctic
OT DANOM — SE Asia
OTATI — Australia
OTAVALENOS — Andes
OTAVALO — W Europe
OTO — Plains NA
OTOE MISSOURIA — Plains NA
OTOMAC — Orinoco Basin
OTOMI — Mesoamerica
OTTAWA — Northeast NA
OTUKE — Central SA
OUACHITA — Southeast NA
OUARSENIS — N Africa
OUCHESTIGOUEK — Northeast NA
OUIBA — Orinoco Basin
OUJE BOUGOUMOU — Northeast NA
OULAD DJERIR — N Africa
OUMAMIOUEK — Northeast NA
OUNIE — N Africa
OURIA — N Africa
OVAMBO (Ambo) — S Africa
OVATIJIMBA — S Africa
OVIMBUNDU — C Africa
OWLAND — C Africa
OY — SE Asia
OYAMPI (Wayapi) — Orinoco Basin
OYANA — Orinoco Basin
OYBEA — Melanesia
OZBEK — E Asia
OZETTE — Northwest Coast NA
P'U NOI — SE Asia
PA KO — SE Asia
PA O — SE Asia
PABINEAU — Northeast NA
PACAAS NOVAS — Amazon Basin
PACAGUARA — Amazon Basin
PACAJA — Amazon Basin
PACAJE — Andes
PACHEENAHT — Northwest Coast NA
PACIFIC ESKIMOS (Alutiiq) — Arctic
PADAM — S Asia
PADAUNG — SE Asia
PADEBU — W Africa
PADHOLA — E Africa
PADLIMIUT — Arctic
PADOUCA — Plains NA
PAEZ — Andes
PAHARI — S Asia
PAHOUIN — C Africa
PAHRUMP PAIUTE — Great Basin NA
PAI — S Africa
PAI TAVYTERA — Central SA
PAIKONEKA — Amazon Basin

PAIPAI (Akwa'ala) — *Mesoamerica*
PAIUTE (Piute) — *Great Basin NA*
PAIUTE SHOSHONE — *Great Basin NA*
PAIWAN — *E Asia*
PAK THAI (Southern Thai) — *SE Asia*
PAKADJI — *Australia*
PAKAGUARA — *Amazon Basin*
PAKHTUN (Pashai, Pashtun, Pathan) — *C Asia*
PAKOH HOE — *SE Asia*
PAKUA SHIPI — *Northeast NA*
PALA — *Far West NA*
PALAUANS — *Micronesia*
PALAUNG — *SE Asia*
PALAWA — *Australia*
PALAWAN — *SE Asia*
PALENQUE (Guarine) — *Orinoco Basin*
PALESTINIANS — *Middle East*
PALIKUR — *Orinoco Basin*
PALIYAN — *S Asia*
PALLIRMIUT — *Arctic*
PALLISA — *E Africa*
PALOUSE — *Plateau NA*
PALTA — *Andes*
PALU'E — *SE Asia*
PAMBIA — *C Africa*
PAME — *Mesoamerica*
PAMIAGIKUK — *Arctic*
PAMIRIAN TAJIKS (Pamirians) — *C Asia*
PAMIRIANS (Pamirian Tajiks) — *C Asia*
PAMPANGAN — *SE Asia*
PAMUNKEY — *Southeast NA*
PANAG — *E Asia*
PANARE (E'napa) — *Orinoco Basin*
PANCENU — *Caribbean Coast SA*
PANCHE — *Andes*
PANDARAM — *S Asia*
PANDE — *C Africa*
PANDIT — *S Asia*
PANDJIMA — *Australia*
PANGAN — *SE Asia*
PANGASINAN — *SE Asia*
PANGERANG — *Australia*
PANGKALA — *Australia*
PANGWA — *E Africa*
PANIYAN — *S Asia*
PANTAGORO — *Caribbean Coast SA*
PANZALEO — *Andes*
PAOAN — *E Asia*
PAPAGO (Tohono O'odham) — *Southwest NA*
PAPEL — *W Africa*
PAPINACHOS — *Northeast NA*
PAPUA NEW GUINEANS (Papuan) — *Melanesia*
PAPUAN (Papua New Guineans) — *Melanesia*
PARAITIRY — *Amazon Basin*
PARAKANA — *Orinoco Basin*
PARAMAKA — *Orinoco Basin*
PARAUJANO — *Caribbean Coast SA*
PARE — *E Africa*
PARESSI — *Amazon Basin*
PARINGNOGA — *Australia*
PARIRI — *Orinoco Basin*
PARNKALLA — *Australia*
PAROJA — *S Asia*
PARSI — *S Asia*
PARUNDJI — *Australia*

PASCUA YAQUI — *Southwest NA*
PASE — *Amazon Basin*
PASHAI (Pakhtun, Pashtun, Pathan) — *C Asia*
PASHTUN (Pakhtun, Pashai, Pathan) — *C Asia*
PASIEGOS — *W Europe*
PASKENTA NOMLAKI — *Far West NA*
PASQUA — *Plains NA*
PASSAMAQUODDY — *Northeast NA*
PASTO — *Andes*
PATAMONA — *Orinoco Basin*
PATASHO — *Central SA*
PATELIA — *S Asia*
PATHAN (Pakhtun, Pashai, Pashtun) — *C Asia*
PATWIN — *Far West NA*
PAUCATUCK EASTERN PEQUOT — *Northeast NA*
PAUGUSSETT — *Northeast NA*
PAUINGASSI — *Plains NA*
PAUISHANA — *Amazon Basin*
PAUMA — *Far West NA*
PAUMARI — *Amazon Basin*
PAUQUACHIN — *Northwest Coast NA*
PAUSERNA — *Amazon Basin*
PAUSHIANA — *Amazon Basin*
PAVAGUA — *Central SA*
PAVIVAN — *S Asia*
PAWAIA — *Melanesia*
PAWNAKA — *Amazon Basin*
PAWNEE — *Plains NA*
PAWUMWA — *Amazon Basin*
PAYA (Pech) — *Mesoamerica*
PAYANSO — *Andes*
PAYS PLAT — *Northeast NA*
PEAR — *SE Asia*
PECH (Paya) — *Mesoamerica*
PECHANGA — *Far West NA*
PEDA — *W Africa*
PEDI (Sotho) — *S Africa*
PEE DEE — *Southeast NA*
PEEPEEKISIS — *Plains NA*
PEGUIS — *Plains NA*
PEHUENCHE (Aravcanian) — *Andes*
PEIGAN — *Plains NA*
PEKI — *W Africa*
PELOPONNESIANS — *S Europe*
PEMBINA CHIPPEWA — *Plains NA*
PEMON (Taulipang) — *Orinoco Basin*
PENAN — *SE Asia*
PEND D'OREILLES — *Northwest Coast NA*
PENDE — *C Africa*
PENELAKUT — *Northwest Coast NA*
PENOBSCOT — *Northeast NA*
PENSACOLA — *Southeast NA*
PENTECOST ISLANDERS — *Melanesia*
PEORIA — *Plains NA*
PEPEHA — *Melanesia*
PEQUOT — *Northeast NA*
PERAK JAHAI — *SE Asia*

PERAMANGK — *Australia*
PERANAKAN — *SE Asia*
PERICU — *Mesoamerica*
PERSIANS — *Middle East*
PETAMINI — *Melanesia*
PETITSIKAPAU — *Northeast NA*
PEUL (Fulani, Fulbe) — *W Africa*
PEWENCHE — *Andes*
PHALABORWA — *S Africa*
PHOENIX ISLANDERS — *Polynesia*
PHOKA — *E Africa*
PHONG — *SE Asia*

Life is short, but a smile takes barely a second.

CUBAN PROVERB

PHOU NOY — *SE Asia*
PHOU THAY — *SE Asia*
PHUAN — *SE Asia*
PIANOKOTO — *Orinoco Basin*
PIAPOCO — *Amazon Basin*
PIAPOT — *Plains NA*
PIAROA — *Orinoco Basin*
PIBELMEN — *Australia*
PIC MOBERT — *Northeast NA*
PICAYUNE CHUKCHANSI — *Far West NA*
PICUNCHE — *Andes*
PICURIS PUEBLO — *Southwest NA*
PIEGAN — *Plains NA*
PIEMONTESE — *S Europe*
PIJAO — *Andes*
PIKANGIKUM — *Northeast NA*
PIKELOT — *Micronesia*
PILAGA — *Central SA*
PILATAPA — *Australia*
PIMA — *Southwest NA*
PIMA BAJO — *Mesoamerica*
PINDE — *C Africa*
PINDIINI — *Australia*
PINDJARUP — *Australia*
PINE CREEK — *Plains NA*
PINGANGNAKTOGMIUT — *Arctic*
PINI — *Australia*
PINOLEVILLE POMO — *Far West NA*
PINTUBI — *Australia*
PIPIL — *Mesoamerica*
PIQUAL SEPT SHAWNEE — *Northeast NA*
PIRAHA — *Amazon Basin*
PIRIOU — *Orinoco Basin*
PIRO — *Southwest NA*
PIRO — *Amazon Basin*
PISA — *Melanesia*
PISCATAWAY — *Northeast NA*
PISCATAWAY CONOY — *Northeast NA*
PISIGSARIFIK — *Arctic*
PIT RIVER TRIBE — *Far West NA*
PITAPITA — *Australia*
PITCAIRN — *Polynesia*
PITJANTATJARA — *Australia*
PITJARA — *Australia*
PIUTE (Paiute) — *Great Basin NA*
PLAINS APACHE (Kiowa Apache) — *Plains NA*
PLAINS CREE — *Plains NA*
PLAWI — *W Africa*

POARCH CREEK — *Southeast NA*
POCOMAN — *Mesoamerica*
POCONCHI — *Mesoamerica*
PODZO — *E Africa*
POGORO — *E Africa*
POHEY — *Caribbean*
POHLIK — *Far West NA*
POHNPEI ISLANDERS — *Micronesia*
POHOY — *Southeast NA*
POJOAQUE PUEBLO — *Southwest*
POJULU — *E Africa*
POKAGON POTAWATOMI — *Northeast NA*
POKOMAM — *Mesoamerica*
POKOMO — *E Africa*
POKOT (Suk) — *E Africa*
POLAR ESKIMOS — *Arctic*
POLES — *C Europe*
POLISHCHUK — *E Europe*
POMAKS — *Middle East*
POMO — *Far West NA*
POMOUIK — *Southeast NA*
PONAPE — *Micronesia*
PONCA — *Plains NA*
PONGAPONGA — *Australia*
PONGO — *W Africa*
PONTIC — *S Europe*
PONTUNJ — *Australia*
POOSPATUCK — *Northeast NA*
POPAYANENSE — *Andes*
POPOLOCA — *Mesoamerica*
POPOLUCA — *Mesoamerica*
POQOMAM — *Mesoamerica*
POQOMCHI' — *Mesoamerica*
PORTARUWUTJ — *Australia*
PORTAULUN — *Australia*
PORTUGUESE — *W Europe*
POTANO — *Southeast NA*

POTAWATOMI — *Plains NA*
POTIDJARA — *Australia*
POTIGUARA — *Amazon Basin*
POTTER POMO — *Far West NA*
POVEN — *Arctic*
POWHATAN — *Southeast NA*
POWHATAN RENAPE — *Northeast NA*
POYA — *Andes*
POYNDU — *Australia*
POZO — *Andes*
PRAIRIE POTAWATOMI — *Plains NA*
PRANJE — *Melanesia*
PREMINGANA — *Australia*
PROVENCAL — *W Europe*
PSHAV — *Caucasus*
PUEBLO — *Southwest NA*
PUELCHE (Guennakin) — *Central SA*
PUINAVE — *Amazon Basin*
PUIPLIRMIUT — *Arctic*
PUISORTOK — *Arctic*
PUKAPUKA — *Polynesia*
PULANA — *S Africa*
PULAP — *Micronesia*
PULAYAN — *S Asia*
PULUSUK — *Micronesia*
PUMAN — *E Asia*
PUME (Yaruro) — *Orinoco Basin*
PUMI — *E Asia*
PUN — *S Asia*
PUNABA — *Australia*
PUNAN — *SE Asia*
PUNEITJA — *Australia*
PUNJABI — *S Asia*
PUNTHAMARA — *Australia*
PUNU — *C Africa*
PUNU — *E Asia*
PURANETERS — *Australia*
PUREPECHA (Tarascans) — *Mesoamerica*
PURI — *Central SA*
PURIGOTO — *Orinoco Basin*
PURIK — *E Asia*
PURUHA — *Andes*
PURUM — *S Asia*
PUSHT I KUH — *Middle East*
PUTHAI — *SE Asia*
PUTHLAVAMIUT — *Northeast NA*
PUYALLUP — *Northwest Coast NA*
PUYUMA — *E Asia*
PWO — *SE Asia*

Q'ANJOB'AL (Kanjobal) — *Mesoamerica*
Q'EQCHI (Kekchi) — *Mesoamerica*
Q'EROS — *Andes*
QAERNERMIUT — *Arctic*
QAHATIKA — *Southwest NA*
QAHTAN — *Middle East*
QALANDAR — *S Asia*
QARARSHA — *Middle East*
QASHQAI — *Middle East*
QAUMAUANGMIUT — *Arctic*
QAZAQ (Kazakhs) — *C, E Asia*
QIANG — *E Asia*
QIMANT — *E Africa*
QINGUAMUIT — *Arctic*
QIZILBASH — *C Asia*
QUAKERS — *Northeast NA*
QUALICUM — *Northwest Coast NA*
QUAMAUANGMIUT — *Northeast NA*
QUAPAW (Akansa) — *Plains NA*
QUDA'A — *Middle East*
QUECHAN — *Southwest NA*
QUECHUA (Runa) — *Andes*
QUEETS — *Northwest Coast NA*
QUERANDI — *Central SA*
QUERO — *Mesoamerica*
QUI (Dulong, Qui) — *E Asia*
QUIANG — *E Asia*
QUICHE (K'iche') — *Mesoamerica*
QUICHUA — *Andes*
QUIENJIANG — *E Asia*
QUILEUTE — *Northwest Coast NA*
QUILIGUA (Kiliwi) — *Mesoamerica*
QUILLACA — *Andes*
QUILLACINGA — *Andes*
QUIMBAYA — *Andes*
QUINAULT — *Northwest Coast NA*
QUINDIO — *Andes*
QYRGHYZ (Kirgiz) — *E Asia*
RABAI — *E Africa*
RABHA — *S Asia*
RACHA — *Caucasus*
RAGLAI — *SE Asia*
RAHANWAYN — *E Africa*
RAI — *S Asia*
RAIAPU — *Melanesia*
RAINBARNGO — *Australia*
RAINTANA — *Melanesia*
RAIS — *Middle East*
RAJPUT — *S Asia*
RAKHINES — *SE Asia*
RAKKAIA — *Australia*
RAMA — *Mesoamerica*
RAMINDJERI — *Australia*
RAMKOKAMEKRA (Canela) — *Amazon Basin*
RAMONA — *Far West NA*
RANA — *S Asia*
RAPA — *W Europe*
RAPA NUI (Easter Islanders) — *Polynesia*
RAPPAHANNOCK — *Southeast NA*
RAROIA — *Polynesia*
RASHID — *Middle East*
RASTAFARIANS — *Caribbean*
RATAGNON — *SE Asia*
RATHAWA — *S Asia*
RED KAREN (Kayah) — *SE Asia*

RED THAI (Tai Deng) — SE Asia
REDDI — S Asia
REDJANG — SE Asia
REGEIBAT — N Africa
RELA — N Africa
REMBARUNGA — Australia
REMO — Andes
RENDILLE — E Africa
RENGAO — SE Asia
RENNELL ISLANDERS — Melanesia
RESIGHINI YUROK — Far West NA
REYESANO — Amazon Basin
RHADE — SE Asia
RIANG — E Asia
RIBE — E Africa
RIF — N Africa
RIJAL AL MA — Middle East
RINCON — Far West NA
RINGARINGA — Australia
RISTEBURA — Australia
RITARNGO — Australia
RIYAM — Middle East
RIZEGAT — C Africa
ROANOKE — Southeast NA
ROBODA — Melanesia
ROCKY CREE — Northeast NA
ROGLAI — SE Asia
ROHINGYA (Arakanese) — SE Asia
ROKA — S Africa
ROLONG — S Africa
ROM — Mesoamerica
ROMA (Gypsies) — Europe
ROMANIANS — E Europe
RORO — Melanesia
ROSEBUD SIOUX — Plains NA
ROSHANIS — C Asia
ROSSEL ISLANDS — Melanesia
ROTINESE — SE Asia
ROTUMANS — Polynesia
ROUCOUYENNE (Wayana) — Orinoco Basin
ROZVI — S Africa
RUCANA — Andes
RUCUYEN — Amazon Basin
RUFIJI — E Africa
RUKAI — E Asia
RUKUBA — W Africa
RUMAI — E Asia
RUMELIAN TURKS — Middle East
RUMSEY WINTUN — Far West NA
RUNA (Quechua) — Andes
RUNBUBURA — Australia
RUNGARUNGAWA — Australia
RUNGUS — SE Asia
RUSHAN — C Asia
RUSSIANS — C, E Asia, E Europe
RUTULS — Caucasus
RYUKYU ISLANDERS (Okinawins) — E Asia
SA DANG — SE Asia
SAAR — Middle East
SABANEQUE — Caribbean
SABASKONG (Onegaming Ojibway) — Northeast NA
SABERI — Melanesia
SABRAS — Middle East
SAC (Sauk) — Plains NA
SADHU — S Asia
SAEK (Xek) — SE Asia
SAFAIHA (Laheiwat) — Middle East

SAFWA — E Africa
SAGADA IGOROT (Lepanto) — SE Asia
SAGAMOK ANISHNAW-BEK — Northeast NA
SAGARA — E Africa
SAGDLIRMIUT — Subarctic
SAGINAW CHIPPEWA — Northeast NA
SAHARWAIS — N Africa
SAHI — W Africa
SAHO — E Africa
SAHTU DENE — Arctic
SAID ATBA — N Africa
SAISIAT — E Asia
SAKALAVA — E Africa
SAKHA (Yakut) — Arctic
SAKIMAY — Plains NA
SAKUYE — E Africa
SALA — E Africa
SALAJAR — SE Asia
SALAKAHADI — Melanesia
SALAR — E Asia
SALASAKA — Andes
SALAWATI — Melanesia
SALINAN — Far West NA
SALISH — Northwest Coast NA
SALISHAN BELLA COOLA — Northwest Coast NA
SALIVA — Orinoco Basin
SALOR — C Asia
SALUAN — SE Asia
SAM TAO — SE Asia
SAMAAL — E Africa
SAMAHQUAM — Northwest Coast NA
SAMAL — SE Asia
SAMALEK — Melanesia
SAMARITANS — Middle East
SAMARZAKAN — Caucasus
SAMBAA — E Africa
SAMBAL — SE Asia
SAMBAS — SE Asia
SAMBIA — Melanesia
SAMBIOA — Amazon Basin

Those who have no fence around their land have no enemies.

BURUNDI PROVERB

SAMBURU — E Africa
SAMI (Lapps) — N Europe
SAMIA — E Africa
SAMISH — Northwest Coast NA
SAMO — W Africa
SAMOANS — Polynesia
SAMOYED (Nenets) — Arctic
SAMPITS — Plains NA
SAMRE — SE Asia
SAMTAL — S Asia
SAN (Basarwa, Bushmen) — S Africa
SAN CRISTOBAL ISLANDERS — Melanesia
SAN'HA — Caribbean Coast SA
SANAPANA — Central SA
SANDAWE — E Africa
SANDIA PUEBLO — Southwest NA
SANEI — E Asia
SANEMA — Caribbean Coast SA
SANGHA — C Africa
SANGIL — SE Asia

SANGIR — SE Asia
SANGO — C Africa
SANGU — E Africa
SANHAJA — N Africa
SANPOIL — Northwest Coast NA
SANSU — E Asia
SANTA CRUZ ISLANDERS — Melanesia
SANTAL — S Asia
SANTANDAR — W Europe
SANTEE SIOUX — Plains NA
SANTIAM — Northwest Coast NA
SANYE — E Africa
SAOCH — SE Asia
SAPARA — Melanesia
SAPO — W Africa
SAPONI — Southeast NA
SAPOTAWEYAK CREE — Plains NA
SAR — C Africa
SARA — C Africa
SARAGURO — Andes
SARAKATSANI — S Europe
SARAMAKA — Amazon Basin
SARCEE — Plains NA
SARDINIANS — S Europe
SARIKOLI — C Asia
SARIQ — C Asia
SARNIA CHIPPEWAS — Northeast NA
SARSI — Northwest Coast NA
SART (Tajiks) — C Asia
SASAK — SE Asia
SATAR — S Asia
SATSUP — Northwest Coast NA
SATURIWA — Southeast NA
SAUGEEN — Northeast NA
SAUI — Melanesia
SAUIANA — Amazon Basin
SAUK (Sac) — Plains NA

SAUK SUIATTLE — Northwest Coast NA
SAULTEAUX — Plains NA
SAUMINGMIUT — Arctic
SAVARA — S Asia
SAVUNESE — SE Asia
SAWAI — SE Asia
SAWOS — Melanesia
SAYISI DENE — Plains NA
SAYYID — Middle East
SCANDINAVIANS — N Europe
SCATICOOK — Northeast NA
SCHAGHTICOKE — Northeast NA
SCHAMATAIRI — Orinoco Basin
SCHIRIANA — Orinoco Basin
SCOTS — N Europe
SCUGOG MISSISSAUGAS — Northeast NA
SEBEI — E Africa
SEBUANO — SE Asia
SECHELT — Northwest Coast NA
SECOTAN — Southeast NA

SECOYA — Amazon Basin
SEDANG (Xo dang) — SE Asia
SEGEJU — E Africa
SEHARIA — S Asia
SEK — SE Asia
SEKANI — Northwest Coast NA
SEKELE — S Africa
SELEPET — Melanesia
SELETZ — Northwest Coast NA
SELKNAM (Ona) — Patagonia
SELKUP — Subarctic
SELUNG — SE Asia
SEMAI — SE Asia
SEMALAI — SE Asia
SEMANG — SE Asia
SEMARIJI — Melanesia
SEMELAI — SE Asia
SEMIAHMOO — Northwest Coast NA
SEMINOLE — Plains, Southeast NA
SEMOQ BERI — SE Asia
SENA — E Africa
SENECA — Northeast NA
SENECA CAYUGA — Plains NA
SENGA — E Africa
SENGSENG — Melanesia
SENOI — SE Asia
SENTINELESE — S Asia
SENUFO — W Africa
SEPHARDIC JEWS — Middle East
SERAHULI — W Africa
SERAMINA — Melanesia
SERBS — C Europe
SERE — E Africa
SERER — W Africa
SERI — Mesoamerica
SERRANO — Far West NA
SESE — E Africa
SEWA — C Africa
SGAW — SE Asia
SHABAR — S Asia
SHACKAN — Northwest Coast NA
SHACRIABA — Central SA
SHADERLI — Caucasus
SHAHSEVAN (Ilsaven) — Caucasus
SHAKE — C Africa
SHAKOPEE SIOUX — Plains NA
SHAMATARI — Amazon Basin
SHAMATTAWA — Plains NA
SHAMBAA — E Africa
SHAMRAN — Middle East
SHANAFIR — Middle East
SHANGANA — S Africa
SHANJO — S Africa
SHANS — E, SE Asia
SHARANAHUA — Amazon Basin
SHARARAT — Middle East
SHARCHOP — S Asia
SHASHI — E Africa
SHASTA — Far West NA
SHAVANTE — Amazon Basin
SHAWANAGA — Northeast NA
SHAWIYA — N Africa
SHAWNEE — Plains NA
SHE — E Asia
SHEGUIANDAH — Northeast NA
SHEIKH — C Asia
SHENABLA — C Africa
SHERBRO — W Africa
SHERENTE — Amazon Basin
SHERPA — S Asia

SHESHEGWANING — Northeast NA
SHETEBO — Andes
SHETLANDERS — N Europe
SHEWA — E Africa
SHI — C Africa
SHILA — C Africa
SHILLUK (Collo) — C Africa
SHINANS — C Asia
SHINNECOCK — Northeast NA
SHIPAYA — Amazon Basin
SHIPIBO — Amazon Basin
SHIRIANA — Amazon Basin
SHLEUH — N Africa
SHLUH — N Africa
SHOKLENG — Central SA
SHONA — S Africa
SHORS — C Asia
SHOSHONE (Shoshoni) — Great Basin NA
SHOSHONE BANNOCK — Great Basin NA
SHOSHONE PAIUTE — Great Basin NA
SHOSHONI (Shoshone) — Great Basin NA
SHUA (Tshwa, Tyua) — S Africa
SHUAR (Jivaro) — Amazon Basin
SHUBENACADIE — Northeast NA
SHUCURU (Shukuru) — Amazon Basin
SHUGNAN — C Asia
SHUI — E Asia
SHUKURU (Shucuru) — Amazon Basin
SHUMA — Plains NA
SHUSWAP — Northwest Coast NA
SHUWA — W Africa
SIAMESE (Thai) — SE Asia
SIAN — SE Asia
SIANE — Melanesia
SIBEA — Middle East
SIBERIAN ESTONIANS — N Europe
SICILIANS — S Europe
SIDAMA — E Africa
SIDAMO — E Africa
SIDI — S Asia
SIERRA MIWOK — Far West NA
SIHANAKA — E Africa
SIKAIANAN ISLANDERS — Melanesia
SIKANESE — SE Asia
SIKON — W Africa
SIKSIKA — Plains NA
SIKUANI — Orinoco Basin
SILA (Sy La) — SE Asia
SILESIANS — C Europe
SIMAA — S Africa
SIMBA — Central SA
SIMONG — S Asia
SIMORE — Melanesia
SINABO — Amazon Basin
SINDAGUA — Andes
SINDHI — S Asia
SINGMUN (Xing Moun) — SE Asia
SINHALESE — S Asia
SIO — Melanesia
SIONA — Amazon Basin
SIOUX — Plains NA
SIPACAPA — Mesoamerica
SIPAKAPENSE — Mesoamerica
SIRAYA — SE Asia
SIRIONO — Central SA
SISE — C Africa
SISKA — Northwest Coast NA
SISSETON WAHPETON SIOUX — Plains NA

SITKA — Northwest Coast NA
SIUAI (Siwai) — Melanesia
SIUSLAW — Northwest Coast NA
SIWAI (Siuai) — Melanesia
SIWANG — SE Asia
SKAGIT — Northwest Coast NA
SKAWAHLOOK — Northwest Coast NA
SKEETCHESTN — Northwest Coast NA
SKILLOOT — Northwest Coast NA
SKOKOMISH — Northwest Coast NA
SKOOKUMCHUK — Northwest Coast NA
SKOWKALE — Northwest Coast NA
SKUPPAH — Northwest Coast NA
SLAVEY — Subarctic
SLAVS — C Europe
SLEB — Middle East
SLIAMMON — Northwest Coast NA
SLOVAKS — C Europe
SLOVENES — C Europe
SNAKE — Great Basin NA
SNAUSI — N Africa
SNOHOMISH — Northwest Coast NA
SNOQUALMIE — Northwest Coast NA
SO — SE Asia
SOBO — W Africa
SOBOBA — Far West NA
SOCIETY ISLANDERS — Polynesia
SODA CREEK — Northwest Coast NA
SOGA — E Africa
SOKAOGON CHIPPEWA — Northeast NA
SOLI — S Africa
SOLIGARU — S Asia
SOLIMAN — Amazon Basin
SOLOMON ISLANDERS — Melanesia
SOLORESE — SE Asia
SOMALI BONI (Aweer, Kilii) — E Africa
SOMALIS — E Africa
SOMBRA — W Africa
SONGHAI — W Africa
SONGHEES — Northwest Coast NA
SONGISH — Northwest Coast NA
SONGO — C Africa
SONGU — Melanesia
SONGYE — C Africa
SONINKE — W Africa
SOOKE — Northwest Coast NA
SOP — SE Asia
SORA — S Asia
SORBS (Wends) — W Europe
SORK — SE Asia
SOROL — Micronesia
SORONGO — C Africa
SOTAKS — E Europe
SOTATIPO — E Asia
SOTHO (Pedi) — S Africa
SOU — SE Asia
SOUEI (Xouay) — SE Asia
SOUNGOR — N Africa
SOUNINKE — W Africa
SOUTHEAST ALABAMA CHEROKEE — Southeast NA
SOUTHERN CHEROKEE — Southeast NA

SOUTHERN CHEYENNE — Plains NA
SOUTHERN PAIUTE — Great Basin NA
SOUTHERN PIEGAN — Plains NA
SOUTHERN SIERRA MIWUK — Far West NA
SOUTHERN TEHUELCHE — Patagonia
SOUTHERN TEPEHUAN — Mesoamerica
SOUTHERN THAI (Pak Thai) — SE Asia
SOUTHERN UTE — Great Basin NA
SPALLUMCHEEN — Northwest Coast NA
SPANISH — W Europe
SPOKANE — Northwest Coast NA
SPUZZUM — Northwest Coast NA
SQUAMISH — Northwest Coast NA

CHILDREN AND PONY IN DUBLIN, IRELAND

*Be happy while ye'er leevin,
for ye'er a lang time deid.*

SCOTTISH PROVERB

SQUAXIN — Northwest Coast NA
SRAGHNA — N Africa
SSINGO — E Africa
STALO — Northwest Coast NA
STANJIKOMING — Northeast NA
STAR CREEK — Southeast NA
STEILACOOM — Northwest Coast NA
STIENG (X. Tieng) — SE Asia
STIKINE — Northwest Coast NA
STILETZ — Northwest Coast NA
STILLAGUAMISH — Northwest Coast NA
STO:LO — Northwest Coast NA
STOCKBRIDGE — Northeast NA
SUA — C Africa
SUAU — Melanesia
SUBANUN — SE Asia
SUBI — E Africa
SUBIYA — S Africa
SUFRAI — Melanesia
SUHUL — Middle East
SUK (Pokot) — E Africa
SUKA — Melanesia
SUKI — Melanesia
SUKKERTOPPEN — Arctic
SUKU — C Africa
SUKUMA — E Africa
SULA — SE Asia
SULOD — SE Asia
SUMBA — SE Asia
SUMBANESE — SE Asia
SUMBAWANS — SE Asia
SUMBWA — E Africa
SUMU — Mesoamerica
SUNDANESE — SE Asia
SUNDI — C Africa
SUNWAR — S Asia
SUQUAMISH — Northwest Coast NA
SURI — E Africa
SURUI — Amazon Basin
SUSQUEHANA — Northeast NA
SUSU — W Africa

SUTENAI — Plains NA
SUTRAI — Melanesia
SUWARKA — Middle East
SUYA — Amazon Basin
SVANS — Caucasus
SWAHILI — E Africa
SWAKA — C Africa
SWAMPY CREE — Northeast NA
SWANGLA — S Asia
SWAZI — S Africa
SWEDES — N Europe
SWINOMISH — Northwest Coast NA
SWISS — W Europe
SY LA (Sila) — SE Asia
SYCUAN — Far West NA
SZEKLERS — E Europe
T'EN — E Asia
T'IN (Htin, Thin) — SE Asia
TA LIANG — SE Asia
TA OY — SE Asia
TABASARANS — Caucasus
TABTULABAL — Far West NA
TABUN — SE Asia
TABWA — C Africa
TACANA — Amazon Basin
TACARIGUA — Caribbean Coast SA
TACATACURA — Southeast NA
TADO — Andes
TADOUSSAC — Northeast NA
TADVI — S Asia
TADYAWAN — SE Asia
TAGABILI — SE Asia
TAGAKAOLO — SE Asia
TAGAL — SE Asia
TAGALAG — Australia
TAGALOG — SE Asia
TAGBANOUA — SE Asia
TAGIN — S Asia
TAGISH — Subarctic
TAGOMAN — Australia
TAHITIANS — Polynesia
TAHLTAN — Northwest Coast NA
TAI (Hmong, Meo, Miao, Mong) — S, SE Asia
TAI DAM (Black Thai) — SE Asia
TAI DENG (Red Thai) — SE Asia
TAI KHAO (White Thai) — SE Asia
TAIMANIS (Taimuri) — C Asia
TAIMORO — E Africa
TAIMURI (Taimanis) — C Asia
TAINO — Caribbean

TAIOR — Australia
TAIRA — Orinoco Basin
TAIRORA — Melanesia
TAISAKA — E Africa
/TAISE — S Africa
TAJIKS (Sart) — C Asia
TAKU — Northwest Coast NA
TALAMANCA — Mesoamerica
TALANDJI — Australia
TALI — Southeast NA
TALLCREE — Plains NA
TALLANES — Andes
TALLENSI — W Africa
TALYSH — Caucasus
TAMA — N Africa
TAMACHEQ (Tuareg) — N Africa
TAMANACO — Orinoco Basin
TAMANG — S Asia
TAMATHLI — Southeast NA
TAMAULIPECO — Mesoamerica
TAMAYA — Melanesia
TAMAZIGHT — N Africa
TAMBAHOAKA — E Africa
TAMBARO — E Africa
TAMBO — E Africa
TAMILS — S Asia
TAMONG — S Asia
TAMOYO — Central SA
TANACROSS — Subarctic
TANAINA — Subarctic
TANALA — E Africa
TANDROY — E Africa
TANG — W Africa
TANGA — C Africa
TANGA ISLANDERS — Melanesia
TANGANEKALD — Australia
TANGARA — Australia
TANGGUM — Melanesia
TANGU — Melanesia
TANIKUTTI — Australia
TANIMBAR — Melanesia
TANKARANA — E Africa
TANKAS — E Asia
/TANNEKWE — S Africa
TANNESE — Melanesia
TANOSY — E Africa
TANUMUKU — Amazon Basin
TAONKAWA — Plains NA
TAOS PUEBLO — Southwest NA
TAPAJO — Amazon Basin
TAPARITO — Orinoco Basin
TAPE — Central SA
TAPIETE — Central SA
TAPIRAPE — Amazon Basin
TAPKO — C Asia
TAPOAJA — Amazon Basin
TARAHUMARA — Southwest NA
TARAHUMARA — Mesoamerica

TARARIU — Central SA
TARASCANS (Purepecha) — Mesoamerica
TAREUMIUT — Arctic
TARGARI — Australia
TARIANA — Amazon Basin
TARIBELANG — Australia
TARMA — Andes
TARO — Melanesia
TARUBURA — Australia
TARUMA — Amazon Basin
TARUMBUL — Australia
TASADAY — SE Asia
TASETSAUT — Northwest Coast NA
TASHILHIT — N Africa
TASIUSAK — Arctic
TATARS — E Asia
TATITATI — Australia
TATS — Caucasus
TATSANUTTINE — Arctic
TATUNGALUNG — Australia
TATUYO — Amazon Basin
TAU — S Africa
TAUADE — Melanesia
TAULIPANG (Pemon) — Orinoco Basin
TAUNGTHU — SE Asia
TAUNGURONG — Australia
TAUSUG — SE Asia
TAVETA — E Africa
TAVGI YAKUT — Arctic
TAWAHKA — Mesoamerica
TAWAKONIE — Plains NA
TAWANA — S Africa
TAWARA — E Africa
TAY — SE Asia
TAYY — Middle East
TCHAMBULI — Melanesia
TCHINOUK — Northwest Coast NA
TE MOAK — Great Basin NA
TEBRANUYKUNA — Australia
TEBU — N Africa
TECO (Cuitlatec) — Mesoamerica
TEDA — N Africa
TEDEI — Australia
TEDONG — SE Asia
TEGLIN — Northwest Coast NA
TEHATCHAPI — Far West NA
TEHEULCHE (Tsoneca) — Patagonia
TEITA — E Africa
TEKASTA — Southeast NA
TEKE — C Africa
TEKESTA — Caribbean
TEKKE — C Asia
TEKNA — N Africa
TELEFOLMIN — Melanesia
TELUGU — S Asia
TEMAGAMI — Northeast NA
TEMBA — W Africa
TEMBE — Amazon Basin

TEMIAR — SE Asia
TEMNE (Timmannee) — W Africa
TEMOQ — SE Asia
TEMUAN — SE Asia
TENANA — Subarctic
TENE — W Africa
TENETEHARA — Amazon Basin
TENGGARESE — SE Asia
TENINO — Northwest Coast NA
TENMA — Australia
TEOCHIU — E Asia
TEPECANO — Mesoamerica
TEPEHUAN — Mesoamerica
TEPETH — E Africa
TEPITI — Australia
TEPPATHIGGI — Australia
TEQUE — Caribbean Coast SA
TEQUISTLATEC — Mesoamerica
TERABIN — Middle East
TERALINAK — Australia
TERECUMA — Amazon Basin
TEREMEMBE — Amazon Basin
TERENA — Central SA
TERIBE — Mesoamerica
TERIK — E Africa
TERNATAN — SE Asia
TERRABA — Mesoamerica
TERRABURA — Australia
TESLIN TLINGIT — Arctic
TESO — E Africa
TESUQUE PUEBLO — Southwest NA
TETON SIOUX (Lakota Sioux) — Plains NA
TETUM — SE Asia
TEUESH — Patagonia
TEVE — S Africa
TEWA — Plains NA
TEWA PUEBLO — Southwest NA
TEWELCHE — Patagonia
TEWI — W Africa
TH WENE — S Africa
THADOU — S Asia
THAGICU — E Africa
THAI (Siamese) — SE Asia
THAI LAO (Lao Isan) — SE Asia
THAKALI — S Asia
THAKUR — S Asia
THAPA — S Asia
THAQIF — Middle East

*Charity sees the need,
not the cause.*

GERMAN PROVERB

THARAKA — E Africa
THARAWAL — Australia
THARU — S Asia
THAUA — Australia
THEDDORA — Australia
THEMBU — S Africa
THEREILA — Australia
THESSALON — Northeast NA
THIN (Htin, T'in) — SE Asia
THLALERWA — S Africa
THLOPTHLOCCO CREEK — Plains NA
THO — SE Asia
THUG — S Asia
THURI — C Africa
THURIBURA — Australia
TIAK — Melanesia

TIATINAGUA — Amazon Basin
TIBETANS — E Asia
TIDOG — SE Asia
TIDONG — SE Asia
TIDORESE — SE Asia
TIGRAY — E Africa
TIGRE — E Africa
TIGUA — Plains NA
TIKAR — W Africa
TIKERAMIUT — Arctic
TIKOPIA ISLANDERS — Melanesia
TIKUNA — Amazon Basin
TILBABURA — Australia
TILLAMOOK — Northwest Coast NA
TIMANAMBONDRO — E Africa
TIMBA SHA SHOSHONE — Great Basin NA
TIMBARO — E Africa
TIMBIRA — Amazon Basin
TIMBU — Central SA
TIMISKAMING — Northeast NA
TIMMANNEE (Temne) — W Africa
TIMORINI — Melanesia
TIMOTE — Caribbean Coast SA
TIMUCUA — Southeast NA
TINGAIAN — SE Asia
TINGAMITMIUT — Arctic
TIO — C Africa
TIONONATI — Northeast NA
TIPAI (Campo) — Far West NA
TIPURA (Moorang, Mro) — S Asia
TIRARI — Australia
TIRIKI — E Africa
TIRIO (Trio) — Amazon Basin
TIRIS — N Africa
TIRURAY — SE Asia
TIV — W Africa
TIWA — Southwest NA
TIWI — Australia
TIYAHA — Middle East
TJALKADJARA — Australia
TJAPUKAI — Australia
TJAPWURONG — Australia
TJERARIDJAL — Australia
TJIAL — Australia
TJINGILI — Australia
TJONGKANDJI — Australia
TJURORO — Australia

TJUUNDJI — Australia
TL'ETINQOX T'IN — Northwest Coast NA
TLA O QUI AHT — Northwest Coast NA
TLAPANEC — Mesoamerica
TLHAPING — S Africa
TLHARA — S Africa
TLINGIT — Northwest Coast NA
TLOWITSIS MUMTAGILA — Northwest Coast NA
TOAKAS — SE Asia
TOALA — SE Asia
TOARIPI — Melanesia
TOBA — Central SA
TOBAJARA — Amazon Basin

TOBELORESE (Tobolese) — SE Asia
TOBIQUE — Northeast NA
TOBOLESE (Toberolese) — SE Asia
TOBOSOS — Plains NA
TOCOBAGA — Southeast NA
TODA — S Asia
TOFALAR — C Asia
TOGEMAN — Australia
TOHONO O'ODHAM (Papago) — Southwest NA
TOJOLAB'AL — Mesoamerica
TOKA — S Africa
TOKELAUNS — Polynesia
TOLAI — Melanesia
TOLOWA — Far West NA
TOLUPAN (Jicaque, Torrupanes) — Mesoamerica
TOMA — W Africa
TOMAGRA — N Africa
TOMBEMA — Melanesia
TOMINI — SE Asia
TONAWANDA SENECA — Northeast NA
TONGA — S Africa
TONGANS — Polynesia
TONGAREVA — Polynesia
TONGASS — Northwest Coast NA
TONGWE — E Africa
TONKAWA — Plains NA
TONKAWA — Mesoamerica
TONOCOTE — Central SA
TONTO APACHE — Southwest NA
TOOSEY — Northwest Coast NA
TOOTINAOWAZIIBEENG — Plains NA
TOPACHULA — Southeast NA
TOPOSA — E Africa
TOQUAHT — Northwest Coast NA
TOR — Melanesia
TORADJA — SE Asia
TORAJA — SE Asia
TORI — W Africa
TORO — E Africa
TOROMONA — Amazon Basin
TORRES STRAIT ISLANDERS — Australia
TORRES MARTINEZ — Far West NA
TORRUPANES (Jicaque, Tolupan) — Mesoamerica
TORY ISLANDERS — N Europe
TOSKS — S Europe
TOSTO — Caribbean Coast SA
TOTBOSOS — Mesoamerica
TOTELA — S Africa
TOTJ — Australia
TOTOK — SE Asia
TOTONAC — Mesoamerica
TOUBOURI — W Africa
TOUBOUS — N Africa
TOUCOULEUR (Tukulor) — W Africa
TOUM (Tum) — SE Asia
TOWA PUEBLO — Southwest NA
TRALAKUMBINA — Australia
TRINITARIO — Amazon Basin

TRIO (Tirio) — Amazon Basin
TRIQUE — Mesoamerica
TROBRIANDERS — Melanesia
TRUKESE (Chuuk Islanders) — Micronesia
TRUMAI — Amazon Basin
TRY (Chli) — SE Asia
TS'KW'AYLAXW — Northwest Coast NA

The feet take a person to where one's heart is.

ETHIOPIAN PROVERB

TSAKHURS — Caucasus
TSARTLIP — Northwest Coast NA
TSATCHELA (Colorado) — Andes
TSATTINE — Northwest Coast NA
TSAUKWE — S Africa
TSAWATAINEUK — Northwest Coast NA
TSAWOUT — Northwest Coast NA
TSAY KEH DENE — Northwest Coast NA
TSEGA — S Africa
TSEKU — E Asia
TSEREKWE — S Africa
TSESHAHT — Northwest Coast NA
TSEYCUM — Northwest Coast NA
TSHASI — S Africa
TSHWA (Shua, Tyua) — S Africa
TSIMIHETY — E Africa
TSIMSHIAN — Northwest Coast NA
TSNUNGWE — Far West NA
TSOGO — C Africa
TSONECA (Teheulche) — Patagonia
TSONGAN — S Africa
TSOU — E Asia
TSUU T'INA — Plains NA
TSWA — C Africa
TSWANA — S Africa
TU (Monguor) — E Asia
TUALATIN — Northwest Coast NA
TUAMOTU — Polynesia
TUAREG (Tamacheq) — N Africa
TUAREG KEL AHAGGAR — N Africa
TUAREG KEL AJJER — N Africa
TUAREG KEL FEROUAN — N Africa
TUAREG KEL IFORAS — N Africa
TUAREG URAREN — N Africa
TUBAR — Mesoamerica
TUBATULABAL — Far West NA
TUBUAI — Polynesia
TUCANO — Amazon Basin
TUGEN — E Africa
TUIRIMNAINAI — Orinoco Basin
TUJEN — E Asia
TUJIA — E Asia
TUKKONGO — C Africa
TUKULOR (Toucouleur) — W Africa
TUKYLOR — W Africa
TULU — S Asia

TULUA — Australia
TUM (Toum) — SE Asia
TUMBEZ — Andes
TUMBUKA — E Africa
TUMBWE — C Africa
TUMEREHA — Central SA
TUNEBO — Andes
TUNG — SE Asia
TUNGUS (Evenk) — Arctic
TUNICA — Southeast NA
TUNUNIRMIUT — Arctic
TUNUNIRUSIRMIUT — Arctic
TUNUVIVI — Australia
TUOLUMNE ME WUK — Far West NA
TUPARI — Amazon Basin
TUPI — Central SA
TUPINAMBA — Central SA
TUPINAMBARANA — Amazon Basin
TURA — W Africa
TURKANA — E Africa
TURKISH CYPRIOTS — S Europe
TURKMEN (Yomut) — C Asia
TURKS — Middle East
TURRBAL — Australia
TUSCANS — S Europe
TUSCARORA — Northeast NA
TUSCOLA CHEROKEE — Southeast NA
TUSHETIAN — Caucasus
TUSKEGEE — Southeast NA
TUTCHONE — Subarctic
TUTSI (Watutsi) — C, E Africa
TUVALUANS — Polynesia
TUVANS — E Asia
TUYUNERI — Amazon Basin
TWA — W Africa
TWANA — Northwest Coast NA
TXIKAO — Amazon Basin
TXUKAHAMAI — Amazon Basin
TYAVIKWA — S Africa
TYOKWE — S Africa
TYROLIANS — C Europe
TYUA (Shua, Tshwa) — S Africa
TZELTAL — Mesoamerica
TZOTZIL — Mesoamerica
TZUTUHIL — Mesoamerica
UAKA — Orinoco Basin
UAKHANIS — C Asia
UALARAI — Australia
UANAN — Amazon Basin
UASHAT MAK MANI UTE-NAM — Northeast NA
UBINA — Andes
UCHECKLESAHT — Northwest Coast NA
UCLUELET — Northwest Coast NA
UDAM — W Africa
UDEGE — E Asia
UDEGEI — Subarctic
UDIS — Caucasus
UDMURTS (Votyak) — E Europe
UGARUNG — Australia
UHUNDUNI — Melanesia
UKIT — SE Asia
UKONONGO — E Africa

UKRAINIANS (Little Russians) — E Europe
UL'CHE — E Asia
ULAD YIHYA — N Africa
ULCHI — Subarctic
ULITHI — Micronesia
ULKATCHO — Northwest Coast NA
UMANAK — Arctic
UMATILLA — Northwest Coast NA
UMBANDU — C Africa
UMEDE — Australia
UMOTINA — Amazon Basin
UMPQUA — Northwest Coast NA
UNALIGMUT — Arctic
UNANGAN — Arctic
UNCOMPAHGRE — Plains NA
UNDANBI — Australia
UNGA — C Africa
UNGARINYIN — Australia
UNGHI — Australia
UNGORRI — Australia
UNJADI — Australia
UNKECHAUG POOSPATUCK — Northeast NA
UNTSURI SHUAR — Amazon Basin
UPERNAVIK — Arctic
UPILA — W Africa
UPPER KISKOPO SHAWNEE — Northeast NA
UPPER KUSKOKWIM — Subarctic
UPPER MATAPONI — Southeast NA
UPPER NICOLA — Northwest Coast NA
UPPER SIMILKMEEN — Northwest Coast NA
UPPER SIOUX — Plains NA
UPPER SKAGIT — Northwest Coast NA
UPPER UMPQUA — Northwest Coast NA
URALI — S Asia
URAMA — Melanesia
URAPMIN — Melanesia
URARINA — Amazon Basin
URHOBO — W Africa
URU (CHIPAYA) — Andes
URUBU (Kaapor) — Amazon Basin
URUPA — Amazon Basin
USHI — E Africa
USINO — Melanesia
USPANTEC — Mesoamerica
USUKUMA — E Africa
UTAIBAH — Middle East
UTE — Great Basin NA
UTINA — Southeast NA
UTU UTU GWAITU PAIUTE — Great Basin NA
UTUADO — Caribbean
UVEANS — Polynesia
UYGURS — C, E Asia
UZBEKS — C Asia
VACAROS DE EL ZADA — W Europe
VADEMA (Doma, Mvura) — S Africa
VADEYEU NGANASANS — Arctic
VAI — W Africa
VAISI — Middle East
VALE — S Africa
VALUNKA — W Africa
VANATINAI — Melanesia
VARLI — S Asia
VASAVA — S Asia

VATWA — S Africa
VEDDA (Wanniyala) — S Asia
VELLALA — S Asia
VENDA — S Africa
VEZO — E Africa
VIDUNDA — E Africa
VIEJAS — Far West NA
VIETNAMESE (Nguoi Kinh) — SE Asia
VILELA — Central SA
VILI — C Africa
VINZA — E Africa
VISAYAN — SE Asia
VLACHS — E Europe
VOLGA TATARS — C Asia
VOLOKHS — E Europe
VOLTAIC — W Africa
VONOMA — E Africa
VOTO — Mesoamerica
VOTYAK (Udmurts) — E Europe
VUGUSU — E Africa
WA — SE Asia
WAAGAI — Australia
WAATA — E Africa
WABAGA — Melanesia
WABASSEEMOONG (Islington) — Northeast NA
WABAUSKANG — Northeast NA
WABIGOON — Northeast NA
WABO — Melanesia
WACCAMAW SIOUX — Southeast NA
WACO — Plains NA
WADAI — N Africa
WADAMAN — Australia
WADANDI — Australia
WADERE — Australia
WADIJA — Australia
WADIKALI — Australia
WADJABANGAI — Australia
WADJALANG — Australia
WADJARI — Australia
WAGERA — C Africa
WAGGUMBURA — Australia
WAGMATCOOK — Northeast NA
WAGOMAN — Australia
WAHGOSHIG — Northeast NA
WAHNAPITAE — Northeast NA
WAHPETON DAKOTA — Plains NA

WAKAWAKA — Australia
WAKELBURA — Australia
WAKHAN — C Asia
WAKHI — C Asia
WAKUENAI — Amazon Basin
WALA — W Africa
WALAMO — E Africa
WALANGAMA — Australia
WALAPAI — Southwest NA
WALBANGA — Australia
WALBIRI (Walpiri, Warlpiri) — Australia
WALGALU — Australia
WALJEN — Australia
WALLA WALLA — Northwest Coast NA
WALLIRMIUT — Arctic
WALLOONS — W Europe
WALMADJARI — Australia
WALMADJE — Australia
WALMBARIA — Australia
WALPIRI (Walbiri, Warlpiri) — Australia
WALU — Australia
WALUWAR — Australia
WAMA — Amazon Basin
WAMBAIA — Australia
WAMIRA — Melanesia
WAMPANOAG AQUINNAH — Northeast NA
WANAMARA — Australia
WANANO — Amazon Basin
WANAPAM — Northwest Coast NA
WANDA — E Africa
WANDANDIAN — Australia
WANDARANG — Australia
WANDJIRA — Australia
WANEIGA — Australia
WANGAN — Australia
WANGARA — W Africa
WANGKAJUNGA — Australia
WANJI — Australia
WANJIWALKU — Australia
WANJURU — Australia
WANKI — Mesoamerica
WANMAN — Australia
WANNIYALA (Vedda) — S Asia
WANTOAT — Melanesia
WAO (Auca, Huaorani, Waorani) — Amazon Basin
WAORANI (Auca, Huaorani, Wao) — Amazon Basin
WAPE — Melanesia

Desire beautifies what is ugly.

SPANISH PROVERB

WAHTA MOHAWK — Northeast NA
WAICA (Yanomami) — Amazon Basin
WAICURI — Mesoamerica
WAIGEO — Melanesia
WAIIEMI — Melanesia
WAILAKI — Far West NA
WAILBRI — Australia
WAILPI — Australia
WAIMIRI — Amazon Basin
WAIRACU — Amazon Basin
WAIWAI — Amazon Basin
WAIYANA — Amazon Basin
WAIYARIKULE — Amazon Basin
WAKA — Melanesia
WAKABUNGA — Australia
WAKAJA — Australia
WAKAMAN — Australia
WAKARA — Australia

WAPEKEKA — Northeast NA
WAPISIANA — Orinoco Basin
WAPPO — Far West NA
WAR — W Africa
WARABUL — Australia
WARAKAMAI — Australia
WARAMANGA — Australia
WARANBURA — Australia
WARAO — Orinoco Basin
WARAY WARAY — SE Asia
WARBAA — Australia
WARDAL — Australia
WARDAMAN — Australia
WARDANDI — Australia
WARE — Melanesia
WAREI — Australia
WARIANGGA — Australia
WARIPERIDAKENA — Orinoco Basin
WARJAWA — W Africa

WARKAWARKA — Australia
WARKI — Australia
WARLPIRI (Walbiri, Walpiri) — Australia
WARNDARRANG — Australia
WAROPEN — Melanesia
WARROAD CHIPPEWA (Kah Bay Kah Nong) — Plains NA
WARRUMUNGU — Australia
WARURA — Amazon Basin
WARUNGU — Australia
WARWA — Australia
WASAGAMACK — Plains NA
WASAUKSING — Northeast NA
WASCO — Northwest Coast NA
WASHOE — Great Basin NA
WASKAGANISH — Northeast NA
WASONGOLA — C Africa
WASTEKO (Huastec) — Mesoamerica
WASWANIPI — Northeast NA
WATERHEN — Plains NA
WATHAURUNG — Australia
WATIWATI — Australia
WATTA — Australia
WATUTSI (Tutsi) — C, E Africa
WATYI — W Africa
WAURA — Amazon Basin
WAUZHUSHK ONIGUM — Northeast NA
WAWAKAPEWIN — Northeast NA
WAYANA (Roucouyenne) — Orinoco Basin
WAYAPI (Oyampi) — Orinoco Basin
WAYORO — Amazon Basin
WAYUMARA — Amazon Basin
WAYUU (Guajiro) — Caribbean Coast SA
WAYWAYSEECAPPO — Plains NA
WAZIMBA — C Africa
WE WAI KAI — Northwest Coast NA
WE WAI KUM — Northwest Coast NA
WEAPEMEOC — Southeast NA

WEBEQUIE — Northeast NA
WEBER UTE — Great Basin NA
WEENUSK — Northeast NA
WEILWAN — Australia
WELAMO — E Africa
WELEGA — E Africa
WELI — Melanesia
WELSH (Cymry) — N Europe
WEMBAWEMBA — Australia
WEMINDJI — Northeast NA
WENAMBA — Australia
WENAMBAL — Australia
WENATCHEE — Northwest Coast NA
WENDS (Sorbs) — W Europe
WERAERAI — Australia
WERIGHA — N Africa
WEST GREENLANDERS — Arctic
WESTERN APACHE — Southwest NA
WESTERN LAMOOT — Subarctic
WESTERN MONGOLS (Kalmyks) — C Asia
WESTERN PENAN — SE Asia
WESTERN SHOSHONI — Great Basin NA
WETAR — SE Asia
WEYMONTACHIE — Northeast NA
WHADJUK — Australia
WHANG (Giai, Nung) — SE Asia
WHAPMAGOOSTUI — Northeast NA
WHILKUT — Far West NA
WHITE KAREN — SE Asia
WHITE RUSSIANS (Belarusians) — E Europe
WHITE TAI — E Asia
WHITE THAI (Tai Khao) — SE Asia
WHITECAP DAKOTA — Plains NA
WHYCOCOMAGH — Northeast NA
WICHITA — Plains NA
WIDEKUM — W Africa
WIDI — Australia
WIDJABAL — Australia
WIILMAN — Australia
WIIMBAIO — Australia
WIK — Australia

WIK KALKAN — Australia
WIKAMPAMA — Australia
WIKANJI — Australia
WIKAPATJA — Australia
WIKATINDA — Australia
WIKEPA — Australia
WIKMEAN — Australia
WIKMUNKAN — Australia
WIKNANTJARA — Australia
WIKNATANJA — Australia
WIKWEMIKON — Northeast NA
WILAWILA — Australia
WILINGURA — Australia
WILJAKALI — Australia
WILLARA — Australia
WILMEN — Australia
WILYA — Australia
WIMMARAO — Australia
WINDUWINDA — Australia
WINNEBAGO — Northeast NA
WINTU — Far West NA
WINTUN — Far West NA
WIRADJURI — Australia
WIRAM — Melanesia
WIRANGU — Australia
WIRDANJA — Australia
WIRI — Australia
WIRNGIR — Australia
WIRU — Melanesia
WISCONSIN POTAWATOMI — Northeast NA
WISHRAM — Plateau NA
WITBOOIS — S Africa
WITOTO (Huitoto) — Amazon Basin
WITSUWIT'EN — Northwest Coast NA
WIYA — W Africa
WIYOT — Northwest Coast NA
WOBE — W Africa
WODA — Melanesia
WODIWODI — Australia
WOGAIDJ — Australia
WOGAIT — Australia
WOGEMAN — Australia
WOGEO ISLANDERS — Melanesia
WOLA — Melanesia
WOLAMO — E Africa
WOLEAI — Micronesia
WOLF CHEROKEE — Northwest Coast NA
WOLGAL — Australia
WOLINAK — Northeast NA
WOLLAROI — Australia
WOLOF — W Africa
WOM — Melanesia
WONGAIBON — Australia
WONGKADJERA — Australia
WONGKAMALA — Australia
WONGKANGURU — Australia
WONGKUMARA — Australia
WONGO — C Africa
WONNARUA — Australia
WONTOAT — Melanesia
WOODLAND CREE — Subarctic
WORIMI — Australia
WORKIA — Australia
WOROR — Australia
WOTJOBALUK — Australia
WOUNAAN — Mesoamerica
WOVAN — Melanesia
WOWONI — SE Asia
WUDJARI — Australia
WULGURUKABA — Australia

WULILI — Australia
WULPURA — Australia
WULWULAM — Australia
WUNAMBAL — Australia
WUNINGAG — Australia
WURADJERI — Australia
WURANGO — Australia
WURUGU — Australia
WURUNDJERI — Australia
WUSKWI — Plains NA
WUTE — W Africa
WYANA — Orinoco Basin
WYANDOTTE — Plains NA
WYNOOCHEE — Northwest Coast NA
X. TIENG (Stieng) — SE Asia
XAM — S Africa
XANEKWE — S Africa
XARAY — Amazon Basin
XARIRAWI — Melanesia

Experience is the comb that nature gives us when we are bald.

BELGIAN PROVERB

XARUMA — Orinoco Basin
XAVANTE — Amazon Basin
XEK (Saek) — SE Asia
XENI GWET'IN — Northwest Coast NA
XERENTE — Amazon Basin
XESIBE — S Africa
XETA (Heta) — Central SA
XHOSA (Nguni) — S Africa
XIBE — E Asia
XIKRIN (Kayapo) — Amazon Basin
XINCA — Mesoamerica
XING MOUN (Singmun) — SE Asia
XIXIME — Mesoamerica
XO DANG (Sedang) — SE Asia
XOKLENG — Central SA
!XOO (!Ko) — S Africa
XOUAY (Souei) — SE Asia
XU — S Africa
YAB ANIM — Melanesia
YADSI — W Africa
YAE (Ye) — SE Asia
YAFI — Middle East
YAGNOB — C Asia
YAGUA — Amazon Basin
YAGUABO — Caribbean
YAHGAN (Yamana) — Patagonia
YAIWAI — Australia
YAKA — C Africa
YAKAN — SE Asia
YAKIMA — Northwest Coast NA
YAKO (Ekoi) — W Africa
YAKOMA — C Africa
YAKUT — E Asia
YAKUT (Sakha) — Arctic
YAMADI — Amazon Basin
YAMAMADI — Amazon Basin
YAMANA (Yahgan) — Patagonia
YAMEO — Amazon Basin
YAMHILL — Northwest Coast NA
YAMI — E Asia
YAMIACA — Amazon Basin
YAMINAHUA — Amazon Basin
YANA — Far West NA
YANADI — S Asia
YANDJINUNG — Australia

YANG — SE Asia
YANGHERE — C Africa
YANGMAN — Australia
YANGORU BOIKEN — Melanesia
YANGURO — Melanesia
YANKIBURA — Australia
YANKTON SIOUX — Plains NA
YANOMAMI (Waica) — Amazon Basin
YANS MBUN — C Africa
YANTRUWUNTA — Australia
YANZI — C Africa
YAO — E Africa
YAO (Man, Mien) — SE Asia
YAORO — Australia
YAP ISLANDERS — Micronesia
YAQUI — Southwest NA

YAQUI — Mesoamerica
YARALDI (Kukabrak, Narrinyeri, Ngarrindjeri) — Australia
YARGO — Australia
YARMBURA — Australia
YARO — Central SA
YARURO (Pume) — Orinoco Basin
YASA — C Africa
YATE — Melanesia
YAULAPITI — Amazon Basin
YAURORKA — Australia
YAUYO — Andes
YAVAPAI — Southwest NA
YAVAPAI APACHE — Southwest NA
YAWANI — Orinoco Basin
YAZGULEM — C Asia
YAZIDI (Yezidi) — Middle East
YE (Yae) — SE Asia
YEI — S Africa
YEKE — C Africa
YEKOOCHE — Northwest Coast NA
YEKUANA (Makiritare) — Orinoco Basin
YELA — Melanesia
YELMEK — Melanesia
YELYUYENDI — Australia
YEMAI — Melanesia
YEMICI — Caribbean Coast SA
YEMRELI — C Asia
YENADI — S Asia
YERAKI — Melanesia
YERAVA — S Asia
YESEY — Subarctic
YESIBE — S Africa
YESKWA — W Africa
YETI — Melanesia
YEZIDI (Yazidi) — Middle East
YHAMAD — Middle East
YI — E Asia
YIMAS — Melanesia
YIR YORONT — Australia
YOKAGHIR — Subarctic
YOKAYO — Far West NA
YOKUTS — Far West NA
YOLNGU (Murngin) — Australia
YOMBA SHOSHONE — Great Basin NA
YOMBE — C Africa

YOMUD — C Asia
YOMUT (Turkmen) — C Asia
YONCALLA — Northwest Coast NA
YONGGOM — Melanesia
YORUBA (Nagot) — W Africa
YORUK — Middle East
YOSKO — Mesoamerica
YOUGHIOGHENY SHAWNEE — Northeast NA
YSABEL — Melanesia
YSLETA DEL SUR PUEBLO — Southwest NA
YUAN (Northern Thai) — SE Asia
YUANZHUMIN (Gaosazhu) — E Asia
YUCATAN MAYA — Mesoamerica
YUCHI — Plains NA
YUED — Australia
YUGUL — Australia
YUGUR — E Asia
YUIN — Australia
YUIT — Arctic
YUKAGHIR (Odul) — Arctic
YUKATEKO — Mesoamerica
YUKI — Far West NA
YUKO — Caribbean Coast SA
YUKPA (Motilones) — Caribbean Coast SA
YUKUNA — Amazon Basin
YULBARIDJA — Australia
YUMA — Amazon Basin
YUMBO — Amazon Basin
YUMBRI — SE Asia
YUNGAR — Australia
YUNNAN — SE Asia
YUPIAT (Yupik) — Arctic
YUPIK (Yupiat) — Arctic
YUQUI — Andes
YURACARE — Amazon Basin
YURAKS — Arctic
YURI — Amazon Basin
YUROK — Northwest Coast NA
YURUNA — Amazon Basin
YUSTAGA — Southeast NA
YUSUFZAI — C Asia
ZACATEC — Mesoamerica
ZAFISORO — E Africa
ZAGHAWA — N Africa
ZAMBALES — SE Asia
ZAMINDAR — S Asia
ZAMUCO — Central SA
ZANDE (Azande) — C Africa
ZAPOTEC — Mesoamerica
ZARAMO — E Africa
ZARANIQ — Middle East
ZARMA — W Africa
ZAYR — N Africa
ZEMMUR — N Africa
ZENTAN — N Africa
ZEZHRU — S Africa
ZHONGJIA — E Asia
ZHUANG — E Asia
ZIA PUEBLO — Southwest NA
ZIGULA — E Africa
ZIMAKANI — Melanesia
ZIMBA –- S Africa
ZINZA — E Africa
ZOMBO — C Africa
ZOQUE — Mesoamerica
ZOROASTRIANS — Middle East
ZULU — S Africa
ZUNI — Southwest NA
ZUWAYAH — N Africa

BOAT VENDOR NEAR BANGKOK, THAILAND

ILLUSTRATIONS CREDITS

COVER: James L. Stanfield

BACK COVER: (upper center) Steve McCurry; (upper right) David Alan Harvey; (lower right) Steve McCurry; (lower center) Jodi Cobb, National Geographic Photographer; (lower left) Ed Kashi; (upper left) David Edwards.

FRONTMATTER: 2-3, Bruno Barbey; 4, Sam Abell, National Geographic Photographer; 6 (top to bottom), Eric Valli and Debra Kellner, George Steinmetz, Robert Caputo, David Alan Harvey, Maggie Steber, Cary Wolinsky, Angela Fisher/ Carol Beckwith/Robert Estall agency, Nik Wheeler/BLACK STAR, Natalie Fobes, 8-9, Robert Caputo.

ASIA: 15, Eric Valli and Debra Kellner; 18-19, Steve McCurry; 20 (upper left), David Edwards; 20 (upper right), Harry N. Naltchayan; 20 (lower left), Bruce Dale; 20 (lower right), Charles O'Rear; 21-23 (both), REZA; 24-25, Jonathan Blair; 26-27, James L. Stanfield; 31, Kenneth Garrett; 32-33, David Edwards; 34 (upper left), Jonathan Wright; 34 (upper right), Jodi Cobb, National Geographic Photographer; 34 (lower), Gordon Wiltsie; 37, Roger Ressmeyer; 38-39, Charles O'Rear; 40-41, Jodi Cobb, National Geographic Photographer; 42, Michael S. Yamashita; 44-45, 46, Steve McCurry; 47, Raghubir Singh.

OCEANIA: 49, George Steinmetz; 52-53, Peter Essick; 54 (upper), George Steinmetz; 54 (lower left), Sam Abell, National Geographic Photographer; 54 (lower right), Jay Dickman; 55, Medford Taylor; 56, Sam Abell, National Geographic Photographer; 58, Belinda Wright; 60-61, Paul Chesley; 62-63, George Steinmetz; 66, Jodi Cobb, National Geographic Photographer; 68, Peter Essick; 70-71, Jodi Cobb, National Geographic Photographer; 72-73, John Eastcott & Yva Momatiuk; 75, Randy Olson; 79, Melinda Berge/Network Aspen.

SOUTH AMERICA: 81, Robert Caputo; 84-85, Lynn Johnson; 86 (upper left), David Alan Harvey; 86 (upper right), William Albert Allard, National Geographic Photographer; 86 (lower), O. Louis Mazzatenta; 87, Stuart Franklin; 92-93, Robert Caputo; 94-95, Alex Webb/MAGNUM; 99, Anna Susan Post; 100-101, Stuart Franklin; 102-103, Maria Stenzel; 104, Stuart Franklin; 106, Loren McIntyre; 108-109, Stuart Franklin.

MESOAMERICA & THE CARIBBEAN: 111, 114-115, 116 (upper), David Alan Harvey; 116 (lower left), Bruce Dale; 116 (lower right), David Alan Harvey; 117, James Nachtwey; 119, Tomasz Tomaszewski; 120-121, 122-123, David Alan Harvey; 126, Cary Wolinsky; 128-129, David Alan Harvey.

NORTH AMERICA: 131, Maggie Steber; 134-135, Bruce Dale; 136 (upper left), Steve Wall; 136 (upper right), Susanne Page; 136 (lower), Stephen Trimble; 137, Maggie Steber; 140-141, Joel Sartore/ www.joelsartore.com; 142-143, David Alan Harvey; 144, Tomasz Tomaszewski; 145, Kenneth Jarecke; 149, 150-151, Bruce Dale; 152-153, Paul Chesley; 155, Dan Dry; 156-157, Dewitt Jones.

EUROPE: 159, Cary Wolinsky; 162-163, 164 (upper left), Sisse Brimberg; 164 (upper right), James P. Blair; 164 (lower left), Alexandra Avakian; 164 (lower right), Anna Susan Post; 167 (upper), Sam Abell, National Geographic Photographer; 167 (lower), Annie Griffiths Belt; 168-169, Tomasz Tomaszewski; 170-171, Dean Conger; 173, Jim Richardson; 175, Lynn Johnson; 176-177, Medford Taylor; 178-179, David Alan Harvey; 180, Farrell Grehan; 183, Thomas Nebbia; 184, Alexandra Boulat; 188-189, James L. Stanfield; 190-191, Gerd Ludwig; 194, Ed Kashi; 196-197, Tomasz Tomaszewski.

SUB-SAHARAN AFRICA: 199, Angela Fisher and Carol Beckwith/Robert Estall agency; 202-203, Chris Johns, National Geographic Photographer; 204 (upper left), Angela Fisher & Carol Beckwith; 204 (upper right), Michael S. Lewis; 204 (lower left), Chris Johns, National Geographic Photographer; 204 (lower right), Angela Fisher & Carol Beckwith; 205, Michael S. Lewis; 207, Angela Fisher & Carol Beckwith; 208-209, Michael & Aubine Kirtley; 210-211, José Azel; 212, Angela Fisher & Carol Beckwith; 214, Michael Nichols, National Geographic Photographer; 217, Maria Stenzel; 218-219, Michael S. Lewis; 220-221, 222, Frans Lanting; 225, David C. Turnley; 226-227, Frans Lanting; 228-229, Chris Johns, National Geographic Photographer; 230, Frans Lanting; 232-233, Ed Kashi.

NORTH AFRICA & THE MIDDLE EAST: 235, Nik Wheeler/BLACK STAR; 238-239, James L. Stanfield; 240 (left), Lynn Abercrombie; 240 (right, both), Ed Kashi; 242, Bruno Barbey; 243, REZA; 244-245, Steve McCurry; 246-247, Jodi Cobb, National Geographic Photographer; 249, Annie Griffiths Belt; 250-251, Michael S. Yamashita; 252-253, REZA; 254-255, 256, Alexandra Avakian; 259, James L. Stanfield.

ARCTIC: 261, Natalie Fobes; 264-265, Sarah Leen; 266 (upper), Richard Olsenius; 266 (lower), Natalie Fobes; 266 (right), Dean Conger; 267, Karen Kasmauski; 269 (left), Dean Conger; 269 (upper right), Natalie Fobes; 269 (lower right), Joanna B. Pinneo; 270-271, 272, 274-275, Maria Stenzel; 276-277, Courtesy Ministry of Tourism and Antiquities, The Hashemite Kingdom of Jordan/Photograph by John Tsantes, Smithsonian Institution; 283, José Azel; 285, David Alan Harvey; 286, Sisse Brimberg; 287, Blaine Harrington; 288, Medford Taylor; 290, REZA; 292, Angela Fisher and Carol Beckwith; 293, Miguel Rio Branco/ MAGNUM; 295, Sam Abell, National Geographic Photographer; 297, Blaine Harrington.

ADDITIONAL READING

BENNETT, LINDA, ED. Encyclopedia of World Cultures. G. K. Hall & Co., 1992.

BLUNDEN, CAROLINE AND MARK ELVIN. Cultural Atlas of China. Checkmark Books, 1998.

COE, MICHAEL AND OTHERS. Atlas of Ancient North America. Facts on File, 1986.

FITZHUGH, WILLIAM W. AND ARON CROWELL. Crossroads of Continents: Cultures of Siberia and Alaska. Smithsonian Institution Press, 1988.

FITZPATRICK, JUDITH M., ED. Endangered Peoples of Oceania: Struggles to Survive and Thrive. Greenwood Press, 2000.

FREEMAN, MILTON M.R., ED. Endangered Peoples of the Arctic: Struggles to Survive and Thrive. Greenwood Press, 2000.

GALL, TIMOTHY L., ED. Encyclopedia of Cultures and Daily Life. Gale Group, 1998.

GERNER, DEBORAH J., ED. Understanding the Contemporary Middle East. Lynne Rienner Publisher, 2000.

GONEN, AMIRAM, ED. The Encyclopedia of the Peoples of the World. Henry Holt and Co., 1993.

HIRSCHFELDER, ARLENE AND MARTHA KREIPE DE MONTAÑO. The Native American Almanac. Prentice Hall General Reference, 1993.

HOPKIRK, KATHLEEN. Central Asia: A Traveller's Companion. John Murray Publishers Ltd., 1994.

JOHNSON, GORDON. Cultural Atlas of India: India, Pakistan, Nepal, Bhutan, Bangladesh, and Sri Lanka. Facts on File, 1996.

LEE, RICHARD B. AND RICHARD DALY, EDS. The Cambridge Encyclopedia of Hunters and Gatherers. Cambridge University Press, 1999.

LEVINSON, DAVID. Ethnic Groups Worldwide: A Ready Reference Handbook. NetLibrary Inc., 1998; The Encyclopedia of World Cultures. Macmillan Publishing Company, 1995.

LEWIS, BERNARD. The Multiple Identities of the Middle East. Schocken Books, 1999.

MALINOWSKI, SHARON AND ANNA SHEETS, EDS. The Gale Encyclopedia of Native American Tribes. Gale Group, 1998.

MAYBURY-LEWIS, DAVID. Millennium: Tribal Wisdom and the Modern World. Viking Press, 1992.

OLSON, JAMES S. The Peoples of Africa: An Ethnohistorical Dictionary. Greenwood Press, 1996.

PRICE, DAVID H. Atlas of World Cultures: A Geographical Guide to Ethnographic Literature. Sage Publications, 1989.

READER, JOHN. Africa: A Biography of the Continent. Knopf, 1998.

ROGOZINSKI, JAN. A Brief History of the Caribbean: From the Arawak and the Carib to the Present. Facts on File, 1999.

SPONSEL, LESLIE E., ED. Endangered Peoples of Southeast and East Asia: Struggles to Survive and Thrive. Greenwood Press, 2000.

STURTEVANT, WILLIAM C., ED. Handbook of North American Indians. Smithsonian Institution, 1990.

WILSON, DAVID J. Indigenous South Americans of the Past and Present. Westview Press, 1999.

You may also wish to consult the following Web sites: Cultural Survival at www. cs.org and Cultures on the Edge at www.culturesontheedge.com.

ACKNOWLEDGMENTS

National Geographic Books gratefully acknowledges the assistance of many knowledgeable people during the preparation of Peoples of the World. In particular we wish to thank Martha Crawford Christian and Michele Callaghan for their excellent editorial comments, Blakely Blackford for her artwork, and Ray Milefsky for his timely advice. We also extend our thanks to Connie D. Binder, Peyton H. Moss, Jr., Lyle Rosbotham, Lisa Thomas, Juan J. Valdés, and Anne E. Withers.

INDEX

301

PEOPLES
OF THE WORLD

PUBLISHED BY THE
NATIONAL GEOGRAPHIC SOCIETY

John M. Fahey, Jr.
President and Chief Executive Officer

Gilbert M. Grosvenor
Chairman of the Board

Nina D. Hoffman
Executive Vice President

PREPARED BY THE BOOK DIVISION

Kevin Mulroy *Vice President and Editor-in-Chief*

Charles Kogod *Illustrations Director*

Marianne R. Koszorus *Design Director*

STAFF FOR THIS BOOK

K.M. Kostyal *Project Editor*

Carolinda E. Averitt *Text Editor*

Greta Arnold *Illustrations Editor*

Suez Kehl Corrado *Art Director*

Melissa Farris *Design Assistant*

Elisabeth B. Booz, Gaye Brown, and Kristen Reed *Researchers*

Carl Mehler *Director of Maps*

Thomas L. Gray, Nicholas P. Rosenbach *Map Editors*

Matt Chwastyk, Jerome N. Cookson, James Huckenpahler, Gregory Ugiansky *Map Research and Production*

R. Gary Colbert *Production Director*

Lewis R. Bassford *Production Project Manager*

Janet Dustin *Illustrations Assistant*

MANUFACTURING AND QUALITY CONTROL

George V. White *Director*

Clifton R. Brown *Manager*

Phillip L. Schlosser *Financial Analyst*

The world's largest nonprofit scientific and educational organization, the National Geographic Society was founded in 1888 "for the increase and diffusion of geographic knowledge." Since then it has supported scientific exploration and spread information to its more than eight million members worldwide.

The National Geographic Society educates and inspires millions every day through magazines, books, television programs, videos, maps and atlases, research grants, the National Geographic Bee, teacher workshops, and innovative classroom materials.

The Society is supported through membership dues, charitable gifts, and income from the sale of its educational products.

Members receive NATIONAL GEOGRAPHIC magazine—the Society's official journal—discounts on Society products, and other benefits.

For more information about the National Geographic Society, its educational programs, publications, or ways to support its work, please call 1-800-NGS-LINE (647-5463), or write to the following address:

National Geographic Society
1145 17th Street N.W.
Washington, D.C. 20036-4688 U.S.A.

Visit the Society's Web site at www.nationalgeographic.com

Composition for this book by the National Geographic Society Book Division. Printed and bound by R.R. Donnelley & Sons, Willard, Ohio. Color separations by Quad Graphics, Martinsburg, West Virginia. Dust jacket printed by the Miken Co., Cheektowaga, New York.

Portions of David Maybury-Lewis's essay "Ethnicity and Culture" were excerpted from *Indigenous Peoples, Ethnic Groups, and the State.* Copyright © 1997 by Allyn & Bacon. Reprinted/adapted by permission.

Library of Congress Cataloging-in-Publication Data

Peoples of the world : their cultures, traditions, and ways of life.
       p.   cm.
    At head of title: National Geographic.
    Includes bibliographical references and index.
    ISBN 0-7922-6400-2 -- ISBN 0-7922-6401-0 (cloth)
      1. Ethnology. I. National Geographic Society (U.S.)

GN378 .P4616 20001
305.8--dc21   2001042785